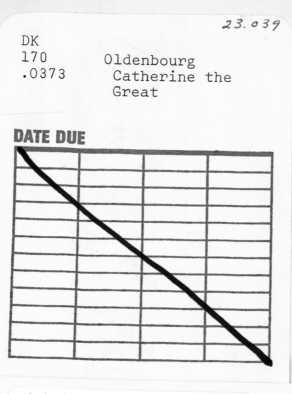

CATHERINE THE GREAT

PANTHEON BOOKS, *A division of Random House, New York*

ZOÉ OLDENBOURG

CATHERINE
THE GREAT

Translated from the French by Anne Carter

CONTENTS

ILLUSTRATIONS

(*between pages 204 and 205*)

These photographs are reproduced with the gracious permission of the Directors of the Russian State Museum of Leningrad, and the State Museum of the Hermitage.

INTRODUCTION

Her contemporaries—men of the caliber of Voltaire and Diderot among them—called her the Star of the North, Minerva, "admirable autocrat, conqueror, peacemaker and legislator"; she was the "Mother Tsarina" of all the Russias, mother of her country, mother of her people, Catherine the Wise; she was the friend of the Enlightenment or, more modestly, an "enlightened despot." She was also the Messalina of the North, the *grosse et vieille Cateau* of the Revolutionary pamphleteers. To history she will always be Catherine the Great, one of the three or four women who have ruled in their own right, for any length of time, over a great nation and who have left behind them a glorious memory of their reign.

She was more than simply a great ruler, and more than a remarkable woman: already she belongs among the half-legendary figures whose lives have been popularized and vulgarized in films, plays and novels with little regard for what they were really like.

Catherine has had no lack of chroniclers, and all of them, objective and impartial scholars, dedicated admirers and passionate detractors alike, have found abundant material in the records left by her contemporaries and by Catherine herself. Few historical characters have, in the course of their lives, been so thoroughly observed, judged and described by their contemporaries, and there are fewer still who have left so much written testimony about themselves. If she had not been an empress, Catherine would surely have been a writer, and she would have occupied an honorable place in literary history (almost certainly in French literary history, since she wrote little in any other language) among the writers of letters and memoirs. The principal subject of Catherine's writing is herself, and it might even be said that it is this wealth of material which makes her biographers' task so difficult. Her character emerges as complex and inconsistent, but then there must be few human beings who would not appear equally complicated if they provided such extensive documentation about themselves.

But paradoxically enough, the picture which history (at least as far as the nonspecialist is concerned) has retained of Catherine is based more on slander and on official panegyrics than on objective research. In the nineteenth century Catherine was the subject of two, diametrically opposite, historical views: in Russia the great sovereign, the ancestress of the reigning tsars, was presented as a woman of genius, a model of all the virtues, or very nearly so. She was thought of as sensitive, kind, generous and intelligent, a ruler devoted body and soul to her adoptive country and with no other object in life than the glory of Russia.* Even after more than forty years of Communist rule, this is still the prevailing picture of her: the Russians are grateful, they do not forget that Catherine's was a great reign, and they show an indulgence which sometimes verges on admiration for the faults of the woman. Catherine may have been a German but she is still a national pride.

Even in Russia, however, the other side of the coin began to appear at an early date. Russian liberals were not kind to an autocrat such as Catherine II.† But it was in the West that the Empress's reputation suffered the worst, a fact which was due largely to the more than understandable resentment felt against her by exiled Polish intellectuals.‡ Very early on, the friend of the *Philosophes*—who was, for all that, violently opposed to the French Revolution of 1789—was presented to the people of Europe as a loose-living, tyrannical and even bloodthirsty woman, and the pamphlets which circulated throughout Europe even in her own lifetime were taken, after Catherine's

---

* The work of one irreproachably objective historian, Bilbassov, was actually banned from publication in Russia.
† Tolstoy was among those who nursed a genuine hatred for a woman he described as "horrible."
‡ Cf. the works of Waliszewski.

death, for authentic evidence. Insofar as the popular imagination interests itself in history at all, the picture it has retained of Catherine II is, generally speaking, that of a virago, guilty of every imaginable crime and viciousness.

In the twentieth century, the publication of Catherine's memoirs made the story of her youth better known and gave rise to another picture which exists alongside that of the imperial tyrant. This shows an innocent young princess handed over to the mercy of an unworthy husband, persecuted, corrupted in spite of herself, and then forced into power almost against her own will or, as another version of the story has it, rising to power through intrigue. As Shaw's *Great Catherine* or the *Petite Catherine* of André Obey, she is a figure of melodrama or comedy. In the West the Russian Empress seems to have suffered from the disrespect attached to Russia in general: a place so extravagantly barbaric that it is hard to take it altogether seriously.

Eminent modern historians have given us a subtler, more objective and undoubtedly more accurate picture of Catherine II. I am thinking especially of Henri Vallotton's admirable book,* and of that by Ian Grey.† (Lavater-Sloman's extremely interesting biography,‡ on the other hand, gives the impression of having been written directly in the tradition of the nineteenth-century historiographers, so blinded does the author seem to be by her admiration for her heroine.) It is with some temerity that I am embarking on a fresh biography of a woman about whom practically everything has already been said. But the whole truth can never be told about any human being whose personality holds the slightest interest.

In this book I shall make no attempt to cover the whole of Catherine II's long and brilliant reign complete with wars, social upheavals, political and economic problems, and cultural developments. It is the woman, more than the empress, that I aim

* *Catherine II* (Paris, Fayard, 1955).
† *Catherine the Great: Autocrat and Empress of All Russia* (London, Hodder & Stoughton, 1961).
‡ M. Lavater-Sloman, *Catherine II et Son Temps* (Paris, Payot, 1952).

to show, and more especially the slow shaping and maturing of the future empress.

The greater part of this book will be concerned with the story of how Catherine came to the throne. It is almost a unique case of a woman achieving supreme power through her own merits, or at least as a result of a series of exceptional circumstances which she succeeded admirably in turning to her own advantage (and this, after all, is the story of every dictator). There can be no doubt that Catherine was a clever politician, and an intelligent and active woman, but in the course of her reign all she did was to canalize, foster and follow the political and economic development of a country which was already expanding fast, and it would be too much to credit Catherine with the initiative for this development. Whatever may have been said of her, Catherine was less a genius than an extremely capable ruler. She continued and—in some directions—surpassed the work of Peter the Great: she was, as we shall see, rather the docile instrument of a ruling class than a sovereign guided by political ideas of her own. But she was a woman: a man in the same situation and possessing the same qualities would certainly have attracted less attention, been less admired and less detested. Apparently women are not judged by the same moral criteria as men; and moreover it must be admitted that, for all the vigor of her character, Catherine was quite capable of using specifically female weapons to further her own position and power.

Her personality is attractive to the extent that she was a suffering, struggling human being; and it is in her *humanity* that I have tried to portray her. That is why this book will be devoted chiefly to the early part of her life—to a time when she had not yet become a sacred cow.

Often she will be allowed to speak for herself, with the reservations that this inevitably brings with it. "One is never so well served as by oneself." Even if she had been a model of integrity, Catherine would have painted herself in her memoirs more beautiful than she was. Moreover, it is by no means certain that she did not consciously manipulate the truth to her own advantage.

Yet it looks as though Catherine's memoirs should be very largely taken as the truth where they concern herself. It is arguable whether Catherine, writing for posterity or for the edification of her grandchildren, would have tended to draw a veil over her lapses (especially over her amorous adventures) and admit only to those which were common knowledge. We know that she kept silent about some of her political intrigues and about her way of solving her financial difficulties: letters from men attached to the embassies of France and England reveal what she (perhaps intentionally) tried to conceal. But it is possible that Catherine, who was madly extravagant and incapable of taking any interest in money for its own sake, had really *forgotten* details of this kind. Might she not, in the same way, have omitted to mention some compromising amorous exploit? It is possible; but a letter she wrote to Potemkin bears out the evidence of the memoirs, and with Potemkin she does seem to have been sincere, and does not appear to have confused her lover with a posterity for whom it was important to leave a flattering portrait of herself.

Lastly, the tone of the memoirs suggests that the author is enjoying retracing her lost youth, that she is seeking above all to justify herself in her own eyes, to *understand* herself, which makes it look as though Catherine was not lying very much, and then only on matters which were comparatively unimportant. She did not publish her memoirs and never finished them, so there is no way of knowing what she would finally have left in. She was writing, chiefly, for herself, and this makes it seem reasonable to trust her on the basic facts, without always accepting her interpretation of them.

In telling the long and complicated story of the events which led to Catherine's accession to the throne of Russia, there are three principal factors to bear in mind: first, the state of Russia in the mid-eighteenth century; secondly, the personality of the Empress Elizabeth, and last, the character of Catherine's husband, Peter.

When the girl who was later to become Catherine the Great came to Russia to marry the heir to the throne, it was already a powerful but chaotic state, lacking a coherent form and still shaken by the aftermath of a political and moral upheaval such as few countries have known in the course of their history. Half a century later when the same woman, now Catherine the Great, died, the country had gained so much in internal cohesion and prestige that it stood as a rival to the greatest powers in Europe. Catherine was one of the builders though not the originator of this transformation. For the Russians, the reign of Elizabeth (which lasted for twenty years) was a period of growing self-awareness, of the blossoming of a powerful national pride. Elizabeth's curious figure, which has been so variously judged, stands before anyone who wants to understand the character of Catherine II. As benefactress or wicked stepmother, as a model to imitate or a warning to be shunned, Elizabeth unwittingly forged the character of the woman who was to succeed her.

In this study of the personality of Catherine of Russia, we are compelled to understand the tragic struggle for power which was played out over eighteen years between three people, totally different from one another, quite unequal in their worth, but all three equally subject to the inescapable doom of kings: rule or perish. We must not forget that Catherine's reign was made possible only by the failure of the man who ought, lawfully, to have reigned in her stead. Peter's character, the reasons for his failure, and the part played in it by Catherine are important factors in understanding Catherine's story.

This story was first and foremost a court tragedy, played out in the halls, corridors and alcoves of the imperial palaces of St. Petersburg and Moscow. This book does not claim to be anything more than a character study, and I shall not dwell on the cruel, extravagant, sometimes even the farcical, side of the life of this court. It seemed unnecessary to stress a picturesqueness (or exoticism) which was absent in the eyes of contemporaries. It is enough for us to know that the intellectual and cultural level of Russians at this period was noticeably lower than that of Westerners of the same social standing. Called upon to line up with the West, the Russians had centuries of leeway to make up, and all in all they did not do too badly. We should remember that precisely because of this lack of tradition and of real culture, the eternal game of ambition, intrigue, hatred and jealousy was more crudely displayed in the Russian court than in any other, and that fear and vanity reigned there more than anywhere else, but not in a way that was essentially any different. However, the woman who was to become Catherine the Great was herself a product of the extremely specialized and supranational society formed by the court nobility, and she had been trained from childhood to play her part in the great game.

CATHERINE THE GREAT

One

Childhood

Her name was not Catherine and she was not Russian.

She was born on May 2, 1729 (April 21 by the Julian calendar), at Stettin in Pomerania. Her father was Christian Augustus of Anhalt-Zerbst, one of the dozens of petty princelings, lacking either fame or fortune, who abounded in eighteenth-century Germany. The family of Anhalt-Zerbst was one of the poorest and most obscure of all the countless German princely families, and Christian Augustus did not even become the reigning prince of Zerbst until thirteen years after his daughter's birth, on the death of his cousin-german, and then conjointly with his elder brother. The future empress explains in her memoirs that "the house of Anhalt did not conform to the laws of primogeniture; all Anhalt princes of the same branch have the right to a share; they have shared so much that there is almost nothing left to share . . ." The Anhalts who "reigned" over the town of Zerbst had—after all, *noblesse oblige!*—their ladies in waiting and gentlemen of the bedchamber, but in fact they were very poor; the Princess (Catherine's mother) managed somehow to get her robes of state and dresses for court mourning, but she was short of sheets, as we shall see further on.

Sophia Augusta Fredericka of Anhalt-Zerbst later said of her parents: "To all appearances they lived very comfortably together although there was a great disproportion between their ages and their dispositions were very different. For example, my father was extremely thrifty, and my mother very extravagant and *generous.*" This contains a strong implication (although the word was avoided out of filial respect) that the father was mean and that his wife, and perhaps his children also, suffered for it. It is a fact, certainly, that Sophia took after her mother in this, and she too was to show herself generous to a fault.

Christian Augustus of Anhalt-Zerbst, a prince without a principality, served in the King of Prussia's army: he was a professional soldier, as were practically all the nobility of his time. He possessed the solid, somewhat unendearing, virtues of his race and caste: a sense of duty, order, discipline, thrift; he had unimpeachable integrity, a meticulous and completely down-to-earth mind, an austere piety with a certain tendency toward mysticism. The Prince attained the rank of major general and commander of the eighth regiment of infantry, and then married —rather late in life, for he was already past forty. The marriage was arranged by his family and the couple hardly knew each other. The girl, though she had little fortune, was of very good family: she was related to the ducal house of Holstein, which was actually divided into a number of different branches, the eldest of which, through a connection with the Swedish royal house, had a claim on the throne of that country. Johanna Elizabeth of Holstein-Gottorp, the Prince of Anhalt's future wife, belonged to the younger branch.

This young, unendowed princess had been brought up at the court of her uncle, the Duke of Brunswick. Prince Christian Augustus was not a brilliant match for her, but he was a fairly respectable one. She was very pretty, but this did her little service—rather the reverse. She was lively, flirtatious and ambitious, and this too was perhaps not altogether for her own good. She was brought up in strict piety, as a member of a noted Lutheran family which yet counted bishops and abbesses among its members. It can hardly have occurred to her to fail in her duties. She was fifteen at the time of her marriage, and her husband twenty-seven years older.

(In an attempt to explain Catherine II's amazing gifts, later historians have attributed some extramarital intrigues to the young Princess Johanna Elizabeth of Holstein-Gottorp, Princess of Anhalt-Zerbst, and credited the future empress with more brilliant fathers than the respectable Christian Augustus. These include Frederick II of Prussia (then heir to the throne and only sixteen years old) and Count Ivan Betsky—who was in fact to become the Princess's lover, but not until fifteen years later. However, it seems likely that Johanna Elizabeth was a faithful wife and a devoted mother. But her marriage certainly did not bring her happiness.)

She was no Emma Bovary, however. Overflowing with vitality, she could not cope with boredom or learn to live on dreams. Condemned to a modest existence in the castle of Stettin (where her husband filled the post of military governor), Johanna Elizabeth worked obstinately at building up for herself a place in the world equal to her ambitions. She had a real talent for making the most of her family connections and of her family's ties of friendship with crowned heads. She did not let herself fall into oblivion. Once a year she went to Berlin to pay her respects at the King of Prussia's court, and poor as she was, for nobility confers more privileges than wealth, she occasionally ate at the same table as the Queen and talked with the sons and daughters of kings. This was a great deal, and yet it was also very little: for all her pride, the young woman had too sharp a sense of reality not to know that she was still a person of very little account.

She was too well born for her own good, and in her eyes social obligations were as sacred as those to her family. At last, eighteen months after her marriage, at the age of seventeen, Johanna Elizabeth brought her first child into the world. She had passionately wanted a son, but the child was a girl: Sophia Augusta Fredericka. Since she could not have foreseen that this daughter would one day outshine all the glory of past Anhalt-Zerbsts, and even of all past, present or future Holsteins, the young mother was bitterly disappointed. The customs of the time left very little allowance for the flowering of maternal feelings in noble ladies, and the baby was handed over to the care of nurses, seeing her mother only on such occasions as the Princess had time to think of her. A year after her first confinement, the Princess of Anhalt finally had the son she had wanted so much. She grew the more passionately fond of her second child because his health was delicate, while little Sophia was a comparatively robust child.

As an old woman, Sophia wrote the story of her childhood and young womanhood. She was not disposed to dwell romantically on her early years, but what she does say about them shows that, even at a very early age, she was a clear-headed, obstinate and self-willed little person, very much taken up with herself.

She did not have a happy childhood; certainly she complains somewhat bitterly of her mother's lack of affection: the classic reaction of the eldest child who feels neglected in favor of her juniors. This undoubtedly affected her character profoundly: all her life she exhibited a dreadful, devouring need for love which was like an unconscious search for the mother love she had lacked.

The children of princes—even of such minor princes as

Christian Augustus of Anhalt-Zerbst—were brought up at first by nurses, and then by their governesses, tutors, and music and dancing masters, and court etiquette was drilled into them as soon as they were old enough to be able to sketch a curtsy. In those days small boys and girls were dressed exactly like miniature adults in coats and waistcoats, stays and low-cut dresses, and on special occasions even wore powder in their hair. When the Princess of Anhalt-Zerbst was entertaining ladies in her salon she taught her daughter to kiss the hems of their dresses. Sophia—or Figchen, as she was generally called—trailed after her mother to balls and receptions, masquerades and firework displays, like a frail, brown-haired doll in her panniered gown, and was already drawing attention to herself by her wit, or at least by her childish forthrightness. On one occasion, when she was four, she found some difficulty in getting hold of a coat which she was supposed to kiss—it belonged to no less a personage than Frederick William I, King of Prussia—and exclaimed loudly: "His clothes are too short. I can't reach them." The King remarked that the child was impertinent: *"Das Mädchen ist naseweis."* Figchen was considered rude and self-opinionated, and her mother often gave her deliberate setdowns in order to correct her faults.

Years later, writing of her first governess, Madeleine Cardel, who taught her how to behave "so that I, and she too, might please my parents," she said: "This made me deceitful for my age. My father, whom I did not see so often, believed me an angel; my mother took very little notice of me." Recalling her mother's affection for her eldest son, she said: "As for me, I was merely tolerated, and I was often cruelly snubbed and not always justly."[1] This is the classic attitude of a jealous child; but the bitterness of being only "tolerated" marked Sophia's character for life. She grew up into a passionately egocentric woman, hungry for love and desperately anxious to be both loved and admired.

Her father "believed her an angel" and she loved him dearly, but she saw him so seldom. He was always busy, and even when he was not, his dignity as a prince and a major general forbade him to indulge in demonstrations of affection toward his family. Her mother, Sophia never forgave for having preferred the boys to herself. A second brother was born in 1734, and when the time came for Sophia to be separated from her family, she thought of him with affectionate regret, but the eldest did not exist for her; she barely mentions him, and then only to remark that he died at the age of twelve (on another occasion she says thirteen) of scarlet fever and that he was lame as the result of an accident which occurred in his infancy. She says a word or two of her mother's grief, without even appearing to be aware that the matter could be any concern of hers.

There is no doubt that the person who inspired her with the most affection—though she could not replace her mother, for the proud little princess was incapable of giving pride of place in her heart to an inferior—was her second governess, Elisabeth or Babet Cardel, a Frenchwoman, the daughter of a Huguenot refugee living in Germany. Sophia describes her enthusiastically as a "model of virtue and wisdom: she had a natural elevation of spirit, a cultivated mind, an excellent heart; she was patient, gentle, cheerful, just, constant, and truly everything that could be desired in a person having to do with children."[2] When the little girl grew up into a woman she spoke of Babet Cardel with deep gratitude, praising her for her occasional severity, and in her old age, writing to such cultivated friends as Voltaire and Melchior von Grimm, she loved to sign herself "Mademoiselle Cardel's pupil."

From Mademoiselle Cardel, Sophia learned not only the French language, which was obligatory at that period for every member of good society in Europe, but also a great deal of French literature, and that of the seventeenth century in particular, such as Corneille, Racine, Molière, La Fontaine, although she does not appear to have relished them overmuch. She had other teachers, too: for German, writing, dancing and music; and since her father was a strict Lutheran, there naturally was a pastor at hand to teach her religion and theology. Sophia was a model pupil: conscientious, hard-working, and gifted with an excellent memory and a naturally inquiring mind. The only subject which left her completely indifferent was music, for which she had so little ear that all her life she never perceived anything in it beyond a succession of meaningless noises.

According to the testimony of those who knew her at this time, young Figchen was a lively, boisterous, tomboyish child. She was fond of energetic games, and especially keen on shooting birds. Her parents had the good sense not to keep her cooped up indoors in the castle of Stettin on the score that she was a princess; she made friends with children of her own age, played in the streets of the town, and seems to have been what a modern child would call "bossy" in dealing with her young playmates, but she was also a good organizer and a natural leader in all their games. Even when she was quite young she was a thoughtful child, fond of reading and of asking awkward questions. Among the things she wanted to know were, why should Titus, Marcus Aurelius and other good men be damned simply because they had lived before the Redemption, what was the precise nature of chaos, and what was circumcision. At one point the atmosphere of strict piety in which she was brought up almost made her fall into "melancholy," thanks to the teaching of Pastor Dowe, who succeeded in instilling into her such a terror of the Last Judgment that the child, who was then seven or eight years old, used to sit crying "in a window embrasure in the dusk" through one whole autumn. When Sophia's governess told him of this state of affairs the pastor gave up talking to Sophia about judgment and salvation, and the little girl does not seem to have been troubled by any further anxieties of a metaphysical nature.

Figchen was a healthy child—relatively so, at least, when compared to the majority of children of princely families, in which consistent intermarriage produced frequent cases of degeneracy. Sophia's two brothers were both sickly children and her little sister died young. For a long time she herself suffered so severely from some kind of eczema or impetigo that every now and then she had to have her hair shaved off because of the scabs on her head. At the age of seven she contracted pleurisy and later suffered from a malformation of the spine which meant that she had to wear a corset day and night for four years. However, by the time she was eleven or so her back had grown straight again, and later on, as she grew into womanhood, her fondness for sports and a healthy outdoor life helped her to acquire robust good health.

All the same, in spite of her precocious intelligence, Sophia at the age of ten must have been more of an irritating nuisance to her mother than a source of pride. Not only was she sickly, and cured with great difficulty of her endless eczema only to find her body twisted "like a Z"; not only was she a tomboy and generally regarded as impudent, but she had the added misfortune of being indisputably ugly. Portraits painted at this time show her with a frankly unpleasant expression, and painters of the period were not in the habit of making their models look like monsters, especially when these happened to be young princesses. Ugliness is a terrible handicap for any girl, however willful and independent her character, and it is reasonable to suppose that it was the knowledge that she was unattractive which drove little Sophia to concentrate on her studies and her reading so that in the absence of beauty she would at least acquire "merit," as she was later to put it.

Two

What Do Little Princesses Dream Of?

Nevertheless, by the time she was about ten she was beginning to regain some hope. She wrote later: "The extreme ugliness with which I had been endowed was leaving me." Slowly enough, it must be admitted, but she was not ill-made; she was tall and slim, with a high forehead and attractive, dark blue eyes, and with her long nose and pointed chin she had a look of breeding if not of beauty. It was in this year, 1739, that her parents took her to a party given by her uncle Adolphus Frederick of Holstein-Gottorp (who was later to become King of Sweden). The Holstein-Gottorps were actually one of the noblest families in Germany, and Princess Johanna Elizabeth, although she had no fortune, considered herself to have married beneath her. She was a sophisticated, worldly woman, and the intrigues of the German and other European courts, official receptions, and points of etiquette occupied a large part of her life, or at least of her thoughts. She was determined to let no one forget that she belonged to the illustrious family of the dukes of Holstein. Thus it was at Kiel, on the occasion of a family gathering, that Sophia met for the first time the young prince Karl Peter Ulrich of Holstein, heir presumptive (or at least one of the possible heirs) to the thrones of both Sweden and Russia.

The boy was a year older than Sophia, and was her second cousin on the Holstein side. In her memoirs she describes him as "really handsome, agreeable and well-bred. . . . Indeed everyone was praising to the skies this boy of eleven years whose father had recently died." In actual fact there was little enough to praise. Peter Ulrich was small, frail and sickly, and anything but well-bred, although as to his looks he was certainly no worse off than Sophia and probably better. The shy orphan boy, lonely and bored with life in a palace where he had no company except that of brutal and tyrannical tutors, was in all likelihood delighted to have a cousin of his own age to talk to. Though his daily life was regulated with an almost military discipline, the young prince had a naturally lively temperament and was not stupid, though he was more childish than his age and the conventions of the time demanded. The sensible Sophia found him very babyish, but she overheard her mother and aunts hinting covertly at a possible union between herself and this boy.

Sophia was a princess, and at an age when most small girls are still thinking about dolls she was already considering her future, in other words, marriage, which was the only future possible for her. "Child as I was," she wrote, "the title of queen caressed my ears. From that time onward those around me used to tease me about him [Peter Ulrich] and gradually I grew accustomed to think myself destined for him."

The words "teased me about him" seem to suggest that at least some indication of a mutual attraction did exist between the two cousins which the adults had noticed.

Sophia was dreaming of marriage. She had seen enough noble, pious and unfortunate ladies in her mother's entourage, as well as among more distant relations, who had been condemned by their want of fortune or their lack of personal charm to a life of chastity. Ugly and "poor" (considering her rank) as she was, the child had a lively fear that she might fail to attract a lover. Noble lineage was not a thing to be taken lightly in the circles among which she moved, and it went without saying that a daughter of the Prince of Anhalt-Zerbst must either marry a prince or remain an old maid. But thanks to her meeting with the heir to the crown of Sweden (or of Russia), Sophia, whose imagination had begun to work at an early age, was dreaming of nothing less than a crown. One day, on the occasion of the marriage of one of her cousins, Princess Augusta of Saxe-Gotha, with the Prince of Wales, had she not overheard her father's major-domo saying to Mademoiselle Cardel: "Well, this princess has scarce been so well brought up as our own, and she is not even pretty, and yet here she is destined to become Queen of England. Who knows what ours might not become?"[1] A queen —why not, when one has one cousin married to the Prince of Wales and another who may become a king?

Indeed, Sophia was not the only one to have her eye on this cousin: her mother had thought of him first. A born intriguer and easily dazzled by the lure of a title, she was the kind of woman who naturally tends to pay court to the great ones of this world, almost through a sense of duty. When her brother was appointed the young Duke of Holstein's guardian she lost no time in paying him a visit and embracing the noble orphan who was destined for such a noble fortune, and when, three years later, the same little duke's maternal aunt ascended the throne of Russia as the Empress Elizabeth I, she at once hastened to remind the new Empress of her existence. Besides, as we shall see, her own connections with the Russian court gave her strong grounds for hope. Sophia's marriage, far from being, as it has often been called, a piece of unexpected good luck falling like a thunderclap on a family of obscure German princes, was the result of years of careful preparation on the part of the Princess of Anhalt-Zerbst. True, she could not be altogether sure of success, but she did her best all the same.

The house of Holstein had strong enough ties with the Russian imperial family to permit the Princess of Anhalt-Zerbst to pay court to the Empress without appearing indiscreet. Peter the Great's eldest daughter had married the Duke of Holstein and had become the mother of little Peter Ulrich. One of Johanna Elizabeth's own brothers, Karl Augustus of Holstein-Gottorp, had been betrothed to Peter's second daughter, Elizabeth. The prince had died a few days after the betrothal took place, but Elizabeth had not forgotten him. It was this very Elizabeth who had now acceded to her father's throne, after a *coup d'état* as spectacular as it was swift, and Johanna Elizabeth, proud of the fact that she had very nearly been the sister-in-law of an empress, could talk of nothing but Russia, Peter the Great and Elizabeth I.

Russia, the Russia of Peter the Great, barbarous Muscovy, now elevated as by a miracle, in the space of a few decades, to the rank of a great European power, was a constant subject of interest among the petty courts of North Germany. To its neighbors this vast country was still something of a mystery, but it was haloed with the prestige of a great military power; it was said to be a land of fabulous wealth, either "barbarous" or "civilized" according to the political opinions of the speaker, but important on account of its size and full of unknown potentialities. Under Peter the Great (who died in 1725) and to an even greater extent under his successors, Germans had enjoyed a privileged position in Russia; they had made vast fortunes there, had been generals, ministers and intimate advisers—some of them very intimate indeed—to the tsarinas. Moreover the two most recent rulers, Anna Ivanovna and then her niece, the Queen Mother Regent Anna Leopoldovna, had themselves been German princesses. It was therefore natural for German princes to look on this great country, if not as a zone of influence, at least as a semi-Germanic territory and a perfectly natural place to turn to in search of a great career.

Elizabeth, it is true, had made a break with tradition: the *coup d'état* which brought her to the throne had been due to a wave of xenophobia which ruthlessly swept away the German soldiers and officials, good as well as bad, in favor of true-born Russians. It is possible that the Princess of Anhalt-Zerbst had imperfectly understood this: she thought that the discredited Germans had been justly punished for their crimes, since such a gracious empress as Elizabeth could not make a mistake. In any case, was not the heir to the throne himself also a German prince, and one of Johanna Elizabeth's own relations?

Whatever the facts, the coronation of Elizabeth and the designation of Peter Ulrich as heir to the throne of Russia were received with great delight, says Sophia, in the family of Anhalt-Zerbst. In all family discussions, the boy was still regarded as the ideal husband for Sophia. There were those who said that the young duke would choose a bride from a more noble family and a more powerful one, but "they could not agree on any other *parti*." "In my own small mind," Sophia was to write later, "I had already bestowed myself on him, and this on account of the fact that of all the matches proposed he was the most eligible."[2]

Sophia's mother had a copy of her daughter's portrait made and entrusted it to General Korff, who was to take it to Russia. Korff and another gentleman from the Russian court, Sievers, had already, on various pretexts, asked to see the young princess, and each had taken a portrait of her to show to the Empress. The girl was perfectly well aware of what was going on, and the excitement went more and more to her head. Empress of Russia! True, she was not the only marriageable girl whose portrait had been sent to Petersburg and Moscow by ambassadors and court envoys, but she was only thirteen and probably did not know this: the knowing looks, whisperings and clumsy attempts at secrecy of the grownups around her must have given her the idea that a great future was almost certainly hers. The ambitions of the woman who was to become Catherine of Russia took root in the dreams of a child infected by her mother's overpowering conceit.

There was no question of love in these dreams of a great marriage: she barely knew the boy she looked on as a prospective husband. Besides, at that period love and marriage did not necessarily go together, even in little girls' dreams. Sophia was even then a sensual creature, though she did not know it, having been brought up in total innocence. At night, tormented by an excess of energy that it never occurred to her to try and fathom, she would sit astride her pillow and gallop in her bed "until [she] was exhausted." Even when as a mature woman she recounted this story, she did not understand the disturbances underlying the game; her sensuality was an unconscious, animal thing, as it is

with children who are not given to daydreaming. She did however have one small flirtation with an uncle, a very young, handsome uncle who might perhaps have felt few scruples in seducing
her if she had not been so totally ignorant of the whole business
of love.

She herself describes the progress of this love affair: the
declarations, at first awkward and then more specific, which
ended with her uncle George Louis asking her to marry him.
The girl answered him in surprise that "my father and mother
would not like it," and in the end she agreed "provided only
that my father and mother make no objection." "After I had given
my consent, my uncle abandoned himself entirely to his passion,
which was extreme: he seized every opportunity of embracing
me, and was skilled at creating them, but apart from a few kisses,
all in fact passed off very innocently."[3] The young girl apparently
found her bashful lover's sighs and groans, and his changes of
mood from bluntness to melancholy, totally incomprehensible.
Perhaps George Louis would have had his way in the end, and he
might even have married his niece, had not a letter arrived from
Berlin which effectively put all thoughts of her fond uncle out of
Sophia's head, and gave her parents something else to worry
about.

Three

The King of Prussia

The letter, which arrived on January 1, 1744, came from Brümmer, grand marshal to the court of the Duke of Holstein (now heir apparent to the Russian throne). Brümmer requested the Princess of Anhalt-Zerbst to set out with all possible speed and secrecy for Russia, taking with her "the princess, her elder daughter." The Princess was not—as some historians have claimed—sufficiently stupid to believe that the invitation was meant for her alone and that her daughter was of no account in it; it seems that what disturbed her most was the somewhat clandestine air about the whole proceeding, which did not suggest an official proposal of marriage. She was acutely aware that she and her daughter would be laying themselves open to becoming the laughingstock of every court in Europe, in the event of the marriage failing to take place. Sophia's father and mother hesitated for a long time. Christian Augustus did not like the idea of seeing his daughter settled so far from home, in a foreign country and a distinctly unsafe one at that. Only recently one German princess, Anne of Brunswick-Mecklenburg, had lost her title of regent and been thrown into prison with her family on the orders of this same Elizabeth. A fresh *coup d'état* might find Sophia herself in the same predicament. At best, the future Empress of Russia would certainly be obliged to change her religion and embrace the Orthodox faith, and this, for a devout

Lutheran like the Prince of Anhalt-Zerbst, was in itself a prospect which raised sufficient obstacles to the marriage.

Brümmer's letter was followed by one from the King of Prussia. The King, still writing to the Princess and not to the Prince, at last explained in so many words that a marriage was in the wind and that in the interests of Prussia everything possible must be done to ensure that Princess Sophia became the wife of the Russian Grand Duke. Sophia's mother, he inferred, could exert sufficient influence on the Empress to dissuade her from any alliance which might be to the disadvantage of Prussia. For once, Johanna Elizabeth was in her element: she had honor, favor, intrigue, and a political role to play, while the stage on which she was finally to deploy the assets nature had bestowed upon her, her beauty, wit, noble birth and knowledge of the world, all treasures hitherto wasted on a dull provincial town, was a magnificent one indeed.

Sophia, seeing her parents' excitement, their private conferences, the hesitations of first one and then the other, was consumed with impatience. She tried to understand, and felt frustrated by the mystery which everybody around her persisted in making of it when she knew perfectly well what was going on. "Well then, miss," her mother told her, "since you are so knowledgeable, you have only to guess the rest of the contents of a twelve-page letter about affairs of state." That afternoon, Sophia brought her mother a note which read:

What is to happen?
Why, Peter III is to be your husband.

Then she set about pleading her own cause, the cause of her young ambitions, with great earnestness. "She told me that there was also a considerable risk involved, considering the unsettled state of affairs in that country. I answered that the good Lord would provide for stability, if such was His will; that for myself, I felt my courage was equal to the risk, and that my heart told me that all would go well. She could not prevent herself from saying: 'But what will my brother George say?' (This was the first time she had spoken to me of that matter.) I blushed and answered: 'He can only wish me good fortune and happiness.' She said no more and went to speak to my father."[1] In her youthful arrogance, Sophia believed that what she said had influenced her parents' final decision, and indeed she may have been right, since they would not have acted against her wishes. In any case, the love of her charming Uncle George was no longer in her eyes enough to make her truly happy.

For the first time in her life Figchen quarreled with her beloved Babet Cardel: her parents had forbidden her to mention to anyone what was in the wind, and as far as the rest of the world was concerned they were merely making an ordinary journey to Berlin. Babet realized that her pupil was hiding something important from her and saw her silence as a lack of affection, in which she was probably right. Later, much later, Sophia would attempt to justify herself in her own eyes by counting up all the proofs of affection she had given her governess: how she had visited her every day when she was sick, had once made tea for her with her own hands, and had given her medicine. Mademoiselle Cardel herself, she recalled, had been "much affected by it." The reason Sophia had not confided in her the secret of the Russian marriage was because her parents . . . and so on. Nevertheless the "model of virtue and wisdom," who no doubt loved the child as if she were her own daughter, believed she had earned greater trust and was deeply hurt. But the child had forgotten everything that was not immediately connected with the splendid future which was being held out to her. She took leave of Babet with tears in her eyes, but still without telling her the truth. Mistress and pupil were never to see one another again.

The Prince of Anhalt-Zerbst and his wife and daughter traveled first to Berlin, where they were summoned to an audience with the King of Prussia, who wanted to see the girl and give her mother some last-minute instructions. Frederick II had every intention of getting the Princess to act as a secret agent for Prussia, and as a loyal vassal, she saw nothing wrong in this—indeed, she regarded it as perfectly natural to do so.

The young king—Frederick was thirty years old at the time—
had recently succeeded his father, the "soldier king" Frederick
William I, of whom Sophia afterward wrote in her memoirs
that he was universally detested, that "people embraced one another in the streets and exchanged congratulations on the death
of this king." Frederick II was a very different man from his
father. He was intelligent, cultured, no less energetic than his
father had been and equally gifted as a soldier, and he was to
become the chief architect of the unification of Germany under
the leadership of the Kingdom of Prussia. He was as able a
statesman as he was a great soldier, and was admired and respected by the German princes, who considered it an honor to
serve under his command. The Princess and her daughter shared
this admiration.

Prussia at this time was in an exceedingly tricky position,
threatened by Austria in the east and Russia in the north. She
was a small country and her territories were dangerously split
up, but her ambitions and growing strength were beginning to
make her powerful neighbors uneasy, and it was vitally important to Frederick that Russia should not be numbered among his
enemies. From the moment she came to the throne Elizabeth
had adopted an openly anti-Prussian policy, and this attitude
was put down to the influence of her chancellor (and minister
of foreign affairs), Count Bestuzhev-Ryumin. For some time
now the Empress had been looking for a suitable bride for her
nephew, and her choice of the young princess of Anhalt-Zerbst
had been influenced by the opposition to the chancellor's party,
who wanted the future wife of the heir apparent to be a "neutral"
person, of noble but not particularly influential family, who
would not be the candidate of either faction. Frederick II had
managed matters so well that Elizabeth's choice had in fact fallen
on the candidate he himself favored, and the reason he urged
the princesses to be discreet was that he had no desire to see
his adversaries thwarting his plans.

The girl and her parents were well received in Berlin. Johanna
Elizabeth seems to have felt some reluctance in presenting her

daughter to the King (it may well have been that she considered her insufficiently attractive); several times she claimed that the child was ill, and then she made the excuse that the child had no court dress. The King had to send the young princess a dress belonging to one of his own sisters before Figchen was at last taken to the royal palace.

At first the young girl (she was not yet fourteen) was "timid and shy," and her shyness grew when she learned that at the state banquet she was invited to the King's own table, while her mother was only to sit at the Queen's. It is not hard to imagine her feelings when she found that she was placed next to the King himself. It was her first appearance in the great world, and thanks to Frederick's tact and consideration, it was a triumph for the child's pride. The young king succeeded in putting her completely at her ease; he talked to her about "opera, plays, poetry, dancing and I don't know what, but anyway a thousand things that one does talk about to entertain a girl of fourteen." Gradually forgetting her shyness, and no doubt feeling her best in the court dress with her hair prettily arranged, Sophia managed to answer intelligently and appear natural and lively, and— as she herself says with pride—"the entire company stared in amazement to see the King engaged in conversation with a child." It was the height of bliss when, after requesting her to pass a dish of sweets to one of the guests, the King turned to him and said: "Accept this gift from the hand of the Loves and Graces."[2]

Such a memory would be enough to give any neglected, insecure girl confidence in herself: she, the ugly duckling, had been identified before the whole court with the Loves and Graces! Frederick was not joking: the slender child with her bright eyes and cheeks flushed with excitement must have been refreshingly young and charming. The King of Prussia was well aware that this was one evening the future Empress of Russia would never forget.

Sophia was soon to realize that the "fortune" she had longed for so much would bring her much unhappiness, perhaps more unhappiness than, in her childish innocence, she could have foreseen. Already, at Zerbst, she had said farewell to Mademoiselle Cardel, without even telling her that she was going away for a long time: at Stettin, mother and daughter had had to take leave of the father who had not been included in the Russian Empress's invitation (it was feared that, as a devout Lutheran, he would have too strong an influence over his daughter).

Officially the Princess of Anhalt-Zerbst was traveling to Russia in order to thank the Empress for the kind favors she had shown to the Princess's family. This pretext meant that she had to travel with as little baggage as possible and with only a very few attendants: one gentleman, Monsieur de Laterf, one lady in waiting, Mademoiselle de Kayn, four maidservants, a valet, a few footmen and a cook. For the period, a traveling suite like this appeared almost poverty-stricken. In order to avoid attracting the attention of the opposition party, which was extremely powerful at the Russian court, the Princess was to travel under an assumed name, and she carried papers made out in the name of Countess Reinbeck.

Sophia wept when she said goodbye to her father. Although she did not realize it, she was never to see him again. Probably she also felt a pang in her heart as she watched the walls of the fortress of Stettin where she had spent her childhood vanish over the horizon. But this was no time for regrets: she was a child, and she was thrilled by the prospect of a long journey and a brilliant new life ahead. She foresaw none of the dangers and disappointments which might await her, and the worst she suffered was from the discomfort of the journey: six weeks, first in a carriage and then in a sleigh, over bad roads in the depths of winter. The princesses left Stettin on January 15, and did not reach Moscow until February 10/21 (since the Russian Church had not adopted the Gregorian calendar Russian dates were eleven days behind those in the West).

The thing that tormented her father and formed the constant although superficial preoccupation of her mother, her change of religion, did not trouble the young girl unduly. Princess Johanna

Elizabeth had done her utmost to minimize the importance of
such a step in her daughter's eyes. Sophia was certainly devout,
but in a rational way, and she was not given to flights of mysticism. She was a dutiful girl and submitted obediently to the will
of her parents. Although she was only thirteen years and ten
months old, she was not giddy, rebellious or romantic by temperament. Baroness von Prinzen, her mother's lady in waiting, remarked of her later, "I watched Princess Sophia grow up and
witnessed the progress she made in her studies; I myself helped
her to make her preparations for her departure for Russia. . . .
From her early youth I merely observed in her a cold, calculating
and serious disposition, but also one that was as far from being
outstanding or brilliant as it was from folly, lightness or extravagance. In short, I had formed the opinion that she would turn out
a very ordinary woman."3

Neither mother nor daughter appears to have spared much
thought for the sickly young prince who was the real reason for
their journey. They were too much accustomed to pay more
attention to the title than to the person who bore it, and Peter
Ulrich of Holstein—or rather, the Grand Duke Peter Feodorovich
—was in fact no more than his title. He himself counted for so
little that never once in her memoirs does Sophia give any indication that she felt either joy or sadness at the thought of her
future betrothed; not once in her letters does the mother remember her little cousin and future son-in-law; she is concerned with
her daughter's fortune, her daughter's change of religion, and
that is all.

To be sure, they already knew that the Grand Duke was no
paragon; that his health was so delicate that it was feared he
might never reach maturity; that he was considered ignorant,
willful and wild. It was said—for nothing escaped the eagle eyes
of foreign diplomats—that the young Grand Duke was unhappy
in Russia and that, despite the change of religion which had
been forced on him, he remained a Lutheran at heart and displayed nothing but contempt for his adoptive country. Sophia can
only have had a vague memory of a nice enough boy she had met

once at a family gathering four years before. It was not of him that she had really been dreaming for these four years, not him that she wanted to marry. It was Russia and the Russian crown, the fabulous realm of Muscovy, the empire of Peter the Great.

Sophia Augusta Fredericka of Anhalt-Zerbst's ideas about this country were conventional, sugared, set pieces and she knew nothing of what it was really like. Her mother proudly showed her the portrait of the lovely, gracious Empress Elizabeth, set in a diamond frame, which the sovereign of all the Russias had sent as a gift to the Princess of Anhalt-Zerbst in return for a portrait of her dead sister, Anne of Russia, who had been Duchess of Holstein.[4] The child had been taught in advance to revere, almost to worship, this magnificent woman with the heavy shoulders and big blue eyes, and wise little Sophia asked nothing better. She was perfectly willing to believe that Elizabeth was a model of all the virtues, Russia a great, noble, wonderful country, and the Orthodox religion a highly respectable one, differing hardly at all from the Lutheran faith.

She was to write later that "nowhere are people more apt than in Russia to notice the weaknesses, faults and quaintness of a foreigner. One may be quite sure that nothing will be passed over, because by nature all Russians have a fundamental dislike of foreigners."[5] Certainly the Europeanized Russia of the eighteenth century was not kind to strangers: it was not an easy place to live, and one even less easy to understand. The child whom her mother's ambition and the intrigues of the King of Prussia had combined to launch on this most perilous adventure was speeding in a sleigh over icy roads, between forests and vast stretches of white plain, exhausted and sick to death of the seemingly endless journey. The country was so huge and the journey so long that in the end Petersburg, and Moscow where the Empress lived, began to seem from a distance like some splendid and terrible mirage, cities of legend rather than reality.

Four

Holy Russia

To what extent was Russia in the eighteenth century a European country? She was, somewhat in the sense that modern Japan or the United States of America is today, although neither of these comparisons is altogether just. To the end of her life, Catherine would use the words Russia and Scythia interchangeably, without any pejorative implications. The Russians were not an Asiatic people, either racially, culturally or, least of all, in their religion, but until the beginning of the eighteenth century they had remained more or less completely cut off from the West.

Racially and linguistically, Russia was a Slav country; through the centuries numerous invasions—some warlike, some peaceful—had given the Russian people strong injections of Mongol, Greek and Scandinavian blood. From the tenth century onward the Great Principality of Russia (the name Russia—*Rus*—is Scandinavian in origin) had been in culture and traditions an offshoot of Byzantium, although it had never, like the Slavs of the Balkans, been directly or indirectly dependent on the Eastern Roman Empire. Situated on the great trade routes to the East, Russia, like the countries of the West, had until the thirteenth century a feudal regime in which various different principalities, such as Kiev, Vladimir, Suzdal and Ryazan, were struggling for the lead. The same period saw the flowering of a number of powerful, autonomous city-states like Novgorod and Pskov. At this time Russia's development appears to have differed very little from that of other medieval countries, but then an unforeseen catastrophe fell on the land. Within a few years the proud, warlike feudal principalities of Great Russia were swept by a Mongol invasion, and the lieutenants of Genghis Khan, after burning cities and spreading terror throughout the land, installed themselves on the Volga, imposing on the conquered country a heavy annual tribute which was to bleed an already devastated land almost white. For three centuries Russia was cut off from the Western world, and her neighbors to the north and west naturally took advantage of her situation. Russia suffered from the Poles, the Swedes, the Lithuanians and the Teutonic Knights almost as much as she had suffered from the Tartars, while in the south she was cut off from Byzantium and from the other Slav countries by the creation of a Tartar kingdom on the Sea of Azov.

Up to the sixteenth century, therefore, the Russian people, harried simultaneously both by East and West, as it were, and with their very existence threatened on all sides, withdrew fiercely into themselves, clinging passionately to their traditions, their language and their past, and drawing courage from the exaltation of their national pride.

The period of the "Tartar Yoke" saw the flowering of the Great Principality of Muscovy. Moscow was neither the oldest nor the most important of Russian cities, but toward the end of the fifteenth century, thanks to the victories won by Muscovite princes over the Tartars, little Muscovy began to grow and extend her territory at the expense of other principalities. Ivan III (1462–1505) freed Russia from the Tartar Yoke and, by marrying Sophia Palaeologina, a descendant of the Byzantine emperors, set himself up as the champion of the Greek Orthodox religion and as the successor to the "Second Rome": Russia was to be the third. His grandson Ivan IV (The Terrible) won from the Tartars the southeast of what is now European Russia, took the title of *tsar* (derived from that of *Caesar*), and became the exponent of an autocracy based on divine right which raised the Tsar to the position of God's representative on earth.

Evidently the Muscovite princes were men of inordinate pride and ambition, and they gained an almost messianic reputation. Their real power was not extensive. Ivan the Terrible weakened and disorganized the country in the course of his desperate struggle against a feudal aristocracy which was jealous of his independence, and after the old dynasty had been wiped out Russia lapsed into a period of black and dreadful anarchy. The "Time of Troubles" lasted for eight years but it took the country a hundred years to recover from it. After a narrow escape from Polish occupation, the Kingdom of Muscovy, morally and materially exhausted, regained a relative peace during the reign of the first tsar of the Romanov dynasty, Michael Feodorovich (1613–1645).

Michael's son, Alexei, made praiseworthy efforts to reorganize the life of the nation: like his illustrious predecessors Ivan the Terrible and Boris Godunov, Alexei was, or at least attempted to be, a reformer.

By the middle of the sixteenth century, everyday life in Russia had reached a level which would have been considered primitive even in the Middle Ages. Not merely was she backward by comparison with the European and Asiatic powers who surrounded her; she was, as a result of continual wars at home and abroad and of an isolation which had begun by being enforced and ended by becoming self-imposed, in a state of decadence which put a stranglehold on the entire moral, intellectual and economic life of the country. The Russians had struggled so fiercely to preserve their faith and their traditions that this faith and these traditions had finally reached a state of stagnation through having been guarded too jealously. This tended to paralyze any new development. Like his father and his predecessors, Alexei realized this and tried to find a remedy. The solutions to the problems facing the country had to be sought outside Russia. Everything had to be refashioned: the whole military, commercial, social and economic structure of the country, and the new forms were to be found, not in other countries where the Orthodox religion was practiced, and (since Byzantium no longer existed) even less in the Moslem East, but in that very Christian West, heretical and basically alien though it was, which was in the full flight of technical and economic growth. But the Russians had a deep-seated horror of the West and an even greater horror of any kind of novelty.

When Peter, the youngest of Alexei's sons, came to the throne, Russia was in the process of "westernizing" herself slowly and timidly, every hint of a reform in this direction being the occasion for more or less violent displays of opposition on the part of the people and the nobles. The gulf seemed practically insuperable, and the "enlightened" boyars who went so far as to learn foreign languages and wear—in their own homes—European costume dared not admit in public to such scandalous practices. It is impossible to begin to understand Russia in the eighteenth century without first taking a glance at the fantastic adventure which was the reign of Peter the Great.

Five

❦❦❦❦❦❦❦❦❦❦

Peter the Great

Peter possessed a peculiar and indisputable advantage over "progressive" boyars such as his mother's adoptive father, Artamon Matveiev, or Prince Basil Golitsin who was the favorite of the Regent Sophia: he was not a *civilized* man. He lost his father at an early age, and his childhood was not a pleasant one: during the regency of his half-sister Sophia he and his mother frequently went in fear of their lives, and in the course of a rebellion of the Archers' Guard (which was devoted to Sophia) the young Peter saw the boyar Matveiev dragged from his arms and torn to pieces by the crowd, and his maternal uncles brutally done to death. Sophia wanted to rule and to rule alone, and she seized absolute power for herself, although nominally acting as regent in the name of her two brothers, of whom Ivan was mentally defective and Peter still a child. She was accustomed to describe herself as "Autocrat," and did her best to let young Peter grow up in ignorance, with the object of making him unfit to reign (for the feeble Ivan presented no threat); she deliberately neglected his education—the great Russian reformer and educator never learned to write Russian correctly (or indeed any other language).

In the absence of teachers worthy of his high rank, Peter, a restless, eager boy hungry for knowledge, sought his teachers where he could find them: literally in the streets. It was in roaming the streets of the "German Quarter" that he discovered his vocation. He made friends with a boy named "Alexashka" Menshikov, a ragamuffin from the Moscow suburbs who made his living by selling hot pies, and went with his friend to the shops and houses of foreign merchants—at first out of curiosity, like the badly brought up lad he was. But he was kindly welcomed there and made lasting and sincere friendships. There he found men to teach him about the arts which interested him most: mathematics, mechanics, geography, astronomy, and even carpentry and metalwork; for to the young Peter the "German Quarter" was paradise, and he wanted to learn to do everything his new friends did, even drinking spirits and smoking a pipe.

This "German Quarter" was like a small European town in the very center of Moscow. It was the district reserved for foreign merchants, craftsmen, artisans and mercenaries, although these were by no means all German. (German—*Niemets*—was the name Russians used to denote Westerners in general, al-

ways excepting the Poles.) The foreign colony included a great
many English and Scots, as well as Dutch and Swiss. They
mixed hardly at all with the life of the people, and the people
ignored and looked down on them as "heretics." The young
Tsar's infatuation with these beardless foreigners with their
short clothes shocked and horrified his mother, the boyars and
the people of Moscow, but Peter was a headstrong boy and he
did not give up his dubious and reprehensible predilections. What
those around him took for the mere vagary of an idle boy was
to be at the root of one of the strangest revolutions known to
history.

Western culture fell on exceptionally fertile ground: Peter
swallowed it all eagerly, and gloried passionately in what he
learned. He became the priest of a new religion, dedicated to
hatred of the past and the salvation of Russia by the West. He
was the disciple of the Swiss Lefort and the Scotsman Gordon,
humbling himself before masters in whose presence he felt like
a barbarian; but he never forgot that he was the Tsar so long
as his detested half-sister insolently disputed the title with him.
Then one day, believing himself to be in danger of assassination
on Sophia's orders, Peter marched on Moscow with his regiment
of "Players," youths from both noble and plebeian families whom
he had trained in military exercises. The people sided with the
young Tsar against the Regent, and Peter, having packed
Sophia off to a nunnery, left his mother to govern in his stead
and set off on a grand tour to study in the blessed West to which
he looked for his country's salvation.

He modestly refused to travel with all the splendor due to
a Muscovite tsar, preferring to go simply as one of Lefort's
servants, under the name of Peter Mikhailov, and stand behind
his master's chair at official banquets. He worked for two years
in the naval dockyards at Zaandam in Holland as an ordinary
workman. He had to learn everything from scratch, starting
right at the beginning. The miracle is that this program, which
would have seemed too vast for five successive generations, was
all but accomplished by Peter in his own comparatively short

lifetime. He reorganized the Russian army on Western lines and transformed Muscovy, from a country constantly being beaten on all fronts through lack of soldiers and equipment, into a military power to be reckoned with in Europe. He created the Russian fleet, and established himself firmly on the Baltic Sea by weakening Sweden and building the city of St. Petersburg on the Neva. He wanted to make this a European city and this, more or less, was what it was from the beginning. He succeeded in attracting to Russia substantial numbers of technicians, craftsmen and overseers from Germany, Holland and England, and in getting them to stay. He built schools, factories and dock-yards, and took a personal interest in them all. He was both general and bookkeeper, legislator and carpenter, and was not above turning his hand to anything—not even the job of executioner. He was terrible and he was indefatigable; he devoted himself to his task with a disinterested selflessness seen in few crowned heads. By the time he died, though his reforms were still partial and incomplete, Russia had definitively broken with her past, had emerged from the economic and social morass in which she had been stuck for a century, and had made a fresh start toward a future which was still unknown but rich in hope.

Peter dominated Russian history, as he still does. He was one of those men who are larger than life and become a legend in their own lifetime. He was great even physically, standing well over six feet tall, and a wax model made during his lifetime and still in existence shows him sitting in his chair dressed in a plain blue-grey caftan, a curious figure, unnaturally tall and broad-shouldered, with dark hair, a pale face, a strong chin, and a hard mouth under the fine black mustache. There is a fixed, even slightly insane expression in his black eyes. The wax mask—molded from the life—and the excellent busts made by the sculptor Rastrelli conjure up the disturbing mobility of the face. All his life Peter suffered from dreadful nervous tics, brought on, it was said, by the scenes of carnage he witnessed as a child. Even in bronze one can see the intentness of his stare, the passionate quivering of the nostrils, and the almost painful authority in the mouth. Revolutionary, prophet, pitiless despot, and devoted servant of the public good, Peter deserves the name Great, if only for his powerful personality and the extent of the reforms which he undertook. But like all revolutionaries, he was also a great destroyer.

His fanatical nature led him to act with the most outlandish cruelty, his inordinate faith in the future allowed him to sacrifice the present lightly: no other tsar, not even Ivan the Terrible, would ever have been guilty of such insensate waste of human life; no other sovereign would ever have made such lighthearted demands for sacrifice of his people. No other sovereign would have so demoralized the society in which he lived.

To Western eyes, to the German princesses who entertained him on his travels (he was so shy in company that he would cover his face with his hands when speaking), to the court of Louis XV (where he saw fit to pick up the little king in his arms and toss him in the air before kissing him on both cheeks), he appeared like some kind of savage, and by doing so gave a poor impression of the general standard of education in Russia. However, we should not forget that the Russians themselves thought him even more uncivilized. Without offense to the worthy merchants and technicians who were his teachers, they need not be supposed to have possessed the refinement of manners customary at Rambouillet, and besides, Peter's character was much too impulsive to bow even to the code of politeness of a man like Lefort. Since he never learned good Muscovite manners (which he despised) or European ones (being, in spite of everything, a Muscovite), he always remained something of a classless person, and even in his knowledge and his passion for study, he retained something of the pedantic amateurishness of the self-taught.

He believed in all good faith that he was working for human progress by forcing his boyars to shave their chins and expose their calves, and he derived a childish pleasure from taking a pair of shears and personally trimming the beards and gowns of those who refused. The boyars—the younger ones and the more tractable among the old—submitted to the transformation, but they did not become Westerners for all that. Those who were sincerely won over to the new religion became, at best, replicas of Peter himself, but minus his genius. Those who were converted by force followed the trend willy-nilly, gradually losing all ties with the past, and frequently all self-respect as well. The court of Peter the Great and his successors presented a spectacle of the most fearful licentiousness and inconceivable brutality of manners: *déclassé* himself, Peter, in westernizing the Russian nobility, succeeded only in creating a shapeless, bastard society, which would need time before it could assimilate the foreign civilization which had been so rudely thrust upon it. As for the people, they would never accept this civilization, and looked on the Tsar as a "German" or as Antichrist.

Although he was successful in bending his court to this new way of life, and managed to surround himself with able and devoted colleagues, chosen partly from among the nobles and partly from among the common people and the foreign colony, Peter himself felt almost as rootless in his way as his boyars. The proof of this can be seen in the touching, willful affection he always retained for his boyhood friend Menshikov, and in his curious second marriage with a daughter of the people, a Livonian named Martha who had been captured in battle and was given to Peter by Menshikov. She was a common and not strikingly virtuous woman whose one great merit appears to have been the calm good humor with which she put up with the caprices of her impossible husband. Peter's private life amply justified the accusations of those Russians who called him Antichrist. He worked off the effects of his exhausting labors in unbridled orgies and monstrous drinking bouts, and one of his favorite (and most innocent) diversions consisted in forcing his more reserved boyars to empty huge goblets of wine at a single gulp. As a result of this treatment the man (or woman) concerned frequently passed out completely, and his courtiers feared it like the plague.

Peter was able to command the almost fanatical allegiance of his associates and his troops, and the admiration if not the love of his people, but—perhaps through no fault of his own— he failed in what should have been one of his most vital tasks, the training of a successor.

Six

Peter's Successors

When he died at the early age of fifty-two, Peter was unable to designate a successor, although he had promulgated a decree according to which the choice of a successor devolved upon the Tsar himself. Doubtless he would have liked to proclaim, like Alexander: "To the worthiest," but no one worthy of taking up the inheritance had appeared, and the choice between the possible candidates emerged as a peculiarly embarrassing one. Peter's only son, the one the whole country had looked on as the Tsar-Emperor's natural successor, was no longer available.

The Tsarevich Alexei, Peter's son by his first marriage to the noble Muscovite lady Eudoxia Lopukhina, had early come out in opposition to his father's reforms, and had become the heart and the pawn of the reactionary party. He was loved by the people and by the nobility. For Peter he was nothing more than a dangerous rival: Alexei's very existence jeopardized the future of the work he had set himself, and without hesitation he had his son charged with conspiring against the safety of the realm

and condemned to death. But even Peter could not face the out-
cry which would have been raised by the public execution of
the heir apparent, and Alexei was killed in prison.

He left one son—a boy who was only eight years old at Peter's
death. By his second wife Peter had only daughters; his elder
brother, the half-witted Ivan V, had died, leaving two daughters,
both married to German princes; there remained Peter's wife
Martha, rechristened Catherine, whom he had married after the
birth of his children and solemnly crowned Empress. Once before, on an impulse of gratitude toward his helpmeet, Peter had
made a will in her favor. On his deathbed he had still not ratified
this will, but Catherine was the former mistress and faithful
friend of the favorite Menshikov, the most powerful man in
Russia after the Tsar. The Emperor's widow therefore ascended
the throne under the name of Catherine I, and left the reins of
government in Menshikov's hands.

Unfortunately Menshikov, although he had been excellent,
in an executive capacity, at carrying out his friend's projects and
wishes during Peter's lifetime, turned out to be totally incapable
of governing alone, and the ignorant, sensual and indolent
Catherine was not the woman to give him any help. Peter's death
therefore marked the beginning of a kind of long interregnum
during which rulers chosen by luck and intrigue, and dominated
by more or less ineffectual favorites, allowed the nation's affairs
to go from bad to worse and ruined the exchequer. Meanwhile,
since it was too late to return to the traditions of the past which
had been so roughly destroyed, the "new" Russia made the best
of what little Western polish Peter had been able to impose on
her. The nobility, army officers, higher civil servants, foreign
and indigenous technicians, and the few intellectuals to be
found in Russia at that time had adopted with the "German"
style of dress something of the Western way of life and thought,
although in a still rudimentary form. The clergy, merchants,
artisans, and poorer people generally, had retained the costumes and manners in use prior to the reforms. Some new men
were developing, after a fashion, in schools and universities

abroad. The people lacked neither strength nor adaptability, and despite the notorious incompetence of successive governments the work of Peter the Great was bearing fruit: Russia was open to new ideas, her transformation into a Western power no longer appeared a sacrilege, and the new capital, St. Petersburg, was becoming the center of a glittering, elegant way of life on the fringe of Europe, the focus of intense diplomatic activity, and a great industrial and commercial city; and in spite of the very real poverty existing behind the glittering façade, in spite of the ignorance and unpolished manners of its "high" society, it was already a European city.

The Russian system of government—since Peter's reign the most autocratic that ever was—rested upon one intolerable equivocation: in principle all power was concentrated in the hands of the reigning sovereign. Peter had weakened every organ of state which was at all capable of playing an effective political role in the country—the Duma, the boyars, the Church, and the provincial governments—to such an extent that during his lifetime there was no law in practice other than the Tsar's good pleasure. Moreover, Peter did pass laws and attempt to make them respected. Now, for fifteen years, Russia was ruled by sovereigns who possessed neither the will to govern nor any political ideas of their own, nor even ordinary common sense. Catherine I, the first of these, allowed herself to be led by the ambitious Menshikov, whose sole objective appears to have been the increase of his own power. Catherine survived her husband only two years, and then the throne went to a ten-year-old boy, Peter, the son of the Tsarevich Alexei. To begin with, little Peter II was also Menshikov's instrument; then he fell into the hands of the rival faction and had his too powerful minister exiled to Siberia. The boy emperor died after a reign of only four years and the Council of Nobility decided to put someone on the throne who would agree to be guided entirely by the nobles. This was Anna, second daughter of the co-Tsar Ivan V and widow of the Duke of Kurland. Anna promised whatever they asked and failed to keep her promises; she governed alone, or rather was herself ruled by her favorite Biron (Bürhen), the son of a German groom. This Biron was for ten years absolute master of Russia; he was a greedy, arrogant adventurer with no views beyond his own personal interests and the enrichment of his family: he reigned by fear. His name became a byword, and Bironism was looked on as one of the worst misfortunes that could befall any country.

After Anna Ivanovna's death Biron made a bid to govern in the name of the new Emperor, Ivan VI, a child two months old; but the child's mother, the Regent Anna Leopoldovna, who was the niece of Tsarina Anna, got rid of her inconvenient minister by simple expedient of invoking an unwritten but nonetheless valid law by which the Tsar had absolute power over the life and property of his subjects. Biron and his family in turn took the road to exile and they were not the last: two years later the Regent herself with her husband suffered the same fate, as did the ministers who had helped that young woman to remove Biron.

This time it was not simply a matter of a palace revolution but of a complete reversal of the balance of power which had existed hitherto and a new orientation for Russian policy. The person this *coup d'état* brought to the throne in December 1741 was the candidate of a frankly nationalist party, and whatever may be said about the exact circumstances of her coming to power, she was at least chosen, backed and approved by the will of the Russian people. This time the "will of the people" had made itself felt in a somewhat rough and ready fashion, by a rising among the regiments of the imperial guard stationed at St. Petersburg. The *coup d'état* took place with such ease and swiftness that foreign observers were able to comment that "in Russia, with a little money and a few casks of vodka, you can do anything"[1]—even make a new emperor. But the very ease with which the revolution did come about, together with the stability of the new government, proves that a lot more was involved than a few casks of vodka. Not one hand was raised in defense of the unfortunate and ineffectual Anna Leopoldovna and the legitimate Tsar, the infant Ivan VI. Peter the Great's second daughter, Elizabeth, ascended her father's throne amid the acclamations of the people, who were weary and heartsick after the tyranny of Biron and the other "Germans."

No sooner was she on the throne than Elizabeth set about proving her good faith to her supporters by trying and finding guilty all the German ministers and higher civil servants who had been in power during Anna's reign, sacrificing even Count Ostermann, who had been one of Peter the Great's ablest and most loyal associates. She spent half her time in Moscow—the *Russian* capital—placed native Russians in every important official position, and altogether inaugurated a policy that was markedly Russian to the point of xenophobia, on the assumption, probably not entirely unjustified, that Russia was already quite adequately "westernized" and had no longer any need to be governed by foreigners. Moreover, Elizabeth openly proclaimed that she had inherited her father's ideas and was continuing his work, and it was on the cult of Peter the Great that she meant to base her own very real and lasting popularity.

Seven

❈❈❈❈❈❈❈❈❈❈

Elizabeth

Elizabeth was a handsome woman of thirty-two and did not seem the type to occupy a throne. Temperamentally she was so timid and apathetic that her supporters, among whom were the

officers of the Preobrazhensky guard, the French ambassador the
Marquis de la Chétardie, and the doctor Lestocq, had to force
her hand in order to make her agree to place herself at the head
of their conspiracy. She finally gave in out of a spirit of self-
preservation, because she was afraid that otherwise the suspicious
Regent would shut her up in a convent. She had no bent for
politics and, something still more unusual, no taste or talent for
intrigue.

She spoke French, German and English fluently, but otherwise was supremely ignorant: Peter the Great had been very
busy re-educating Russia, but he seems to have taken little
interest in the education of his own children. In many ways
Peter himself had remained a boor all his life, and his wife, who
had once been a washerwoman, never managed to rid herself of
a certain vulgarity which, for all her pearls, ermine and brocade,
gives her, in all her portraits, something of the air of a peasant
in disguise. But Elizabeth was at least able, by reason of her
beauty, charm and imposing presence, to take her place with
dignity at official ceremonies and court balls. Yet she too had
been prodigiously badly brought up, and taking her parents'
unfortunate example, she indulged in a moral laxity verging
on licentiousness pure and simple.

From her earliest youth (after one proposal of marriage,
which came to nothing on account of the death of her suitor)
she plunged, with superb shamelessness, into a succession of
amorous adventures of, for a princess, the most degrading kind,
choosing as her lovers coachmen, lackeys, church cantors and
others of base extraction, although there was no lack of good-
looking young men either at court or in the city. Elizabeth's
fondness for common men may be partly explained by her
mother's humble beginnings, and also by a perverse desire to
roll in the gutter as a kind of revenge for the humiliations inflicted on her by her father's successors. Kept in the background,
continually suspect and spied upon, fearing for her liberty if
not her life, Elizabeth had spent sixteen years champing at the
bit, looking back nostalgically to the days when she was a small,

petted princess, and feeling particularly sorry for herself, it would seem, because she was always short of money. (In her memoirs, Catherine makes us vividly aware of this restrospective bitterness of the Empress's. She reminded everyone in season and out of season that there had been a time when she was forced to count every penny and take care not to get into debt, and she was as proud of it as any common woman who has come up in the world and tells everybody that she used to work with her hands.) However that may have been, Elizabeth consoled herself for her relative poverty and real insecurity by taking lovers. Her enemies accused her of seducing her young nephew, the little Tsar Peter II (who was actually in love with her), and of having, in the absence of hard cash, rewarded the officers of her guard who raised her to power with her personal favors. Since she was a sociable person, not unduly proud, and liked to enjoy herself, her conduct lent a semblance of probability to these rumors.

At the time of her *coup d'état*, however, she had been living for several years with the handsome Alexei Razumovsky, a Ukrainian peasant who as the possessor of a fine voice had been elevated to the position of cantor in the princess's private chapel. Elizabeth had made him her chamberlain, and when she became Empress she conferred on him the title of count and rained all imaginable honors on his head, but he was not personally ambitious and never showed the slightest inclination to interfere in affairs of state. Persistent rumors that Elizabeth had secretly married him give some reason for supposing that this marriage actually took place.

One aspect of Elizabeth's extravagant disposition emerged in her piety, for she was devout in a thoroughly Russian way: she attended divine service as regularly as her somewhat irregular mode of life permitted, observed fasts, venerated the icons and relics; altogether, for the Russian people and for the Muscovites in particular she came very close to the memory of the tsarinas in earlier times, whose religious duties had been their principal occupation.

Loved by the people—the people of the capital cities at least, and these were the only ones who counted in practice—adored by the soldiers for whom she embodied the living memory of Peter the Great (and whatever the feelings of the people may have been with regard to this prodigious and terrible reformer, his popularity with the army had been enormous), Elizabeth rose to power on the crest of a tremendous wave of popular acclaim which she had in no way sought to provoke.

Once seated on her father's throne, clad in the imperial purple with the crown upon her head, this sovereign in spite of herself could not have taken her role more seriously; she believed wholeheartedly in her divine mission and in her inalienable rights; she really *governed* and did so with more good sense and coherence of ideas than anyone might have expected or than she is generally given credit for. To begin with, and this in itself was a cause of satisfaction to the people, she was wise enough not to mingle business with pleasure and her favorites remained "Emperors of the Night" (the nickname given to Razumovsky). Control of government was in the hands of an experienced politician, Count Bestuzhev-Ryumin, a gruff, cunning, not particularly engaging but thoroughly capable man who retained the Empress's confidence for nearly sixteen years. Elizabeth supported him and kept him in power against winds and tides— in other words, in spite of the manifold intrigues of foreign ambassadors. It is these latter who have left the most unprepossessing portraits of the lighthearted Empress: the Marquis de la Chétardie actually went so far as to become Elizabeth's lover in order to convert her to the political interests of Louis XV, while Frederick II did his utmost to bribe the Tsarina's entourage. Because Elizabeth very quickly put out of her head the services, both of a public and a private nature, rendered by La Chétardie, and because all her life she professed an unconcealed dislike of Frederick II, French and German diplomats persisted in regarding her as a woman who was both stupid and ridiculously easily swayed, whereas in fact her chief defect as far as they were concerned was precisely that she refused to allow them to influence her.

In her memoirs Catherine II, who is not always kind to Elizabeth, pays tribute to the Empress's "great intelligence," spoiled, according to her, by a defective education and the abuse of pleasure; and this seems a fair enough judgment. Catherine lived in Russia for almost the whole of Elizabeth's reign; she was to remain under this woman's domination for eighteen years, watching her moods and whims, trembling, plotting, weeping and rejoicing, in fact as much a slave to her as the meanest of her servants. Twenty years later, as an absolute sovereign herself, she remembered with pride a particular answer or a particular action which had won her some slight token of the Empress's favor. Catherine had to serve her apprenticeship in the hard school of the courtier, always in danger, and more in danger than anyone else at court, before she reached the throne which had haunted her dreams as a small girl.

When Sophia of Anhalt-Zerbst came to Russia, Elizabeth had already been on the throne for nearly two years. The little princess and her mother had built up a somewhat idyllic picture of what the gracious sovereign would be like: a friend of their family, brought to power by her own courage and the will of her people—an idea which the Princess of Anhalt-Zerbst, who had been bitterly disappointed in Elizabeth, was to re-create ten years later with the nicely calculated flattery of the courtier desirous of restoring herself to favor.

Elizabeth was really beautiful; her one defect, and she is said to have forbidden it to appear in her portraits, was a small bulbous nose inherited from her mother. But all the portraits concur in showing with equal fidelity her magnificent, candid blue eyes, her small, firm mouth, broad forehead, and dignified bearing, and probably no portrait could ever quite convey the physical attraction of her splendid body, which was agile and graceful despite an early tendency to fat. She was a tireless dancer, a keen horsewoman, and could wear men's clothes with such distinctive elegance that even when she was over forty-five she could still dazzle her young and ambitious rival, the Grand Duchess Catherine.

Elizabeth's vanity was such that she never wore the same

dress twice (true, she spent a good deal of her time in a dressing gown) and would sometimes change her clothes as often as three times a day. Though the fifteen thousand dresses her enemies accused her of possessing is probably an exaggeration, it is certain that she owned several thousand. She literally smothered herself in jewels and precious stones, and was in the habit of wearing a watch on her bosom which was set in a case studded with outsize emeralds, rubies or sapphires to match the color of her dress. She was naturally fair, but to make herself still more beautiful, she dyed her hair, eyebrows and eyelashes black, because, according to traditional Russian folklore, she who was to be "the fairest of them all" must have hair as black as a raven's wing. Conscious that she could never hope to rival her father in the intellectual sphere, she was determined at least to have the glory of being the loveliest woman in her empire, and the worst insult anyone could pay her was to cast aspersions on her beauty. (Her savage treatment of the Countesses Lopukhina and Bestuzheva, both of whom were implicated in a dubious plot to put Ivan VI on the throne, has been put down to the fact that these two ladies, although both were of a respectable age, had dared to state publicly that their beauty surpassed that of the Empress.)[1]

Inordinately, even hysterically vain of her appearance Elizabeth certainly was, and another of her defects was that she was excessively fond of balls, entertainments and indeed any occasion which gave her an opportunity to shine in public. Just as her father had tried to force his court to dress "in the German fashion" and drink foreign spirits, Elizabeth compelled her courtiers, even old gentlemen crippled with gout, to dance quadrilles and minuets for hours on end. Dancing was an art in which she knew herself to be without a rival, and on occasion she enjoyed making others appear ridiculous in order that her own splendor might shine out more brilliantly.

At a time when she was still trembling for the success of the plot in which she had become implicated and in which she risked gaining or losing everything, she had made a vow before the icon of Saint Nicholas that if ever she ascended the throne she would abolish the death penalty. She kept her word, for in any case she was a sentimental woman and, in her own way, a good one. After allowing the powerful men of the previous regime, principally the two Annas' German advisers, to be condemned to death, she then indulged in the more refined torture of a mock execution (Count Ostermann even saw the executioner's ax brandished over his head) before granting them a reprieve and commuting the death sentence to one of deportation for life. But in the painful affair of the Countesses Lopukhina and Bestuzheva, mentioned earlier, and their associates, she did not allow the accused to escape so lightly: convicted, if not of conspiracy, at least of subversive talk, these unfortunates first endured a flogging and then had their tongues cut out in public.[2] As for the Brunswick-Mecklenburg family—the ex-Regent Anna, her husband and her children—after two years of liberty under strict supervision, they were sent into exile and dragged from one prison to the next, while the little prince Ivan VI was taken from his parents at the age of six and condemned to a life sentence of solitary confinement, a penalty which had never been inflicted on anyone in Russia before that time. Apart from this, Elizabeth's reign did not witness a single death penalty, and although there is no denying that some sentences of corporal punishment and imprisonment amounted more or less to a delayed sentence of death, Elizabeth had good reason to believe herself, in all good faith, a merciful sovereign.

She was not as totally uninterested in affairs of state as foreign diplomats exasperated by her slowness and negligence would have us believe, but she was extremely lazy. She would only attend to them when she felt like it, by fits and starts, between balls, bouts of drinking and the consequent attacks of liver trouble—for she drank a great deal—and was in general content to allow her ministers to govern for her. But in fact, it was common knowledge that one word from the Empress would be enough to send the current minister to join the families of Menshikov, Biron, Münnich, Ostermann and other fallen powers whom the Russian people had branded with the name of *vremenshchiki* (temporary ones) in their icy desert.

Arriving in Petersburg with the (carefully concealed) intention of overthrowing the all-powerful Bestuzhev, Princess Johanna Elizabeth hoped to find the Empress gentle, understanding and easily swayed, and she was to learn at great cost to herself that, beneath her apparent carelessness, Elizabeth was one of the most difficult people to manipulate because she was also the most unpredictable, self-willed, suspicious and authoritarian. She was, in short, after barely two years on the throne, the complete type of petticoat tyrant.

Eight

❰❁❰❁❰❁❰❁❰❁❰❁❰❁❰❁❰❁❰❁

The Child of Kiel

Elizabeth was on the throne, but for all that, the matter of the succession was still far from settled. Peter the Great had been unlucky in his heirs, and among the common people it was sometimes said that this was the vengeance of the Tsarevich Alexei and a just punishment on an unnatural father. Himself sprung from a family more than somewhat degenerate—Peter's eldest brother, Feodor, was so sickly in body that he was condemned from infancy to an early death and his second brother, Ivan, was a hopeless idiot—Peter appears to have bequeathed to his descendants something of the degeneracy of a worn-out line and the imbalance of his own nature. Alexei had been a weakling and suffered from a chronic nervous complaint; his sons by Catherine did not survive; and although, as frequently happens, the daughters were more robust, even so Anne, the eldest, died of tuberculosis at the age of twenty and Elizabeth, who alone inherited her father's vitality, was almost certainly unbalanced mentally. The deficiencies of her education alone are not sufficient to explain odd streaks in her character.

The Romanov dynasty was dying out. The idiot Ivan had two daughters, the youngest of whom, Anna Ivanovna, died without issue. Catherine, the elder, was the mother of the same Anna Leopoldovna whom Elizabeth sent into exile. This Anna at least possessed the doubtful advantage of being prolific: she was brought to bed in her prison regularly once a year and died in childbirth after five years; but the existence of descendants in the rival branch of the family was a source of embarrassment rather than comfort to Elizabeth.

She herself was unmarried. She had been betrothed as a young girl to Prince Karl Augustus of Holstein-Gottorp, the brother of the Princess of Anhalt-Zerbst, but the young man had been carried off by smallpox almost on the eve of the wedding. He had been handsome and Elizabeth had loved him, but she did not mourn him long and consoled herself with other, less exalted lovers. She did not find a husband during the reign of her cousin Anna Ivanovna, and after being offered to a dizzying number of suitors, both illustrious and obscure, one of the loveliest girls in all Russia resigned herself happily to spinsterhood. Once Empress, she had no idea of taking an official lord and master, although she did not, for all that, lay claim to the title of Virgin Queen like her illustrious namesake Elizabeth I of England. Since she was unmarried she could have no heirs, but scandalmongers claimed that she had eight children of her union with Razumovsky.

Her sole heir was therefore the only son of Peter the Great's eldest daughter, Anne, who had married Karl Frederick, Duke of Schleswig-Holstein. Elizabeth had loved her sister dearly and would have been only too happy to adopt her orphan nephew, but he was a sickly child, brought up in Germany, and furthermore, his right to the throne was theoretically greater than Elizabeth's own and he might easily become the tool of insurgents.

He was the grandson, and the only grandson, of Peter the Great. In the eyes of the people he represented the dynastic succession which was the only link between the people and power. Elizabeth knew only too well the power that was in a *name*, in the remotest hint of legitimacy; she was to remember it throughout her reign and hand down this fear to her successor and rival, Catherine II. The power of a dynastic right was great indeed, so great that it could make the dead rise from their tombs.

Little Karl Peter Ulrich of Schleswig-Holstein was the grandson of Peter the Great and the son of the Duke of Holstein. Through his father he had a claim to the crown of Sweden, through his mother to that of Russia. But in his case a mixture of the noble and ancient blood of the German princes with that, not so ancient or so noble but still sufficiently illustrious, of the Romanovs and the peasant blood of Catherine I did not have happy results. Peter Ulrich was a puny little boy, prone from infancy to fevers, convulsions and fainting fits, excessively nervous, unbalanced and, it seems, not over-bright at his studies, although his poor health may have been largely responsible for this.

He had never known his mother, who died when he was three months old. While still very young he was taken away from his nurses to undergo all the rigors of a princely education such as German princes in particular were accustomed to inflict on their sons: intensive study, strict discipline and subjection to a rigorous, almost military etiquette. To add to his troubles, his future claim to the throne of Russia obliged him to study the Russian language and the Orthodox religion, to which the child took a rooted objection long before he was ever actually proclaimed heir to the throne.

L'Enfant de Kiel, as he was known (in French) at the court of the Empress Anna, constituted a threat to the ruling family in Russia, and Anna was given to observing spitefully in her execrable Russian: "And that little devil of Holstein is still living."[1] He did live, managing somehow to stay alive, although the little flame of life was constantly flickering in his skinny body subjected to a training it was ill-equipped to endure.

Karl Frederick of Holstein does not appear to have taken much interest in his son. Like the majority of noble parents of the period, he left him in the hands of tutors, doctors and servants. Until he was seven, Peter Ulrich was looked after by French governesses, but although he spoke faultless French, he was always more at home in German. When he was seven years old his serious education began. It included military training, and the child was taught by officers of his father's guard who, between lessons, would put him to stand guard and practice— with miniature weapons—all the soldier's trade. Before he was nine Peter Ulrich had been promoted to the rank of sergeant.

Not that this game went against his inclinations; indeed, he greatly preferred it to his Latin, Swedish or Russian lessons. Whenever his father organized parades in the castle courtyard, as he was very fond of doing, little Peter Ulrich would desert his books and tutors and rush to the window, jumping up and down excitedly. Thick curtains had to be hung over the lower half of the windows before the little prince could be persuaded to sit still. Much later he told his tutor Stehlin that "the happiest day of his life" was when Duke Karl Frederick gave a great reception to celebrate his birthday and the little prince mounted guard in the banqueting hall in his sergeant's uniform, gaping enviously at the succession of dishes which came to the table. His father, the Duke, watched him with a smile, and after the second course, he had the little sergeant, who had stood stoically at his post suffering all the torment of Tantalus, relieved from duty, solemnly promoted him to the rank of lieutenant and allowed him to sit down at the table among the guests. Whereupon the child was so carried away by excitement and happiness that he promptly found himself unable to swallow a mouthful.[2]

As a soldier's son, born with the taste for battle in his blood, the child was probably quite happy with these stern pleasures and would have been only too glad if he had been allowed to take part in parades every day and look forward to more periods of guard duty; but unfortunately he was not strong enough to make a good soldier and his father, a cultured man who spoke fluent Latin, expected more of him than a simple military training. Peter Ulrich hated Latin, just as he hated all other forms of learning with the exception of music, for which he had a talent which was regrettably neglected.

Careless and exacting though his father may have been, he was a father none the less. But in 1739, when Peter was only eleven, he died. His cousin and guardian, Prince Adolphus Frederick of Holstein-Gottorp, had too many other worries and he abandoned the little prince to the care of the *Oberhofmarschall* of the ducal court, Brümmer. For the child this marked the beginning of the classic martyrdom suffered by a defenseless orphan left at the mercy of adults who, for some inexplicable reason of their own, make him their scapegoat. The young duke's French master, Monsieur Millet, observed that Brümmer was more fitted for breaking horses than for supervising the education of a prince. He was certainly an extraordinarily boorish individual, whose sudden rise at the court of Holstein remains a mystery. Foreign diplomats, always ready to spread scandal, even hinted that Brümmer had formerly been the Duchess Anne's lover and was therefore the little duke's real father—a rumor devoid of substance, and one moreover which is scarcely borne out by Brümmer's decidedly unfatherly behavior toward his pupil.

We may wonder why this man took such delight in tormenting a child who—if he lived—might one day become King of Sweden or Emperor of Russia. In his own interest he should have been more gentle. Probably the explanation of his behavior lies no deeper than his brutal "horse trainer's" nature.

If by ill-treatment he hoped to harden and temper the child's character, he arrived at a totally opposite result. Peter was a weakling in spirit as well as in body and Brümmer's system only succeeded in weakening him further still, turning him into a small hunted animal, restless, suspicious and unnaturally timid.

When, as often happened, the young prince had done badly at his lessons, Brümmer would appear in the ducal dining room at dinnertime and threaten his pupil with the direst punishments as soon as the meal was over. This terrified the child to such an extent that he could scarcely eat and would leave the table retching and vomiting. This problem his masters would often dispose of by simply depriving him of food for a whole day at a time as a punishment. Worse still, the hungry child was compelled to stand by the door with a picture of a donkey hung around his neck and a bundle of canes in his hand, watching while his courtiers dined before his eyes—and this when he was nearly fourteen years old. To encourage him to work better—he was undoubtedly incorrigible—they compelled him to kneel for hours on dried peas until (according to Stehlin) "his knees grew red and swollen."[3]

Peter Ulrich spent his life shut up in his palace and was not allowed to play with children of his own age: his only companions were the daughters of Brümmer's mistress, Madame Brockdorff, a vulgar, peevish woman who ruled the roost at the ducal court of Holstein. Even these young persons he only saw for the purpose of dancing quadrilles, and he did not enjoy dancing. In bitter sarcasm he once remarked: "I'm sure they want to make a dancing master of me, and that's all I need to know." In fact, though he did learn to dance a quadrille quite creditably, his mind rebelled more and more against the other subjects that they were trying to drive into his head by dint of whipping and humiliating him. Sometimes, too, Madame Brockdorff's bad temper was enough to earn him a beating, without the need for bad marks in Latin.

However, a day came at last when, at the age of fourteen, Peter Ulrich left his castle at Kiel, which had been nothing more than a prison to him, and his native Holstein, of which he was supposed to be the ruler, and accompanied by his master and tormentor Marshal Brümmer, was taken to St. Petersburg because his maternal aunt Elizabeth, now Empress of Russia, had expressed the desire to be a mother to him and make him heir to the Russian Empire.

Nine

❦❧❦❧❦❧❦❧❦❧❦❧❦❧❦❧

Elizabeth and Her Nephew

Impulsive and sentimental as she was, Elizabeth was eager to love her sister's only child as if he were her own son. She had never set eyes on him, and when she did, it was a bitter disappointment. She was not a patient woman and he was not an easy child to love (though later she was to give startling proof of the genuineness of her attachment to little Peter).

He was not an attractive child: short for his age, puny, awkward and shy. His aunt never seems to have succeeded in making friends with him, nor does he appear to have offered her the slightest affection. He was horribly homesick, and what is more, still under the thumb of the formidable Brümmer, and he saw the Empress merely as one more tyrant, a tyrant whose reactions were totally unpredictable and who was the more to be feared in that she was more powerful than the rest.

Elizabeth, though no bluestocking herself, was appalled at the child's ignorance. She tried to overcome it by giving the boy new tutors, more suited to his temperament. The Saxon Stehlin, a likable dilettante whom Elizabeth herself often made fun of, undertook the boy's education along lines which today seem perfectly reasonable: teaching him natural history by taking him hunting, history by studying collections of old coins, mathematics and the mechanical sciences by making scale models, and so on. But despite his small stature, Peter was no longer a small boy; his spirit had already been broken by bad teaching and he gained little from Stehlin's lessons except a lifelong fondness for making models. Moreover Elizabeth, who was passionately fond of dancing, made her nephew take perpetual lessons in quadrilles and minuets and the young duke had to drop his other lessons whenever the dancing master and the violinist presented themselves in his apartments. He loved music, and his great delight was playing the violin, but he was badly taught and never learned to play properly, so that he was reduced to practicing on his own and improvising as best he could, or playing his favorite tunes unaccompanied.

His health was so delicate that to make any sustained effort was quite beyond him: throughout the autumn of 1743 he hovered between life and death. On October 12, Stehlin wrote: "He is extremely weak and has lost the taste for everything which pleased him during his illness, even for music. Once on a Saturday, when there was music being played in his Highness's antechamber after dinner and the *castrato* was singing his favorite air, he said, in a barely audible whisper, 'Will they stop playing soon?' The Grand Duke was lying with half-closed eyes, and breathing with difficulty. Her Majesty was informed at once and hurried to his side. She burst into tears and had to be forced away from the Grand Duke's bedside."[1]

The child's nerves, already shattered by constant illness, were further threatened by the violent scenes which the frightful Brümmer continually inflicted on him. Stehlin also reports that one day Brümmer went so far as to attack the young duke with his fists. Peter ran to the window with the intention of calling the grenadiers of his guard to his rescue, then fled into his own room and returned armed with a sword, shouting at Brümmer: "This will be your last piece of insolence. The next time you dare to raise your hand to me I will run you through with this sword." The Prussian diplomat Pezold mentions in his letters that the Grand Duke hated his tutor so much that he had already threatened, at Kiel, to "put a ball through his head."[2] Nevertheless the Empress continued to trust Brümmer, and young Peter had every reason to think that he had gained very little by his change of country and guardian.

If anything, he had lost rather than gained, for however unhappy he had been at Kiel, he was even more so in Russia. His was the kind of introverted nature which cannot bear any thought of change, and besides, he was homesick.

One of Elizabeth's main grievances against her nephew was the youth's open dislike of all things Russian. He never learned to speak Russian properly and felt nothing but contempt and distaste for the Orthodox religion in which he had been instructed on his arrival in Moscow. He was given a discreet course of instruction by the urbane and extremely eclectic court chaplain, Simeon Todorsky, and in December 1742 Karl Peter Ulrich was solemnly admitted to the Orthodox Church under the name of Peter Feodorovich. "From things which the Grand Duke himself has sometimes said, with his customary petulance," wrote Pezold on December 15, "one may conclude that he will not be a fanatical believer, and on the very day he agreed to become a member of the Greek Church, talking in the presence of the Austrian and Prussian ambassadors, Botta and Mardefeldt, on the subject of priests [*Pfaffen*], he said that one promised them a great many things that one could not perform."[3] On another occasion (October 12, 1742) Pezold wrote: "The young duke still knows practically no Russian and very little of the Greek religion, but for this last, as for all the customs of the country, he at all times displays such scorn that he is less and less liked." It was a sad beginning for a future ruler.

Thus, Elizabeth had removed from the throne a family hated by the people for their German origins, only to find that her own heir was every bit as German as the Brunswick-Mecklenburgs had been, so delicate that it was doubtful whether he would ever live to be a man, and to crown it all, cursed with the most unfortunate possible character: stubborn, distrustful, at once timid and violent, and as incapable of feeling affection as he was of inspiring it in others. In those first few months Elizabeth must have realized that this boy was a living disaster. Since he was her nephew and closest living relative, she could only accept him for what he was and hope that with time and perhaps —who knew—under the influence of a judiciously selected wife, the young prince's character might gradually improve.

Early in 1744, Elizabeth finally announced her choice of a future grand duchess. Foreign ambassadors, and Pezold in particular, referring to her choice, explain it by the fact that the Princess of Anhalt-Zerbst did not belong to a powerful family and was therefore unlikely to play any part in politics through her relatives. Nevertheless, as we have seen, this choice had been directed by political maneuvers.

The Empress had considered one of Louis XV's daughters as a possible wife for her nephew, but the degenerate little prince, heir to a problematical throne and destined at best to reign over a barbarous nation, was not a good enough match for a daughter of France. The King of Prussia, Frederick II, when sounded by the party in opposition to the chancellor Bestuzhev, declined to expose his sister to such an unenviable fate. Bestuzhev himself, on the other hand, suggested to Elizabeth the daughter of the Elector of Saxony, Augustus III, who was then King of Poland and a friend of the house of Austria. Frederick II, who opposed the chancellor's policies, gave Elizabeth to understand, through the intermediary of his supporters at the Russian court, that she would be wiser to choose an outsider, a candidate who would not play the game of any party.

Elizabeth had lent herself to this maneuver with a good grace, and she may well have thought that since young Sophia was without grand connections, she could be sent back to Zerbst with a consolation prize if she failed to please, without the risk of international complication. Elizabeth too wanted a grand duchess she could look on as her own creature. It seems clear that she was completely unaware of the King of Prussia's secret designs, and she did not know that Sophia's mother considered herself to be, if not Frederick II's creature, at least under an obligation to him.

Ten

Cinderella at Court

In her memoirs Sophia remarks, not without some bitterness, that although her mother spent what little money she had on her own toilette, she neglected to buy dresses for her daughter, who did not even possess sheets of her own. The princesses left Germany in January 1744, traveling as the "Countess of Reinbeck" and her daughter, and it was under this name that they crossed the Russian border.

The travelers were taken unawares by the northern winter, which was much more severe than in Germany. Little Sophia's feet were so numb and swollen that she had to be carried from the sleigh when they stopped for the night—a fact which her mother does not appear to have even noticed, unless she was deliberately trying to keep it quiet. Although Catherine, thirty years later, could still remember her swollen feet, Princess Johanna Elizabeth does not dwell upon this detail and appears chiefly concerned to justify her actions in the eyes of her family, for her mother, sister and aunts were sure that she was setting out on a fool's errand and in doing so risking both her child's reputation and her happiness.

Yet although in her first letters to her family the young mother, herself somewhat frightened, is attempting above all else to convince her noble relatives that her daughter will never be forced to give up the Lutheran faith against her will, her tone changes when the princesses arrive at Riga (January 25/February 6). The moment their sleigh was across the bridge over the River Dvina and into Russian territory they were welcomed by salvos of cannon fire, and the Empress's chamberlain and relative, Simeon Kirilovich Naryshkin, a former ambassador in London, came to meet the travelers, putting at their disposal a suite of rooms in the town hall and such a train of servants for their stay in Riga and for the rest of the journey that the poor German princess was literally intoxicated by it. Henceforth she could talk of nothing but the magnificent receptions, the respect with which she was treated, the sumptuous appointments, the splendor of the guards' uniforms and the extravagant number of servants assigned to her service.

It was she, much more than her daughter, who was the dazzled Cinderella, thrown into a flutter by the unexpected grandeur which had fallen on her. "Among the sleighs, there is one used by her Imperial Majesty. It is scarlet, decked with silver and lined within with marten fur; there are silk cushions and covers of the same stuff." She enumerates the servants: "There are I don't know how many cooks and scullions . . . a confectioner, a man to make the coffee, eight footmen, two grenadiers, two furriers . . . and I can't tell how many sleighs and grooms."[1] To her husband, she writes in her curious German, dotted with words in French, that everything is done with such grandeur and magnificence (*mit viehler Grandeur und Honneur zugegangen ist*) and that she is surrounded with such a to-do (*bei allen fracas so mich environiert*) that she feels as though in a dream.[2]

All the same, she adds (for she is writing to a father anxious about his daughter's well-being): "Our daughter is in such good health and spirits that even I am astonished."

By a series of forced marches they arrived in St. Petersburg on February 3/14, and the Princess's wonder knew no bounds when she set eyes on the Winter Palace. She felt as though she were already a queen. "I had no sooner reached my apartments than a thousand people were presented to me. My tongue was dry with cold. . . . I dine alone with the gentlemen and ladies assigned to me by her Imperial Majesty; they attend me like a queen." She is already complaining of the number of courtiers paying court to her. "When I retire to my inner apartment I am almost swooning, but to the honor of the Russians, I must say that they are people of great wit. I have met former generals of Peter the Great. I can never tire of hearing them talk of their creator, as they call him."[3]

She was young (only thirty-two) and pretty, and her conversation was sparkling; she was abreast of all the gossip of the court and all court intrigues; she let it be known (and was allowed to believe it) that she had an important political role to play, and foreign ambassadors—La Chétardie in particular, who was in the habit of equating his talents as a seducer with diplomatic ability—paid court to her. She was simultaneously triumphant and impatient, because she knew that nothing had been accomplished until she succeeded in conquering the Empress.

Despite the intrigues of ill-wishers (she was probably right in seeing schemers everywhere), she decided to make all speed to Moscow, traveling day and night in order to arrive in the old capital before the Grand Duke's birthday.

She practically ignored her plain little daughter's existence, though she did write to Frederick: "My daughter bears fatigue admirably: like a young soldier who scorns danger because he has not met it, she rejoices in the grandeur which surrounds her"; and to her husband: *"Figchen southeniert die fatige besser als ich* [Figchen bears fatigue better than I]."[4]

She was taken on a tour of the city of St. Petersburg, and the courtiers showed her the route taken by Elizabeth from the Preobrazhensky barracks to the Winter Palace to accomplish her *coup d'état*. In describing it she makes one remarkable observation: "It is incredible that her Majesty could have endured so long a walk, and that she was not betrayed."⁵ The *coup d'état* had taken place two years earlier. The famous route must also have led Sophia to indulge in some private reflections on the instability of imperial power, and the means to come by it. In her memoirs she tells how, near Riga, their train of carriages had passed another, with lowered blinds, and guarded by soldiers. It was the former ruling family of Brunswick-Mecklenburg being escorted from the place where they had been living in provisional liberty to an unknown destination and a harsher prison.

Eleven

Sophia

Writing in her memoirs of this period of her life, Catherine-Sophia does not dwell at any length on her own personal thoughts and feelings. She notes a few strictly practical details: the sleigh which overturned in the night on the road from St. Petersburg to Moscow; her frozen feet; the sleigh she had difficulty in getting into (they told her, "You must straddle it," and the expression, which was new to her, made her laugh uproariously); the way the Russian ladies recommended her to do her hair, which turned out to be treacherous advice since the Empress did not like it. She does not fail to mention the meeting with the convoy carrying the unfortunate Anna Leopoldovna into exile, but if she felt a moment's dread lest the same fate should befall herself, she says nothing of it.

Having reached the peak of honor, she seems to have thought of nothing but her growing ambitions and her tenacious desire to reign at all costs. She is much more communicative when it comes to relating court intrigues. Like her mother, she had the taste for intrigue in her blood. Yet in these first months of her long and difficult rise, calculating and ambitious though she was, she was still only fourteen.

No doubt she stood up to the fatigues of the journey much less well than her mother claimed, but she suffered even more from her mother's neglect, and she appears to have been much less dazzled by the magnificence spread before her eyes. Toward the end of January, two weeks before their arrival at St. Petersburg, she wrote to her father from Königsberg:

MY LORD,

It was with all imaginable joy and respect that I received the letter by which your Highness does me the honor to inquire after my health. . . . I beg you to assure yourself that this advice and exhortation will remain forever engraved on my heart, as the seeds of our holy faith will in my soul, to which I pray God to lend all the strength it will need to sustain me through the temptations to which I expect to be exposed. In answer to your Highness's prayers and those of my dear Mama He will grant that grace which, in my youth and weakness, I should not dare to hope for without such timely aid. I commend myself to it and hope to have the consolation of being worthy of it, and likewise of continuing to receive good news of my dear Papa, and I am, as long as I live, and in an inviolable respect, my lord, your Highness's most humble, most obedient and faithful daughter and servant,

SOPHIA A.F.P. D'A.Z.

(Augusta Fredericka, Princess of Anhalt-Zerbst)

At Königsberg in Prussia, this 29 January, 1744[1]

Princes in those days evidently did not take their children's education lightly, and in the smaller German courts, effusive family greetings were out of place. Sophia barely permits herself one "dear Papa," at the end of her letter, among a welter of "my lords" and "Highnesses." This letter, no doubt read and corrected by her mother, has nevertheless a ring of true feeling about it: at that moment, at least, the young girl brought up in the Lutheran faith must have felt the temptation to renounce her faith as a misfortune. Christian Augustus of Anhalt-Zerbst felt a good deal of anxiety on the subject, as did his family and that of his wife.

The Prince of Anhalt-Zerbst had given the matter a good deal of thought before he consented to this Russian adventure, and although he had agreed in principle, he still placed the salvation of his daughter's soul above his hopes of a good marriage. When he said goodbye to Sophia he had given his wife a letter "Pro Memoria" in which he set down for his daughter his ideas on the way she should behave herself. It is these fatherly exhortations that Sophia promises to keep "forever engraved on her heart."

Her father began by asking whether it was not possible for her to "follow the example of the Princess of Brunswick [the wife of the Tsarevich Alexei] and keep her own religion, or at least adhere to the *Bauernglaube*, or peasant faith." Neither of these two courses was in fact open to her: the ruler of Russia could not be anything but Orthodox and the "peasant faith" (which meant observing the general principles of Christianity without following any specific dogma) was completely out of the question.

"Upon no account," wrote Prince Christian, "would I have my daughter compelled or advised to adopt an alien religion in which she herself can perceive errors. Since all men live by their faith, it is upon her own prayers to God, her own endeavors, meditations and will, that her decision must depend . . . and it would be better for her to renounce power than to act against her conscience." He also insisted that his daughter should always have a Lutheran Bible, a prayer book, and other Lutheran books, and that she should pray to God to keep her in that faith until she died.[2]

These instructions, accompanied by advice of a more practical nature on the subject of how she should behave to the Empress, the Grand Duke, the court and so forth, may well have provided young Sophia, to begin with at least, with some kind of moral code to which she tried to conform. She was mature enough to realize who was more genuinely fond of her, her father or her mother, and who had her real interests at heart. She loved her father. The Princess of Anhalt-Zerbst wrote to Frederick II after their departure from Stettin: "This separation has moved her extremely. Her great youth enabled her to overcome the first surge of feeling which, at her age, cannot properly be called more than fondness." Sophia's grief may have been deeper than her mother, in her anxiety to reassure the King of Prussia as to her daughter's good intentions, had realized.

The child must have felt all the more homesick at this sumptuous foreign court—so very ostentatiously and insolently sumptuous—in that her mother was monopolizing all the attention of the Russian courtiers for herself and no one took much notice of the daughter, while her mother, absorbed in her social success, forgot her completely. She herself said that she thought herself "a complete frump." Her pride must have suffered badly; she was afraid to show herself in public (the more so because she was short of clothes), and wondered whether the Empress and the Grand Duke might not reject her because she did not possess a pretty face. True, in Berlin, Frederick II had appeared captivated by her wit and charm, but she knew very well that Frederick desired her marriage to the Grand Duke, while many people at St. Petersburg did not.

Mother and daughter reached Moscow on February 20. Sophia had leisure to contemplate the splendor and poverty of the old capital, the "Moscow of white stone," as the Russians called it proudly, although in actual fact the white walls of the Kremlin were made of nothing more than painted brick. Palaces built of wood painted to look like stone stood cheek by jowl with wretched hovels surrounded by ramshackle fences; the roads were broad country lanes with a covering of dirty snow; men and women wearing costumes that were still almost Oriental rubbed shoulders with gentlemen in powdered wigs riding on horseback or in carriages; there were a hundred churches with gilded domes, and crowds of tattered beggars; and elegant little sleighs sped along the frozen river among the ragged children sliding on the ice. The princesses' cortege had to pass right through the city in order to reach the Empress's palace. Now that Sophia had arrived in Moscow she waited, not without some apprehension, for the moment when she would be presented to the already legendary Elizabeth.

Although her mother describes the interview in a few brief sentences, stressing only the fact that the Empress was compelled to withdraw into the next room to hide the weeping brought on by Johanna's resemblance to her dead brother whom Elizabeth was to have married, Sophia has left us a lively portrait of the Empress herself, whose striking beauty she freely acknowledges. She remarks on her grace and dignity and her ease of movement, "although she is exceedingly plump," and she also records the way her hair was arranged, with a black feather falling to the left of her face, and the blaze of gold embroidery and diamonds. Elizabeth was literally covered in diamonds, at least as far as her waist, and her ample white bosom and heavy shoulders were decked in massive necklaces and set in a dazzling frame of precious stones.

Elizabeth had the smiling courtesy of a real princess. She possessed the knack of putting people at their ease, and when she liked, she could display a remarkable degree of tact. The princesses of Anhalt-Zerbst were completely won over by her gracious manner and even more by the tears she shed for the fiancé of her youth. As for the person who was, if such he can be called, the real hero of the hour and the real object of the princesses' journey, the very most that can be said is that he did not make a very strong impression on either mother or daughter. The mother mentions him only in passing; the daughter, in her memoirs, is somewhat more communicative: she describes her young cousin as a little boy only too delighted to find someone he could talk to at last. (He was a year older than she but much younger in character, and she admits to finding him "very childish.") Peter was frequently accused of dissimulation but in fact he appears to have been ridiculously transparent, and his wife was to remark later on that he was "as discreet as a cannon shot," so there can be no doubt that his pleasure was genuine.

Nevertheless, when Peter expressed his delight at having a relative of his own age and one who came from his own country to whom he could talk freely, and promptly confided to her that he already loved another, he managed to freeze his young cousin's heart at their very first meeting. It was a sufficiently wise and practical young heart, to be sure, and no doubt Sophia had made up her mind in advance not to expect too much, but after all, she was only fourteen. The disconcerting boy announced that he was in love with a young lady named Lopukhina whose mother had recently been disgraced (we may wonder whether he was aware of the horrible circumstances attending her "disgrace") and exiled to Siberia. It was a significant choice: feeling oppressed himself, Peter was full of sympathy for the daughter of oppressed parents. While his future wife was still speechless at this untimely confession, the boy went on to say that he was perfectly ready to marry Sophia "to please his aunt." "I blushed as I listened to him," Sophia wrote, "and I rejoiced that I had at least won his confidence."[3] It had been one of her father's parting recommendations that she should respect the Grand Duke as her "master, father and sovereign lord," and seek to win his love through "meekness and docility."

It is unlikely that she thought of love at all at that time, although her brief affair with her uncle must already have opened her eyes a little. Even if she did not yet regard in the light of a lover, but simply as a friend, the prince who was presented to her and whom she must marry at all costs if she wished to become an empress, she must surely have thought to herself that there would never be another man in her life and that she had better make the best of this one.

All the same, she was quite intelligent enough to see that it was not the Grand Duke but the Empress whom she had to please. The marriage of princes was a matter for their parents, ministers and other powerful persons, and she wanted terribly badly for this marriage to be a success. From the very first day, leaving to her mother the intoxications of social successes, she devoted herself with praiseworthy application to the study of the Russian language and the Greek Orthodox religion. We have no means of knowing how earnestly she prayed to God for strength to withstand the temptations to which she was exposed. We do not know how heavily the "holy Lutheran faith," which such a short time before she had sworn never to abandon, weighed on her soul. Certainly she did have scruples, but as her spiritual adviser she was given a man chosen with the express purpose of lulling such perfectly natural apprehensions as a young Protestant might be expected to feel.

This was the same Simeon Todorsky who had been charged with the Grand Duke's religious education, although there he had met with less success. He was a courtier as well as a priest and by no means rigidly or fanatically Orthodox. During the reigns of the German sovereigns, he had been noted for the great toleration with which he regarded the Lutheran faith. He had lived for a long time in Germany and had taken part in theological debates between exponents of the Pietist doctrine and supporters of the critico-historical theories of the mathematician Christian Wolff. Converted to the idea that the external forms taken by different cults were all relative, Simeon Todorsky was one of the religious "progressives" of whom there were many in the eighteenth century, and it goes without saying that he did not represent the real spirit of Orthodoxy, which was always rabidly conservative.

Sophia listened to him willingly, for he spoke perfect German, was well versed in all the various Christian doctrines and was, moreover, an agreeable companion and entertaining talker. She regarded him as one of the holiest men in the Greek Church. Agreeably surprised by the conversation of this indulgent preacher, the girl immediately wrote to her father that there was no doctrinal difference between the two faiths, that "the external dogma is very different, but the Church is forced to adopt these measures by reason of the brutishness of the people. . . . I trust I have not acted with undue precipitancy in this matter, the more so in that, after the fundamental articles of our belief, I have faithfully consulted your Highness's instructions."[4] To this Prince Christian replied, in German: "You must not regard this test lightly; you should examine yourself seriously as to whether the feelings which excite you are really those dominant in your heart, or whether they are not, without your knowing it, a natural consequence of the kindness shown you by the Empress and other persons highly placed at the Russian court. For, weak creatures as we are, we mortals often see only that which is before our eyes, but the Lord knows our hearts and our secret motives and, in His perfect justice, deals out His blessings accordingly."[5]

There was, naturally, a considerable difference between the state of mind of a grave and pious father and that of a young girl of fourteen who was much more concerned with her own worldly future than with the salvation of her soul, but Sophia was no hypocrite for all that. It was just because she was an intelligent and sensitive child that she had been able to accept Todorsky's subtle casuistry so completely and discover for herself a religion "above religion" which already had something in common with the deism of Rousseau. She was delighted to find that the best representative of this Greek Church which she had believed to be so backward could be so broad-minded and tolerant, and superior in this to her own father. (Later on, she was to speak with some bitterness of Lutheran fanaticism.)

Encouraged by her mother (who was afraid that her father's influence might present an obstacle to her conversion and hence to the marriage) Sophia made up her mind. If the truth were told, the "external dogma" so necessary by reason of the "brutishness of the people" was to repel her more than a little, especially as neither the Empress nor her court appeared to regard it as the mere remnant of a barbarous superstition. The interminable services with their Oriental pomp, far exceeding even that of the

Catholic Church; the richness of the churches with their gilded
iconostases, holy icons encrusted with gold and precious stones,
blue clouds of incense, thundering choirs; the brocaded episcopal
vestments sewn with thousands of tiny seed pearls; the monotonous litanies, the endless genuflections and all the slow, complicated, thoroughly medieval ceremonial of this church which she
had been persuaded was so close to the Lutheran, all this might
appeal to young Sophia's aesthetic sense, which was in fact
highly developed; but if she had ever had a sincere belief in the
faith of her childhood, that sincerity must, at this period, have
had its wings clipped.

Sophia had flung herself eagerly into the study of the Russian
language: her teacher, Adodurov, had nothing but praise for his
pupil's intelligence and zeal. In fact Sophia paid dearly for her
enthusiasm and it might even have cost her her life. The child
had formed the habit of getting up in the night to study her
lessons and sitting down to her books and exercises in her nightgown and bare feet. She caught cold. At first her mother, who
was terrified in case her daughter should be taken for an invalid,
told her to hide her illness. The neglected chill turned to pneu-
monia. Sophia developed such a fever that she was unconscious
for hours at a time and the doctors insisted she should be bled.
Johanna Elizabeth would not hear of it on any account, claiming
that excessive bleeding had already caused the death of her
brother who had been betrothed to Elizabeth. In the end the
Empress, who had complete confidence in her doctors, had the
girl's mother put out of the room and sat down to nurse her
herself.

Sophia recovered consciousness in the Empress's arms. It
seems as though, through all the insults she endured at Elizabeth's hands, Sophia always retained a certain gratitude to the
big woman, at once harsh and gentle, who at that moment had
behaved in a more motherly way than her own mother.

For several days the young invalid hovered between life and
death. The reason for her illness became known in the court and
in the city, and those who supported the match made sure that
the affecting spectacle of a little princess who loved Russia so

much that she would spend her nights learning the Russian language did not go unnoticed by the public. This was a card which Sophia was to play often enough in the future, and her first attempt proved a master stroke: from the first month that she lived in Russia she was already, as far as this was possible, popular.

During her illness, when the worst was feared, the Princess of Anhalt-Zerbst had talked of calling a Lutheran pastor to her daughter. Sophia, barely conscious, declared that she had no need of one, and that she would prefer to speak with Simeon Todorsky. This delighted the Empress and the whole court. The strange thing is that in her memoirs, Catherine represents this as an example of her own cunning: luckily, she seems to say, I had that much presence of mind. What was my mother thinking of? A Lutheran pastor would have created the worst possible impression. It is possible that the hard years at Elizabeth's court had wiped any suggestion of spontaneous feeling from Catherine's heart, and that she is not altogether doing herself justice here. There seems little reason why she should be glad of the presence of a strange Lutheran minister, when she so much enjoyed hearing what Todorsky had to say.

However that may be, Sophia, ill and desperately afraid of being sent home again to Zerbst on account of bad health, did not lose her advantage and continued to play the part of a model little princess. Often she would take advantage of her weak state to lie with her eyes shut pretending to be asleep so that she could listen to the conversations of the ladies who watched by her bedside. Luckily for her, French was more commonly spoken at the Russian court than Russian. Her mother was no longer admitted to her room, a fact which did not displease Sophia in the least—indeed, quite the reverse. On the other hand she relates with undisguised bitterness how she was no sooner on the road to recovery than her mother sent one of her ladies to ask for a particular piece of pale blue cloth with silver flowers which had been a present from her uncle. The girl parted with the cloth very unwillingly, saying that she would have preferred to keep it, and that her uncle had given it to her especially because he knew how much she wanted it. The mother's conduct made a very bad impression, and Elizabeth promptly offered her future niece several lengths of blue silk woven with silver, all much finer than the stuff in question.

Meanwhile the chancellor Bestuzhev and those who favored the Saxon marriage were jubilant, and were already writing to the Elector of Saxony to spy out the land. Frederick II, too, was already thinking about a new candidate, the daughter of the Duke of Darmstadt, and Brümmer had already drafted a letter to the Duke to be used in case the Princess of Anhalt should die. Elizabeth, however, announced that it would do no one any good, and that if she had the misfortune to lose such an adorable child, then "the devil take her if she would ever have any princess of Saxony!"⁶ Evidently as far as the Empress was concerned Sophia had fully succeeded in her aims.

In the end Sophia's naturally robust health triumphed over the illness, and perhaps over her doctors. In her joy, Elizabeth presented the girl with a diamond-studded snuffbox and her mother with a ring worth, said Princess Johanna Elizabeth, at least one thousand thalers. A month and a half after her arrival in Moscow the Grand Duke's little betrothed was at last able to go out and appear in public. "At last," she wrote later, "on April 21, 1744, my birthday, on which I entered my fifteenth year, I was in a condition to appear in public for the first time since my dreadful illness. I cannot imagine that the world found me a very edifying sight, for I had got as thin as a skeleton, I had grown taller, my features had lengthened, my hair was falling out, and I was mortally pale. I myself thought I was quite terrifyingly ugly and I could not recover my countenance. That day the Empress sent me a pot of rouge and commanded me to put some on."⁷

At the beginning of May, Sophia wrote to her father:

MY LORD,

I make so bold as to write to your Highness to ask your consent to her Imperial Majesty's intentions with regard to me. I can assure you that your will shall always be my own, and that no one shall make me fail in my duty to you. Since I can find almost no difference between the Greek faith and the Lutheran, I am resolved (with all due regard to your Highness's gracious instructions) to change, and shall send you my confession of faith on the first day. I may flatter myself that your Highness will be pleased with it and I remain, while I live, with profound respect, my lord, your Highness's very obedient and very humble daughter and servant.

SOPHIA A.F. D'A.Z.

Zerbst, 14 (3) May 1744

P.S. I humbly beg your Highness to present my respects to my uncle and tell him that I will write to him by the first post, since my hand is too weak to permit me to do so today.[8]

The hand was weak and the spirit perhaps a little distracted, since the girl dates her letter from Zerbst, the town which she had left six months before yet may still have longed for in her heart. "I am resolved," she wrote, "*to change*," and one can feel the hesitation behind her words, her fear of hurting her father and possibly, but only possibly, some regret for the Lutheran faith to which she was trying to cling by persuading herself that there was "almost no difference" between it and the Orthodox faith. She was very well aware that her own family would always regard her as a renegade, and as yet she did not know what her new family was to be.

Twelve

❮❖❮❖❮❖❮❖❮❖❮❖❮❖❮❖❮❖❮❖❮❖

Young Love and Court Intrigue

After her great surge of tenderness toward the sick child, Elizabeth returned to her normal occupations of balls, receptions, pilgrimages. Sophia was never admitted to her intimate circle. The Grand Duke Peter, on the other hand, was beginning to see in his young cousin the soul mate and haven of peace that he had lacked all his life. Sophia complains mildly that the coming of spring has put an end to the Grand Duke's attentions, since he preferred to go walking or hunting in the country around Moscow, but she adds that "he came sometimes to dine or sup with us and then his childish confidences to me continued." She admits, too, that "at that time the Grand Duke opened his heart to me more than to anyone."

In fact it seems that to begin with, Peter, though not in love —with Catherine he was never that—was deeply and sincerely attached to his future wife. Catherine later denied that there was any reality in this attachment, and yet her mother is unlikely to have been lying when she wrote to her husband: "I would never have believed that the Grand Duke, who was not in doubt as to your consent [to the marriage], could have been so affected by your letter. If all the vows of your future son-in-law should prove true, you will undoubtedly be the happiest of men."[1] Peter had in fact gone almost mad with joy when he learned of the Prince of Anhalt-Zerbst's consent to his marriage with his daughter; he leaped about like a child, smothered the letter in kisses and insisted on reading it aloud to everyone on the slightest excuse.

"I saw clearly that he would have left me without regret; for my own part, seeing his inclination, he was more or less indifferent to me, but the crown of Russia was not." These words were written more than thirty years after the events just described, by a woman who wanted to prove to herself and to the whole world that her husband had never had the slightest feeling for her, and that she had consequently been fully justified in not loving him. For all that, there was a considerable understanding between the two children, and there can be no question that it was Peter who loved the most.

It was at the convent of Troitsa, to which Elizabeth, accompanied by the Grand Duke and the two princesses, was making a pilgrimage, that a most painful scene occurred between the Empress and Sophia's mother. This scene was a direct result of the Marquis de la Chétardie's scheming, and of Johanna Elizabeth's indiscretion in allowing herself to chatter somewhat too freely with him.

The day this happened the betrothed pair were sitting indoors on a window ledge, swinging their legs and laughing and joking together, when Lestocq, the Empress's doctor and intimate adviser, came up to them. He told the girl gruffly: "You can go and pack your bags, for you'll be taking yourself off home at once." Such unjustifiable insolence toward the Grand Duke's affianced bride left both children gaping, and the boy said: "Your mother may have done something wrong, but you have not!" Sophia answered that it was her duty to follow her mother. This is the moment when, she says, "I saw that he would have left me without regret." Can it have been true? The young prince already regarded her as his only friend in the midst of a hostile court. But it is very likely that he did not manage to sound sufficiently eager on this occasion. Proud and sensitive as she was, Sophia often mistook shyness for indifference; and Peter, too, might well have thought that Sophia would leave him "without regret."

The two children were still sitting there, trembling and bewildered, when they saw the Empress Elizabeth emerge from her apartment followed by the Princess of Zerbst, who had "red eyes and her face wet with tears." Like two naughty children, the young people immediately jumped down from the window sill on which they had been perched, and at this childish gesture the Empress smiled and kissed them both, and by so doing gave them to understand that she did not hold the daughter responsible for the mother's errors.[2]

But it had been a close thing. Elizabeth had read La Chétardie's private correspondence (the French ambassador was on leave at the time but still in possession of letters of credit from his government), correspondence in which the careless marquis spoke in the lightest possible terms of the Empress and compromised the Princess of Anhalt-Zerbst—who was his friend—by allowing it to be hinted that she aimed to serve the King of Prussia. La Chétardie was expelled from the country. The Princess received one of Elizabeth's customary dressing-downs (for the Empress was never able to control her tongue when she was angry), and Sophia had reason to believe that her mother's carelessness would ruin the fruit of all her efforts.

The projected marriage was not abandoned, but the Empress cooled considerably toward the Princess of Zerbst and the young Grand Duke became more and more impatient, since he no doubt believed that a whim of his aunt's would deprive him of his little playmate and friend—for Peter was still very much a child and the sensible Sophia, however good her intentions, never seems to have succeeded in taking him seriously.

Some rumors of the Saxon match must have got abroad at the court of Moscow. At all events, the betrothed couple went in constant fear of being separated and, to help fate along, they invented a game which consisted in publicly proposing the following toast: "May God grant that what we hope for will happen soon" (what they hoped for was, of course, their marriage). One day at dinner the ambassador of Saxony, Baron Herzdorf, having penetrated the Grand Duke's innocent ruse and wishing to please him, proposed that they should drink a health in Russian (he was thinking of the now famous one beginning: "May God grant . . ." "If you knew the real meaning of that phrase," Peter retorted more innocently than ever, "then you ought rather to say 'May God grant that *what we do not hope for* will happen soon,'" alluding to the secret hopes of the court of Saxony.[3]

But after all, Elizabeth was less changeable than her enemies would have her: once her mind was made up that her nephew would marry the Princess of Zerbst, she had no intention of going back on her word, and although greatly displeased with the mother, she continued to show favor to the daughter, the "adorable child" she had been so afraid would die. Sophia had managed to touch her Orthodox heart by her willingness to prepare herself for her "conversion," and in her respect for the Empress, Sophia descended to the most blatant flattery. When the Marquis de la Chétardie complimented her on her coiffure she even declared that "to please the Empress [she] would do her hair in any fashion that she might like." She would never have permitted herself to slander her Majesty in the privacy of her own drawing room, as her mother had done; she knew that walls had ears, and furthermore she did sincerely admire Elizabeth. At this period the Empress was fonder of her future niece than she was of her nephew, and thought she could place great hopes in the influence of this pearl among princesses over the future Peter III.

This influence was already making itself felt, to such an extent that even the stern Brümmer judged it advisable to ask the girl to assist him in "chastising and correcting his Grand Duke." Sophia very wisely answered that this was none of her business and she had no wish to "make herself odious" to the young man by constantly remonstrating with him. Indeed, part of the secret of his affection for her lay in her extreme indulgence of his whims and the patience with which she listened to confidences which she herself found "childish."

All the same, she was probably the only person who ever really tried to win the young prince's friendship and confidence, and her good will may not always have been entirely due to self-interest.

Thirteen

The Grand Duchess Catherine

At last the Empress fixed the date for the official betrothal for June 29, the feast of Saints Peter and Paul. On the eve of the ceremony, the young princess was formally to abjure the Lutheran faith and to be admitted to the Orthodox Church.

She herself wrote later: "I read aloud fifty quarto pages in the Russian language with, although I did not understand them, great correctness and an unimpeachable accent [we may take leave to doubt this, since all her life she retained a strong German accent], and after this I recited the creed by heart." This in itself is an indication that she regarded the whole thing in the light of a piece of schoolwork or, at best, of a performance from which she emerged with credit: of her private feelings, not a word. But her mother does give, however discreetly, a hint that her daughter felt some hesitation when the moment came to take the decisive step.

"On that day [the eve of the ceremony] she was continually obsessed by thoughts of religion and discovered engaged in prayer or meditation, and I thought her *a little moved*. I was watching her so closely that not one sigh, not one tear, could escape me. I spoke to her and she assured me, which I could see clearly, that she was only disturbed by a true contemplation of the mysteries of religion. She slept soundly all night long, which was an undoubted mark of the tranquillity of her soul."[1] The secretive child would not admit to her mother any grief she might feel at abjuring her faith, but she might well have been more open with her father. At all events those few furtive tears, laid to the charge of an excess of religious exaltation, did not weigh heavily on the mother's conscience, or on the daughter's determination. Whether it was the effect of tranquillity of soul or simply of exhaustion after three days' fasting, Sophia slept well and when she awoke was taken, after confession, still in her undress, into Elizabeth's room, for the Empress herself wished to prepare her nephew's future bride for the great day.

The Princess of Anhalt-Zerbst takes a good deal of pleasure in describing this feminine ceremony, and describes the "*adrienne*" just like the Empress's own, "made of Tours silk encrusted with decorative trimmings of silver along all the seams." Sophia, wrote her mother, wore a white ribbon on her head which was otherwise very simply dressed, with her hair unpowdered; her only jewels were the large pendants and the brooch which her Majesty had given her during her illness. She was a little pale, and the splendid parure heightened the natural pallor of her skin. "I must say," the Princess adds, "I thought she was lovely." This last remark sounds perfectly sincere: Johanna Elizabeth had always regarded her daughter as plain, and now, seeing her on the point of attaining the highest honors, she could not help changing her mind. Beautiful Sophia probably was not, but she was slender and elegant, with a touch of youthful grace. A skinny little brunette with a pale face and blue eyes.

The girl's admission into the Orthodox Church earned her the approval of the court: she stood up straight and proud and recited her lesson, which she had learned well, with such confidence that the Empress, who cried easily, and all the court after her, shed a few sentimental tears. All the great ladies of the court had coveted the honor of standing godmother to the new convert, and Elizabeth, in order to avoid jealousy, satisfied them all by choosing for this high office a venerable nun, eighty years old, with "an odor of sanctity among the people," as the Princess of Anhalt-Zerbst puts it, and who, moreover, possessed the advantage of no longer having a single living relative.

The ceremony was not, of course, a proper baptism, since the Orthodox faith formally recognizes only one baptism, even if that is a heretic one. The ceremony was more in the nature of a confirmation: as the Princess of Anhalt-Zerbst describes it, "the forehead, eyes, neck, throat and the palms and backs of the hands are anointed with oil. The oil is wiped off with a piece of cotton immediately after application."

While the ladies and even the gentlemen of the court were shedding a few tears, the young convert took care to do no such thing for fear of appearing grief-stricken or exhausted: "As for me, I stood it very well, and everyone praised me." On that day, Sophia Augusta Fredericka of Anhalt-Zerbst received, in exchange for her three Christian names, the first name of Catherine to which was added the Russian patronymic Alexeievna (that of Christianovna would have been too Germanic and after the sad memory of Anna Leopoldovna would, moreover, have made a very bad impression). Sophia was a very common name in Russia, but Elizabeth would not have it because it had belonged to her aunt, the Tsarevna Sophia, the formidable rival of the young Peter the Great. (". . . my own was disliked on account of its connection with the sister of Peter the Great who bore the same name."[2]) But the same situations crop up again and again in history, with only slight variations, and her change of name did not prevent this Sophia from avenging the other Sophia on Peter the Great's grandson.

The docile convert was bombarded with presents: immediately on her exit from the church, the Empress presented her with "a brooch pin of brilliants and a necklace to the value of a hundred and fifty thousand rubles."[3] The girl was so exhausted that she was unable to appear at the banquet. The next morning—the day fixed for the official betrothal—Sophia (no, Catherine, henceforth and for always) was presented with a portrait of the Empress "studded with brilliants" and another of the Grand Duke which was "equally valuable." The story of the next few days, as it flows from the pen of the Princess of Anhalt-Zerbst, is little more than a catalogue of jewels each finer and more valuable than the last, a description of solemn processions, fine points of etiquette and allusions to the maneuvers of various schemers.

At the same time, Johanna Elizabeth writes to her husband (whose absence at such a time appears somewhat surprising, although it can be explained on the grounds that this was, after all, merely a betrothal and the Prince's attachment to the Lutheran faith was well known): "It is indeed painful to us to see our daughter so far away from us . . . even if she is to be mistress of one of the greatest fortunes in the world. We may console ourselves with the thought that we are leaving her among a people who love her already, and to the care of the best and kindest of mothers."[4]

For the betrothal ceremony, Elizabeth wore the imperial crown and mantle, and she left the Kremlin palace "under a canopy of solid silver carried by eight major generals," followed by the Grand Duke and his betrothed. The procession descended the famous Kremlin steps, the Krasnoie Kriltso, and crossed the square to the cathedral "on foot" (it would have been pointless to do anything else, as the cathedral was immediately opposite). Both sides of the square were lined with regiments of the guards. The two young people were placed on a velvet-covered dais in the center of the magnificent church with its massive pillars and walls painted all over with frescos, and were betrothed by Archbishop Ambrose of Novgorod. Then the Empress had them proceed to the exchange of rings. These rings, wrote Princess Johanna Elizabeth, were "real little monsters, both of them, and each must have cost fifty thousand *écus*."[5]

There was great popular rejoicing. Salvos of cannon announced the glad news to the good people of Moscow. Inside the Kremlin palace there were some difficulties and complications: the Princess of Anhalt-Zerbst could not be allowed to sit at the imperial table, which was reserved for Elizabeth, her nephew and Catherine, who had already been proclaimed Grand Duchess, and since she would not eat with the other ladies of the court she had to dine "in a kind of incognito" in a private room with a glass window giving onto the main banqueting hall. It should be said in all fairness that Elizabeth had gone out of her way to be polite to a woman whom already she despised: at the climax of the ceremony she had prevented the Princess from kneeling before her, saying "our situation is the same, and our vows are the same."

The Princess wrote in her memoirs: "The entire ceremony lasted for four hours during which it was impossible to sit down for a moment. . . . It would certainly be no exaggeration to say that my back was numb from all the bowing I had been obliged to do as I embraced all the numerous ladies, and that there was a red mark the size of a German florin on my right hand from all the times it had been kissed."[6]

The betrothed pair were exhausted as well, but there was still the ball in the evening. "At the foot of the throne was a carpet on which only the Empress, my mother, myself and the Princess of Hesse of the ladies, and of the gentlemen only the Grand Duke, the ambassadors of England, Holstein and Denmark, and the Prince of Hesse, were permitted to dance." Catherine adds that they were almost suffocated by the heat and the crowd, since the room was so constructed that the single huge pillar in the center which sustained the roof filled a fourth part of the room.

"From my betrothal to the moment of departure [Elizabeth was leaving on a pilgrimage to Kiev] there was not a day on which I did not receive presents from the Empress, of silver and jewels, cloth and so forth, indeed everything that one can imagine, the least of which was worth from ten to fifteen thousand rubles. In fact, she showed me extreme kindness."[7] Before her betrothal the young princess had been on the verge of a nervous breakdown as a result of the attitude taken by her family in Germany, who disapproved of the match and predicted the direst future for Sophia; now, she was able to laugh at her fears, for everything smiled on her. She had the Empress's favor, presents, pocket money—thirty thousand rubles, of which she hastened to send something to her father so that he could use it for the care of her sick brother; the Grand Duke showed increasing tenderness toward her, and if he was not precisely the young man of her dreams he was, after all, a highly eligible prince and one she could hope to mold to her own liking, since he was little more than a child.

To prevent her niece from growing bored, and also with the object of helping her improve her Russian, Elizabeth gave her a whole court of her own, with chamberlains, courtiers and ladies in waiting, all of them young and gay, so young in fact that the Princess of Anhalt-Zerbst evinces some displeasure at it: this "court" was too giddy and noisy for her taste. Naturally Sophia-Catherine and the Grand Duke were the last to complain. The Grand Duke had his own court, and after their marriage they would become official leaders of the "young court," as opposed to the "old court" which was the Empress's.

The young couple still amused themselves chiefly with children's games: they would spend hours laughing and prancing about, and even a year later Catherine was still romping like a mad thing with her ladies, playing blindman's buff or taking the lid off the big harpsichord and using it as a toboggan to slide along the floor. For the Grand Duke, Catherine was his loyal playmate and his surest refuge from the harshness of his "pedagogues": he was well aware that his fondness for his fiancée could not help but please the Empress.

Catherine saw less and less of her mother, who was vexed to see her daughter take precedence over her on public occasions. "My daughter conducts herself very intelligently in her new situation," the Princess wrote; "she blushes each time she is forced to walk in front of me."[8] Instead she attached herself, or tried to, to her young cousin the Grand Duke. Her mother had gathered about her a circle of friends of whom the Empress and the rest of the court disapproved, and it was not long before her intimacy with the chamberlain Betsky, brother-in-law of the Prince of Hesse, caused a scandal. "While she was with them in her own apartment," Catherine writes, "the Grand Duke and I were busy kicking up a row in the antechamber, for we neither of us suffered from a lack of childish high spirits."[9]

Fourteen

❧❧❧❧❧❧❧❧❧❧❧❧❧❧❧

A Journey to Kiev, Family and Other Troubles

Elizabeth was to make a pilgrimage to Kiev, the oldest and holiest of all Russian cities. She traveled in great pomp with all her court, the Grand Duke, his fiancée and their respective courts, innumerable servants, and a train of carriages and carts over half a mile long. It was a truly imperial cavalcade. "At every halt there were eight hundred horses."

The Grand Duke, availing himself of his rights as Catherine's future husband, had elected to travel in the same carriage as the princesses of Zerbst and there was no getting him out of it. To the great annoyance of Catherine's mother, the pair insisted on filling the carriage with other young people as youthful and giddy as themselves and the whole journey passed in continuous games and laughter from morning to night. It was at this point that Catherine began to be troubled by the realization that her mother and her future husband would never get on well together. During one halt, at Koseletz, Peter was indiscreet enough to attempt to go through the Princess's box. She scolded him angrily and the young man, "leaping about," says Catherine, "to make me laugh," clumsily knocked against the lid of the box and spilled the contents all over the ground. This led to a furious scene which Catherine tried to calm by pointing out to her mother that the Grand Duke had not done it on purpose; the Princess's anger was promptly turned on her and the girl burst into tears. Peter sprang to the defense of his betrothed and let loose a furious tirade against his future mother-in-law, while she in turn raged at him for a spoiled child.[1] From that day the rift was complete. Catherine was constantly torn between the two and, since she seems to have felt a good deal more sympathy for the Grand Duke who had taken her part than for her mother who was continually scolding her, she was very unhappy.

She was distracted from her own troubles by the magnificent spectacle of Kiev, "on the edge of the Borysthenes" as she describes it—in other words, the Dnieper. "The city of Kiev can be seen to perfection from the other side [of the river]." She was probably more impressed with the sight than she lets us see in this stark phrase, to judge by the effect on her of the solemn processions and religious services in the Pechersky Monastery. "I have never been more impressed in my life than I was by the extraordinary splendor of this church in which all the images are covered with gold, silver and jewels."[2] She does not say whether she felt any stirrings of religious feeling in the face of all this magnificence.

The Empress was welcomed by the citizens of the old town with all the baroque pomp and extravagance of the period, including *tableaux vivants* depicting historical and allegorical subjects. A young student in the guise of an old man bearing a crown and scepter came to meet Elizabeth, riding in an antique chariot drawn by winged horses. He announced that he was Kiy, the legendary founder of the city, who had descended from the Elysian Fields to greet his "heir."[3] But *tableaux vivants* and fireworks were as nothing compared with the solemn splendor of the religious processions and services, as they were seen in this the holiest of Russian cities at a period when the Church was immensely, almost indecently rich and the people pious to the point of fanaticism.

There, for the first time, Catherine was able to see what these people were really like and to get to know a Russia which lay outside the life of the court. She could watch thousands of men and women from all classes of society, including crowds of wandering pilgrims, for in no country was pilgrimage more wide-spread, or closer to ordinary vagabondage, than in Russia. There were white-bearded ascetics, loaded with iron chains; monks in black habits and hoods; peasants dressed in rags or in their Sunday best—and at that period peasant costume on festive occasions was highly varied and picturesque; merchants and citizens whose long caftans, flowing beards and leather boots made them look as though they had walked right out of the times of ancient Muscovy; women wearing rich, medieval headdresses, and peasant girls with kerchiefs on their heads and bundles on their backs. Above all there were the beggars, the countless, pitiful and eternal crowd of beggars singing psalms and stretch-ing out their hands for alms. All this the little princess could see from her velvet-cushioned carriage, and she watched, curious and no doubt compassionate, eager for each new spectacle that met her eyes, while her companions, her mother and the Grand Duke, paid no attention at all: the one too wrapped up in her own affairs, the other despising the barbarous land in which he was condemned to live.

On her return to Moscow Catherine continued to make prog-ress in learning her job as a grand duchess. "My gratitude and respect for the Empress was extreme. I regarded her as a divinity, free from all defects; and she too was used to say that she loved me almost more than the Grand Duke. She liked to hear good spoken of me, but I was very timid in her presence. The Grand Duke loved me passionately and everything conspired to give me hope for a happy future."[4]

Unfortunately a sudden cold blast came to interrupt the gaiety of the Moscow court: one evening, while a play was in progress, the Empress took it into her head to send her adviser Lestocq to the Grand Duchess's box to inform her that she was piling up a great deal too many debts. "When she [Elizabeth] was a princess she had no more funds than you and a whole house-hold to maintain and she took care not to have any debts, because she knew that no one would pay them for her."[5] Poor Catherine:

the tears sprang to her eyes. She had fallen abruptly from her pinnacle—she, who had thought herself the Empress's spoiled child, at liberty to spend what she pleased and shower presents on her ladies in waiting, her mother and even the Grand Duke himself. She was a naturally generous person and was never so happy as when giving presents. The ultimate humiliation came when the Grand Duke, who went in great fear of his aunt, agreed with what Lestocq said and added his own reproaches to his overextravagant betrothed—he, who was always the first to demand presents!

As a woman of fifty and an all-powerful empress, Catherine justifies these youthful extravagances as best she can. She had come to Russia poor, she says, so poor that she possessed only three or four dresses and a dozen shifts, and had not even any sheets of her own but was compelled to use those belonging to her mother. And she had to soothe her mother's irritable temper with expensive presents and to win the friendship of her women and the confidence of the Grand Duke. She was never to get over the affront of having been publicly reprimanded in the most humiliating way by a woman who was as practiced in the art of wounding as in that of charming others.

In addition, her mother was becoming increasingly unhappy and discontented because her enemies were ousting her from the Empress's favor, and the Grand Duke, who was sincerely fond of her, had caught the measles. "He grew considerably taller during his illness, but remained very childish."[6] Decidedly too childish in fact, for his favorite pastime consisted in "enlisting" his *valets de chambre*, his footmen, his gentlemen and his entire household, Catherine included, and giving them all a "rank." As he grew older his teachers were finding him increasingly difficult to handle; understandably enough, considering that he was sixteen and tired of being ordered about. Catherine, the only person he trusted, gave in to all his whims and never contradicted him for fear of making him cross.

It is difficult to tell whether this extreme meekness filled Peter with gratitude or contempt or both. Perhaps he thought that she really did love him—indeed, she may have. For a great many years yet they were to retain an almost unconscious affection for one another, like that felt by prisoners who have shared the same chain.

Fifteen

《◇《◇《◇《◇《◇《◇《◇《◇《◇《◇《◇《◇《◇

A Catastrophe

Toward the end of December 1745 the Grand Duke was traveling between Moscow and St. Petersburg, when during a halt at Khotilovo he fainted without warning in his fiancée's apartment. Almost at once he developed a high fever. The next day, Brümmer refused to allow the princesses to enter the invalid's room: the Grand Duke showed all the symptoms of smallpox. Fearing infection for herself and her daughter, the Princess of Anhalt-Zerbst decided to continue the journey. Catherine, whose courage was not the least of her virtues, wanted to remain with her future husband, but although she wept and pleaded she was forced to obey her mother. The two women departed, leaving the young man in the care of his tutors and two ladies in waiting.

No sooner was Elizabeth informed than she set out with all haste for Khotilovo, meeting the princesses on the road in the middle of the night. The Empress asked for news of the invalid and then continued on her way at top speed. Throughout the whole course of the terrible disease she did not leave her nephew's bedside, running the most appalling risk of catching the smallpox herself and losing, if not her life, at least her precious beauty. Her behavior on this occasion, whether it proceeded from real affection or from a simple sense of duty, tells us a great deal more about Elizabeth than all the gossip of courts and ambassadors.

That Catherine was terribly anxious we can scarcely doubt: anxious for a boy of whom, although she often found him irritating, she had become genuinely fond, and anxious for her own future, since with the Grand Duke dead she would lose forever all hope of becoming Empress. She wrote to Elizabeth (in Russian) letters full of solicitude, begging to be told the state of Peter's health. In actual fact these letters were written by her Russian teacher, Adodurov, and she merely copied them out, but this does not necessarily prove that she was deceitful, merely that she was eager to please. All the same, she took care not to admit the truth to the Empress.

None of Catherine's anxiety is allowed to show in her memoirs and this suggests that her sufferings may not have been very acute. She has a great deal more to say about squabbles with her mother over their respective apartments and about her meeting with the Swedish statesman Count Gyllenborg and the sensible advice which he gave her. We shall return to this advice later. Thoroughly pleased with herself, the "fifteen-year-old philosopher," as she calls herself on this occasion, does not give the impression of a girl half dead with worry about the man she loves.

Nevertheless, for Peter if not for Catherine, this disease was to prove a terrible misfortune, a misfortune which shattered perhaps forever their chances of loving one another and lost Peter all hope of a happy life.

Peter had never been handsome. A portrait dating from before his illness (a sketch for an official portrait, preserved in the historical museum of the Kremlin in Moscow) shows us the face of a youth quite degenerate, certainly, but not coarse: it is thin, bony and hollow-cheeked, with high cheekbones and a pointed chin; the big blue eyes are rather long and heavy-lidded, giving him a somewhat languishing expression, and he has a slight, gentle smile which could be inane or could be merely shy. With his fine eyes and fresh complexion this rather unremarkable youth was still not unpleasing: but after the smallpox nothing remained of the delicate freshness which was at least capable of inspiring some tender feelings and to which Catherine had perhaps not been totally indifferent. The wretched young man's face was so pitted and swollen as to be altered out of all recognition.

Catherine saw him for the first time after his illness when Elizabeth brought him back to St. Petersburg. The meeting took place in "a great hall between four and five o'clock in the evening, when it was more or less dark." She says that Peter had grown taller still but that his face was "unrecognizable." They had shaved his hair and he was wearing an enormous wig which disfigured him even more. The poor boy went up to his betrothed and asked her whether she still knew him. She was unable to disguise her involuntary horror and disgust. "He had become quite hideous."[1]

Was Sophia of Anhalt-Zerbst the kind of girl to whom any prince must always seem handsome? At all events, she seems to have displayed more personal grief at the idea of marrying an ugly man than pity for her disfigured playmate. Elizabeth, aware of the girl's distress, surrounded her with attentions and bent over backward to please her, even doing her the honor of dining alone with her "on the throne" on February 10, the anniversary of the Grand Duke's birth. (Peter was still in no fit state to appear in public.) She complimented her on her famous letters in Russian, made her speak the language, praised her accent, praised her beauty and altogether did everything she could to comfort her, perhaps fearing that under the influence of an unconquerable aversion to her future spouse, the little princess might beg her parents to withdraw their consent to the match. Catherine, we may be sure, had no such intention. She was already sufficiently spoiled by court life to place the good graces of the Empress above her own private joys and sorrows. This dinner left her very happy because "everyone complimented her."[2]

As for the Grand Duke, Catherine tells us that she and her mother saw him frequently since their apartments were adjoining, but she observes scornfully that he appeared to be avoiding her company and made excuses to remain in his own room, surrounded by his childish playthings. Catherine must have been very young—or very hard—for it is not difficult to imagine the young man's state of mind when he found that he had become an object of revulsion to the girl he was to marry.

The expression "inferiority complex" was unknown in the eighteenth century, and perhaps after all it does not explain a great deal, for it makes little difference what finishes off an animal already wounded. Peter had been weak and helpless from childhood. Condemned by the quirks of dynastic law to bear a crown he had never sought, this boy, so little cut out to reign, hardly deserves history's condemnation. The majority of historians have presented him as a monster, a sadist, an imbecile or a brute; in fact, he was none of these things. The monstrous thing was the disparity between his capabilities and the role he was called upon to play.

It is fairly clear that the smallpox, coming as it did almost immediately after a serious and belated attack of measles, must have had a profoundly disturbing effect on his delicate constitution. He was still growing, and the fact that he had grown much taller caused comment after the smallpox, as well as after the measles. In fact, from a boy who was small for his age he had become, in the space of a few months, a tall man, resembling in his long thin figure his ancestor Peter the Great. This abnormally fast growth, coinciding with two exhausting illnesses, must already have ruined what little nervous equilibrium he still possessed. His weak state following the illness, combined with the certainty that he had become hideously ugly, had thrown the young prince back once and for all into his childish universe, the eternal refuge of the weak.

From that moment on, either because he entertained no more

illusions as to Catherine's feelings for him or because he felt guilty about his unsightly appearance, he sought the company of servants in preference to that of his future bride, and very bad company it was. Catherine speaks bitterly of the "old servants who are the Grand Duke's favorites," and these vulgar persons gave him their views on how a husband should treat his wife: they let him know the husband should be the master, that his wife should not utter a word in his presence and so forth. According to Stehlin these unlikely preceptors—one of them, Romberg, had formerly been a Swedish dragoon—indulged in the most scabrous talk in the Grand Duke's presence and the boy, who had reached the most critical period of puberty, listened to them avidly. Elizabeth heard of it, probably from Peter himself, since the boy was a perfect sieve and would repeat everything he heard quite thoughtlessly to all and sundry, and she issued orders that his servants were not to corrupt the child's mind in this way, but it seems unlikely that her commands were obeyed: the men knew too well that their conversations did not displease the Grand Duke.[3]

Catherine, for her part, made praiseworthy efforts to regain her future husband's confidence, and he continued to confide in her: she was, after all, the only being to whom he felt really close, and as Catherine says, without appearing to realize just how how pathetic an avowal she is making: "I resolved to keep the Grand Duke's confidence, so that he could at least regard me as one person of whom he could be certain, and to whom he could tell all *without fear of the consequences to himself*." Ever since his arrival in Russia, Peter, who was a dreadful chatterbox, had known that he was surrounded by spies and lived in constant fear of having whatever he said reported either to Brümmer, to the Empress, or to one or another of the various ambassadors and ministers, for he was less simple-minded than might have been imagined. But the fear merely worried him; it did not make him prudent. His fear of Elizabeth was more justified than Catherine in those first months could have believed, but she was soon to learn, to her own cost.

But though Catherine, like the wise and adaptable girl she was, "studied to win the friendship of any [she] merely suspected of being ill-disposed toward [her]," Peter appears to have adopted a completely opposite attitude and delighted in shocking and annoying everyone. While Catherine became more and more Russian, Orthodox, anti-Prussian, indeed all that could be desired of her, even leaving the choice of her hairstyles to the Empress, Peter retreated more and more into himself and his nostalgia for his German Lutheran childhood, becoming, as he grew older, more German than the Germans themselves. True, the life he was forced to lead was no joke and he had a good deal to complain of, but Peter the Great's grandson had inherited his grandfather's stubbornness and his tendency to form one fixed idea, without his capacity for reconciling his own desires with the realities of life.

Catherine, however, appears to have lost what little feeling she might have had for her future husband, and excused herself by pleading Peter's increased coldness toward her. Her friendship became increasingly a thing of calculation and interest. Peter, who was probably less stupid than she gave him credit for being, could not help but realize this and from that winter onward the gulf between the couple widened continually.

Elizabeth, increasingly anxious for the future of the dynasty, made up her mind to have the marriage solemnized as soon as possible, so that there could be a new heir to the empire. Now despite—or perhaps because of—his rapid growth, Peter, who was now sixteen, was still at the awkward age and not physically ripe for marriage. His doctors endeavored to explain this to the Empress, but she, as prudish and naïve in conversation as she was the reverse in practice, pretended not to understand. Furthermore she was in a considerable hurry to get rid of the Princess of Anhalt-Zerbst, who could hardly be sent home to Germany while her daughter was still unmarried. The wedding day was fixed for August 21, 1745, just a year and a half after the young princess's arrival in Russia.

Sixteen

❦❦❦❦❦❦❦❦❦❦❦❦

Their Imperial Highnesses

Catherine was generally considered a girl intelligent beyond her years. Count Gyllenborg, whom she had met once before in Hamburg and who had now turned up in Petersburg during the Grand Duke's illness, had formed a high opinion of her capabilities. As he had done at Hamburg, where "he was continually expressing such fine sentiments and noble maxims as are calculated to inspire a young person, with the object of elevating [her] mind," this distinguished man devoted a good deal of his time at Petersburg to guiding the young princess's thoughts away from the worldly vanities which seemed likely to absorb her completely, and directing her mind toward serious reading, as a way of forcing her to keep her integrity. At that time Catherine, whose chances of ever ascending the throne were threatening to disappear, needed moral support and some kind of philosophy more than ever. She read, or at least tried to read, Plutarch's *Parallel Lives* and Montesquieu's *Considerations sur les Causes de la Grandeur des Romains et Leur Décadence*, and if she was not yet sufficiently mature to understand these works, at least she made a real effort to learn to think and reflect for herself.

In order to show Gyllenborg that she was not simply an empty-headed little girl, she drew for him a verbal picture of herself under the title of "Portrait of a Fifteen-Year-Old Philosopher." This literary essay has not survived. Catherine says that she burned it in 1758 with some other papers at a time when she feared a search would be made of her apartments as a result of circumstances extremely hazardous to herself. Before burning the manuscript, she says, she reread it and "was astonished at the deep knowledge of myself that it showed."[1] She had always been extremely lucid—self-satisfied, it is true, but well aware of her faults, chief of which was a profound, deep-rooted and tenacious egoism.

Count Gyllenborg returned her essay to her, accompanied by a dozen pages of advice calculated to elevate and strengthen a young girl's mind. Catherine, who desperately needed a guide, resolved to follow this advice to the letter, but we do not know how far she succeeded. Life at the court of St. Petersburg was not designed for philosophers, especially when the philosophers were only fifteen.

Her character was still very childish: she was fond of creating an infernal din with her young ladies in waiting, organizing games of blindman's buff in her apartment in the evening. Thinking herself already mistress of her own household, she amused herself by allotting official positions to her companions: one was to guard her jewels, another to care for her clothes, another to look after her ribbons and so forth. The chief lady in waiting, major-domo of this miniature court, made short work of putting the little girl who wanted to play at being a grownup in her place, and to Catherine's great chagrin, all the young ladies in waiting had to resign their offices. Under the supervision of the strict and tiresome Mademoiselle Schenk, she felt like a repressed child in revolt against her elders.

She was still so innocent that even on the eve of her marriage she did not know the difference between a man and a woman. Her ladies in waiting, although they lived in the midst of an extremely licentious court, were also perfect innocents themselves, and at night before going to sleep the girls would chatter for hours, racking their brains to think what this difference was all about. It was Catherine, the boldest among them, who

promised to ask her mother for some facts so that she could
explain it to them. She was in for a disappointment: the Princess
of Zerbst refused to answer her questions and scolded her daughter for her unladylike curiosity.

Obviously Peter did not share her ignorance. His gentlemen
in waiting could hardly have failed to enlighten him. But he
was little more than an overgrown child and, considering his
age, altogether backward in his sexual development. Like a child
who hears and repeats obscene remarks without understanding
them, Peter was to go to his new wife's bed without the faintest
idea of what was expected of him. He was, however, not insensitive to female charms, and Catherine records that when she was
eleven and the princesses of Anhalt-Zerbst were visiting Kiel,
he "paid court" to her mother, who was "then very lovely," and
it was this completely innocent and childlike fondness for pretty
women which made the artless Elizabeth believe that her nephew
was already a man.

It is difficult to tell exactly what were the Grand Duke's real
feelings for his bride on the eve of their marriage. Catherine
complains bitterly of being "too little loved." On one occasion,
when he had to move his lodgings for a short while, Peter sent
a servant to tell her that he lived too far away to come and visit
her often. She insists that only her "vanity and self-esteem"
suffered, but the incident was wounding enough to make her shed
tears in private. The perfect candor with which she speaks of
her self-esteem suggests that there can have been no question
of any other feeling, a fact which justifies Peter's attitude. As
no doubt often happens with weak characters, especially those
that have been deprived of love, he probably wanted to be loved
unconditionally, without making the smallest effort to make
himself loved, and even behaving downright disagreeably if he
felt like it, in a continual effort to put to the test the love he
believed to be his due.

Catherine was no patient Griselda, to say the very least. On
the other hand, it would be hard to blame the Grand Duke, who

was too clear-sighted not to see that she loved his title rather than himself.

Moreover, it is only fair to say that Peter's reproaches to his future bride were not always totally unreasonable: for example on one occasion, during Lent, the Grand Duke sent his dwarf to ask after Catherine, and the dwarf found the girl and her women at prayers "fulfilling exactly the prescriptions for Lent according to our rite." The dwarf told the Grand Duke and he, "who was less than devout," was outraged and promptly reproached Catherine for her excessive devotion. Since he was well aware that this devotion contained a large admixture of hypocrisy, whether conscious or unconscious, and of flattery to Elizabeth, his irritation seems, when all is said and done, fairly understandable. All his life Peter was to be incapable of adapting himself and was never to see anything more than base opportunism in the flexibility of others.

The future was to prove that Catherine's "opportunism" corresponded purely and simply to an instinct for self-preservation. Neither she nor Peter was able to forget the fate of their fellow German, the Regent Anna Leopoldovna. The little prince Ivan VI was still alive and Elizabeth was keeping him in reserve, not, to be sure, as a possible future monarch but as a threat to hang over Peter's head. In the final analysis, even the child whose birth the Empress desired so strongly already represented, for its future parents, a possible promise of disgrace or even of exile. No doubt the betrothed couple were not consciously aware of all this, but they were quick-witted enough to sense it, and Peter in particular, because he hated the land in which he was compelled by his aunt's will to live. Catherine records that the Grand Duke was frequently in the habit of saying that it was an accursed country, that he could never live in it and was sure he would die there. He knew what he was talking about.

Meanwhile, the court at St. Peterburg was making ready, in feverish excitement and an atmosphere of balls, intrigue, argument over points of etiquette and wild expenditure, to celebrate the first imperial marriage ever seen publicly in Russia.

Seventeen

❦❦❦❦❦❦❦❦❦❦❦❦❦❦❦

The Wedding

By a few weeks before the wedding, it had become quite clear that the event was, to all practical purposes, without precedent. The young imperial house of Russia had never celebrated a proper royal marriage and Elizabeth wished her nephew's wedding to be a real national festivity. Peter the Great had imposed on his court the manners of the guardroom or, at best, of an upstart bourgeoisie, and it had made little progress in refinement under the rule of his immediate successors. Now Elizabeth was aiming to model it upon the court of Versailles. She was still a long way from success but her admiration for French civilization, which was shared at that time by the whole of Europe, was sincere. She was not deficient in either intelligence or taste, and she was striving to bridge as best she could the gaps in her father's work. She was determined to make Russian high society, at least on the surface, civilized and refined, and from the moment of her accession she had begun to fill St. Petersburg with French professors, artists, musicians and craftsmen.[1]

She therefore wrote to Versailles asking for precise information about the recent wedding of the Dauphin and to the court of Dresden for information about the nuptial celebrations of Augustus III of Saxony, the son of the King of Poland. The Empress's emissaries returned to Petersburg armed with detailed descriptions and voluminous folders of sketches and designs. At the wedding of the heir to the Russian Empire the very latest rules of etiquette and the most subtle details of ceremonial customary in Western courts would be observed with, if possible, even greater magnificence, for despite the disastrous state of her finances, Elizabeth always managed to find money when it was a matter of making a show.

The Princess of Anhalt-Zerbst, who was present at the wedding—feeling bitter and humiliated because the last few months had been a real nightmare for her—comforted herself by describing the splendor of the occasion for the benefit of her German relatives. Womanlike, she dwells particularly on the details of her daughter's costume, which Elizabeth herself had insisted on helping to arrange. "She even placed the imperial crown upon her head. She [Catherine] was unpowdered; her dress, or at least her gown, was of the most shimmering cloth of silver I have seen in my life, and encrusted with glittering embroidery all over the underskirt."[2] This wedding dress is still on view in the Kremlin museum: though the "shimmering" cloth of silver is very tarnished now, it has a wide skirt like those worn by Velásquez's infantas. The short-sleeved bodice, covered with silver embroidery, is made to encompass a ridiculously small waist, and the whole dress is very small, for Catherine was still growing at the time. An immense cloak of silver lace with a broad flowing train is fastened to the shoulders. "This fine decoration," says her mother, "and the superb jewels with which she was covered gave her an appearance which I can only call charming. A little rouge had also been put on her cheeks. Her complexion had never been lovelier. Her hair was a bright but lustrous black which heightened her air of youth and added to the advantage of dark hair the gentleness of fair."[3] She adds that Elizabeth had a similar dress but made of "chestnut-coloured Naples silk," while the Grand Duke was dressed in garments "exactly like those of his intended" (as far as color and the design of the embroidery were concerned, that is) with "the buttons, sword and all the decorations of brilliants."

So the young couple, dressed in white and silver and smothered in jewels, were led with great ceremony to the Kazan Cathedral; the description of the masters of ceremonies, the gentlemen of the bedchamber, the carriages, and the footmen going before and behind each gentleman of the court is enough to make one's head reel, for Johanna Elizabeth had a good memory and she was not one to take matters of etiquette lightly. She forgets nothing, not even the number of footmen accompanying each courtier or the livery they wore. In addition there were twenty-four carriages; the bride and groom (although this appears contrary to Orthodox usage) were together, in the Empress's carriage, to which the young bride's mother was not admitted. The Princess of Zerbst does not bother to describe the beauty of these carriages with their huge wheels covered in gilding, drawn by six white horses and literally dripping with gold, their side panels and doors covered in paintings depicting mythological scenes. She had seen enough of them.

Seeing so much gold, so many pearls and jewels, lavished even on the trappings of the horses, the people of Petersburg, those at least who were lucky enough to catch a glimpse of the procession between the regiments of guards lining the route, must have thought that the Tsarina and her court really belonged to a world apart where common mortals might not enter. They cheered the young royal couple very properly, and not without some affection for the two fragile, overawed young people in their shimmering garments encrusted with silver and diamonds.

On the eve of the ceremony the young bride was nervous and depressed: her mother came to reassure her and talked to her about her future duties. They wept together and parted, says Catherine, "very affectionately." After the months of misunderstandings and mutual indifference amounting almost to animosity, mother and daughter found themselves friends again on the eve of a separation which was likely to be forever. Her daughter's exalted position would not be enough to save the Princess of Anhalt-Zerbst, compromised simultaneously by her intrigues with the Prussians and by her connection with Count Betsky, from an ignominious dismissal.

For the young bride the wedding ceremony was nothing but one long, painful ordeal, and her beautiful dress was "horribly heavy." One curious detail emerges: during the sermon which preceded the blessing one of the ladies of the court, Countess Chernysheva, took it into her head to whisper to the Grand Duke under her breath that he should on no account turn his head while the couple were in front of the priest, since whoever looked around first would be the first to die. The young man indignantly told her to mind her own business and stop talking nonsense, and he promptly told Catherine what she had said. She seems to have regarded this merely as one more proof of her husband's indiscretion which might easily have provoked a quarrel between herself and Countess Chernysheva, but the indiscretion may well have sprung from the best of motives.

After the religious ceremony came the banquet, and after the banquet the ball. After only half an hour's dancing the impatient Empress decided to take the bride to her bedchamber.

The bride was bedded very quietly by comparison with the usual customs of those days. The Princess of Anhalt-Zerbst remarks that Elizabeth was preceded *only* by the masters of ceremonies, the grand master of the court, the grand marshal, and the grand chamberlain of the Grand Duke's court, and was followed *only* by the young couple, holding hands, the Princess Mother, her brother, the Princess of Hesse, the grand mistress, a few ladies in waiting and other, as she calls them, *Frelen*. The men left the nuptial apartments as soon as all the ladies had entered.

The bride was undressed. "Her Imperial Majesty removed the crown; I resigned to the Princess of Hesse the honor of putting on her shift [no doubt it was an honor to which the poor disgraced mother was not bidden], and the grand mistress put on her dressing gown." She adds in some surprise: "Excepting this ceremony there is much less attached to the undressing of the young couple than there is at home; no man dares enter after the groom has gone into his room to put on his nightclothes. There is no dancing or garlands, and no garter is given away."⁴

On this point, Russian ways were more reticent than those customary in the West.

The Princess is lost in admiration when she describes the apartments set aside for the young couple. "The bedchamber in poppy-colored velvet, verging on scarlet, the bed embroidered with pilasters and garlands in raised silver work,"[5] and more in the same vein. She may have been trying to convince herself that at least her daughter had not lost everything in this venture and that such luxury could to some extent justify a marriage of which her family disapproved. Certainly she had no illusions about her son-in-law or her daughter's future happiness, nor, certainly, about the advantages she herself could hope to gain from the marriage. The crowning insult came when the bride's father was not even invited to the wedding, and the Princess had been obliged to swallow this truly inconceivable affront.

Desperate but still hopeful, she had written lies upon lies to her husband, giving him to understand that he would be invited, that the invitation was on the point of being dispatched, that he would be invested with the order of Saint Andrew, and then, since this was impossible because he already possessed the order of the Black Eagle from the King of Prussia, that his son would receive the decoration in his stead, all promises which may have existed only in her imagination. After her quarrel with the wife, the Empress had refused point-blank to receive the husband, and in the end Christian Augustus was told that they dare not invite him out of consideration for public opinion in Russia, which was strongly against "German princes," although the Princes of Hesse, Holstein and others were living peaceably at the court at the time. Altogether, beneath the silver lace and the diamonds and the "little imperial crown" Catherine was nothing but a poor girl bought for the sole purpose of providing the son of the house with heirs.

The little bride was left alone with her fears in her bed of scarlet velvet with the embroidered pilasters. She claims that she waited there for more than two hours, wondering whether she should get up or stay in bed. Her husband was in no hurry

—he was probably as frightened as she was—and was waiting for his supper. He came to her at last. Of her wedding night Catherine says nothing except to quote one remark of Peter's: "It would amuse the servant to see us both in bed together."[6] No doubt he was thinking of his valet's coarse jokes, but in the rest of her narrative Catherine states explicitly that he had neither the intention nor the desire to fulfill his marital functions, and that he still regarded her as nothing more than a playmate. The innocent Catherine probably found this rather comforting than otherwise.

The marriage, although not consummated, was nonetheless followed by a series of festivities each more brilliant than the last. Splendid presents were given to the bride and there were balls, masquerades and entertainments. On August 30, the feast of Saint Alexander Nevsky, which fell two days after the wedding ceremony, Elizabeth went with her entire court to the monastery dedicated to this national hero, saint, prince and warrior. There, after salvos of cannon, a *Te Deum* and a "triple discharge" by the guns of the fleet, the Empress had the little boat which her father had once built with his own hands, the famous "grandfather of the Russian fleet," solemnly taken out of the museum where it was kept. On this occasion the humble wooden boat, half eaten away by time, was to be the hero of the feast in memory of the saint of the Neva and of Peter the Great. Elizabeth was intent upon reminding everyone that she wished to perpetuate the line of direct descent from Peter the Great and that her nephew's marriage was an event on a national scale.

As the cannon boomed out, the Empress herself, dressed in naval officer's uniform, stepped into the wooden boat and piously kissed the picture of her father which had been placed there. Then the vessel, which was no longer seaworthy, was taken on a triumphal barge to the fortress of Saints Peter and Paul, preceded by four galleys with drums beating and trumpets blowing. Elizabeth followed the reliquary barge, standing upright in her boat which carried the imperial standard, and the whole court

followed her down the Neva in boats and barges to the sound
of martial music. Petersburg, a maritime city with its many
canals always busy with gondolas, was an ideal place for processions on the water and this one was of an exceptional splendor
and solemnity, since it was at the same time something in the
nature of a pilgrimage. The cannons of the Admiralty and of
the fort fired salvos and the boats carrying the court replied with
trumpet blasts. Elizabeth conducted the humble worm-eaten boat
in triumph along the broad, splendidly decked river, past the
palaces of stone and brightly painted wood that stood all along
the low banks, and followed it respectfully, proclaiming herself
the heir and the first servant of the Great Builder.[7]

The young couple, however, were not enjoying themselves.
The endless quadrilles bored them the more because they had
to dance them with "crippled and decrepit old people" (at least
this was how they appeared to a fifteen-year-old girl), since
only high officials were permitted to take part. Moreover, Catherine discovered that her new principal lady in waiting, Madame
Kruse, was a real dragon who forbade her companions to speak
to her "in low voices" and kept everyone away from her. At
present her only real pleasure was in her talks with her mother,
and even her mother was on the point of leaving her. With the
Grand Duke, she says "it was all childishness";[8] he amused
himself playing soldiers, surrounded by his servants, while Catherine was no longer free to play games with her ladies, and her
laments prove that she too was still a child at heart.

Eighteen

❖❖❖❖❖❖❖❖❖❖❖❖❖❖❖

The Newlyweds

Sophia of Anhalt-Zerbst cannot have possessed a very amiable character or a very good heart: a naturally likable person does not continually talk about her efforts to make people like her, and someone endowed with real natural goodness remembers those about her for other reasons besides the troubles they have caused her. Now, Sophia was probably genuinely fond of her mother even though her mother really was frivolous and selfish, but throughout the entire first half of her memoirs she does nothing but complain about her and lay emphasis on her own gentleness, patience and filial devotion. Her mother's frequent fits of bad temper were a perpetual subject of irritation to Catherine, yet her mother had good reason to be bad-tempered, as the young girl herself admitted.

Princess Johanna Elizabeth was too young to be the mother of a grown-up daughter and too lively to be the wife of a stern, middle-aged husband. She had hoped, in coming to Russia, to find worthy employment for her intelligence and charm, and now she was leaving the Russian court after a stay of twenty months, mortified and humiliated, her illusions faded forever, and she could not even take with her the consolation of having established her daughter's happiness. Yet she was probably not altogether such a bad mother as Catherine, and her historians after her, generally make out.

But although Catherine, without blaming her mother, betrays scant pity for her, she does emphasize the fact that during the weeks preceding their separation, talking to her mother was her one pleasure. She was unhappy and, with the natural selfishness of a child, thought much more about her own sorrows than those of her mother. The wedding night, or rather the revelation of the physical obligations of marriage, had come as a somewhat brutal shock, since the Princess of Anhalt-Zerbst had waited until the very last moment before enlightening her daughter on her duties as a wife. The revelation may have come as too much of a shock, or possibly it was the thought of being bound for life to a man she did not love, or even the change in the conditions under which she lived, but Catherine was so unhappy that she clung to her mother like a sick child.

They spent as much time together as they could, exchanging confidences and recollections. Johanna Elizabeth was making ready to leave. The Empress had given her sixty thousand rubles to pay her debts, but when this amount had been spent, there were still debts amounting to seventy thousand rubles remaining. This was a further headache for Catherine, who promised her mother to take over the debts. The Princess of Anhalt-Zerbst left, "showered with gifts" after all, because in spite of every-thing Elizabeth was anxious to keep up appearances. Before she left, the Princess obtained an audience with the Empress and asked forgiveness on her knees for all the trouble she had caused her. Elizabeth unkindly declined to forgive, but she made it quite clear that things would have gone much better had the Princess adopted such an attitude of humility from the outset.

Catherine wept a great deal. In order to avoid the worst agony of parting, the Princess of Anhalt-Zerbst left the palace of Tsarskoie Selo very early in the morning, without saying goodbye to her daughter. They were never to see one another again; and Catherine appears to have recovered—or discovered —her mother only at the very moment when she was about to lose her. Elizabeth tried to alleviate the young woman's grief by granting her permission to "frequent the Empress's dressing room, that is to remain as long as [she] liked, at about twelve in the morning or five or six in the evening with her ladies in waiting."[1] It was a poor consolation; and the poorer in that more often than not Elizabeth remained invisible. It was, however, Catherine observes with resignation, "a kind of favor." Even that was not to continue for long.

Thus, at the age of fifteen and a half, Catherine found herself completely alone, without friends or support, without even the mother who had been such a trial to her but whom she loved in spite of everything, in a strange court, in a strange land, compelled to sleep every night in the bed of a boy whom there can be no doubt she was growing to dislike more and more.

She herself allows us a glimpse of her thoughts during those first few days of her marriage. "I told myself: if you love that man you will be the unhappiest creature on earth, since your character is such that you would demand your love returned. This man scarcely even looks at you; when he talks to you it is of practically nothing but dolls, and he pays more attention to any other woman than he does to you. You are too proud to complain, so proceed with caution, if you please, in the matter of kindness toward the gentleman: think of yourself, my lady."[2] This much is quite clear: the young bride was determined never to show any fondness toward her husband for fear of being hurt. A reasonable enough attitude, since Peter would no doubt have made her suffer horribly if she had loved him. His was one of those demanding and self-centered natures for whom love is, above all else, the need to dominate.

If, instead of a more or less calculated and self-interested friendship, she had felt a real affection for him, if she had thought of him first and herself afterward, then she might well have succeeded only in ruining herself with him. Even a mother's self-abnegation would not have been enough to melt this heart, forever arrested at the most infantile stage.

Catherine's main grievances against her husband appear somewhat contradictory: he "talks of nothing but dolls" and he "pays more attention to any other woman" than to herself; but what, in fact, were the attentions which Peter heaped on other women? Seven years after her marriage Catherine was still a virgin, and so was Peter. Catherine, extremely ignorant in these matters, was continually seeing betrayal in the passing infatuations of a boy who wanted to pass for a man in the eyes of the world. Both of them were so young that they went from one misunderstanding to another, from one sulky quarrel to the next. Catherine, nettled, pretended to be scornfully indifferent to the way her spouse would ogle this or that lady of the court, and Peter may well have taken this feigned indifference for the real thing and amused himself by affecting a cynicism which was not in his nature.

What does emerge very clearly, as much from Catherine's own evidence as from that of foreign diplomats residing at the Russian court, is that Elizabeth's attitude toward her nephew and niece had altered strangely since the Grand Duke's marriage and the departure of the Princess of Anhalt-Zerbst. It was as though, once the Grand Duke was married and the dynasty (so she believed) assured, the Empress began to regard the young couple as a tedious nuisance, rivals for power whom it would soon no longer be necessary to harbor and who must, above all else, be prevented from growing dangerous.

Catherine complains bitterly of the annoyances which she and Peter were compelled to endure during their first year of marriage: she had become attached to her first lady in waiting, Maria Zhukova, and the young woman was promptly dismissed from court. Her first chamberlain, Zahar Chernyshev, was removed and sent on a diplomatic mission to Ratisbon because it was feared that the young man was falling in love with the Grand Duchess. She admits that this persecution was not aimed at her alone and that all the members of the "young court" who had the misfortune to find favor either with herself or with the Grand Duke were liable to find themselves, on various pretexts, either disgraced or dismissed. It is true that the young couple, taking advantage of the privilege accorded them by protocol of maintaining their own court, were endeavoring to inject a certain amount of gaiety into it and to attract people who would amuse them. Elizabeth was afraid that the young court might become a center of unrest, but neither Catherine nor Peter nor their empty-headed young friends had any such idea in their minds.

Peter and Catherine each amused themselves in their own way. Catherine danced and chattered with her ladies and the young men of the court, not forgetting to make a display of religious zeal to please the Empress, which irritated the Grand Duke beyond measure. Peter organized rather childish games, including a puppet theater, a spectacle which Catherine says "was the most insipid thing in the world." But as usual he went too far. The Grand Duke conceived the idea of using the drill which he had obtained for the purpose of drilling holes in the floor of his theater, to pierce a number of peepholes in the forbidden door separating the room where the shows took place from the Empress's private dining room. In this way he was able to watch his aunt dining in company with a dozen of her intimate friends, including the master of the royal hunt, Razumovsky, who was wearing "a brocaded dressing gown." Peter found this idea so irresistibly funny that he invited all his friends to enjoy the show, and even summoned Catherine and her ladies. Catherine, terrified, refused to have anything to do with the game, and impressed on her husband how indiscreet he had been, but by that time he had let at least "twenty people" into the secret.

The consequences of this silly joke were not long in coming: Elizabeth burst in in a furious rage with her nephew, declaring that "henceforth she could only regard him as an ungrateful wretch; that her own father, Peter the First, had also had an ungrateful son whom he had punished by disinheriting him; that when the Empress Anna was alive, she [Elizabeth] had always shown her the respect due to a crowned head and one anointed of the Lord, and that she [Anna] would never have supported such pranks, and put any one who showed her lack of respect in the fortress." At last, putting the incident back in its proper perspective, she added that "he was nothing but a small boy and she would teach him how to behave." When Peter in turn lost his temper, his aunt "let fly at him with the most shocking insults and abuse, displaying as much contempt as anger."[3] Catherine, like a good little girl, watched the scene in horror, still on the verge of tears, and she adds, not without some satisfaction, that she herself was not scolded but, on the contrary, congratulated on having taken no part in what the Grand Duke had done.

When Elizabeth had gone, the young couple looked at one another, he shamefaced, she terrified. Peter said: "She was like a fury; she didn't know what she was saying." Catherine: "She was fearfully angry."[4] Whether or not they knew the manner of his death the ghost of the Tsarevich Alexei hovered over them, and the mention of the fortress forced the young people to think seriously about their position. At this stage Peter does not appear to have been greatly disturbed by his aunt's threats, but gradually, as he saw that people were beginning to avoid him, he himself became increasingly fearful and suspicious, and took refuge more than ever in his childish amusements.

As for Catherine, in spite of her sincere and praiseworthy desire to please the Empress, she drew the latter's anger upon herself for something which was not her fault. She shared a room with the Grand Duke and, nine months after the wedding, still showed no signs of pregnancy. In the end Elizabeth realized that the marriage had not even been consummated, and she blamed Catherine, reproaching her for not having succeeded in arousing the Grand Duke. "She said . . . that it was through my fault that my marriage had not yet been consummated," and Catherine adds naïvely that a woman cannot be the cause of this. Whatever recourse might be open to a woman in this position, Catherine, ignorant, shy and already determined in advance not to give way to any tenderness toward her husband, can clearly not have been a very inviting spouse. Moreover, Peter must have thought her unattractive: at least she claims that he often praised other women's beauty (sometimes in her presence) and compared her with them—to her disadvantage, naturally. Or was this merely an easy way of making her lose her temper?

Nineteen

Politics and Play

In subjecting the Grand Duchess to one frightful scene (Catherine thought she was on the point of assaulting her physically), Elizabeth was moved by other grievances than the latter's involuntary sterility. She accused her of no less a crime than spying for the benefit of the King of Prussia.

In February 1744, while the great train of sleighs was carrying them from Petersburg to Moscow, and before they had seen the Empress and her court, the princesses of Anhalt-Zerbst had had the opportunity to peruse a document addressed to them by Monsieur Scryver, the secretary of the legation in Berlin. This paper, Catherine says, was "really interesting" because it gave the princesses an idea as to who were the most important people at court and the degree of favor in which the various favorites were held. Needless to say, the secretary of the legation judged people and events entirely from the point of view of the interests of the King of Prussia, and he outlined a complete course of action for mother and daughter.

In this way Sophia had learned that the Russian court was divided into two parties: that of the chancellor Bestuzhev, who "was for the courts of Vienna and of Saxony, and for England," and that represented by the Marquis de la Chétardie, the court of Holstein and the Empress's intimate adviser Lestocq, which "stood for France, her protégé Sweden and the King of Prussia."[1] All these *foreigners*, Catherine observes (writing a great many years after these events when she had had time to change sides),

were putting forward as future chancellor Count Michael Vorontsov, one of the principal agents, together with Lestocq and
La Chétardie, of the conspiracy which had placed Elizabeth on
the throne. The object of this second party was the overthrow
of Bestuzhev. The hatred of Frederick II and La Chétardie for
the chancellor can clearly not have been motivated by their zeal
for Russia's interests, and the Princess of Anhalt-Zerbst, arriving in a land of which her daughter was one day to become the
ruler, therefore made herself, although she was completely unaware of the fact, the agent of a foreign power which Elizabeth
regarded as an enemy.

To begin with, as good Germans mother and daughter had
failed to realize the indelicacy of their behavior; they owed the
King of Prussia gratitude and respect, they felt obliged to further
his interests, and felt that Russia could hardly fail to gain from
an alliance with Prussia. The chancellor was presented to them
as an adversary, even as a personal enemy, an altogether detestable person who had cunningly succeeded in worming his
way into the confidence of the too susceptible Empress. The
letters of German diplomats contain open execration of the
chancellor; they state that Elizabeth is inviting universal contempt by allowing herself to be led by such a knave. Frederick
II declared that Bestuzhev was so venal "that he would sell the
Empress herself if he were offered a good enough price," a
reproach which the chancellor does not appear to have deserved,
as he was always crippled by debts and Frederick would have
been the first to have leaped at the chance of paying them.

Catherine could scarcely help sharing the prejudices of those
around her. For a long time Bestuzhev was her *bête noire*, the
prime cause of all her miseries, but being both too young and too
cautious, she had never become personally involved in any intrigues against the chancellor. Her mother, relying on La
Chétardie, who thought himself and was generally thought by
others to possess more credit than he actually had, had allowed
herself to be drawn into saying and doing things which did no
harm to Bestuzhev but a great deal to herself.

Once the Princess was out of the way, her daughter remained

as her Imperial Highness the wife of the heir apparent, and in theory the first personage in the Empire after the Empress herself and the Grand Duke. To begin with, Elizabeth was genuinely fond of her, but it can only have taken her a few months to realize that the girl was less candid than she pretended to be. It was only natural that she should suspect her of sharing her mother's views. These suspicions may have had some foundation: Johanna Elizabeth had in fact tried to draw her daughter into political intrigue, and Prince Adolphus Frederick of Holstein-Gottorp (elder brother of the Princess of Anhalt-Zerbst) had sent his niece a cipher for use in secret correspondence, in order that she might be able to get confidential information through to him—for the benefit, naturally enough, of the King of Prussia. Catherine, as much from prudence as from native honesty, refused to use the code. Her father's instructions, her own principles and her personal feelings all encouraged her to show scrupulous loyalty to Elizabeth. Moreover, she knew that Bestuzhev's department was adept at deciphering coded letters. But once the Empress's suspicions were aroused, she did not stop halfway: urged on no doubt by Bestuzhev, she openly accused her niece by marriage of "betraying her to the King of Prussia."

Catherine describes the scene for us, adding a melancholy comment to the effect that in the two years she had been in Russia this was *the first time* that the Empress had spoken to her in private and without witnesses. The aunt whom the Princess of Anhalt-Zerbst had described to her husband on the eve of the betrothal ceremony as "the best and most loving of mothers" rained the cruellest reproaches on the head of the young Grand Duchess, accusing her of conspiring with her mother, saying that her "shifts and schemes were well known and that she knew all." Moreover Elizabeth was a woman, and carried away by her fierce temper, she flung all her accusations pell-mell at Catherine, claiming that she reserved all her attentions for the Grand Duke's "valets" and that "she had not forced me to marry against my will, and that she knew very well I loved another; in fact, a thousand horrors of which I forget the half."[2]

The poor girl burst into horrified tears and backed toward the door. "I saw that she was upon the point of hitting me . . . I knew she beat her women, her servants and sometimes when she was angry, even her gentlemen in waiting." Elizabeth was a tall, heavily built woman with an impressive bearing and Catherine only a fragile girl of fifteen.

From that day onward the Empress, acting on her chancellor's advice, forced on the Grand Duchess a new entourage, all charged to keep her under strict supervision, and a set of new rules by which she was henceforth to regulate her conduct. These rules, dictated by Bestuzhev, were apparently aimed at consolidating the mutual affection of the married couple, but in fact they were intended to render them politically harmless.

The Grand Duchess was expressly given into the charge of a "noble lady" who was to take care "to watch constantly with all her power over the marital fidelity of their Imperial Highnesses." This lady, Maria Semenovna Choglokova, *née* Hendrikova, was Elizabeth's first cousin and a great favorite of hers. She and her husband were known to be devoted to Bestuzhev. On the other hand, the Grand Duke's "pedagogues" and tyrants, Brümmer and Bergholz, were sent back to Holstein on suspicion of harboring Prussian sympathies, a measure of which the young man himself would have been the last to complain, had not the two Germans before their departure painted a sad picture of the fate which was to be his once he was left at the mercy of Bestuzhev's creatures. As the head of his household—in other words, as watchdog—he was given Prince Basil Repnin, who was actually a very worthy man with high moral principles which he lived up to, but who was soon to lose his job.

As for Catherine, she was terrified to find herself placed under the tutelage of a new dragon, more powerful than the Mademoiselle Schenk or Madame Kruse of whom she had so often complained in the past.

The Grand Duchess's duties were presented to her in the following manner: "Her Imperial Highness has been selected for the high honor of being the noble wife of our dear nephew his

Imperial Highness the Grand Duke, heir to the Empire, and the said Grand Duchess [i.e. Catherine] has been elevated to her present dignity of Imperial Highness with none other but the following aims and objects: that her Imperial Highness might by her sensible behavior, her wit and virtue, inspire a sincere love in his Imperial Highness [the Grand Duke] and win his heart, and that by so doing may bring forth the heir so much desired for the Empire and a fresh sprig of our illustrious house."[3] In fact these recommendations were designed, first and foremost, to curb the young girl's pride. The other points in the famous "Instructions" were aimed at preventing Catherine from showing too much familiarity toward her courtiers, pages, and ladies and gentlemen in waiting, at preventing her from meddling in any way in "political affairs," and from writing to anyone at all, on any pretext, except through the intermediary of the Council for Foreign Affairs; even to her father and mother she was in future only to write letters transcribed from a model given her by the chancellery, without being permitted to add a single word to them. Peter, for his part, was subjected to the same strict supervision.

Catherine hated and feard Bestuzhev; years later she wrote of him: "He was infinitely more feared than loved, excessively given to intrigue, suspicious, firm and fearless in his principles, not a little tyrannical, an implacable enemy, but a friend to his friends, whom he only abandoned when they turned their backs on him. In addition, he was not easy to get on with and often overscrupulous." By the time she wrote these words, the chancellor was already dead, but long before his death he had ceased to be her enemy. In this verdict she does justice at the same time to an enemy and a friend. During the early years of her life in Russia Catherine suffered much from this man's persecution, not because he felt any personal enmity toward her, but because he saw her as a possible opponent of his policies. For in contrast to the majority of courtiers, to Peter, to Catherine, and to the other ministers, who were frequently ambitious or interested, Bestuzhev-Ryumin was a statesman and a man of political ideas.

His great idea, which he called "the system of Peter the Great" and which Elizabeth shared with him, was to preserve the alliance with the house of Austria and with England, in order to curb the power of Turkey, Russia's traditional enemy, and to check the expansion of Prussia and the Scandinavian countries, Russia's rivals in the north and west. Catherine had to pay homage to the chancellor's powerful personality: "Bestuzhev's enemies were numerous, but he made them all tremble. He was helped by his position and his character, which gave him an infinite advantage over the backstairs politics [politicians]."

Meanwhile, the chancellor was trying by all means to discredit the Grand Duchess and the Grand Duke, and his spies reported the young couple's slightest actions and behavior to him without fail. Peter was known to be frankly pro-Prussian and anti-Russian and anti-Orthodox, and knowing his character, Bestuzhev could scarcely help fearing the accession of such a sovereign to the throne. (He was not the only one to do so.) His hope was that the Grand Duke would have a child who, if he were brought up along the proper lines, could be designated heir instead of his father. As for the little German Grand Duchess, the chancellor was in no doubt that she, at the bottom of her heart, shared her mother's and her husband's views. He did not yet know her.

Catherine endeavored to avoid compromising herself in any way. But she was young and gay, loved company and was not yet interested in politics. Above all, she was furious to find that she was being prevented from enjoying herself. Her husband was so difficult to love, and her amusements so innocent! The Grand Duke, she said, had among his "servants" three young men—two brothers and a cousin—by the name of Chernyshev. They were charming and gay and the Grand Duke liked them a great deal. For once Catherine shared her husband's tastes: the young couple had become very friendly with these three young men. Andrei, the eldest of the Chernyshevs, was a particular favorite with Peter and Catherine, and with her he had fallen into an attitude of innocent flirtation.

One day, while the couple were still engaged, Andrei, who

may well have thought that Peter paid too little attention to the girl, had told him laughing: "She isn't my betrothed, you know, she's yours." Peter laughed a great deal at this, and ever afterward, they talked of Andrei Chernyshev familiarly among themselves as Catherine's "betrothed." After the marriage the Grand Duchess and the young officer felt that it was more proper to address one another as *matushka* (mother) and *synok* (my son). It was a half-amorous but extremely innocent friendship, but people at court began to gossip. One day Catherine's faithful servant, Timofei Evreinov, took the young woman aside and warned her of the risk she was running. "You talk of nothing and seem to be interested in nothing but Andrei Chernyshev." When the girl protested the innocence of her feelings the worthy man answered: "What you call kindness and affection, because the young man is faithful to you and serves you, others call love."[4]

The word was out and Catherine had sense enough not to take offense at the clear-sighted Evreinov's words. Frightened, she examined her feelings and began to fear that she was in fact in love. In order to avoid compromising the Grand Duchess young Andrei, on Evreinov's advice, pretended to be ill and asked for leave of absence from court. Peter was not let into the secret and worried for a long time over his friend's supposed illness.

Andrei Chernyshev returned after several months' voluntary exile, and an incident occurred at court at the memory of which Catherine seems more troubled and regretful than she would doubtless have been willing to admit. It happened during a concert: the Grand Duke was fond of the violin and often played the instrument himself. Catherine, who hated music in general and her husband's in particular, was deathly bored, and retired to her own room. This gave onto the great hall of the Summer Palace, which happened to be full of scaffolding at the time as the ceiling was being repainted. As luck would have it, there was no one in her room, something which did not often happen. She opened the door, and seeing Andrei Chernyshev at the far end of the hall full of workmen, beckoned him to her.

They did not say much. Andrei, who may have been in love or may simply have given way to the temptation of finding the

two of them alone together, asked Catherine to let him come into her room. She refused and confined herself to talking with him through the half-open door. Fortunately for her, she happened to look around and saw the chamberlain Devier standing behind her at the other end of the room. She had had a lucky escape, but the next day the three Chernyshevs were posted as lieutenants to a distant regiment, which all but amounted to being placed under arrest, and she lost track of them for a long time. From this moment on the Grand Duchess was placed under the supervision of Madame Choglokova. Elizabeth's accusations that Catherine "loved another" were therefore founded on very real rumors and possibly feelings. Catherine was not the only one to suffer from the disgrace of the Chernyshevs. Peter missed his friends as much as she did. To him also their removal appeared as an undeserved punishment.

The Grand Duke and Duchess were not to be allowed to make themselves the center of an independent court, composed of devoted friends and faithful partisans. Only spies were now tolerated among their entourage.

Twenty

❧❧❧❧❧❧❧❧❧❧❧❧

Russia

A year after her marriage it was still doubtful whether Catherine-Sophia of Anhalt-Zerbst, the Grand Duchess Catherine Alexeievna, lawful wife of the heir to the throne of Russia, could be

sure of ever reigning. She wanted to rule, and like the sensible and conscientious girl that she was, she strove to make herself worthy of it. Apparently too this sensible child had managed, in all innocence, to arrive at a simple, indeed a brilliant piece of intuition: namely, that to reign in Russia it was necessary to try and get to know Russia and to make the Russians like her.

In this apprenticeship she was lucky in having before her eyes a model which was the more valuable in that she had to copy it at all costs or risk losing all hope of becoming Empress. Elizabeth herself was ostentatiously Russian, she was Russian by temperament and conviction, fanatically Orthodox, a "progressive" Russian nourished on the ideas of Peter the Great, but able to reconcile her father's Western ideas with her people's national pride. But whereas Elizabeth was always a divinity, allowing herself to be worshipped from afar, Catherine's immediate entourage was composed either of subordinates or of people incapable of sharing her ideas. The Grand Duke hated everything Russian and at the risk of displeasing him, Catherine chose to please the Empress and, insofar as this was possible, the people.

Certainly Simeon Todorsky had influenced her a great deal at the time of her conversion, but the main sentiment this cosmopolitan priest seems to have inspired in her was profound indifference to the "external forms" of religion, and though she may not have realized it at the time, with regard to religion itself. Her Russian teacher, Adodurov, though obliging and sincerely devoted, was never more than a servant. Confident of her own judgment, the girl presumed to follow her own line of conduct without asking advice of anyone.

In her memoirs she remarks continually on her own progress in "the affections of the people," and ascribes all the credit to her efforts to appear obliging and friendly toward everyone. Her "public" extended, as yet, no wider than the court, but the girl put so much fervor into her religious observances and so much concentration into her studies of the Russian language that she was already beginning, through the court, to gain the sympathies

of the people of both capitals. At this time she honestly believed in the importance of the will of the people, and in the duties of a sovereign. She wanted to become Russian in order to be worthy to rule over Russia.

Obviously she still did not know the Russia whose history she had so early set herself to study. The court was little more than a kind of parasitic plant or artificial flower blooming on the body of the great Russian Empire, a real little state within a state: brilliant, self-centered, useless, and totally divorced from the deeper life of the land whose resources it exploited unscrupulously. The gap between the court and the rest of the country was greater in Russia than anywhere else.

In June 1741 (the year of Elizabeth's accession) the English ambassador, Finch, wrote: "The majority of the nobles are *hardened* Russians. . . . They are indifferent to Europe and hate foreigners."[1] He adds that the Russians would like to see Petersburg and all the lands won from Sweden vanish overnight, so that they could live at Moscow, near to their own lands. If this was the attitude of a large part of the nobility, it is not hard to imagine that of the rest of the people.

Those words were written only sixteen years after Peter the Great's death. When Catherine became Grand Duchess of Russia, Peter the Great would, if he had lived, have been a little over seventy, and many of his friends and former opponents were still alive. The "Muscovite" past, which was already becoming a legend, was still very close: fundamentally the country had not changed.

The life of the common people was exactly the same as it had been in the time of the Muscovite tsars, with the difference that Peter the Great had created a new tax, which was imposed on the entire population and considerably restricted the already limited freedom of the small landowner. Peter's successors, who possessed neither his disinterestedness nor his flair for organization, were incapable of turning the extra resources provided by the new taxes to anything more useful than indulging in a spate of unbridled luxury and filling the pockets of their ministers

and favorites. The common people were wretchedly poor and no one thought of doing anything to help them. Catherine still knew nothing of these people, though they were to make their presence felt in a brutal enough fashion during her reign: for her they existed only on paper. Much later she was still able to write shamelessly, and perhaps in all sincerity, that in Russia "every peasant has his turkey in the pot" every Sunday, and that though men died of overeating they never died of hunger.

The peasants represented ninety-five percent of the population and the life force of the nation, which was mainly agricultural. Russia was rich: rich in grain, in cattle, in leather, furs, and wood for building. Russia's wealth of basic materials seemed inexhaustible, and for centuries she had a flourishing export trade. The primary resources of the country, still more or less untapped, were considerable. Lastly, unpaid slave labor constituted an inestimable source of wealth, one almost impossible to assess and a veritable gold mine for the classes which exploited it. But the greatest confusion reigned in the administration and in the country's finances and communications. The general standard of living was low, and the exploitation of natural resources insufficient and rudimentary. Society was divided into classes between which barriers were raised which it was, for all practical purposes, impossible to overstep. There was a rich and powerful clergy which had almost nothing to do with the life of the people beyond exploiting them; a middle class of merchants and craftsmen who clung to their old habits and distrusted Western "novelties"; and lastly a nobility, more privileged than the other classes because it held in its possession most of the power and land, but still liable to compulsory military and civil service. When later on Catherine spoke of the people or of her "subjects," it would always be the nobility she had in mind as the only subjects who really counted.

She realized very quickly that a gulf would always separate her from the *people*, properly speaking: Russia was not like Zerbst or Stettin, where she had been able to play in the streets with the neighbors' daughters and where the young prince was not so very different from the wealthier citizen, nor the rich citizen from the artisan. The people here appeared to be a completely abstract concept. Crowds would sometimes gather along the route to watch her carriage pass by, but they were a motley and often wretched collection with no identity of their own. Catherine knew that these people were poor and oppressed and she promised herself that one day she would do something to improve their condition, for a tsarina was surely all-powerful, but she soon realized that the will of these people counted for nothing. There was one other element, closer and easier to observe, whose support, as Elizabeth had proved, was something to be preserved. This was the army, and in particular the regiments of the imperial guard on permanent duty at the court. Under Elizabeth the army had been freed from the control of Germans; it was rabidly nationalist and the Grand Duke was already widely known to be unpopular in military circles. Catherine did not possess the means to keep in close touch with the regiments of the guard; all she could do was to seize every possible opportunity to display her attachment to the Russian language and court.

She very quickly obtained such a reputation for being Russian and Orthodox that the Russian people began to realize it, and this attracted sympathies which she needed the more in that her husband delighted in shocking and outraging public opinion. Neither she nor anyone else could be in any doubt that Peter hated Russia and the Russians, since what force of character he possessed was entirely negative, a strength of protest, blind, stubborn and total. But did Catherine really love Russia? Had she, at least, some reason to love it?

Everything suggests that this country with which, from a distance, she had believed herself in love had cruelly disappointed her. She had realized very quickly that all the brilliance and ostentatious wealth of Elizabeth's court was nothing but a sham. In this country people seemed to be cheating all the time: sumptuous clothes and dirty linen, magnificent audience chambers covered in gilding, velvet and precious inlays, and living rooms which were all too often totally devoid of furniture. The courtiers displayed an insolent luxury in their clothes, their carriages and the livery of their servants. "The Empress herself," writes Catherine, "loved fine clothes excessively . . . and everyone modeled themselves upon her example. The days were taken up with gaming and dressing. As for myself, I made it my principle to please the world in which I had to live, I adopted their way of life . . . I wanted to be Russian so that the Russians would love me."

The houses were poor: in Moscow nearly all of them, even the palaces, were made of wood painted and carved to suggest the appearance of stone. In Petersburg, only in the main streets and along some of the quays were there any stone buildings; all the rest was merely "wooden baroque, and more disagreeable than it is possible to describe." Inside, the houses were whitewashed or papered with poor wallpaper, and because they were mostly built in haste, they were exceedingly uncomfortable: doors did not shut, stairs wobbled and threatened to collapse, walls oozed with damp. On the occasion of the wedding of Leon Naryshkin, the Grand Duchess, conducting the bride to the nuptial chamber, had to traverse "cold passages and unheated staircases, and pass through a still unfinished gallery (for they were always building and rebuilding endlessly) built of wet timber from which the water dripped continuously on all sides." But worst of all was the heating system: great antiquated stoves, mostly in need of repair, with cracked tiles that meant that rooms were always full of acrid smoke which made the air almost unbreathable, and even that was not all. These stoves were a constant fire hazard, and since the houses were made of wood, fires raged through them from top to bottom. Elizabeth's palace in Moscow, a vast building containing hundreds of rooms, was completely destroyed in a matter of a few hours.

Moscow was the city for fires: in winter the houses burned as a result of accidents with the heating apparatus; in summer, because of the heat and the dryness. The smallest spark in a bale of straw could destroy a complete district. "From my windows," Catherine writes, "I often saw two, three, four or even five fires at the same time in different parts of Moscow." The inhabitants, used to this periodic scourge, took it as a matter of course and spent their lives moving house and rebuilding. The Empress herself set the example, and for two months she, with her nephew and niece and her entire court, lodged, or rather camped, in improvised and uncomfortable dwellings.

Furniture was a luxury, as it had been in the West during the Middle Ages, and each time the court changed its place of residence, which was often, as Elizabeth was always traveling between Petersburg and Moscow, all the household movables had to be carried along with the baggage. After the great fire, when the young imperial couple moved into the Choglokov household, they noticed that the house (although its owners were high in favor at court) contained no furniture at all. Elizabeth, who spent fortunes on her clothes, had so little furniture that after the birth of Catherine's first child she was compelled to have the furniture from her own personal apartments taken into the Grand Duchess's room, and the reception was no sooner over and the guests departed than the furniture was whisked away again, leaving the young wife in an empty room.

Necessaries were lacking but luxuries abounded. To wash in, Elizabeth had a solid gold basin studded with precious stones. There were numerous mirrors, set in molded silver frames and decorated with massive gilding. Audience chambers contained mirrors covering entire walls, which, considering the size of the rooms and the height of the ceilings, was an unnecessary extravagance. (Ever since the time of Peter the Great the imperial palaces had been adorned with a plethora of mirrors and looking glasses, for it should be remembered that a mirror was an object of superstitious fear in ancient Russia, something to be hidden in a corner, always covered with a cloth and always very small, only to be looked in alone, safe from all evil eyes. For Peter and his followers the freedom to look at their own reflections was something of a remarkable discovery, and they thought of it as a sign of progress. Even in Elizabeth's time the mother of her favorite Alexei Razumovsky, who was a woman of the people, thought she would die of fright when she saw the rooms with their walls of mirrors.)

It is true that even in the West there still existed a certain disparity between the luxury displayed for show and the relative poverty of daily life. Even the Versailles of Louis XV, to say nothing of that of Louis XIV, would shock us today by its discomfort and lack of hygiene. Moreover the Russians, "westernized" though they were, did insist on taking frequent baths, a custom which had fallen into disuse in the West and was not revived until the nineteenth century. We even find the Grand Duke Peter demonstrating his hostility for all things Russian by refusing to take a bath. Nonetheless Catherine, who came from a provincial German town which could certainly not have rivaled Versailles or London or Vienna, was profoundly shocked by the poverty and discomfort which reigned in Russia even in the imperial palaces. This poverty was clearly not the result of impoverishment, since the display of external wealth was, on the contrary, excessive, but lack of organization and, more than anything else, of a real absence of civilization. It was as though the Russians, in their wish to become "civilized" in the Western manner, had borrowed only the most superficial appearances from the West, a brilliant façade behind which lay nothing but emptiness.

Catherine, a serious and educated girl for her time, found no one to whom she could talk. Her mind, eager for intellectual nourishment, was starving. When she wanted to read she found that there were not even any books, that no one could lend her any, and that she could not buy them. However much she loved fine clothes, dancing and childish games, she also sought more serious occupations; but she could find nothing but faro and gossip. She lost a good deal of money at cards; she listened to the gossip because it gave her an insight into the workings of court intrigue; she prayed—because she had to—but none of this prevented her from growing profoundly bored, and considering that she had fallen into exceedingly "barbarous" surroundings.

Barbarous, and moreover hostile: had not her mother endured

the worst humiliation; was not she herself ceaselessly under suspicion, reprimanded, surrounded by spies, at the mercy of a capricious and distrustful empress? No, she too had little cause to love Russia or the Russians, apart from one or two amiable ladies in waiting, a few pleasant young chamberlains, who were disgraced as soon as she showed any liking for them. This cold, uncomfortable and inhospitable country could hardly please her, but for the fact that she had taken it into her head that one day she would rule over it and that she must therefore get used to it at all costs. Moreover, she had no intention of going back to Zerbst to become the object of her family's humiliating pity. (Time and again she says that she was too proud to bear being pitied.)

Two years after her marriage and her mother's departure came a terrible blow: her father, who had not been allowed to come to her wedding and whom she had not seen since she left home, died suddenly at Zerbst at the age of fifty-six. For a long time she had received only unsealed letters (she could not even be sure that she did receive all those he sent her), and it was long since she had been free to slip a single word of affection or personal feeling into the rare official communications which she was compelled to copy out from a model already written for her. She was cut off from her family completely. Now her father had died, perhaps believing her to have become a stranger forever, without one word of tenderness between them.

Catherine mourned him deeply. She shut herself up in her apartment and wept for a week. Her dragon, Madame Choglokova, gave her to understand that she would not be allowed to mourn for more than a week "since her father was not a king." "I answered that this was true and he was not a king but that he was my father, and she replied that it was not fitting for a grand duchess to weep for a longer time for a father who was not a king."[2]

Christian Augustus of Anhalt-Zerbst, although not granted the honor of himself leading his favorite child to the altar, had at least insisted on sparing what he could from his meager resources to provide her on her wedding day with a chest full of splendid dresses made of the fine brocade for which the town of Zerbst was famous—gowns less rich than those Elizabeth was able to give her, but they were the best the Prince could do. Before he died he must have had ample time to indulge in belated regrets and remorse, for his daughter's future seemed to be painted in gloomy enough colors, and at all events, the present was sad.

Although Catherine was extremely cautious and avoided the temptation, she did sometimes manage to smuggle messages through trusty friends and some time later she succeeded in sending a clandestine letter to her mother. In this letter she asks the Princess of Zerbst to send her brother the young prince to her, for she missed her family terribly. "Allow the boy to make the journey," she wrote. "You cannot believe how much good it will do him to be here. You will say that *the taste has changed*, and you will find this advice strange, but believe me, it is right."[3] It is clear from this that in those first years, Catherine found Russia very little to her taste. She needed all her determination and powers of deception to be able to conceal her boredom, contempt, perpetual irritation and depression.

Twenty-one

∗∗∗∗∗∗∗∗∗∗∗∗∗∗∗

The Court

"By the day following our arrival [at Reval, during one of the Empress's journeys] everyone had begun gaming: the Empress's favorites, including Count Razumovsky and Countess Shuvalova, were excessively fond of it, and moreover, it was a necessity at a court where there was no conversation, where everyone cordially hated one another, where slander took the place of wit, and where the slightest word might be taken for high treason. Dull maneuvers passed for cleverness, and it was pointless to discuss art or science since everyone was ignorant of them, and one could wager that at least half the company was unable to read, and I am not sure that a quarter of them could write."

How Babet Cardel's pupil must have felt out of place among all these so-called fine ladies and gentlemen! She, who had taken such pains to acquire merit, must have felt like a pearl cast before swine, and these years of her youth were for her a time of contemptuous misery.

Everything went wrong: when traveling, their lodgings were wretched—Catherine was compelled to dress herself "next to the stove where they had just baked the bread," and when Elizabeth compelled her court to camp out in tents, she had to wade through puddles. There were no fixed hours for meals. On one ceremonial occasion for which everyone was "exceedingly dressed up" this splendor went for nothing because the draft had blown out all the torches. When at last they were able to stop in an imperial palace, a house built by Peter the Great, the rooms were so small that they could not live in them and still had to put up tents. Balls were "deathly boring," and the company of the Grand Duke, who would never be parted from his menservants, was hardly more entertaining. Madame Choglokova had nothing agreeable to say and was continually observing that "the Empress would not approve of such remarks" or "her Majesty would not like that." When they went to watch a naval parade they saw nothing but cannon smoke, and they had scarcely sat down to an alfresco dinner before it began to rain in torrents. When they went to Rogerwick, on the Baltic Sea, the place was intolerable because of the pebbles, and as they had to camp there for several days Catherine developed an ailment in her feet that took four months to disappear. The Grand Duke organized parties in his house at Oranienbaum, at one of which everyone, courtiers and servants alike, was compelled to join in military exercises and "the ball was very poor and very badly organized, while the men were irritable and bad-tempered from all the incessant military exercises." Catherine began to feel "a great deal of melancholy" and "tendencies toward hypochondria that often reduced me to tears."[1]

Speaking of this period of her life she says: "The life I led for eighteen years would have been enough to make any ten other people in my place go mad and twenty more die of misery." She grew thinner. It was feared that she was growing consumptive, but for all her apparent fragility she had an iron constitution. She looked for and found remedies for her unhappiness. For many years these remedies were the solitary pleasures of horseback riding, hunting, fishing and reading. Later on came the joys and, to an even greater extent, the sorrows of love, but the object of her love was never her husband.

She despised the society in which she lived, but she was not utterly fixed and blind in her prejudices: quite the reverse, in fact. She was gifted with a great capacity for sympathy and took a lively interest in the people around her. She was able to praise Prince Repnin, who was the Grand Duke's governor for a time, unreservedly for being "not merely a man of honor and probity but also a man of wit, and very gallant, full of candor and loyalty."[2] She became greatly attached to the excellent Madame Vladislavova, who was given to her as her first lady in waiting, although this lady was dedicated to the interests of Bestuzhev; she was to have a devoted friend in the person of Leon Naryshkin, gentleman of the bedchamber at the Grand Duke's court, an enterprising young man who was extremely witty and amusing; and she was also to display a sincere attachment to those of her servants who served her faithfully. She knew how to make people love her and many paid the price in disgrace and exile for their devotion to the Grand Duchess's person.

But the court, the unbelievably boring court where everyone hated everyone else and had no intelligent conversation, the brutish, stupid court, Catherine despised and detested as she was coming, more and more, to detest the Empress herself.

Elizabeth, so ill-educated that she did not even know that England was divided from the Continent by the Channel, was yet able to pass for a cultivated woman among the high society of Moscow and St. Petersburg. It is time to look and see who in fact were the nobles, the innumerable "counts" who made up the court. Count Razumovsky was a simple peasant from the Ukraine whose only asset was a fine voice and a good figure (Catherine says: "He was one of the handsomest men I ever saw in my life"). He was one of the most notable personalities at the court, holding the honorable office of master of the royal hunt and never interfering in politics. A good man and a model of discretion, he was nonetheless an "upstart peasant" for all that. The brothers and sisters of Catherine I who had come to Russia after the death of Peter the Great were peasants too, of such humble origin that they did not even possess a family name, only Christian names. When they were elevated to the rank of counts and countesses, names had to be specially made up for the occasion: Skavronsky, Hendrikov and Efimovsky. Catherine compains bitterly of their vulgarity and ignorance. Her duenna, Madame Choglokova, had been born a Hendrikov. The Empress Anna Ivanovna had given her groom, Biron, the title of Duke of Kurland, and although he himself was in exile, members of his family were still allowed at court, and they were anything but a distinguished family.

Counts Ostermann, Shuvalov, Bestuzhev, Lopukhin, Rumiantsev—their names were endless. Peter the Great, having suppressed the very words *boyar* and *boyarina*, had been forced to find some other title to bestow on his favorites and high officials, and "count" was in fact the German *Graf*. Peter had bestowed it recklessly, and his successors imitated him on a grand scale. Nationals of foreign countries were made counts or barons indiscriminately: there were merchants and technicians like Count Tolstoy, otherwise a German merchant named Dick, the ancestor of the great writer; Count Ostermann, the Tsar's secretary and man of affairs; Baron Shafirov, a converted Dutch Jew who became head of the department of German affairs; Count Lestocq, a doctor and the son of a Huguenot refugee from Hanover; and many others, including Russians of low birth and others who belonged to authentically noble families like the Lopukhins and the Chernyshevs. The title of prince (*kniaz*) was really Russian and was reserved for a few very ancient families. (The Romanovs, for instance, were never princes and were looked down on by the real nobility.) The majority of these families were still powerful: the Trubetskois, the Sheremetevs, the Repnins, the Volkonskys, the Obolenskys, the Dolgorukys, the Golitsins. Although the title of prince did not have quite the same value in Russia as in the West, owing to the fact that all members of the family had the right to use it, it was rare and did to some extent provide a guarantee of ancient nobility. Even Peter the Great would have felt some scruples in giving it away freely, although he did bestow it on his friend Menshikov, the least aristocratic of all his favorites. Menshikov became a prince and so, later, did two of Catherine's favorites.

At all events this nobility, part authentic but uprooted, and part improvised, must have seemed to those of ancient blood like Catherine, Peter and their German relatives to be curiously coarse and superficial. Perhaps they did not always take due account of the difference between a "Count Razumovsky" and a "Prince Golitsin." The difference, a very real one in the eyes of the Russians, might sometimes escape a foreigner's notice. The court nobility, whether it liked it or not, was dependent on the Empress. Noble princes like Sheremetev and Trubetskoi were compelled to give precedence on ceremonial occasions to a peasant like Razumovsky, while the more opportunist flattered and imitated him. Moreover, although Alexei Razumovsky lacked education, he did possess a natural nobility: a man who held for so long the invidious position of imperial favorite must have been able to disarm slander and calumny. Elizabeth's worst enemies never accused Alexei of anything worse than limited intelligence, while at the same time paying due homage to his "virtuous and honest character."[3] But the second great favorite, Ivan Shuvalov, in other respects a fine and reasonably cultivated young man, brought his uncles, both coarse and ambitious men, to power at court.

The court had long been dominated by men who lacked culture

or traditions and were rewarded with vast fortunes by careless sovereigns, and seemed at its most Russian in its passion for the most unbridled prodigality. The courtiers would throw their money out of the windows, and in the end Elizabeth herself imposed some reductions on them, not out of any spirit of economy but simply because the ladies of the court were appearing in such splendid clothes and sumptuous carriages that she was afraid they would outshine her. The great lords might not possess any furniture and might live in hovels, but they would give banquets on feast days for hundreds of people, with silver dishes on the table and forty, fifty and even eighty successive courses.

They indulged in the most extravagant whims: one day the brother of the favorite Razumovsky had the idea that his guests would enjoy listening to the song of the nightingale in the woods on his estate, and since the river was in flood and the wood out of reach, he had his peasants build a dike and a dam all in the space of a few hours so that in the evening the ladies and gentlemen were able to cross the river dry-shod to be entertained by the delights of the nightingales' song in the moonlight. The desire to dazzle was so strong and the imagination so capricious that it was not unusual for great lords (like magicians served by a free and unlimited supply of labor) to amuse themselves by transforming a field into a lake or a mountain overnight, or building a triumphal arch or a pleasure pavilion right in the middle of a forest. The story of the famous House of Ice, although it actually occurred during the reign of Anna Ivanovna, is typically Russian: to amuse the Empress her courtiers decided, in the middle of winter, to build a palace at Petersburg made entirely of ice. Walls, roof, doors, windows, pillars and balconies were all carved out of ice and then sprayed with water to give the whole edifice a fine gloss. Furniture, dishes, kitchen utensils, were all made of ice, and nothing was missing, except of course heating and the people to live in it. Then, with great pomp, two servants, both clowns, were solemnly married and the couple installed in their new home with the Empress's blessing. They were found in the morning frozen to death, but this was merely an unimportant detail: the diversion had been unique of its kind, and the pillars, sculptures and furniture carved out of ice had glittered magnificently in the winter sunshine.

Elizabeth built no houses of ice, but she bent the court to her whims with a truly feminine capriciousness, continually traveling between the two capitals when each journey involved fantastic expense and was an ordeal for everyone. She camped where she pleased (and everyone else was obliged to do the same) and arranged the hours of day and night to suit herself: dining in the morning, sleeping all day or not at all, eating meals in the middle of the night. At court one lost all sense of time. Sometimes the Empress would be seized by a sudden desire for order and then she would send to tell her nephew that he was wrong to stay up late with his friends, and to tell her niece that she was taking too long to do her hair and was liable to be late for Mass.

She had an immoderate fondness for dancing, so the court danced all the time. She loved masquerades, and so they went about in disguise. Every Tuesday she held a ball at which the gentlemen had to dress like ladies and the ladies like gentlemen. Catherine records: "There could be nothing more hideous, and at the same time more entertaining, than the figures cut by the men got up like this, and nothing more wretched than the women dressed as men. The only person these garments suited to perfection was the Empress herself, and she was very beautiful in them. For the most part at these masquerades the men were in a vile humor and the women went in constant peril of being knocked over by the monstrous giants who managed their vast panniers so clumsily that they were always bumping into you."[4] She tells how she herself and Countess Hendrikova were embarrassed in this way: the two women were caught up in the skirts of the tall, imposing Monsieur Sievers, and they both fell down under the weight of his hoops and were unable to get up. Catherine was fifteen at the time and she thought it was all very funny, but although this kind of horseplay might have been all very well for a girl of fifteen, it is easy to imagine how infuriating it must have been to grave councilors and court officials and even to young gallants when they were compelled to make themselves ridiculous in this way. (One Prince Repnin in the time of Ivan the Terrible had preferred death to the "dishonor" of taking part in a masquerade, but Peter the Great had succeeded in reducing to nothing both the noble pride and the simple vanity of his courtiers. The nobility of the court were not only, for the most part, ignorant and madly conceited. Like any society which has lost its ancient traditions and has not yet found new ones, they were completely without principles and profoundly amoral.)

When Catherine saw her for the first time, Elizabeth was thirty-four; she was still very lovely, but already much too fat. She ate and drank vastly, was given to staying in bed for days on end, would occasionally bestow her favors on any agreeable young man at the court right under the nose of the too easy-going Razumovsky, and altogether led the most irregular kind of life. As a result her celebrated beauty was beginning to desert her. At all events, she began to persecute the ladies of her court in a curious fashion. One day in the winter of 1747, she took it into her head to command all these ladies to shave their heads, and sent them "ill-combed black perukes, which they were to wear until their hair grew again." The women and girls wept bitterly, but they obeyed. The ladies of the town, less harshly treated than those of the court, did not have to shave but they too were forbidden to show themselves in public without these black wigs, and the wigs, put on over their own hair, made them look ridiculous enough. The reason for this capillary revolution was that the Empress, unable to get the powder out of her hair, had decided to dye it black over the powder, but the dye had not taken very well. She had been obliged to shave her head, and she did not wish to be the only one with a shaven head.

Fortunately for the Grand Duchess, she was spared: Elizabeth took pity on her pretty hair, which was only just growing again after a serious illness. Apparently the Empress was not jealous of the skinny, unattractive girl, although a year later she did forbid her to appear in a particular white dress with gold trimmings, making the excuse that it was too similar to that of the order of Alexander Nevsky, but in fact because it was too pretty. Once the Empress publicly cut off a knot of ribbons which the lovely Madame Naryshkina, who was a great deal too elegant and dignified, was wearing on her head; and on another occasion two ladies in waiting, who were also imprudent enough to look too pretty, had half their hair shaved off close to their heads. "These young ladies," says Catherine, "claimed that her Majesty had torn off some skin with their hair."[5]

Had Elizabeth limited her despotism to the realm of gowns and coiffures, Catherine would not have complained too much, but unfortunately Catherine found herself virtually a prisoner in this court which she already regarded as insipid, exhausting and vulgar; and worse still, she was a prisoner who enjoyed an apparent freedom which was strewn at every step with pitfalls.

Twenty-two

Troubles for the Grand Duke and Duchess

In retrospect it is tempting to see people and things in the light of events which occurred after the period described. Once the Grand Duke had been eliminated from her life forever, Catherine rarely gives a hint of what their relationship must have been in the first years of their married life. But by reading attentively, we can see that there was a good deal of friendship, or at least solidarity, between them, and very often Catherine, who is Peter's principal accuser and the chief prosecution witness against him, evinces for her husband a pity which history was later to refuse him.

Self-centered as she was, she naturally dwells much more on her own troubles, but she makes it clear that the Grand Duke's were no less. She lays the responsibility for the young man's moral degradation squarely on the Empress: he was weak, and yet he was systematically deprived of every friend to whom he showed any fondness—and not all of them were unworthy of his friendship—and reduced to the company of vulgar and uneducated servants.

Following the removal of the Chernyshevs, who were so effectively hidden that only a lucky chance followed by a piece of real detective work on the part of Evreinov was able to trace their retreat, it was learned that "three or four pages of whom the Grand Duke was very fond had been arrested and taken to a dungeon. . . . As soon as it became noticed that he had a fondness for any one more than any other, they were removed."[1] The Grand Duke's uncle, the Prince-Bishop of Lübeck, was also sent away, as were all the gentlemen from Holstein in his suite, beginning with Brümmer and Bergholz, whose loss was not greatly felt, and all his servants, among them his major-domo, Kramer, "a gentle, steady man who had been attached to the Grand Duke from birth and was a sensible person able to give him much good advice. His removal made the Grand Duke weep very sincerely." The Grand Duke liked his valet, the rough old Swede Romberg, so Romberg too went to the fortress.

For lack of friends of his own age—since all to whom he became attached were sent away—the homesick boy took refuge more and more in the company of his father's old servants and found even this poor comfort denied him. If Elizabeth thought that in this way she could keep him from intriguing with Prussia and make him less German, she achieved the completely opposite result: nothing and no one could influence Peter Ulrich—constraint less than anything.

As for Catherine, she fought and struggled and strove to

appear meek and hide her real feelings, but in vain: she speaks bitterly of the little Kalmuk girl who did her hair so well, of her dear Maria Zhukova, her Finnish maid and even the faithful Evreinov, who were all taken away from her because she had shown some fondness for them. Elizabeth distrusted all friends of her nephew and niece, for even the humblest servants could be used as messengers, listen at doors and give warnings, and might be dangerous in case of a conspiracy. She was fearful and suspicious, so much so that she used to make her chamberlain, a man named Chulkov, who had been elevated to the position because of his strange power of doing without sleep, lie outside her door every night. She was not afraid of the Grand Duke himself so much as of those who might try and use him for their own ends.

She had another reason, too, for wishing to isolate the young couple as much as possible: she thought that if the young people were reduced to each other's company they would end by falling in love and producing an heir. It was a somewhat simple-minded but not altogether ridiculous calculation. Catherine herself admits: "In his distress, the prince, who was parted in this way from everything for which he so much as began to form an attachment, being unable to open his heart to anyone, turned to me." Their intimacy, which the marriage (a marriage still unconsummated) had destroyed instead of strengthening, was in this way knitted together by force of circumstances. But if Peter was turning once again to Catherine as the only friend he could trust, Catherine found this renewal of friendship hard to bear.

Her husband bored her; she felt nothing but pity for him. They had few tastes in common except for the company of other young people, and this was a pleasure practically denied them. Peter was what would be called today morbidly introspective, incapable of getting outside himself and taking an interest in the ideas of others. He would stride up and down his wife's room talking to himself for hours on end, absorbed in "minute" details of military procedure, lost in a world where Catherine could not follow him. If she tried to talk to him about her own interests he appeared totally indifferent. She liked to read, she says, and he read too, but his reading was "stories about highway robbers or romances." What romances, Catherine does not say, but they are unlikely to have been serious novels. These days, Peter would have been an avid reader of comics.

"Yet there were times when he would listen to me," she says, "but it was always when he was unhappy."[2] This was often enough, because he was exceedingly timid and constantly afraid of some plot or intrigue which might mean that he would end his days "in the fortress." Endowed with a lively though limited imagination, he must have brooded over this gloomy prospect incessantly. He had some perspicacity, says Catherine, but little judgment; he was incapable of disguising his thoughts and feelings, and he lived in fear of betraying himself and of making new enemies. Rapidly losing his way among the complicated values of the court, he no longer knew whom to try to please, or against whom to plot (and he was the last man in the world to be capable of intrigue). He came to value his wife's good sense more and more, and she did her best to reassure him.

Meanwhile, he tried to amuse himself as best he could. He was eighteen and the marriage had still not been consummated. The reason for this, according to foreign diplomats, and Castéra in particular, who were less discreet than Catherine, was a physical defect that any rabbi or a surgeon could easily have put right, but the Grand Duke could not bring himself to face the operation. Peter's character was still quite infantile; his pastimes at all events were indubitably so. He had a passion for toy soldiers and "other children's toys," probably miniature cannon, model forts and so on, since Catherine says that some of his toys were very heavy. He used to hide himself to play with them, and the only people in his confidence were Catherine, naturally, and her first lady in waiting, Madame Kruse. Madame Kruse even went to the lengths of secretly procuring toys for the Grand Duke.

He used to play with them in the evenings in the connubial bedchamber, spreading the whole collection out on the bed, talking endlessly as he invented battles or dramatic engagements in which his wooden soldiers were the heroes. Catherine would listen to him, sometimes amused, but more often irritated because these games, in which she could not take part, prevented her from sleeping or reading in peace. The young couple had to hide like children from Madame Choglokova, who on one occasion actually came and knocked on their door at midnight. Catherine and Madame Kruse hurriedly bundled all the toys under the bedclothes.

The young couple were kept under increasingly strict supervision: in the early autumn of 1747 the Empress informed them that in future no one would be allowed to enter their apartments or speak to them without the express permission of Monsieur and Madame Choglokov; the "ladies and gentlemen" of the young court were no longer permitted to cross the threshold of the grand ducal chamber and no one, not even their servants, was allowed to speak to them except in a loud voice so that all might hear. "The Grand Duke and I . . . both grumbled and told each other what we thought of this kind of imprisonment which neither of us had deserved."[3] But not even this could drive the Grand Duke to find solace for this unfair treatment in the arms of his wife. He found a new enthusiasm and a less harmless one than the childish games just described. Now he began to train hunting dogs.

He used to keep them hidden in an alcove off Catherine's apartment and she found their barking and their smell exceedingly disagreeable. Moreover, Peter was a very bad trainer and appears only to have liked his dogs because they provided an outlet for his helpless grudge against the world. He beat them cruelly. Sometime later, Catherine witnessed one very painful scene: "I saw him holding one of his dogs up in the air by its collar while one of his boys, a Kalmuk by birth, held it up by the tail. It was a poor little English King Charles and the Grand Duke was beating the dog with all his strength with the butt end of a whip. I tried to intervene on behalf of the wretched animal, but that only made him redouble his blows and I retired to my chamber in tears, unable to bear a scene which struck me as cruel in the extreme. In general tears and screams, far from inspiring

pity in the Grand Duke, only made him angry: pity was a sentiment which his nature found painful, even intolerable."

Is this passage alone enough to prove that Peter was a sadist?
He had no occasion, nor perhaps desire, to inflict such treatment
on his fellow men, but behavior of this kind certainly indicates
that his character was mean and above all desperately weak. The
words "pity was a sentiment which his nature found painful"
show that Peter was not by nature cruel or insensitive, merely
embittered. As the hare in the fable enjoyed frightening the frogs,
so Peter's frenzied make-believe cruelty was his revenge, his way
of making himself feel strong.

He had however another passion, more endearing perhaps, but
still unfortunate: he loved music. No one, it seems, had bothered
to teach him properly and his wife says that "he did not know a
note. . . . He had a good ear and the beauty of his music consisted entirely in the violence of the sounds he drew from his
instrument." He played the violin, then, to some extent by ear
and played rather badly. If this is the case, and supposing he
really did have a good ear, one wonders how he could bear his
own playing, unless he was so irretrievably plunged in his dream
world that he could not hear the noise he was making. In any
case it is certain that his violin brought him only a very incomplete kind of satisfaction. He was twenty years old by this time,
and he must have suffered increasingly on account of his impotence. Catherine suffered too. For a long time the young woman
apparently attributed her husband's coolness toward her to the
liking he showed for other women, and this gave rise to an incurable resentment. Time and again in her memoirs, she betrays
a jealousy she will not admit to openly. "I told myself that with
this man I was bound to be very unhappy . . . and that I should
have reason to die of jealousy, which would do no one the least
good." Five years after this, observing that her husband was extremely attracted to the Princess of Kurland (one of Biron's
daughters) she got up from the table with a bad headache and
wept bitterly—from anger, she insists, not from jealousy, for she
was too proud to bear being pitied. It was her pride that Peter

wounded continually, and perhaps involuntarily, since he was
not only unable to hide the interest he felt in any pretty woman
but would confide his feelings to Catherine herself, and to all
appearances he treated her like a sister or a comrade and never
as a woman with whom he could envisage simply falling in love.

Twenty-three

(◆(◆(◆(◆(◆(◆(◆(◆(◆(◆(◆(◆

The Apprentice Years

Catherine was so lonely, so lost, so desperate for affection that she
would probably have forgiven her unattractive husband all his
faults if he had at least condescended to show some semblance of
what might be called tenderness toward her. Meanwhile, she
floundered in conjectures. Did she believe her husband had
mistresses? Perhaps to begin with she did, but she herself tells us
that seven years after their marriage the Grand Duke was still
so innocent that it was necessary to resort to the good offices of a
pretty, complaisant widow who was charged by Madame Choglokova with the duty of enlightening him. Peter drove Catherine
mad, if not with jealousy at least with rage, when he was not even
capable of deceiving her.

Moreover, as time passed, the Grand Duchess was emerging
from her chrysalis and "growing more beautiful before one's
eyes." People told her so, and though distrustful of flattery, she
began to believe it. "I was tall [not very: to judge by her dresses
she cannot have been more than five foot three] and I had a

slender waist; all I lacked was a little flesh, for I was very thin. [How she must have envied Elizabeth's splendid *décolletages!*] I liked to go without powder, for my hair was of an exceedingly fine brown, very thick and strong."[1] Portraits painted at this period show a charming figure, not exactly pretty but attractive and elegant, with bright eyes and a firm, intelligent little mouth. At all events Peter, with his tall, gangling body and hopelessly pockmarked face, was decidedly a great deal less good-looking than his wife.

Since she had no hope of pleasing her husband, Catherine may have tried to attract others, but she does not appear to have done so. She had been brought up on very strict principles and the episode of her loving friendship for Andrei Chernyshev had made her cautious. She had no intention of loving her husband, but it never entered her head to love another. However, even at this period she inspired some tender feelings in others: Count Kyril Razumovsky, the brother of the favorite, sighed for her secretly and the Swedish ambassador thought her pretty enough to make her feel embarrassed in his presence. But Peter was still the only man of whom she dared to think.

One tiny incident in her memoirs shows that Catherine did for a long time retain for her husband the kind of sisterly affection which led her to make excuses for him and feel sorry for him. She tells how one day, during a meal at Tsarskoie Selo, when General Buturlin had finished telling a funny story, Peter burst out thoughtlessly: "Oh, the son of a bitch will make me die of laughing today!" Peter spoke Russian very badly and practiced it mostly with his new servants, who were common men of the people, and among the common people the term "son of a bitch" (*sukin syn*), which is both vulgar and insulting, was little more than a term of friendly abuse. The worthy general, however, was rendered practically speechless and was to remember the affront until the day he died, which was some time after Peter. "And yet," says Catherine, "it was merely the stupid blunder of a young man, carried away with the intoxication of laughter, who has been forced into bad company because that is what his dear aunt and her subordinates surround him with. Truly, the young man deserved more pity than resentment."[2]

In order to get rid of the Grand Duke's people from Holstein, Elizabeth had declared a short while after his marriage that he no longer had any need of "pedagogues" or supervisors. In fact, as anyone could see, after Brümmer's departure the Grand Duke had been placed under stricter supervision than ever, and later on this foreign prince was to be virtually deprived of all contact with countries outside Russia. Nevertheless he remained, by right and title, Duke of Holstein. The Empress was therefore compelled, if only for form's sake, to allow him to deal with the affairs of a state of which he was the ruler.

Peter received periodical reports from the ministers of his duchy and had to sign papers and give orders. There is no denying that from the outset the young man took his responsibilities as Duke of Holstein very much to heart. From the spring of 1746 he surrounded himself with a veritable court in miniature, which formed his council of state. Its members included the privy councilor Pehlin, the councilor Löwenbach, the secretaries von Brambsen and Zeiss, the officers von Schil and Katzen, and others. Looking on Russia as a land of exile, Peter tried to form the closest links possible with his native land: he had even had a model of the city of Kiel, which he loved, he said, more than the whole Russian Empire, brought to him from Holstein.

Elizabeth, seeing how eagerly her nephew seized on the opportunity to flee from Russia, even if only in imagination, would not allow the young duke to install a miniature Duchy of Holstein right in the middle of St. Petersburg. The Empress cared so little for the Duchy of Holstein that by virtue of a treaty concluded with Sweden in 1745, she ceded the whole town and lands of Schleswig, a hereditary appanage of her nephew, to Denmark. This was a tragedy for Peter, but he was not permitted to protest. From that day on it was his dream to reconquer Schleswig.

The Grand Duke's new governor, Prince Repnin, a worthy man whose patriotism was never questioned, saw nothing wrong in encouraging the young man in his new activities and did not oppose the Grand Duke's fondness for playing at soldiers. This time it was not a matter of toys: Peter fetched regiments of German soldiers from Holstein, built a small fort, organized parades and so on. Repnin, seeing that these occupations coincided with the young man's real interests, doubtless regarded them as the best way of counteracting the desperate childishness of the Grand Duke's character. But Elizabeth was worried—and with reason—at her heir's obstinately Germanophile tendencies, and also at the bad impression the Grand Duke's German entourage was having on public opinion.[3] Altogether she disapproved of this "dummy soldiering" and in 1747 she sent the Holsteiners back home, leaving Catherine to bewail their departure, since for the future Peter had to make do with his wooden soldiers, his dogs and his violin.

Not that this had cured him of his passion for Holstein. For seventeen years successive Danish ambassadors, supported by the ambassadors of France and Austria, by Elizabeth herself and by Bestuzhev, urged him to renounce his duchy, which was a poor land, far away and without interest for Russia, in exchange for the counties of Oldenbourg and Dalmenhorst. Although the exchange was a thoroughly advantageous one from all points of view, Peter consistently refused to give up his paternal inheritance. In 1750, when Count Lynar supposed that Peter, once Emperor of Russia and with other cares in his head, would give up his title, Bestuzhev told him that on the contrary the Grand Duke's first objective, once on the throne, would be to make war on Denmark in order to recover Schleswig: in which judgment the old chancellor showed considerable psychological insight.

Not only did the future Emperor of Russia prefer his city of Kiel to the entire Russian Empire; he had also developed a burning, almost fanatical admiration for King Frederick of Prussia, on whom he had never even set eyes, and who was regarded by Elizabeth and Bestuzhev as an enemy to be destroyed. This admiration which he proclaimed at the top of his voice caused even Frederick to smile. "I am his Dulcinea," he said, speaking of Peter. It was the youthful admiration of a boy in search of a hero on whom to model himself, but poor Peter possessed none of Frederick's virtues, nor even his faults. Yet this passion, like the rest of the Grand Duke's "ideas," was to prove singularly tenacious.

Peter, then, was champing at the bit, and meanwhile devoting his energies to games which only served to dull and coarsen his character. By the time he was twenty-three, he had begun to show an increasingly noticeable fondness for the bottle, although Catherine seems to be exaggerating when she says that the Grand Duke had developed the drinking habit while still a child in Kiel. No one mentions having seen him drunk or mentions his taste for wine before 1750. Whatever else it may have been, the life the Grand Duke was compelled to lead was of no value as a training for sovereignty. Elizabeth must have been aware of this, but she was afraid above all else of putting too much power and freedom of action into the hands of a prince so undisguisedly hostile to her country, and one who might turn out to be a possible rival, for she had not forgotten the way in which she herself had come to the throne.

Already in 1747 the Prussian ambassador, Finckenstein, was writing to Frederick II: "One may wager that the Grand Duke will never reign in Russia. To say nothing of his bad health which threatens him with an early death, the Russian people hate the Grand Duke to such an extent that he runs a great risk of losing the crown even should it pass naturally to him after the death of the Empress."[4] On this subject the Prussian ambassador is hardly the person who could be suspected of willfully blackening the picture.

If the Grand Duke could not be sure of ever coming to the throne, Catherine was even less so. However, while there was no other heir and no other possible claimant, she could reasonably hope that the crown would nevertheless pass "naturally" to her husband and therefore to her. Meanwhile she spent her enforced leisure in reading, meditating and cultivating her mind, although timidly enough as yet, for she was young and inexperienced. What time she did not devote to riding, which had become her

favorite pastime and one in which she was making rapid progress, or to shooting duck on the lake, she employed in reading,
and she read a great deal—a great deal, at least, for the circles
in which she lived.[5]

She began by obtaining novels. The French novels of the
seventeenth century were still fashionable at the time: D'Urfé's
Astrée, Polexandre by Gomberville, *Le Grand Cyrus* by Madame
de Scudéry, and Desmarets's *Clovis*. Catherine says that while
out walking she always had a book in her pocket, but she soon
tired of novels. Next she stumbled on the letters of Madame
de Sévigné and says that they "entertained her considerably." A
long and unrewarding history of Germany, written by Father
Barre, canon of Sainte-Geneviève, interested her because it was
about Germany. She read Péréfixe's *Histoire d'Henri le Grand*
with passionate interest and was particularly attracted by the
personality of the good King Henry. Henri IV became for her
the model ruler. She read Brantôme too, and liked him very
much, although he seems odd reading for a young woman (or
rather a young girl) as puritanical as she still was. Brantôme,
like Madame de Sévigné, "amused her considerably." These are
almost the sole comments which her memoirs give us on her
reading. Later, in her voluminous correspondence, she often re-
calls her admiration for Henri IV and we may guess that from
her youth, with her eminently realistic and practical nature,
Catherine preferred fact to fiction and history to romance.

After the learned, moral and conventionally respectable works
of such authorities as Fathers Barre and Péréfixe, Catherine
discovered the works of great contemporary writers such as
Montesquieu, Voltaire and Bayle, and they opened out new
horizons for her. Thinking of the future, telling herself that one
day she would have to govern a great nation or at least help her
husband govern it, she began thinking more and more about
politics—its objects, laws and ethical basis. As a child of her age,
she was a sincere believer in progressive theories, in the doctrines
of the *Philosophes*, and dreamed of using her influence to put
Voltaire's and Montesquieu's principles into practice. She was

only twenty, after all, and her dreams were generous—for she did not lack generosity—and impractical. But though she could dream such dreams over a book in the (relative) solitude of her room or in some corner of the park, contact with those around her quickly forced her to measure the gulf which separated her dreams from reality. Catherine was also, more than anything else, a clear-sighted woman, gifted with merciless common sense.

For a long time—over ten years—she persisted in giving the Grand Duke good advice and in trying, with infinite patience, to influence his elusive and obstinate character. She knew only too well that she was nothing by herself, that her charm and popularity and what support she was able to command for herself were of only secondary importance. What came first, the thing that really counted, was the ascendancy she could gain over the Grand Duke; but as she observed toward the end of Elizabeth's reign, when her rupture with Peter was virtually complete: "A strong character cannot easily advise a weak one, for the very character of the weak makes them incapable of following, or even appreciating, the other's suggestions."[6] There can be no doubt that she is thinking here of the Grand Duke and that the "strong character" is herself.

There was yet another reason for her despair at the indifference Peter showed toward her on all occasions: it was always possible that another woman, more attractive than herself, might in the end succeed in inspiring some lasting feeling in the Grand Duke, leaving the Grand Duchess in the unenviable position of a Maria Theresa of Spain or a Marie Leczinska of Poland. Catherine's marital happiness seemed increasingly precarious, and after seven years of a marriage that was no marriage at all, the young woman remarks bitterly: "One might say that he paid court to all women; only she who bore the name of his wife was excluded from his attentions." It must be added that Peter was a poor Don Juan and never succeeded in impressing the object of his attentions, but Catherine's pride suffered none the less for that.

When Sophia of Anhalt-Zerbst arrived at the Russian court she was every bit as innocent as the Archduchess Marie-Antoinette years later, who was too simple to understand the role played by Madame Du Barry in the life of Louis XV. It can only have been on the eve of her marriage, or even later, that she realized the position of Count Razumovsky. Gradually, too, her eyes were opened to many other scandals, public and private, including the one in which her own mother had been involved, and they must have saddened and disgusted her a great deal. Yet she still had to live in this court where licentious behavior was not merely tolerated but even encouraged by the Empress's own conduct. Later on she witnessed the machinations of the new favorite, Ivan Shuvalov, against another presentable young man, Colonel Beketov: both favorites sharing and quarreling in public over the Empress's good graces and each supported by his own clique.

Choglokov, who was the Grand Duke's governor as his wife was the Grand Duchess's, was a notorious libertine. On one occasion he managed to seduce one of Catherine's ladies in waiting, Mademoiselle Koshelev, and got her with child. Scandalized, the Empress at once informed the outraged wife, who generously forgave him and obtained her husband's continuation in his job. This little domestic scandal kept the whole of the "young court" occupied for a week. They were hoping to see the Choglokovs dismissed, but only the young lady was sent home. A little while later Choglokov dared to raise his eyes to the Grand Duchess herself. Without abandoning her own principles, Catherine realized exactly how little these principles were regarded by those around her. Even Maria Choglokova herself, who had been placed before Catherine as an example of marital fidelity, also ended by deceiving her volatile husband. Catherine, who was still not concerned to attract any man in particular, began to flirt a little, hoping to please and yet afraid of it, as she knew the danger any romance she might embark on could mean for herself and, even more, for her lover.

What precisely were these dangers? The Empress often

threatened the Grand Duke with "the fortress," and so did Madame Choglokova, who treated the lad of over twenty like a small child when he refused to do as she told him. Catherine may not have feared imprisonment for herself, but she was certainly afraid of being ignominiously sent back to her native country. She did her utmost to avoid displeasing Elizabeth, but to no purpose, for the Empress was a woman whose reactions were impossible to foretell. One day (according to Catherine) she sent her chamberlain Afzin to the Grand Duchess with orders to tell her that "her Imperial Highness had said at table that I was overloaded with debts, that everything I did was stamped with the mark of foolishness, and yet I still imagined I had a great deal of wit . . . that I deceived no one and that all the world knew of my perfect foolishness . . . and he added, with tears in his eyes, that he said this to me on the Empress's orders but that he begged me to pretend that he had not told me that he had been ordered to say it."[7] Catherine treats it lightly in her memoirs, but at the time the knowledge that she had gone to so much trouble to win the Empress's confidence only to be rewarded with pleasantries of this kind must have been a hard pill to swallow. Certainly the young woman no longer had any idea of regarding Elizabeth as "a divinity free from all defects." She was even beginning to seek other protectors, less highly placed, no doubt, but also less capricious.

She was still keeping out of political intrigues, but at heart she still belonged to the pro-Prussian party. She merely behaved with more discretion than her husband. In 1748 she received a cruel warning: Count Lestocq, the Empress's councilor, who did not always treat her respectfully but whom her mother had recommended to her on her departure as a reliable friend, was suddenly disgraced. "Coming one day into her Majesty's apartments," she says, "I approached Count Lestocq and spoke a few words to him: he told me, 'Don't come near me.' I took this for a joke on his part because he was in the habit of saying to me, 'Charlotte, stand up straight!' and by that he meant to allude to the manner in which I was treated. I was about to answer him in the same tone, but he added; 'I am not joking. Go away from me.' This upset me a little and I said, 'And are you avoiding me?' He said again, 'I told you to leave me alone.' "8

The next day she learned that Lestocq had been taken to the fortress and accused of intriguing on behalf of the Prussians. Coded letters to him from the Prussian ambassador, Finckenstein, compromised him gravely and compromised the Grand Duchess also. (Finckenstein had written among other things: "You yourself told her Imperial Majesty that if the Princess of Zerbst had listened to your advice and that of Brümmer, she would have led the Grand Duke by the nose: say, then, what your advice was?"9 One might well ask, and it is hard to see why Catherine should have needed to "lead the Grand Duke by the nose." But in Elizabeth's eyes these letters could prove complicity between Lestocq, the Grand Duchess and the King of Prussia.) Lestocq, whom Catherine pitied and claimed was innocent, was interrogated by a special commission composed of Bestuzhev himself, General Apraxin and Count Shuvalov. The affair began to have all the appearance of a treason trial. Lestocq was tortured but confessed to nothing and was condemned without proof, or rather exiled and deprived of all his property without formal condemnation. Catherine observes sadly: "The Empress was not strong enough to deal justice to an innocent man; she would have feared such a person's resentment and it is for this reason that, in the course of her reign, no one, guilty or innocent, has left the fortress without being exiled at the least."10

Now the young woman was well aware of the Empress's fondness for Lestocq, who had been her private physician for years and was one of the principal architects of her rise to power. If such a man could be ousted from the imperial favors from one day to the next and suffer the most appalling treatment, who at court could be certain of keeping their freedom? (It does not, however, appear that in this affair there is any reason to accuse Elizabeth of inconsistency. Lestocq was undoubtedly guilty of a secret understanding with the Prussian ambassador and Bestuzhev had been only too delighted of the excuse to destroy an enemy.)

From that day forward Catherine, who had been in danger of becoming personally implicated in an affair of high treason, feared the terrible chancellor even more than she had done before. She saw Bestuzhev's creatures everywhere. She could not move a step without arousing suspicion, and she and her husband were openly and insolently persecuted. She had given up aspiring to the Empress's favor and was now looking to the chancellor, but he was not an easy man to win over. She never saw him face to face and he was forewarned against her. However, in the end she realized that Bestuzhev, although vindictive, proud, and cunning, and moreover "always drunk," was only interested in people insofar as they could serve or endanger his political objectives. She found herself in the process of gradually modifying her own beliefs, and making it clear that she did not share her husband's ideas or harbor any sympathies for the King of Prussia. At the same time the King, informed by his ambassadors of his former protégée's intelligent and prudent course of action, tried by all means to make her his ally.

In this way, still living under close surveillance, spending her days riding around the countryside on horseback or reading and her evenings dancing or listening to the Grand Duke's chatter, the young Grand Duchess began to play a part in the game of Russian politics, in a secondary but far from negligible capacity. Even foreign courts were already realizing that it was wiser to concentrate on this cautious but sensible young woman than on her unreliable husband.

But time was passing, and eight years after their marriage the grand ducal couple were still without an heir. The Empress was forty-two, and her health was failing. In 1749 she was almost carried off by a strong "attack of constipation," to the great anxiety of the court and the terror of the young Grand Duke and Duchess, who were already seeing themselves threatened with exile or imprisonment as a result of a palace revolution in favor of the imprisoned prince Ivan VI. Clearly Elizabeth had no thoughts of releasing the Duke of Brunswick's son from the fortress of Schlüsselburg. He was, after all, the offspring of the family she had dethroned. But Peter had no children and the consequences if the throne passed irrevocably to a pair of Germans who were indifferent or even hostile to the interests of Russia might be disastrous. To Elizabeth, as to Bestuzhev and his followers, the young couple's sterility appeared increasingly in the light of a catastrophe.

One day while the Grand Duke was out hunting, he found himself alone in the woods with a certain Lieutenant Baturin of the Butirsky regiment. Suddenly this officer, proclaiming great devotion to the person of the Grand Duke, dismounted from his horse, flung himself on his knees before Peter and swore that "he acknowledged no other master and would do anything he commanded." Peter was terrified. He promptly set spurs to his horse, leaving his faithful subject all alone on his knees in the middle of the wood, and hurried off to tell the whole story to his wife. His terror increased when he learned that Baturin had been arrested and taken before the secret chancellery set up to judge crimes against the state. Had Peter simply allowed himself, if not actually to join in a conspiracy, at least to lend his tacit support to the conspirators who wished to bring him to the throne, no one would have been any the wiser and Baturin would not have been betrayed. As it was, the officer was accused of intending to kill the Empress, set fire to the palace, and in the resultant horror and confusion, put the Grand Duke on the throne.[11]

Peter was certainly not the man to place himself at the head of any conspiracy, whatever its chances of success. He was cowardice personified. But this incident, of no account in itself, showed him that there were people on his side, that he was no longer a child forced to tremble before his aunt for the rest of his life. "From that time forward," says Catherine, the only witness and the best, "I saw the thirst to rule growing in the Grand Duke's mind: he was dying for it but he made no attempt to render himself worthy of it."[12]

Twenty-four

❧❧❧❧❧❧❧❧❧❧❧❧❧

Love and Reasons of State

"At our court [the young court]," Catherine writes, "there were two chamberlains named Saltykov." The younger, Sergei, had recently married one of the Empress's ladies in waiting, Matrone Petrovna Balk; the elder, Peter, was a stupid person of repulsive appearance and "one of the greatest telltales," and was engaged to the same Princess of Kurland who had been courted by the Grand Duke. Catherine, only too glad to see one of her rivals married off, herself embroidered a wedding gown for the bride-to-be.

The Saltykov family was one of the most ancient and noble in Russia, although its members did not bear the title of prince or the singularly devalued one of count. Sergei Saltykov was a good-looking young man of twenty-six with a large number of feminine conquests to his credit.

Catherine was becoming frankly pretty. She herself realized this with astonishment and an innocent vanity. "One day," she writes, "I was watching her [Elizabeth] dance a minuet (this was during one of the celebrated masked balls where the women were dressed as men and vice versa) and when the dance ended and she came up to me, I took the liberty of remarking that it was fortunate for the women that she was not a man, for her picture alone, painted thus, would be enough to turn many a head. She took what I had said out of the real feelings of my heart in very good part, and answered in the same tone, the most gracious in the world, that if she were a man, it would be to me that she would present the prize.

"I bent to kiss her hand at the receipt of such an unexpected compliment. She embraced me and the whole company was trying to make out what could be between the Empress and myself."[1] Possibly Elizabeth's words were inspired by mere politeness toward a young woman whose sincere admiration had touched her, but in any case Catherine was beginning to think herself pretty. She speaks with a childish pride of one ball in particular at which she outshone all the ladies of the court: she was wearing a simple white dress with "very small hoops," adorned by a single rose which "imitated nature to perfection." She had another rose in her hair, which was tied in a queue at the back of her head by a white ribbon, and a white gauze ruffle at her throat. She was the belle of the ball and everyone was in raptures at the simplicity of her costume; she was admired and the Empress herself deigned to put a patch on her cheek. Catherine was prouder of this imperial patch than of everything else put together.

"They said I was as lovely as the day and perfectly dazzling. . . . To tell the truth," she adds, "I have never thought myself extremely beautiful, but I was pleasing and I think this was my strong point."[2]

She was pleasing because there was a man who pleased her and because she could sense that this man admired her.

Sergei Saltykov was certainly not Catherine's first love. She had felt something more than friendship for Andrei Chernyshev, the charming young man who paid so dearly for the friendship the grand ducal pair felt toward him. Her faithful Evreinov had enabled her to find out where the brothers were hidden and for some time she had maintained a secret correspondence with Andrei through the good offices of an intelligent maidservant, Catherine Petrovna, and for this boy she took risks that she dared not take to write to her parents. But when Sergei came on the scene she quickly forgot the faithful and unfortunate Andrei.

She writes: "He was as handsome as the day and there was certainly no one to equal him either at the great court or still less at our own. He lacked neither wit nor that turn of knowledge, manners and ability which the great world, and the court in particular, can give."[3] It is the judgment of a woman in love. Sergei was neither as handsome nor as witty as she would have him, but this was the way she saw him. He had charm and gaiety and knew how to talk to women. He was the kind of young man whose passions are easily aroused and who goes straight to the point without letting any obstacles deter him. Two years before his affair with the Grand Duchess he had fallen heavily for Matrone Balk, one of Catherine's ladies in waiting: he had seen the girl in the park, playing on a swing, and had at once asked for her hand, which he obtained. It was a pretty love story and much talked about at court, but for Sergei, Matrone was simply another of his numerous conquests.

The Grand Duchess was so charming, so obviously bored and so strictly watched that she was a natural victim for any young *roué*. Saltykov courted her according to all the rules of seduction, beginning by openly seeking the friendship of her "dragons," the Choglokovs, who alone were in the position to facilitate his approach to the Grand Duchess. It was in the Choglokov house that Sergei managed to obtain frequent interviews with the object of his passion.

Catherine had grown used to Maria Choglokova and often went to visit her; she was not a very clever or educated woman, but she was young, pretty, not malevolent, and a good mother to her family. Maria was pregnant and ill and Catherine writes that she was able to amuse her. Sergei Saltykov visited the Choglokovs with his friend Leon Naryshkin and Catherine accompanied her friend Princess Gargarina. The master of the house was always present at these meetings between the young people, and Sergei Saltykov—Catherine records this with admiration and gratitude—had found an ingenious way of lulling the vigilance of their common enemy. He discovered that Choglokov had a leaning toward poetry, and pretended to take an interest in his literary compositions, although he was "the dullest man and the least endowed with wit and imagination." This lover's ruse worked like a charm: on his new friend's insistence Choglokov would go and sit in a corner, absorbed in the composition of some new lyric. Leon Naryshkin, who was aware of his companion's projected gallantry, would compose the music for these songs and sing them with the author, and meanwhile the conversation in the room could go on unchecked and the lovers were able to say whatever they liked.

The affair began like a French farce. During one of these improvised concerts, Sergei summoned up courage to declare his passion and was not too badly received. At first Catherine did not answer, then she began reminding the young man of his obligations to his wife. He poured out the classic excuses: "He began to tell me that all that glittered was not gold, and that he was paying dearly for a moment's blindness." Catherine allowed herself to fall into the trap like any schoolgirl. She pitied him, tried to discourage him, and took more and more pleasure in listening to him. She saw him almost every day. Clumsily and without conviction she tried to make him believe that she loved another. "How do you know? Perhaps my heart is already occupied elsewhere." Naturally he did not believe a word of it. He was too experienced not to know that his prey was already his. During a hunting party arranged by Choglokov on one of the islands at the mouth of the Neva, Catherine was induced to confess her love.

She did not say it in so many words. Catherine was twenty-three, but where emotions were concerned she was still a child and like any inexperienced girl in the same circumstances, she was afraid of committing herself. She listened to the seducer with a delight which she does not admit but which it is not hard to divine, allowing him to paint in glowing colors the joys that their secret liaison would bring them. She was compelled to admit that Sergei was "preferable" to other men at the court. She pretended to laugh, and when he insisted that he would not leave her until she told him he was "tolerated," she answered like the heroine of a Marivaux play: "Yes, yes, only go away." This was at once followed up by a "No! No!" which neither he nor she took seriously.[4]

Then while they were at supper, a wind came up from the sea which "made the waters rise so high that they reached as far as the steps of the house, so that the sea water covered the island several feet deep." The storm meant the hunters could not get back to their boats and forced them to stay where they were until three o'clock in the morning; and in the midst of the cheerful chaos brought about by the incident Sergei had plenty of time to talk of love and Catherine leisure to listen and realize that she would not resist him. She was very frightened, "dissatisfied," she says, with herself, and afraid as much for her safety as for her virtue. It may well have been on the day following this episode of the flooded island that she finally lost the virginity which had been a standing reproach to her for eight years.

There can be no doubt that she was immediately head over heels in love with her first lover, and at this stage she does not appear to have felt any other anxiety beyond the fear of finding her secret discovered and her love shattered. Certainly she felt no remorse; it is hardly likely that she should have when she was making the man she loved happy. Sergei was frivolous and cynical and Catherine, happy in her first love, thought of nothing but pleasing her lover.

It was Sergei Saltykov who, once he had attained his object, began advising his mistress to be cautious. He repeated to her what the Grand Duke had said to his *valet de chambre*, Bressan: "Sergei Saltykov and my wife are fooling Choglokov, making him an accessory to their desires and then mocking him." Peter was not disturbed by any considerations of his honor as a husband, and may have thought the affair nothing more than a flirtation carried to unusual lengths. It amused him to see the detestable Choglokov made a fool of. But other people less disinterested than the Grand Duke had also noticed Sergei's attentions: there was still the Empress's anger to be feared and the young courtier had no desire to see his career in ruins. Now it appears from

Catherine's own statements, as well as from those of the French diplomat the Marquis de Castéra, that Elizabeth may have been less blind than she was generally thought to be, and Saltykov's undertaking not as difficult or dangerous as he himself imagined.

Castéra's story, which is similar to Catherine's own, reads like a tale from Boccaccio: there is a stupid young Grand Duke who is incapable of fulfilling his conjugal obligations, a charming Grand Duchess, extremely bored by her enforced chastity, a clever and gallant "M. de Soltikoff" who succeeds in seducing the Grand Duchess during a hunting party and hastens to make up for the Grand Duke's impotence. Then in the course of a gay dinner where everyone is telling doubtful stories and drinking heavily, he persuades the young simpleton until, encouraged by his companions, he finally resolves to undergo the operation which will make it possible for him to enjoy the pleasures of marital and extramarital intercourse. Thus "M. de Soltikoff" and the charming Grand Duchess are enabled, with perfect safety, to provide the Empire with an heir.[5]

What is absolutely certain is that it was precisely at this time that Elizabeth instructed the Choglokovs, and Madame Choglokova in particular, to procure her an heir at all costs. She held her cousin responsible for the sterility of the young couple and reproached her for neglecting her duties. The result was that Madame Choglokova was compelled to "bestir herself and carry out the Empress's orders to the letter." Catherine herself mentions neither the operation nor Saltykov's part in it, but she does indicate that Peter finally lost his innocence with a certain Madame Groot, the pretty widow of a painter. This was arranged through the good offices of Madame Choglokova, who spent "several days" in persuading the young widow and "promising her I don't know what," and then in instructing her in what was expected of her and exactly what the matter was she was to lend herself to. Peter's valet, Bressan, was given the job of acting as go-between and the undertaking was crowned with success.

By that time Catherine was probably already pregnant by Sergei Saltykov, and not only pregnant but already neglected, for the young man had become "inattentive and sometimes stupid, arrogant and dissipated." Catherine's happiness had lasted only a few weeks. There were a few delightful hunting parties where everyone was dressed in the same costume, "grey underneath and the rest blue with a black velvet collar." In this way couples were able to mix and mingle without anyone's being able to identify the lovers from a distance. Then Saltykov and his friend Naryshkin went away to the country for three weeks to avoid rousing suspicion; and also, no doubt, because Sergei was already tired of his naïve and demanding mistress.

To the misfortune of being so swiftly deserted was added—at least so may reasonably be supposed—the still greater one of having, out of prudence and duty, to endure a man she did not love and who did not love her, and whom she found all the more repulsive because she was in the process of discovering all the joys and miseries of love with another man. It may well have been from that moment that she began to hate Peter. Peter, on his side, never felt anything for Catherine physically but aversion. There is no reason to suppose he was not intelligent enough to understand the pitiful role he was being compelled to play.

It is not suggested that Peter was impotent, but he was very probably sterile. The many serious illnesses which had made his childhood one long martyrdom would in themselves be enough to account for that. Supposing his doctors were in a position to state with certainty that the Grand Duke would never produce children, they can only have done so under the seal of the greatest possible secrecy. At all events, Peter had numerous mistresses, yet he has never been credited with being the father of natural children, while the woman who lived intimately with the Grand Duke for seven years and was his "favorite sultana" married after his death and at once produced a child. Everything points to the conclusion that the reason Elizabeth did not reward Madame Choglokova for her trouble in the affair of Madame Groot was precisely because the Grand Duke's initiation into the art of love was not followed by a pregnancy. Madame Groot did not have the honor of giving birth to an imperial bastard. The

Grand Duchess, on the other hand, did have a miscarriage in December 1752, three or four months after her affair with Saltykov began.

It all looks as though the couple had both been put to the test, as it were, and the test had proved conclusive. Catherine, at least, was normally constituted and capable of giving the Russian Empire the heir it so badly needed.

No doubt she herself cared very little about the future of the dynasty; at that time she was preoccupied solely with her own love affair and the way in which she could keep a lover who was growing cooler every day, although he explained his behavior by the need to avoid arousing suspicion. It was this love affair which inspired the young woman to take the first steps toward reaching an understanding with Count Bestuzhev. Thinking the chancellor was ill-disposed toward Sergei, she plucked up her courage and went so far as to approach the man whom she regarded as her worst enemy. She sent one of her friends, Bremse, to the chancellor with the mission of conveying to him that the Grand Duchess was "less far from him than formerly." Delighted to find the Grand Duchess becoming one of his supporters and possibly hoping to hold her by making himself an accomplice in her love affairs (thanks to his spies he knew everything about her "as though he had been living in [her] room"), Bestuzhev offered his services, gladly granted an interview to Saltykov himself and promised to tighten the screw on the Choglokovs and make Madame Vladislavova "as gentle as a lamb." In short, he said, "she [Catherine] will see that I am not such an ogre as I have been painted to her." Thus the confidence inspired by love finally gave the Grand Duchess the opportunity to become the ally of a man whom she had hitherto feared like the plague.

Bestuzhev thought that he was playing a subtle game, but in fact, in the complex maneuvers of politics and court intrigue, where there was often only a step between the highest favor and total disgrace, it is difficult to say which of the two gained most from their alliance. At all events, Catherine saw with astonishment that her bugbear had suddenly been transformed into an indulgent and urbane protector: he was actually offering to watch over Catherine and her lover under the very noses of the people he himself had given the task of supervising the young woman. She records that "he gave him [Saltykov] a good deal of advice which was as useful as it was wise. All this made him very intimate with us, without any living soul being any the wiser."[6]

But Catherine was to have more surprises yet. No sooner was the secret alliance with the chancellor concluded than Madame Choglokova herself made the most surprising about-face. The scene Catherine describes (and she is for obvious reasons the only person who does so) is certainly an extraordinary one, but there is no reason to believe she is making it up. Catherine hardly ever lies, at least in her memoirs, and the incident is so compromising that when the Russian Academy of Sciences was editing the Empress's works in 1907, they did not dare publish this passage.

Madame Choglokova, "who had always," says Catherine, "kept in mind her favorite business of watching over the succession," took the young woman aside and gave her a long lecture on marital fidelity in general and her own in particular, obviously in order to avoid being accused of immorality. She ended by saying "that there were sometimes circumstances of an overriding importance which should be made an exception to this rule."

The inference was clear: It is your duty to give an heir to the Empire. Now, your husband is sterile, therefore . . . Believing it was a trap, Catherine refused to understand. Then Madame Choglokova told her: "You shall see whether I love my country and how sincere I am: I have no doubt that you have looked favorably on someone. I leave you to choose between Sergei Saltykov and Leon Naryshkin, and if I am not mistaken, it is the latter."

Catherine cried out: "No, no, not at all!" "Well then, if it is not he, it must be the other." And Madame Choglokova added, "You will see that I shall not be the one to stand in your way." Catherine still pretended not to understand, so steadfastly that

Madame Choglokova "scolded" her, and not only that day but on other occasions, "in town as well as in the country."[7] Three months later, in consequence of this feigned incomprehension, Catherine once more became pregnant.

Maria Choglokova's behavior appears so strange that there have been suggestions that it was inspired by some personal interest: her husband was at that time in love with the Grand Duchess, and Choglokova might have hoped by this means to eliminate a rival; but however bottomless the depths of human stupidity, it is hard to believe that a woman could bring herself to take such an extraordinary step from pure jealousy. Moreover, there can be no doubt that Maria Choglokova would not have dared act as she did if she had not been certain of at least the tacit approval of Elizabeth herself, or possibly of the chancellor, who could have passed the idea on to her as if it had come from the Empress herself. There are several indications in Elizabeth's previous behavior with regard to Catherine and Saltykov which seem to show that the Empress had known of her niece's escapade from the beginning and had knowingly encouraged it. Moreover, she was quite intelligent enough to realize that her nephew, although the true grandson of Peter the Great, was in fact merely a symbolic heir. The succession could equally well be assured by a child who merely appeared to be legitimate, especially if his real father were a young nobleman of authentic Russian stock.

Catherine was therefore put in the way of becoming pregnant —for it was already known that she was capable of it—and, to this end, of keeping her lover. This was not as easy as it might have been. The handsome Sergei was at his wits' end to find excuses for seeing as little of Catherine as possible. She heaped reproaches on him. He answered her with good and bad reasons and protestations of sincerity, just as every Don Juan tired of a conquest has done since love began. She was in love, inexperienced, and asked nothing better than to believe him. "He gave me such good and sufficient reasons for it that since I saw and spoke to him, my thoughts on this subject [that of his inconstancy] have faded away." It was therefore Catherine, with the connivance of Choglokova (and possibly of Bestuzhev and the Empress), who had to find ways and means of making Sergei Saltykov finally provide the Grand Duke with a son.

It is clear that the succession was among the least of Catherine's worries, but at last she was pregnant beyond all shadow of doubt, for the second time. It never seems to have occurred to her to take care of herself. Instead of resting she set off with her husband and the young court to Lubertzi, one of the Grand Duke's estates, which lay some twelve versts from Moscow (a verst is a little less than a mile). This country excursion was about as exhausting as it could be: the house was falling to pieces, they had to put up tents in the courtyard, and the Grand Duchess slept in a *kibitka* (either a nomad's tent or a covered wagon), and was moreover unable to sleep on account of the noise made by the masons, for the house was in the process of being rebuilt and they were working day and night to get it finished quickly.[8] By day, Catherine dashed around the countryside in a gig, trying to keep up with the hunt. When she returned to Moscow her condition made her very tired. "I slept until midday every day and it was all they could do to wake me for dinner," she says.[9] But in spite of this she was obliged to lead an exhausting social life. On June 29, 1753, she was seized with pains after a ball and had another miscarriage, more serious than the last. For nearly two weeks she was so ill that her life was believed to be in danger. It was six weeks before she was well again.

Elizabeth's hopes had come to nothing, for the time being at least. In spite of all Madame Choglokova's efforts and the various tests to which the couple were submitted, the heir was still not forthcoming. Catherine had experienced her first love affair: it was ordinary and a little sad, but lovely because it was the first. Sergei Saltykov did not desert her and she, though she doubted him, did her best to persuade herself that he still loved her. As for the Grand Duke, Catherine is silent on the subject of their relations at this stage, and Peter wrote no memoirs.

He was now twenty-five. His association with Madame Groot

and the marital intercourse he was able to have with Catherine
had in no way improved his character. It seems that for him the
discovery of love was only a source of fresh humiliation, and
there is nothing astonishing in this, if one thinks of what must
have been Catherine's state of mind at the time. In his bitterness
he tried, even more than ever before, to take refuge in the imaginary world he had made for himself, and in drink. It was at
this time that he began drinking in earnest. His favorite servant,
a Ukrainian, obtained wine and strong liquor for him, and Peter
spent his nights drinking with his servants, Kalmuk boys who
got drunk and refused to obey his orders. Drunk himself, he
tried to bring them to order by beating them, but he cannot have
done so very severely, since it had no effect and the Grand Duke
still called Catherine in to scold his disrespectful Kalmuks.

This fondness for drink, which Peter took care to hide from
his aunt's spies and from Choglokov in particular, would not be
enough in itself to make the Grand Duke appear abnormal, but
there are other, more serious indications. It is Catherine again
who recounts the story of the rat which was solemnly hanged for
"criminal actions deserving of the extreme penalty according to
military law." The rat had eaten two soldiers made of paste and
he was hanged only symbolically, having already been killed by
a dog. Catherine roared with laughter at the seriousness with
which her husband explained the affair to her, and Peter was
mortally offended.[10] What we know of the Grand Duke's character shows that he was extravagant, quarrelsome, an unbalanced
dreamer, but he does not appear to have been mad to the point
of taking "crimes" and "punishments" of this kind really seriously. But, like many maladjusted people, he must have been
able to become passionately absorbed in the imaginary world of
his made-up games, and admittedly this world was a singularly
uninteresting one.

At this period his wife had already had two miscarriages. He
probably did not believe himself the author of either of these two
pregnancies. He was certainly aware of Catherine's liaison with
Saltykov, just as he was by no means unaware of his wife's next

affair. For a long time yet he was to regard his spouse as a friend and ally, and a friend who had the additional advantage of being obliged to give in to all his whims without a murmur. But it is hard to imagine that he enjoyed his role of the complaisant husband, the father on paper, and one day he was to rebel against it.

Twenty-five

The Succession Ensured

In February 1754 (seven months after her second miscarriage, that is) the Grand Duchess was again in an interesting condition. This time she was not allowed to imperil the future of the dynasty with hunting parties and excursions into the country.

Sergei Saltykov had become, officially, one of the Grand Duke's close companions and an even closer one of the Grand Duchess. He and Leon Naryshkin formed part of the little circle which met daily in the Choglokov's house, under their auspices, and no one thought any longer of finding their presence suspicious or of sending them away. Early that winter Elizabeth's residence in Moscow, the Annenhof palace, burned down. Catherine was an eyewitness, and the incident made a big impression on her. She recounts that when the fire broke out she left the palace "at three o'clock precisely, and at six no trace of the building remained." This building, with the outbuildings which surrounded it, covered an area two or three versts in circumference. Such swift destruction is a record even for a wooden palace and suggests that at best the building can have been little more than a ramshackle collection of planks. The Muscovites were used to accidents of this kind: some at least of the furniture was got out very quickly by detachments of soldiers, and the people inside the palace had plenty of time to escape. Catherine remarks: "Then I saw an extraordinary thing: an amazing number of rats and mice were coming down the stairs in single file, without even appearing to hurry very much."

The Grand Duke and Duchess had no alternative but to find somewhere else to live, and Elizabeth billeted them in the Choglokov house. "The wind blew through it in all directions, the doors were half rotten, the floors split open, leaving gaps three or four inches wide, and in addition there were vermin everywhere."[1]

Catherine was afraid for her books, which were a literally irreplaceable treasure, especially in Russia, but by good fortune they were brought back to her unharmed the day after the catastrophe. While furniture was being got out, an immense number of bottles of wine and liqueurs had been discovered in the Grand Duke's cupboards. Elizabeth was less fortunate: all her dresses, numbering four thousand in all, were burned. She was thoughtful enough to tell Catherine that of all her clothes, the only dress she really regretted was one made from a piece of cloth the Grand Duchess had given her. Decidedly the Empress knew how to find the right word or gesture to win back her niece's heart. Catherine was always ready to forget the whims of the tyrant and remember only the charm and beauty of the woman, and Elizabeth had strong reasons for taking care of the person to whom she looked for an heir to the Empire.

Catherine's life was not a cheerful one that winter. She complains, naturally enough, of the discomfort of the lodgings in which she lived after the fire. She caught cold and fell into a state of "hypochondria" for emotional rather than physical reasons. She describes one evening in particular which she spent alone with Madame Choglokova, the one waiting for her husband

and the other for her lover. Despite his promises Sergei had not managed to slip away from a certain banquet and when he returned it was late at night. Maria Choglokova kept repeating: "There, they've deserted us!" which was exactly what Catherine thought herself.

From the way she speaks of Sergei at this time one might almost imagine that he and not the Grand Duke was her husband. At that period their liaison must have received some official sanction, and when Catherine became pregnant for the third time Sergei Saltykov was still allowed to frequent her society and was accepted as her intimate companion. There is no incident at court about which she does not add "Sergei Saltykov told me" or "I told Sergei Saltykov."

Not long after Easter, Choglokov, who had been so hated and mocked by all the young court and by Catherine in particular, died of a stomach complaint, and only then did Catherine realize that she had been very fond of the man, or at least of his family. She wept a great deal and sincerely shared the widow's grief. This was the end of the role of watchdog to the Grand Duchess, which Maria Choglokova had fulfilled at first strictly and later with only too much complaisance. Making her recent widowhood an excuse, the Empress released her cousin from her employment and Catherine passed into new hands: those of Alexander Shuvalov, the uncle of Elizabeth's young favorite, who was to take Choglokov's place.

At first Catherine was terrified on two counts: first, because Alexander Shuvalov was head of the "State Inquisition," in other words the secret police, and secondly because he suffered from a facial tic which contorted his features hideously whenever he expressed the slightest emotion. Catherine complained bitterly about this, saying that it was a strange idea to force a pregnant woman to see such a man continually and what if the child were to have a tic like that. Moreover, for her first lady in waiting the Grand Duchess was given Countess Rumiantseva, an old enemy of her mother's and, worse still, "the sworn enemy of Sergei Saltykov." Catherine protested at this and her objection carried.

This time, terrified of being separated from her lover, she had the presence of mind to use her condition as a weapon and threatened her entourage with another miscarriage. They humored her.

When the court removed to Petersburg Catherine "died of fright" in case Sergei Saltykov (and, she adds for form's sake, Leon Naryshkin) should be left behind in Moscow. But she was to be allowed to keep Saltykov. During the journey Alexander Shuvalov and his wife watched her so closely that Sergei was unable to get near her. Only once, at Princess Gargarina's suggestion, the lovers were granted "such a little thing, a few minutes' conversation."[2] When she arrived in Petersburg and was settled in the Summer Palace, Catherine had only one idea in her head, one thing that haunted her: she thought that everything was being done to separate her from the man she loved. However, he was still there, he continued to see her, and she no longer complained about him. She did not even think of doubting him or reviling him any more: the fear that a separation was probably imminent made her forget all other concerns.

"It was nearly a mortal blow to me," she says, "when I learned that the apartment being made ready for my confinement adjoined and formed a part of the Empress's own suite." It was nearly a mortal blow because, as she herself says, her friends (and Sergei among them) would no longer be able to visit her freely. She would be "isolated, with no company, and wretched as a stone."[3]

On September 20, 1754, nine years after her marriage, the Grand Duchess Catherine Alexeievna bore a son. "There was great rejoicing in the city and in the Empire at this event."

The Empress herself was present during the long and painful labor, as also were the Grand Duke and the Shuvalovs. No sooner was the baby bathed and swaddled, and anointed by the Empress's confessor, than Elizabeth carried him off in her hurry to show to the rest of the court the heir that had been so long awaited. Her haste was understandable, but from then on the little prince never left the Empress's apartments, and the young mother had no cradle next to her bed. "I remained on my bed of suffering [her labor bed], and this bed was placed opposite a door through which I could see daylight, while behind me there were two big windows which did not close properly, and two more doors to the right and left of the bed. . . . No sooner was the Empress gone than the Grand Duke also departed and so did Monsieur and Madame Shuvalov, and I saw no one else until three o'clock. . . . I was sweating a great deal and I begged Madame Vladislavova to change my linen and put me to bed; she replied that she dared not. She sent several times for the midwife, but she did not come. I asked for something to drink but I received the same answer."[4]

Once the child had been taken from her womb alive, no one took any further interest in the young mother. They left her lying for hours on her labor bed, exposed to terrible drafts, dying of thirst and crying as if her heart would break. Finally someone thought to put her to bed, and she says, "I saw no other living soul all that day, nor did anyone send to inquire after me. The Grand Duke, for his part, did nothing but drink with anyone he could find, and the Empress was busy with the child."[5]

Considering that he probably did not believe himself the father of the child, the Grand Duke's behavior was, if not very considerate, at least understandable; especially as he had never taken much interest in the subject of an heir that was chiefly wanted in order to disinherit him. But on Elizabeth's part, such total disregard for a woman in childbirth can only prove hostility or contempt at the very least, a hostility and contempt which were the more unjust in that Catherine had done her best and it was not for Elizabeth to reproach her for the manner in which her child had been conceived.

After little Paul's baptism, the Empress appointed Sergei Saltykov as envoy to take the news of the birth of the baby, of which he was in all probability the father, to the court of Sweden. The irony of his mission may well be interpreted as a punishment, for foreign courts were well aware of the liaison and Sergei could hardly help but feel somewhat ridiculous in his role of bearer of good tidings. The fact remains that he was hastily removed as soon as it was no longer necessary to humor the Grand Duchess.

Twenty-six

《❖《❖《❖《❖《❖《❖《❖《❖《❖《❖

Paul Petrovich

A new life was beginning. From the day of his birth the little boy Catherine had borne in agony was a symbol. He represented a hope, a tool, a threat, a formidable weapon in the cruel game being indulged in by the adults who surrounded him. No one thought of the child's real interests or needs.

Like all baby princes, and even more than most, the Tsarevich Paul Petrovich was a child watched over too closely, mollycoddled, surrounded by a whole swarm of nurses, maidservants, doctors and valets, and deprived of real affection. It is hard for a nurse to grow fond of a child whose health is an affair of state and who, if he so much as sneezes, is likely to lose her her post. Paul did not know his parents: from the moment he was born Elizabeth had made it clear to the Grand Duke and Duchess that they had no claim on their son. The Grand Duke hardly seems to have minded this, but the young mother did, although admittedly even her feelings were modified by the fact that she was already worn out by her labor, by the rheumatism she had contracted from being in a perpetual draft and by the neglect she had suffered after the birth of the child everyone was busy making such a fuss over.

She was anxious, nevertheless, and since she could not see her son, she did at least make some attempt to find out how he was, although "secretly" because, she says, "to ask for news of him would have been regarded as casting doubts on the care the Empress was taking of him."[1] Another mother might perhaps have been less respectful of court etiquette, might have begged and entreated, but Catherine was too much a princess and, in any case, too beaten and humiliated. Just as, through no fault of her own, her marriage had been a failure, so she was now in the process of failing in her first experience of motherhood: she was not given the chance to become fond of her child.

In the end she did manage to see him from time to time, and she describes with horror how little Paul was "placed in an extremely warm room, swaddled in flannel and laid in a cradle lined with black fox fur. Over him was a coverlet of quilted satin, and over that was one of rose-colored velvet lined with black fox. Many times after that I myself saw him put to bed in this way, with the sweat pouring from his face and his whole body, so that when he grew older, if he got in the slightest draft, he would catch cold and it would make him ill. Besides, there were a great many old women about him who, as a result of instructions which they did not comprehend and lack of common sense, did him infinitely more harm than good both physically and morally."[2] For a mother, even as indifferent a mother as Catherine, this was a perpetual heartbreak and yet she dared say nothing. She was much too frightened of the Empress.

She was not permitted to see her baby until forty days after her confinement, so that little Paul was a six-weeks'-old baby, an age at which a child's face is already well formed and he is beginning to smile. His mother admitted to finding him "very handsome," but she was only able to look at him for the few moments while the prayers at the churching ceremony lasted. Then once again she did not see him for weeks.

On the occasion of his baptism there were banquets, balls, illuminations and fireworks. The people rejoiced at the birth of an imperial heir, the courtiers wondered what changes this birth would bring in the Grand Duke's position, and the happiest of them all was undoubtedly Elizabeth.

This amazing woman, the possessor of an affectionate nature which had been deprived of the joys of motherhood, seems to have behaved as though Catherine had brought the child into the world solely for her benefit. The mother was paid off with a present of a hundred thousand rubles and a few trifling jewels ("a wretched little necklace and two miserable rings which I would have been ashamed to give to my maids").[3] To add insult to injury, five days after Catherine had been given the money the Empress sent to fetch it back because there was not a penny left in her coffers, and it was not refunded until three months later. The explanation of this was that when the Grand Duke learned that his wife had received a present and he had had nothing, he regarded it as a reflection on his marital misfortunes, or as a piece of deliberate malice, and demanded a similar present: so the hundred thousand rubles changed hands. Altogether Elizabeth considered she had paid off the parents and was quit of them. She had, after all, been keeping them lavishly at the expense of the state for years. She herself meant to be a mother to the child.

She began by taking her new role very seriously and had little Paul's cradle put in her own room. "Whenever he cried she ran to him herself," but it was too late for her to play mother. Absorbed by her own pleasures, her balls and banquets, and occasionally by affairs of state, she left little Paul to the care of his nursemaids and contented herself with supervising and terrorizing them. Paul was wrapped up, fed and pampered a great deal too much, and grew up into an exceedingly delicate and nervous child. Nevertheless Elizabeth's love for her grandnephew was so obvious and fierce that the French diplomat the Marquis de l'Hôpital hints in his dispatches to the French court at the possibility that the Tsarevich Paul might be a child of whom Elizabeth herself had been brought to bed clandestinely and whom she had succeeded in substituting for the one born to the Grand Duchess.[4] Since this dispatch was written three years after Paul's birth Elizabeth's fondness for the child was evidently more than a flash in the pan, and this belated spark of maternal feeling made the Empress behave more harshly than ever toward the child's real mother, who was in any case resigned to it and, as we shall see, was soon consoled.

For the Empress, the Tsarevich Paul's existence represented something quite other than simply the joy of bringing up a little grandnephew: it had opened up new political perspectives. She was now forty-five years old and, although her health was precarious, she could still hope to live for a long time, long enough to watch the child grow up. Now this woman, although she sometimes seemed to be totally preoccupied with her ball gowns and her love affairs, was no comic-opera empress: she had kept alive the cult of her father's memory and she meant to be faithful to the ideas of Peter the Great. She had few ideas of her own, but those she did have were simple and clear and she clung to them. In home affairs she was, as her father had not been, stubbornly pro-Russian, fanatically Orthodox, and she followed the example of Louis XIV in "doing penance on the backs of others" in her persecution of the Catholic, Protestant and Jewish minorities in the western provinces, and in encouraging the administration to convert the Tartars and Kalmuks of the eastern provinces by force. In foreign affairs she held, with an exemplary fidelity, to the alliance with the house of Austria, in the hope of forming with it a solid block which would be able to break the power of the Ottoman Empire to the south and east and put a brake on the expansion of the Kingdom of Prussia in the west.

This policy, which was directed by Bestuzhev, was to gain Russia access to Constantinople and the Balkans and ensure her an ever increasing influence in Poland and the countries of the Baltic. In Elizabeth's eyes Prussia was therefore Russia's natural enemy, and for twelve years Prussia had been ruled by Frederick II, a great captain, an autocratic monarch and a politician of genius, against whom the combined efforts of the Empress Maria Theresa and Elizabeth seemed likely to prove powerless. Frederick was making every effort to divide Russia and Austria; he had little hope of altering Elizabeth's attitude, for she stuck with a truly female obstinacy to her fixed personal hatred for him, but he was still hoping, with some justification, to find an ally in Elizabeth's successor. Elizabeth was very well aware of the part played by foreign diplomats and, even worse, by foreign money in her own rise to power. She saw in the Grand Duke an openly declared Prussian and in the Grand Duchess a concealed one.

Now the birth of little Paul altered the situation completely. It became clear that if the Empress lived long enough, she would disinherit the Grand Duke in favor of his son, and Elizabeth could be relied on to bring up the child with completely opposite ideas to those of his parents.

Up to the age of eight Paul was a complete stranger to his parents: for his mother as well as his father he was a rival, and even a potential danger. In disinheriting the parents there was no certainty that Elizabeth would be satisfied with sending them back to Holstein. In the event of Paul's accession to the throne the fate of a claimant as incontestably legitimate as Peter would be sealed. The events that followed were to show that for Peter there was only one possible destiny.

Meanwhile, Elizabeth doted on baby Paul and looked after him as well as she could. Catherine loved him from a distance, but not very passionately because her thoughts were elsewhere. The Grand Duke ignored his existence altogether. The still open question of whether Paul was in fact the legitimate heir of the Romanov dynasty recurred time and time again. All the evidence suggests that he was not, and that he was known not to be, otherwise Catherine would surely not have dared to hint at it so broadly in her memoirs. However, there have been claims that Paul had an undeniable resemblance to the Grand Duke, physically as well as in character. On the first point the matter is debatable. True, they were both ugly, but Paul's face with its flat cheekbones, big slanting eyes, and small snub nose like a Pekinese is only very faintly reminiscent of the long, attenuated visage of his supposed father. The character resemblance, too, can just as well be explained by the similarity of the situations in which the two men found themselves, by Paul's desire to copy a father he idealized but never knew, and by the common ancestry of Peter and Catherine who were, after all, second cousins.

Whoever was his real father, young Paul was marked from birth by that heaviest of inheritances, a tottering throne waiting for the strongest to seize it.

Twenty-seven

❧❧❧❧❧❧❧❧❧❧❧

Love and Politics

It is doubtful if Catherine ever got over the shock which she sustained from the birth of her son and the neglect she experienced after her confinement. She, who had a right to the highest honor and regard, was treated like a mere tool whose use has been outworn, like a servant dismissed without so much as a thank-you. The sufferings of her pride stifled those of thwarted mother love in her heart.

The hundred thousand rubles with which they thought to pay her for her pains, and which they took back again a few days later, the jewels unworthy of a maidservant, the insulting dismissal of her lover, the marriage of her friend Princess Gargarina, which was hurried forward so she too would be out of reach of the Grand Duchess, and more than all this, the sheer physical exhaustion following her painful labor and the lack of care she had experienced—all this had plunged her into such a state of wretchedness that she swore never again to leave her apartments.

She read avidly. She read Voltaire's *Histoire Universelle*, Montesquieu's *Esprit des Lois* and the *Annals* of Tacitus, and it was her reading of this last book, she says, which brought about "a strange revolution" in her mind. The Roman historian's bitter, disillusioned pessimism suited her frame of mind. She admits: "I was beginning to see the black side of most things and to look for deeper and more heavily ingrained motives underlying the various interests in things as they appeared to me." She spent the winter of 1754 to 1755 in a tiny room leading off her apartment, driven out of her own bedchamber by the cold and the unbearable proximity of the Grand Duke, who did nothing but smoke, drink and create a hideous uproar with his menservants.

Between Christmas and Lent there was a continual round of festivities at court and in the city, "and all this was *still* on account of the birth of my son."[1] She was irritated by rejoicings from which she was excluded, and perhaps by the very existence of the son who brought her no joy. Sergei Saltykov (of whom the chancellor, faithful to his role as the lovers' protector, obtained news for her) had returned from Sweden and there was now talk of sending him as ambassador to Hamburg. He had come back but was far from ardent. Catherine arranged a meeting and went to a great deal of trouble to welcome him, but although she waited until three in the morning, he did not come.

It was clear now that she had nothing more to hope for from Sergei: he had failed to meet her, she says, "through lack of ardor and attentiveness to me, without any regard for what I had suffered for so long, solely on account of my fondness for him." She still loved him. She attributed her own disgrace to the scandal provoked by their love affair, and when she wrote to reproach him, he came back to her. "It was not difficult for him to soothe my feelings, because I myself was eager for it."[2] It was he who finally encouraged her to appear again in public.

But Catherine seems to have harbored no more illusions: she

had hardened herself against love and in future she would not be any man's plaything. She had had enough of figuring permanently in the light of a victim. "I resolved to make those who had caused me so much suffering know that I had no intention of letting anyone offend against me with impunity." She made up her mind that in future she would be hard, acid and mocking, and she succeeded, avenging herself in this way on her fickle lover, the insolent courtiers, and the spies and watchdogs of the Empress and the whole world. She was still young, still naïve in spite of her twenty-five years, and her enforced hardness still had something of an air of childish rebellion.

But the wound to her pride and her disappointment in love drove her to seek for power, what little power she could gain at court, and she launched into politics and intrigue.

She made her reappearance at court, dressed in a magnificent gown of blue velvet embroidered with silver, looking prettier than she ever had, with her head held high, her eyes bright and a hard smile on her lips, thoroughly resolved to return insult for insult and regard no one's feelings. For her first "victims" she chose the Shuvalovs, the guardians who had been imposed on her by Elizabeth. This family was then at the peak of its power, thanks to Ivan Shuvalov's liaison with the Empress. Catherine began by being doubly pleasant to all those who were hostile to the Shuvalovs and succeeded so well in heaping scorn on her enemies that, disconcerted and fearing for their future, they hastened to try and win the sympathies of the Grand Duke.

Peter tried to reason with his wife, clumsily as always. He poured out reproaches like a child, telling her that she was growing unbearably proud and unpleasant but failing to give any precise reasons. Catherine describes the scene, from which she emerged victorious; she had the upper hand throughout, since Peter was half or more than half drunk and was in any case too feeble to hold his own with anyone. Catherine dismissed him scornfully, telling him to go back to his bottle. She no longer had any feeling for the man beyond a kind of contemptuous pity, mingled with irritation, and treated him like a clumsy and tiresome colleague whom she was forced to include in her calculations and to whom she had to give the benefit of her advice.

Peter did still ask her advice, in spite of the "dreadful unkindness" of which he complained, in spite of the intrigues of his friends, the Holsteiner Brockdorffs and the Shuvalovs. He had a great deal of admiration for his wife's practical good sense and had once nicknamed her Madame Resourceful, but by mutual consent neither of them appeared any longer to consider themselves man and wife.

With her heart still smarting from her unfortunate passion for Sergei Saltykov, Catherine was now a ready victim for a new seducer, for, as she was later to write to the man who was the great love of her life, "it is my misfortune that my heart cannot rest content, even for an hour, without love." That was true, at least, from the time when she finally discovered love.

"I walked with my head held high, more like the leader of a strong faction than someone oppressed and humiliated."[3] As yet the "strong faction" did not exist except in her dreams, but the court was beginning to realize that the young Grand Duchess possessed character, that she might become a person to fear, or to treat with care. The Grand Duke, whom it was becoming difficult, on account of his age, to treat as an irresponsible child, abandoned himself more and more to his passion for his Duchy of Holstein, and brought councilors, soldiers and finally an "entire detachment" from that country. He was only able to see them furtively in small sections but he persisted so fiercely that in the end it became impossible to thwart his wishes: he was, after all, Duke of Holstein, and this title did give him certain rights. Astonishing as it seems, the Shuvalovs, whom he promised to reward for this service with his future favor, even allowed him with the greatest secrecy to import troops from Holstein. Now, although the Empress may have been unaware of this move of her nephew's, or at least have wearily closed her eyes to it, the people, and in particular the regiments of the guard stationed at Oranienbaum, the Grand Duke's residence, were only too well aware of the arrival of the German troops, and the effect on them was disastrous. Public opinion was alerted, and the officers of the guard grumbled openly that the "accursed Germans" were in the pay of the King of Prussia. The future Emperor was beginning to get the reputation of a traitor to Russia, something which amounted to a contradiction in terms. Catherine did everything she could to make it quite clear that she disapproved of this state of affairs, and managed things so that everyone was aware of her disapproval. She considered her husband's whim a "piece of childish imprudence . . . harmful to the Grand Duke's well-being."⁴

At last, caught up more and more in court intrigue, anxiously watching her own interests and mindful of public opinion, the Grand Duchess was beginning to think increasingly as a Russian and to take the interests of her new country to heart. This was already becoming known among the officers of the guard and in the regiments stationed around the capital; and since the Grand Duke was decidedly doing his best not to be and the soldiers needed someone to acclaim, she was already becoming popular. The Grand Duchess's patriotic feelings were also noted in foreign courts and Frederick II was beginning to fear he would lose an ally. He worked on the Grand Duchess through the classic intermediary of the *corps diplomatique*: not in this case the Prussian ambassador, which would have been unwise, but the English ambassador, since England was, in fact, on the point of concluding an alliance with Prussia.

The new English ambassador, Sir Charles Hanbury-Williams, called the "Chevalier Williams," came to Russia at Whitsun in the year 1775.⁵ Sir Charles at once set about the conquest of the Grand Duchess. He was a man of middle age and, despite his aristocratic charm, could not hope to win the young woman's heart himself, but he concentrated on gaining her confidence through his conversation, charming her by his wit and worldly wisdom and by subtle flattery. Finally, perhaps with the deliberate intention of pleasing her fancy, he introduced her to a young man whom he had brought with him. This young man was Count Stanislas Poniatowski, a young Polish nobleman with whom Sir Charles had formed a somewhat equivocal but undoubtedly perfectly innocent friendship.

Catherine's affair with Sergei Saltykov had already resulted in her being written down in the amorous catalogue of European courts as a "susceptible" young woman of whom a handsome youth might have high hopes. Her passion for Saltykov had been used to obtain the heir who had been too slow in making an appearance; now her emotional weaknesses were to be used for political ends. Hanbury-Williams's plan succeeded admirably as regards the Grand Duchess's heart, but its political results were somewhat dubious because Catherine enjoyed none of the influence with which she was credited.

Stanislas Poniatowski has since been reckoned one of the best-looking men of his time. At the age of twenty-three his extreme good looks, allied to a genuinely cultivated mind, refined manners, and a sweet and open disposition, must have made him irresistible. Stanislas belonged, through his mother, to the noble Czartoryski family who were the declared enemies of Augustus II of Saxony, the present ruler of Poland. Stanislas's father had formerly embraced the cause of Charles XII of Sweden and Stanislas Leczinski. Charles's defeat and Leczinski's exile had ruined the Poniatowski family, and Stanislas, although sincerely attached to his native country, had spent most of his life in foreign courts. Before he became friendly with Hanbury-Williams, the young man had lived in Paris and had for a long time been a frequent visitor to Madame Geoffrin's salon. He had taken a great liking to her and used to call her "Mother." The effect this boy, clad in all the seductive appeal of Parisian sophistication, must have produced on Catherine may well be imagined. Williams recommended his protégé to her, saying that the young man belonged to the pro-Russian party in Poland and hoped to make his fortune in Russia. Catherine considered that the handsome Pole was well worth her interest.

He was, in fact, all the more worthy because the Grand Duchess had recently learned that in Sweden and in Dresden, Sergei Saltykov had been paying court to "every woman he met."

Moreover Leon Naryshkin, who had played the part of go-between for Sergei so admirably, now constituted himself Stanislas's protector.

Leon had been a close friend of Catherine's for as long as four or five years, and a perfectly honorable one, despite the fact that he was in general a loose-living young man. He occupied a good position at court, chiefly because he was related to the Tsarina, and was a gentleman of the bedchamber at the young court. Catherine said of him later: "He was a natural Harlequin . . . he did not lack intelligence, he knew something about everything, and he had a unique way of looking at everything. He could sustain an argument on any subject, whether art or science . . . and by the time he had finished no one could make head or tail of the string of words that flowed from his mouth, so that in the end everyone would burst out laughing."[6] He was a strange young man with a talent for never taking anything seriously and making everything into a joke; he believed in nothing beyond the pleasure of laughing and enjoying himself in good company. He was goodhearted—a very good friend to Catherine. Deciding, quite logically, that only another lover could console the young woman for the loss of her first, he set himself to find her this new love. He was not at all averse to the Pole, but Catherine, who was in no way frivolous, still had no thought of betraying the man who had deserted her.

She merely records that Leon Naryshkin had been taken ill and had written her several elegant and witty letters which delighted her. Later on he admitted that the letters were in fact dictated by his "secretary," his new friend Stanislas Poniatowski, who "did not stir from his house." Stanislas, in his own memoirs, is less discreet. He recounts how Leon Naryshkin, finding him altogether too backward, practically locked him up in the Grand Duchess's bedchamber by force.

The fact is that for the first and last time in his life, Stanislas was desperately, passionately in love. For all his good looks and his wit, there was nothing of the adventurer about him; he was a pure, shy, sentimental boy, brought up by an extremely pious mother according to the strictest principles. He states in his memoirs that he had never known a woman before he met Catherine. He was romantic: Sir Charles had talked to him about the virtuous and unfortunate Russian Grand Duchess; he admired her before he had even met her, and the moment he saw her he was lost.

At this period Catherine was at the height of her beauty, or rather, in Stanislas's own rather muddled phrase, "She was at that time of beauty which is ordinarily the height for any woman who has one." He draws a conventional but charming picture of her: ". . . with her black hair she had a dazzling fairness, the liveliest coloring, very eloquent big blue eyes, a rather prominent mouth that seemed to call for kisses, perfect hands and arms, a slim waist, tall rather than short, with an easy gait that yet contained the most perfect nobility, and a laugh as gay as her humor."[7] But for the determination of his friend Leon Naryshkin, Stanislas would probably have been content to worship this dazzling, intelligent and exciting Grand Duchess from a distance, but a day came when his friend forced him into a position where he had no alternative but to conceal himself in Catherine's apartment or else risk compromising her seriously. He does not appear to have found it difficult to obtain a hearing. Taken by surprise, the young woman offered no resistance. "I cannot deny myself," the deserted lover wrote many years afterwards, "the pleasure of noting even the very clothes I found her in that day: a little gown of white satin with a light trimming of lace, threaded with pink ribbon for its only ornament."

"My whole life was devoted to her, much more sincerely than those who find themselves in such a situation can usually claim."[8] The young Pole was at the height of bliss. As for Catherine, she was certainly not averse to a new lover who was honest, tender and sincere, and three years younger than herself, but she was less deeply involved with him than she had been with her first love. Stanislas did not have Sergei Saltykov's defects, but neither did he possess the qualities which had made her love Saltykov.

With Sergei she had been the backward and rather foolish virgin in the hands of a professional seducer, while with Stanislas the roles may have been to some extent reversed. Catherine was no seductress, but she did possess a degree of experience in love, she was disillusioned, bitter, determined to let no one else play with her heart, and she was dealing with a boy who, for all his charm, seemed predestined to serve as her plaything. He was to be the only one who remembered their love. Catherine remains very discreet on the subject; she merely remarks that her favorite little dog, which was generally very suspicious of strangers, would leap fearlessly onto Stanislas's knee, and that this gave rise to some malicious comment.

Speaking of this period of her life, she confines herself to a narrative of court intrigue in which the handsome Pole is involved only by accident. She talks of preparations for war against Prussia, of her riding lessons, and of the Grand Duke's whims and love affairs, and she recounts with obvious pleasure her secret, nocturnal escapades with Leon Naryshkin. She would creep out furtively, disguised as a man, and jump into the faithful Leon's carriage, to be taken to his home. There she would meet Stanislas and Naryshkin's sister-in-law Anna. "The evening was spent in the maddest hilarity it is possible to imagine," and such escapades occurred two or three times a week throughout the winter of 1755 to 1756. There is not one word of love, and however understandable Catherine's discretion, it is obvious that Poniatowski did not occupy the exclusive place in her thoughts that Saltykov had done.

For her this new love was a pleasure, and one of a high order; but it was not the great love of her life. It did not make her forget more serious matters such as her position at court, the influence she could build up and the supporters she could attract. Politics had taken over, and it is hard to tell whether her close collaboration with Williams was due to the English ambassador's friendship with Stanislas, to her own desire to play a part in politics, to her admiration for the ambassador's intelligence, or to the pounds sterling which the obliging Sir Charles placed at her disposal through the intermediary of the English consul, Wolfe.

Should we regard the Grand Duchess at this time not simply as a woman who could be seduced but also as one who could be bought? Or was she really a sincere friend of Frederick II, only a more astute one than her husband, and trying, with the advice of Hanbury-Williams, to do what she could to help the King of Prussia? At the beginning, before the alliance between England and Prussia was concluded, she told Sir Charles that Frederick's heart was "the worst in the world"; but once the alliance had become a fact as a result of the treaty of Westminster, she showed herself favorably inclined toward the King of Prussia. She made contact with Field Marshal Apraxin, and the Grand Duchess's party succeeded in persuading the Empress that a winter campaign against Prussia would be disastrous. At the beginning of the Seven Years' War (which was not yet called by that name) Catherine was among those who considered the war untimely and useless, and she does not appear to have changed her mind as time went by. She kept up a secret correspondence with Field Marshal Apraxin, who was in command of the Russian army, and Frederick II even entertained hopes of bribing this officer through the intervention of the Grand Duchess.

But at the beginning of 1757 Catherine was writing to the chancellor Bestuzhev to "urge General Apraxin, once he has defeated the King of Prussia, to confine him within his former boundaries."[9] Clearly the Grand Duchess was playing a complicated, even somewhat inconsistent game, and in politics she was still only an amateur directed by her personal preferences and immediate interests. No matter: she was still serving her apprenticeship, and meanwhile she managed to make herself felt so successfully that the French minister for foreign affairs, the Abbé de Berny, wrote to the ambassador, the Marquis de l'Hôpital, that he was quite prepared to come to the assistance of the Grand Duke and Duchess if they needed money, and that he intended to do this "without the Empress's knowledge."[10] This was entirely due to its being common knowledge in France that the Grand Duchess was calling on the English ambassador for her personal expenses.

Catherine may have been as yet simply a woman who knew how to use her influence to assist her love affairs and obtain what money she needed, but in Russia and abroad the courts were watching her with interest, realizing that, sooner or later, she would be someone to be reckoned with.

Twenty-eight

ॱ॑ॕ॑ॕ॑ॕ॑ॕ॑ॕ॑ॕ॑ॕ॑ॕ॑ॕ

An Odd Couple

Catherine was in fact one of the most spendthrift of women; later she laid the blame for this on Elizabeth's taste for luxury. Coming to Russia as a poor relation, she had taken to spending money so lavishly that the Empress had to reproach her continually for the extent of her debts.

In her memoirs and in her letters Catherine makes numerous excuses for herself, recalling, on every possible occasion, the 70,000 rubles worth of debts left by her mother. It is true that when this frivolous and unfortunate woman died in 1760, the debt was found to have increased considerably; but before 1760, with her annual allowance of 30,000 rubles, occasional presents such as the 100,000 rubles she received when Paul was born, and "loans" from the English ambassador (on November 11, 1756, for instance, she had 44,000 rubles), Catherine would have been hard put to it to claim that it was her mother's debts which were crippling her budget.

She was a great gambler and on occasion lost more than half

her annual allowance at cards (in 1760 her losses reached the sum of 17,000 rubles).[1] Moreover she was simultaneously careless, optimistic and indifferent where money was concerned—money spent, at any rate, for she allowed herself to be robbed to the most exorbitant extent. Finally, she was generous almost to a fault, and in this extravagance she behaved more like a Russian than a German. She wanted to dazzle people; she loaded her entourage with presents; she arranged splendid entertainments and rivaled the Empress herself in the richness of her clothes. Then at the mildest reproof she excused herself by pleading her mother's 70,000 rubles and the expensive tastes of her ladies in waiting. Later her love of spending was to develop Homeric proportions, but even as early as this it was already one of her dominant vices. She knew very well, too, that money breeds money, and that spending it was the surest way of winning hearts. For the present she was chiefly out to enjoy herself, and she meant to give even her amusements the grandeur and brilliance that was singularly lacking in those of the Grand Duke.

The woman in love who used to slip out at night by a side door, disguised as a man, to meet her young lover was at the same time cultivating her friendship with Hanbury-Williams, conversing with diplomats and ministers, and making herself a reputation as a confirmed Anglophile. It was considered (still according to the Marquis de l'Hôpital) that "Mr. Williams had left a deep layer of English principles at the bottom of the Grand Duchess's heart and mind such as only time can erase."[2] Here the influence of Stanislas was only indirect. That young man was not sufficiently wide in his interests to let himself be contaminated by "English principles"; he was maneuvering to get his Czartoryski relations restored to their inheritance, and was plaguing the courts of Russia, Poland and Saxony with his attacks on King Augustus of Poland.

As for the Grand Duke, he was living carelessly, dividing his time between Petersburg and his residence at Oranienbaum where he had billeted his regiment of Holsteiners. He was completely "enfranchised," and no longer contented himself with sighing, more or less platonically, after various ladies of the court: he had mistresses, invited "singers" and loose women to his private suppers, and smoked and drank ceaselessly to such an extent that Catherine says "from then on he began to smell almost constantly of a mixture of wine and tobacco smoke, which became really unbearable to those who came near him." In fact, he appears to have found a remedy for his troubles in debauchery, and even more in wine than in the company of women. But ever since the birth of the Tsarevich Paul, he had been associating with one woman who could, all things considered, be called the woman in his life.

This woman was not a beauty or a great coquette but an ordinary young girl of very little account, stupid, ugly, slightly hunchbacked, with a squint. Her name was Elizabeth Vorontsova and she was a niece of Bestuzhev's rival, the vice-chancellor Michael Vorontsov. Elizabeth made up in spirit for what she lacked in beauty or brains; she loved laughing, drinking, shouting and singing, but otherwise there is little good to be said of her character. In the end Peter developed a sincere and permanent attachment to her and his choice may perhaps be explained by his inferiority complex: the Grand Duke might have hoped that an ugly girl would love him for himself, and apparently his hopes were not disappointed. But to begin with, Elizabeth Vorontsova was no more than "favorite sultana." She had rivals and occasionally quarreled with her lover. Once the Grand Duke even went so far as to ask his wife's advice on the way he should decorate his room to please Razumovsky's niece, Madame Teplova, and he is also known to have had an affair with a singer. The one he found too demanding (it was to Catherine again that he complained: "Just imagine, she's written me a letter four pages long and thinks I ought to read all that, and what's more, answer it") and the other, no doubt, too easy. It was always to Elizabeth Vorontsova that he returned, and she became his official mistress, living in hopes of the day when she might look forward to being something more.

At this point, paradoxically enough, the grand ducal couple

seem to have been on reasonably good terms. It is Stanislas Poniatowski who describes the state of their relationship: he tells how, disguised as a tailor, he went in a little covered carriage to visit his mistress at Oranienbaum where she was living with her husband. It was nighttime and in the middle of the woods his carriage met that of the Grand Duke, who was accompanied by Elizabeth Vorontsova and his suite, "all of them half drunk." The little carriage aroused some suspicion but everything passed off as well as could be imagined. In the end the Grand Duke, who liked Poniatowski, told him: "Aren't you a fool not to have taken me into your confidence in time?" He went further than this and actually burst into his wife's room, dragged her out of bed, hardly giving her time to put on a dressing gown, and took her to Stanislas, saying to Catherine, "Well, there he is! Now I hope everyone will be pleased with me."[3]

It was Peter who arranged meetings for the two lovers, bringing Stanislas into his room at Oranienbaum by means of a disused staircase. The four of them, the Grand Duke, Elizabeth Vorontsova, the Grand Duchess and Stanislas, would dine there together and after the meal Peter would withdraw with his mistress, saying to the other two, "There now, my children, you don't need me any more, I think." And when the young Pole was threatened with dismissal from court as a result of his imprudent behavior and diplomatic *gaffes*, it was to the Grand Duke, among others, that Catherine appealed in her efforts to avert the threat. In his own curiously tortuous way Peter did his best. He hinted to the Austrian ambassador, Count Esterhazy, that the French were secretly agitating for Poniatowski's removal, thus betraying their agreement with Austria, since Stanislas was well known for his Austrian sympathies. In the end the Grand Duke's overcomplicated maneuvers proved worse than useless, but his clumsiness does not appear to have been intentional.

We may wonder whether Catherine found her husband's attitude at all shocking or if, on the contrary, she approved of his cynical good-fellowship. As Stanislas does not appear to bear any grudge against Peter, we can assume that in this matter Catherine was in agreement with her husband. They seem to have come to a tacit understanding not to interfere with each other's affairs, and to this understanding Peter remained faithful until the day when, either through love of Vorontsova or love of power, he made up his mind to treat his wife as an enemy. Catherine for her part was rapidly freeing herself from the notions of morality which had been instilled into her as a child, though all her life she was to keep up her pretensions to being a moral woman.

Poniatowski has left us a portrait of Peter which even in its scornful irony is somehow touching: "Nature made him a mere poltroon, a guzzler, an individual so comic in all things that seeing him, one could not help thinking, 'Here is the very type of *Arlecchino finto principe*.' In one of the outpourings of his heart with which he frequently honored me he observed, 'See, though, how unhappy I am. If I had only entered into the service of the King of Prussia I would have served him to the best of my ability. By this present time I should, I am confident, have had a regiment and the rank of major general, and perhaps even of lieutenant general. But far from it: instead they brought me here and made me Grand Duke of this damnable country.' And then he railed against the Russian nation in his customary ridiculous manner, yet at times really very agreeably, for he did not lack a certain kind of wit. He was not stupid, but mad, and as he was fond of drink, this helped to addle his poor brains even further."[4] What Stanislas took for a comic trait and a sign of madness, Peter's regret at having inherited the Russian Empire rather than serving as an officer in Frederick II's army, shows, on the contrary, that the unfortunate Grand Duke was not devoid of common sense. Stanislas himself was one day to become a king, to the greater misfortune of his country and his own unhappiness, and yet he perhaps never understood that not all heads are made to wear a crown.

Meanwhile Peter, fenced in by his determination to ignore all those around him, his adoptive country and his future obligations, was immersing himself ever more deeply in every resource open to the weak and escapist. He soaked himself in drink and in the society of people who were socially and intellectually his inferiors, and retreated completely into a world of his own making. It is Catherine who most cruelly exposes her husband's pointless boasts: he even went so far as to claim that *when his father was alive* he had held a military command and had cleared the "gypsies" out of Holstein. In his mind the time when his father was alive had become a kind of halcyon period, but at that time he had been less than ten years old. Catherine calls him a liar, but this kind of thing does not even deserve to be called lying.

"If the Empress should die," wrote the Marquis de l'Hôpital on November 1, 1757, "we shall see some sudden revolution, for the Grand Duke will never be allowed to come to the throne and will surely be prevented." On November 30 he wrote: "The Empress has plans for Paul Petreowitz [*sic*], if she lives long enough to bring him up."[5] Catherine, however, observes that from 1749 onward the Grand Duke had shown a great eagerness to reign. How was he to reign, one may ask, when he was doing everything he could to make himself detested? It is arguable that the explanation of Peter's feelings is to be found in the Grand Duke's confidences to Poniatowski: he hated Russia and only wanted to reign in order to be rid of his aunt's control. He was nearly thirty, but his character was still so infantile that even ambition was beyond him.

The fact is that there was a very real threat: people at court were talking, secretly but earnestly, of the possibility of putting little Paul on the throne and sending his parents back to Holstein. For Catherine such a solution would have been a catastrophe. She had been preparing herself for her role of Empress of Russia for thirteen years; was she now to lose everything in favor of a child which she had brought into the world only to see him taken away from her? She had won herself solid support in Russian political circles: the chancellor Bestuzhev was now among her friends; he helped her, intervened on behalf of her lovers, and she kept up a confidential correspondence with him. She had established friendly relations with the head of the army, Field Marshal Apraxin, with whom by the chancellor's connivance she was secretly corresponding. She was already thinking of leaving herself one way out, which was to have herself appointed regent, or at least a member of a council of regency, should the Grand Duke be deprived of his rights to the throne.

The Grand Duke himself she treated more and more like a younger brother to be advised, guided and occasionally scolded, whose confidences she had to listen to and whose love affairs she must approve. Sometimes she would also try to force a rupture with a mistress who was gaining too much ascendancy. Peter no doubt believed that by tolerating his wife's lovers he was earning the right to complete freedom himself. He was not content with openly courting his wife's ladies in waiting; he made her listen to the progress of his affairs and would sometimes ask her advice. Everything Catherine allows us to see of their relationship at this point indicates that the Grand Duke still felt a trust in her that he accorded to no one else, not even to his great favorite Brockdorff, a man who did his best to widen the rift between Peter and his wife.

Catherine gave her husband honest or at least well-meant assistance in the affairs of Holstein. She did so well, and succeeded so well in penetrating the fiscal, administrative, judicial and other complications which put such panic into Peter's idle brain, that ever afterward it was always Catherine the Grand Duke sent for whenever his secretary, Zeiss, came to present him with any papers to do with the affairs of his duchy for signature. As a sensible woman, Catherine regarded this occasional chore as good training for both her husband and herself, and she told him as much. She said that he should regard this task merely "as a specimen of the kind of thing he would have to control one day, when the Russian Empire fell to his lot." Peter promptly "repeated once again what he had told me very often . . . that he did not feel that he was born for Russia: that he did not suit the Russians or the Russians him, and that he was convinced he would die in Russia."[6]

Catherine succeeded in raising his morale so effectively that she managed to persuade him to take an interest in Russian affairs. The Grand Duke asked Shuvalov to request the Empress to allow him to attend her conferences of ministers. Elizabeth was actually perfectly willing to agree to her nephew's wish, but it was arranged that the Grand Duke should attend only those meetings where she was present in person. She went with him several times, but after that neither she nor he attended again. Elizabeth only interested herself in business by fits and starts, and preferred to spend her days in sleeping and her nights in revelry. Thus her nephew's shy attempt to take an interest in the affairs of the country he was one day to govern fell flat. Later on, he made such objectionable use of his right to attend ministerial conferences that Elizabeth's lack of enthusiasm becomes highly understandable.

One day when the Empress was questioning Catherine about the Grand Duke's life, the younger woman started to talk about the affairs of Holstein and immediately perceived that her artless confidence had produced the most unfortunate effect in Elizabeth's mind. The poor Grand Duchess, who had done nothing but faithfully perform her duties as the Grand Duke's wife and a future ruler, began to see increasingly clearly that she was living on top of a volcano. The Grand Duke was not trusted and neither was she. She racked her brains trying to understand the intrigues which were going on around her and to guess what enemies were working for her downfall.

She did not lack enemies, and the most dangerous was undoubtedly Elizabeth herself, or rather the insoluble situation created by the Grand Duke's unfortunate character. Not only the Empress but the court, the army and public opinion in both capitals were living in a state of growing anxiety. A future with Peter as Emperor was beginning to seem more and more a disaster to be averted at all costs, but there seemed no practicable way of avoiding it.

Russia, faithful to her alliance with Austria, had been at war with Prussia since September 1756. It was the first war of Elizabeth's reign, and the Russian generals, who still remembered with pride the victories of Peter the Great, were not ill-pleased that their long period of inactivity had come to an end at last. But money was lacking for the army as it was for everything else. The troops were ill-equipped and the men badly trained, and Field Marshal Apraxin, who though an old and experienced general was also a slow and timorous one, dared not begin operations until the spring of 1757. Russia was sending her armies against the greatest general of the age, against the best-equipped and best-disciplined army in Europe, at a time when the Empress's precarious state of health meant a strong likelihood that the throne would soon fall to Frederick's most fervent admirer.

Faced with the necessity for an offensive which would restore Russia's prestige among her allies and his own with the Empress, Bestuzhev appealed to the Grand Duchess and asked her to write herself to the Field Marshal and make him understand that she at least was in no way pro-Prussian. To please the chancellor, Catherine did so. She wrote secretly, without the Empress's knowledge, in order to give Apraxin confidence. She had written him other letters too, although she was to swear later on that there were only three of these, all highly inoffensive. This may be true, but she was certainly forced into playing a double game, because her great friend Hanbury-Williams was still on the scene with his "enlightened" counsel and his offers of money, to encourage her to be nice to the King of Prussia. Moreover, she too admired Frederick.

Twenty-nine

❧❧❧❧❧❧❧❧❧❧❧❧❧❧

New Threats

It was at this point that the old chancellor, despairing of ever obtaining the good will of the Grand Duke, sent the Grand Duchess a secret memorandum containing a proposal that on the death of the Empress, Catherine should be included in the government and Bestuzhev himself given supreme command of the regiments of the guard, as well as of the ministries of war, foreign affairs and the navy. Catherine rejected these proposals as unrealistic. Already she may have been hoping for more.[1]

But the secret correspondence into which she had gradually allowed herself to be dragged was beginning to look increasingly like a plot being hatched behind the Empress's back. Elizabeth undoubtedly had her suspicions. She was only forty-seven but she was haunted by the fear of approaching death. She was beginning to show signs of the suspiciousness of elderly people when they think those around them are already burying them before their time, and become doubly watchful because they are afraid of being set on one side.

The Russian armies had finally unleashed a vigorous attack on the Prussians. In July 1757 they had taken Memel and in August they inflicted a crushing defeat on the enemy at Gross-Jägersdorf. This was great news for the whole country, or at least for that class of it which took some part or some interest in public affairs. The Russians' national pride, always lively and sensitive, had badly needed this confirmation of Russia's strength. The victory was celebrated in the capitals by *Te Deums*, festivities and popular rejoicing. The Grand Duchess took care to show her patriotic sentiments by giving a great entertainment in the gardens of Oranienbaum and at the same time did what she could to assuage the Grand Duke's disappointment. For Peter the defeat of the invincible Prussian army was a terrible blow. It is open to question whether Catherine's delight was as sincere as she pretended. On the whole it seems likely. Catherine was a soldier's daughter, and as professional soldiers place their swords at the disposal of foreign kings and serve them faithfully, so she set herself to serve her new country with all the loyalty of which she was capable. She would never be guilty of German nationalism.

At all events, joy soon turned to disappointment. Instead of following up his victory, the Field Marshal retreated, and so precipitously that his retreat took on all the appearance of a rout. There was great scandal. Apraxin was recalled on the spot and replaced by his lieutenant, a German named Fermor.

Everyone, as Catherine herself says, was looking for what was behind it. It looked simple enough on the face of it: the Field Marshal, having received reports that the Empress was gravely ill, had believed that she was dying and had ordered the retreat with the object of pleasing the Grand Duke because he, like everyone else, knew that the Empress's death would be the signal for the immediate end of the war. Obviously Elizabeth could not forgive this speculation on her own death, and whatever may have been Apraxin's real reasons, she believed he had been guilty of treason and ordered the old general to retire to his estates and await his trial. Then she set about hunting for his accomplices.

General Fermor, who succeeded Apraxin, at once very decently tried to clear his predecessor by pointing out that the soldiers had not been paid, that they were short of weapons and clothes and were dying of hunger. By prodigies of courage and endurance they had succeeded in beating the enemy, but the effort had proved too much of a strain and Apraxin had found himself compelled to withdraw in order to avoid disaster. Being unable to supply his troops in enemy territory, he had had no alternative but to retreat as fast as possible to the Russian border. But neither Elizabeth nor the Russian court, nor any foreign court, could apparently understand that it was possible for men to die of hunger, or that lack of food could be an argument of any weight in military strategy. Even Catherine herself twenty years later could not understand it, and did not venture to excuse her friend Apraxin's conduct.

Moreover, his imprudent behavior had exposed Elizabeth personally to the greatest danger. In seeking out "traitors" the first people Elizabeth would suspect would be the Grand Duke and Duchess, and the Grand Duchess rather than the Grand Duke because he was too closely watched on account of his known convictions to be able to make the smallest move in favor of his idol Frederick II. Catherine could very easily be suspected of intrigue and hypocrisy.

Catherine was carrying her second child at the time and her pregnancy was already so far advanced that she no longer appeared at court. This time, of course, the birth of her child was not a great event looked forward to impatiently by the whole nation. Indeed, there was so much gossip about it that the Grand Duke himself, not to be thought stupid, felt obliged to declare before witnesses: "I don't know how it is that my wife becomes pregnant." Admittedly he was a more than tolerant husband, but this could not go on forever, and his preference for Elizabeth Vorontsova was becoming more and more marked. Catherine was more than hurt by these aspersions on her honor; she was terrified. She told her friends, and Leon Naryshkin in particular: "Make him swear an oath that he has not lain with his wife, and tell him that if he swears such an oath you will go and tell it to Alexander Shuvalov as Grand Inquisitor of the Empire." Either because he feared a scandal or because he really could not swear that the child was not his own, Peter refused. Catherine does not commit herself one way or the other, but she does say: "This remark of the Grand Duke's, uttered so imprudently, made me very cross."[2]

In fact the Grand Duke was now in possession of a dreadful weapon against her. It made no difference whether he was flagrantly and notoriously unfaithful to her: if he accused her of misconduct, she was lost. In her inmost heart, she came to a decision: "It was a matter of either perishing with him or through him, or of saving myself and my children and perhaps the state from the catastrophe which the prince's moral and physical qualities seemed all too likely to provoke." It is clear that she had no desire to perish, either *with* Peter or *through* him.

At this period, however, Peter was still trying to show his wife that he looked on her as a friend: true, he was drunk at the time and chose the most ridiculous way of showing it, but the gesture does in itself suggest that the Grand Duke may have retained more affection for his wife than she perhaps believed. When Catherine felt her first labor pains coming on, the Grand Duke was informed, and he burst into his wife's room at two o'clock in the morning, dressed in the uniform of the Holstein guards, booted and spurred and wearing an "enormous sword" at his side. He announced solemnly that the duty of *an officer of Holstein* (he took care not to say a Grand Duke of Russia) was to "defend the ducal household against all its enemies according to his oath," and he added that "it is in a crisis that one knows who are one's real friends."[3] The Grand Duke's enormous sword was obviously not much help against the pangs of childbirth and in the end Catherine, Madame Vladislavova and the midwife managed to persuade him to leave the room, insisting that the Empress would be horrified if she arrived to find her nephew clad in the detested uniform of Holstein.

After a protracted labor, Catherine was delivered in the presence of the Empress and the Grand Duke (who had changed his clothes) of a girl and expressed a wish to call her Elizabeth. The Empress chose the name Anne in memory of her elder sister, the Grand Duke's mother. This time Peter seemed delighted at becoming a father and gave orders for great celebrations, not only in his own apartments in Petersburg but also in Holstein.

This second child, like the first, was promptly taken away from its mother, but Catherine was resigned in advance and did not suffer too much. She did, however, make arrangements to have a large screen placed in her room and installed behind it "a sofa, some mirrors, portable tables and a few chairs." Here she could entertain her most intimate friends in private without the knowledge of the Empress or the Shuvalovs. Whenever one of her watchdogs appeared, the screen was drawn across, and if anyone happened to ask what it concealed they were told that it was the commode.[4] Thanks to this useful stratagem, Catherine was able to spend her weeks of enforced idleness very cheerfully. She still had Stanislas Poniatowski with her since, although the Polish court had long been demanding his recall, he had managed to delay his departure on the excuse of illness, hoping to put off indefinitely the moment of parting from the woman he adored and the child he had every reason to believe was his own.

In spite of the chivalrous manifestations of delight on the part of the Grand Duke, Poniatowski was so widely believed to be the father of Princess Anne that on the day of her churching, Catherine found herself alone in the chapel with Alexander Shuvalov the only other person present.

The handsome Stanislas departed at the end of 1758 but Catherine's heart did not break: new dangers were threatening her, and she had no time to abandon herself to her grief. Stanislas had been nothing more for her than a happy, tender relaxation from the cares and intrigues which were occupying her thoughts to an ever increasing extent.

Preparations for Apraxin's trial were going forward with the slowness habitual to Russian trials, and Catherine was living in a state of terror as a result. The chancellor Bestuzhev, whose credit had dwindled considerably since the semirupture between Russia and England and the alliance concluded with France, was also afraid of being implicated in the so-called treason. The allies, France and Austria, were infuriated by the Field Marshal's withdrawal and attributed his action to Bestuzhev's intrigues. The old chancellor's anti-French sentiments were well known and the French and Austrian ambassadors were busy trying to oust him from the Empress's favor. There was some truth in their accusations, and obviously Bestuzhev, seeing that his power was declining, was flirting with the young court far beyond the limits allowed by the touchy and suspicious Empress. It was true that any moment Elizabeth might succumb to another stroke, and that the Russian army, which had been left by Austria to carry the full weight of the war, was short of proper equipment and supplies and only stood up to the strain of the campaign thanks to its soldiers' exceptional powers of endurance. It was true, too, that the chancellor had firm English sympathies and was trying to maintain himself in power by holding the balance between today's adversaries and the allies who through the whim of a new emperor might become tomorrow's enemies.

The man who for fifteen years had directed Russia's foreign policy and made the whole court tremble before him, who had earned the implacable hatred of the courts of France and Prussia, was now paying the price for his past glory. He was losing the support of the Austrian court and, with the departure of Williams, that of England also. Practically everyone at court was his enemy. The vice-chancellor, Michael Vorontsov, eager to step into his shoes, and the brothers Peter and Alexander Shuvalov, long the opponents of the chancellor, were all intriguing with foreign ambassadors, persuading the allies that Bestuzhev alone was responsible for the so-called failure in the Russian army, that he was in the pay of the English, or even of the Prussians. Moreover, in a confidential interview with the Empress the Austrian ambassador, Count Esterhazy, succeeded in making her believe that her chancellor was betraying her in favor of the young court, hinting that he and the Grand Duchess must have sent Field Marshal Apraxin secret orders, and that the retreat of the autumn of 1757 was therefore nothing less than treason.

It is easy to suspect treason in every setback or failure on a military level, especially when it concerns an ally. Elizabeth listened to Count Esterhazy's insinuations because her enfeebled health made her fear the worst: it was not for nothing that she made the unsleeping Chukhov keep watch outside her door. She remembered the way she herself had seized power, and she had watched on the night when, upon her orders, soldiers had dragged the Regent Anna Leopoldovna from her bed and taken her off to prison.

Sensing his danger, the Grand Duke, who was first to be threatened since logically his only reason for betraying the Empress would be to place himself on the throne, hastily set about cultivating the friendship of the Shuvalovs, and also that of Michael Vorontsov, the uncle of his beloved Elizabeth. Acting on the advice of these men, he went in person to see his aunt and succeeded in melting her heart by asking her forgiveness for his errors of conduct for which, he claimed, Bestuzhev's wicked counsels were alone responsible. He knew, or his advisers knew, that the Empress was at that time so incensed against the chancellor that blackening the old man was a sure way to please her. There is no doubt that Peter would have been capable of selling his best friends in order to save himself, and he had never loved Bestuzhev.

With Catherine it was different. She was too loyal to betray a friend and she could not have done so even if she had wanted to, because she was already far too deeply compromised. Furthermore she was kept in ignorance of what was brewing: she had only recently recovered from her confinement—custom did not permit her to reappear in public until six weeks after the birth —and saw no one apart from her happy little group of faithful friends. Of these, Poniatowski had long been discredited and threatened with dismissal, the ebullient Leon Naryshkin was the last man to concern himself with politics, and Leon's sister-in-law, Anna Naryshkina, and Madame Siniavina were both young women much more interested in enjoying themselves than in meddling in intrigues.

Catherine was a naturally cheerful person who much pre-

ferred laughing and talking in good company to indulging her
vanity or dressing up in fine clothes, and provided she had two
or three amusing young people around her she found it easy to
be happy. So she thoroughly enjoyed herself during the enforced
retirement which followed her confinement, but without forgetting that she was more or less officially in disgrace. The
court avoided her. It did not even occur to her to ask to be
allowed to keep the newborn child who was almost openly
regarded as a bastard. Apraxin's trial was still pending, and
since torture was usually allowed as a method of interrogation,
he might easily be persuaded to compromise her seriously.

Then one Sunday, February 15, 1758, when the young court
was to celebrate a double wedding, Catherine received a short
note from Poniatowski telling her, in the greatest secrecy, that
Bestuzhev had been arrested the previous day, and with him
her jeweler Bernardi, an adjutant named Elagin, and Adodurov.
Catherine decided, with a good deal of understatement, that "I
could not flatter myself that this affair did not concern me more
closely than it appeared."

The chancellor's arrest had been kept a secret from her.
Stanislas had taken a serious risk in warning his mistress and
giving her time to make hasty preparations. She had been
expecting Bestuzhev's disgrace for a long time, without for a
moment considering severing her connection with him, either
wholly or for the sake of appearances. The arrest of the three
other people mentioned in the letter proved that the Grand
Duchess was now being aimed at directly. Bernardi was her
personal jeweler and more than that: besides undertaking to
deliver certain letters of the Grand Duchess's to their destina-
tions, he had acted as an intermediary to the court in London
in order to collect the subsidies Catherine was being offered
and on occasion demanding (although this is a fact she is careful
not to admit in her memoirs). Elagin, formerly one of Razumovsky's adjutants, was a close friend of Stanislas. "He had,"
says Catherine, "always shown a marked zeal and attentiveness
toward me" (such attentiveness, indeed, that they were believed

to be lovers). Adodurov, as we already know, was Catherine's Russian teacher, who had always remained attached to her, and three years earlier she had obtained Bestuzhev's interest for him.

Consequently Catherine dressed and went to Mass "with a dagger in her heart." Not a word was said to her, and she dared question no one. She tried to put on a good face during the wedding celebrations—one of the grooms was in fact her friend Leon Naryshkin—but toward evening she could stand it no longer and plucked up courage to speak to Marshal Trubetskoi, who was one of those on the special commission set up to examine the Bestuzhev affair. "Have you found more crimes than criminals, or have you more criminals than crimes?" she asked him. The marshal replied: "As to crimes, we are still looking for them."[5]

The next day a note was brought to her from Bestuzhev. He begged her to be calm, as he had had time to "throw everything in the fire." She managed to smuggle a note back to the old man couched in exactly the same terms: she too had "burned everything." By this she meant the letters written to her by the chancellor, and in particular the one mentioning his proposal of associating her in the government. She tried to communicate with the prisoner through devoted servants and obliging guards, and Poniatowski, seeking a way to prove his devotion to his mistress, took an active part in this secret correspondence— somewhat too active, in fact, for he was suspected and the attempt was soon discovered.

Preparations for the trial were still going forward laboriously, since there does not really seem to have been any serious failure in the exercise of his duties of which the chancellor could be accused, and there was talk of the crime of high treason. Bestuzhev was said to have intended to "sow discord between the Empress and their Imperial Highnesses," a sufficiently vague crime and not an easy one to prove. But while they were still looking for accusations against him, and seeing that the most obvious motive for the impeachment—and the true one—was the secret understanding between the chancellor and the Grand

Duchess, Catherine was now living in a state of constant apprehension for herself, her friends and her servants. One day she summoned her valet Chkurin and ordered him to collect all her account books, papers, letters, and "anything which might look like a paper of any kind" and made a great holocaust of them in the fireplace.[6]

She regarded the threat so seriously that she gave up seeing her friends for fear of bringing trouble on them, and she hardly dared appear at court for fear people would turn their backs on her. The Grand Duke himself, she said, pretended not to know her, not out of hostility but simply because he dared not speak to her. In fact, she was so obviously in disgrace that a rumor began to spread to the effect that she was on the point of being sent back where she came from.

In her memoirs she defends Bestuzhev fiercely, since he was guilty only of having put his trust in her. She explains the situation clearly enough: the Marquis de l'Hôpital bore a grudge against the chancellor for his English sympathies and Count Esterhazy thought he was not being sufficiently energetic in furthering the interests of Austria. The allied ambassadors put pressure on the vice-chancellor Michael Vorontsov and the Shuvalovs. While Count Bestuzhev thought "like a patriotic man and was not easy to lead," Vorontsov and the Shuvalovs were "open to suggestion by the two ambassadors." Catherine reports that fifteen days before Bestuzhev's arrest, the Marquis de l'Hôpital had presented Vorontsov with an ultimatum: "If you have not removed the grand chancellor within fifteen days, I shall have to address myself to him and in future deal directly with him alone." Vorontsov "took fire" at this and hastened to demonstrate to Elizabeth that "her glory was being adversely affected by Count Bestuzhev's reputation in Europe."[7]

Even when she was an empress and thought herself an even better ruler than she was in reality, Catherine could still pay nothing but tribute to the farsightedness of the old man who had been able to see, in the fragile and somewhat frivolous Grand Duchess, a woman capable of taking the reins of government into her own hands. He had hoped, it is true, to govern with her and through her, but he had certainly counted on the Grand Duke's being eliminated in one way or another; clearly he could not share his plans with the Empress. It was in this way that a conspiracy, or the preliminary sketch for a conspiracy, developed which looked to Elizabeth like treason, although it was in actual fact directed against the Grand Duke. The Empress was unable to resign herself coolly to the idea that her own death was considered to be so close, so imminent that she was already being discounted and men were already making plans for a future which did not include her.

She preferred to believe in treason pure and simple. The Grand Duchess, who was after all a German, had been bought by Prussia through the intermediary of England. The chancellor, whether because he had been bribed or because he wanted to ingratiate himself with the Grand Duchess, was playing the Prussian game. The Grand Duke counted for nothing in the intrigue and so did not disturb Elizabeth for the moment. However dissatisfied she was with him, she could still see no way of disinheriting him in favor of a minor.

Thirty

❦❦❦❦❦❦❦❦❦❦❦❦

The Turning Point

Catherine's memoirs came to an abrupt end after a very detailed description of an incident which was perhaps one of the most important events in her life. Her entire future was at stake and she knew it. She laid her cards on the table and risked everything on one throw. Once she had won this she had only to follow the path she had laid down for herself and which, she claims, was forced on her contrary to her own wishes.

She is looking for excuses for herself and she finds them, for her subject matter is the elimination of the Grand Duke and her own rise to power. By the time she wrote her memoirs, she already knew how the story would end.

She does not say exactly what it was that she was accused of. No one says, but everyone knew, and the Grand Duke first of all, kept informed as he was by the enemies of Bestuzhev and Catherine. Catherine remarks, as though by accident, on her husband's sudden hatred for her, a hatred which she says was cultivated by the Shuvalov clan and the Vorontsova girl. She does not say what she is accused of and instead it is she who makes accusations. She counterattacked. Seeing her friends in prison and knowing herself on the point of being convicted, through their confessions, of venality, of conspiring with the enemy and finally of plotting against her own husband, she made up her mind to write a letter to the Empress.

"I set myself to write my letter to the Empress in Russian, and I made it as pathetic as I could."

In this letter, "I began by thanking her for all the favor and kindness she had shown me on my arrival in Russia, adding that, unhappily, events proved that I had not deserved them, since I had drawn on myself the hatred of the Grand Duke and her Majesty's very obvious displeasure; that in view of my wretchedness and the fact that I was dying of boredom in my room, where I was deprived of even the most innocent amusements, I begged her instantly to put an end to my miseries by dismissing me, in whatever fashion seemed best to her, and sending me back to my family; that as for my children, since I never saw them, even though I lived with them in the same house, it had become a matter of indifference to me whether I stayed under the same roof with them or several hundred leagues away; that I knew she took such care of them as surpassed that which my feeble abilities would permit me to give them; that I dared entreat her to continue in this, and that in this assurance I would spend the rest of my life among my own family, praying to God for her, for the Grand Duke, for my children and for all those who had been kind or unkind to me, but that the state of my health had been reduced through grief to such a condition that it was necessary for me to do what I could at least to save my life, and to this end I begged her to allow me to go to a spa, and from there to my family."[1]

Inwardly triumphant, she handed this letter to Alexander Shuvalov, who was her worst adversary at the time and whom she had already given to understand that she was longing only to return to her own country. She was perfectly well aware that by this move she was putting her enemies' backs to the wall, and that once faced with the alternative of sending the Grand Duchess away, Elizabeth would be forced to make a decision. The Empress would certainly recoil from a family scandal of this kind, and the threat of departure was a piece of blackmail from which much was to be gained.

She made the Grand Duke's and the Shuvalov's refusal to allow her to go to the theater serve as a pretext for her decision to write the letter. Her first victory came when Shuvalov hastily made a carriage ready for her. Catherine went to the play and noticed with a malicious pleasure that the Empress was not there. "I think my letter prevented her." All she had to do now was wait. She waited, with growing impatience, seeking every opportunity of disconcerting and disarming her opponents.

It was now the first week in Lent. Catherine "performed her devotions," which meant that according to the Russian custom, she spent a great part of her day in church, for the services during the first week were very long. This proof of her attachment to the Orthodox faith does not appear to have disarmed her enemies, for not long afterward Madame Vladislavova, to whom she had been very close for four years, was taken away from her, giving her a fresh excuse for a demonstration of grief. She announced to those around her that "being tired of suffering and seeing that my patience and gentleness serve for nothing except to bring everything that concerns me from bad to worse," she could only promise Madame Vladislavova's replacement "all possible ill-treatment, even blows." Otherwise she lived on her nerves, refused to eat and wept incessantly, until her women grew alarmed (for she was very well loved by her servants) and began to fear for her health, even indeed for her life.

At this point she feigned illness, and indeed, as a result of fear and nervous tension, she really was ill. She took to her bed and demanded a confessor. Admittedly the confessor she asked for was the Empress's own, who happened to be the uncle of one of her waiting women, Catherine Ivanovna. Forewarned by his niece, he took the initiative in the plan, with the object of acting as intermediary between Elizabeth and Catherine. It was not an easy matter to obtain an audience with the Empress, but the Grand Duchess simulated illness so well and called so convincingly for a confessor, that she carried her point despite the opposition of Shuvalov, who at first would hear of nothing but a doctor.

The priest, prejudiced in her favor from the outset, agreed to everything she said, and going to the Empress, painted the young woman's sufferings in the most vivid colors. He urged her to grant the Grand Duchess the interview she was expecting, which was to decide her fate. The cunning and tenderhearted old man also encouraged Catherine to persevere in her supposed desire to return to her own country, knowing that she would never be sent away, since the Empress could not justify such a step "in the eyes of the public."

At last the long-awaited day came: Elizabeth ordered Alexander Shuvalov to inform the Grand Duchess that she would be received "the following night," for Elizabeth was an incorrigible night owl.

Catherine summoned up all her strength, left her bed, dressed and waited for midnight when Shuvalov was to come and fetch her and take her to the Empress. Worn out and suffering from nervous exhaustion, the young woman went to sleep on a sofa. When they finally came for her, it was half past one in the morning.

She was to hear her sentence. This was the only kind of trial to which a person of her rank could be subjected, but Catherine had at least managed to make Elizabeth understand that she would not let herself be condemned without a hearing.

The arguments that she set out thirty years afterward in describing this incident may not have been those she had actually prepared to use on the Empress, but she meant to make it clear to herself and to posterity that she had acted within her rights, that she was totally innocent, and that she was the most loyal and sincere as well as the most noble, kind and sensitive young woman that ever was. Her only fault was that she did not love her husband because he had never been able or even wished to make her love him. But that this husband was altogether contemptible she was the first to recognize. "She [Elizabeth] knew it so well that it was already many years since she had been able to spend so much as a quarter of an hour in his company without being moved to disgust, anger or grief, and that when he was mentioned in her presence she burst into bitter tears and talked of the misfortune of having such an heir." Was evidence required, Catherine had the proof in her hands, since she afterward had access to Elizabeth's correspondence. On one occasion Elizabeth wrote: "My nephew has displeased me extremely," and on another: "My nephew, devil take him, is a monster."

All things considered, Catherine contemplated her dismissal (she says) with "a very philosophical eye"; she was able to rise above vulgar feelings. "Happiness and misery are in each person's heart and mind; if you feel unhappy, then rise above this unhappiness and act in such a way that your happiness depends on no single event." Let no one believe that she was greedy for power and grandeur. For fifteen years she had done nothing but act as the perfect wife of the most unworthy husband, she had "given him the most sincere devotion that a friend or even a servant can give to his friend or master," for lack of a tenderness which he did not deserve she had lavished good advice on him, and it was not her fault that God had made her a woman and a desirable one, and therefore exposed to temptation.

She claimed to be "a frank and loyal knight with a mind in-

Peter the Great, from the portrait by A. Gelder

I

Princess Elizabeth Petrovna (the future Empress Elizabeth) at sixteen,
by I. N. Nikitin, about 1720

II

Princess Sophia Augusta Fredericka of Anhalt-Zerbst
(the future Empress Catherine II), by Anna-Rosina Litchewski, 1742

III

Grand Duke Peter Feodorovich and Grand Duchess Catherine Alexeievna
when betrothed, by G. C. Groot, 1744 (or early 1745)

IV

Empress Elizabeth Petrovna, by P. Rotari, 1745-50

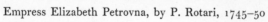

V

Empress Elizabeth Petrovna in a black domino,
copy by G. C. Groot of his portrait done in 1748

Ivan Ivanovich Shuvalov, favorite of the Empress Elizabeth,
by D. G. Levitzky

VII

Grand Duchess Catherine Alexeievna, by G. C. Groot, about 1745

VIII

Count Alexei Petrovich Bestuzhev-Ryumin, chancellor, by Serdukov

Grand Duchess Catherine Alexeievna on horseback,
by G. C. Groot, about 1748

Grand Duchess Catherine Alexeievna,
by G.C. Groot, about 1748–50

Tsarevich Paul Petrovich
when three or four years old,
painter unknown

Gregory Orlov, by F. S. Rokotov

XII

Empress Catherine Alexeievna in mourning dress
(after Elizabeth's death and when pregnant with the
future Count Bobrinsky), painter unknown, spring 1762

Grand Duke Paul Petrovich, by F. S. Rokotov, 1761

Empress Catherine II, by S. Torelli, between 1762 and 1765

Marble bust of Prince Gregory Alexandrovich Potemkin,
by Shubin, 1791

XVI

Potemkin, Prince of Taurida

XVII

Empress Catherine II wearing the uniform of
the Preobrazhensky Regiment, by Erickssen, 1762

Catherine II walking in the Tsarskoie Selo Park, by Borovikovsky

XIX

Grand Duke Paul Petrovich, by F. S. Rokotov, about 1765

XX

Alexander Dmitrievich Lanskoi, favorite of Catherine II,
by D. G. Levitzky, 1782

XXI

Empress Catherine II, by F. S. Rokotov, 1779

Catherine II, Legislatrix, by D. G. Levitzky, 1783

Bartolommeo Rastrelli, famous Italian architect
who worked for Elizabeth and Catherine,
by P. Rotari, before 1762

XXIV

Count Alexander
Matveievich Dmitriev-Mamonov,
favorite of Catherine II,
by M. Shibanov, 1787

Catherine II in travel dress, by
Shibanov, 1787. This portrait and
Mamonov's were painted on the
occasion of the Empress's long
journey to the Crimea.

XXV

Emperor Paul I, by E. Shchukin

Portrait of Princess Catherine Roma-
novna Dashkova in exile during
Paul's reign, painter unknown. Princess Dashkova was exiled by Paul, as
were most of the participants in the
coup d'état of 1762. After Paul's
death, Alexander I abrogated the
sentences and the exiled came back
to Petersburg.

Grand Duke Constantine Pavlovich,
by L. Miropolsky, 1786. The second
of Catherine's grandchildren, whose
name was later to be used as a pretext for revolution by the Decem-
brists.

Catherine the Great, by Lampi, 1794

XXVIII

View of the Kremlin from the Stone Bridge, by De la Barthe, about 1790

XXIX

View from Ivanovsky Square in the Kremlin, of the Archbishop's House, the Savior's Tower, and the St. Nicholas Church, by De la Barthe, about 1790

Podnovinsky suburb in Moscow during a popular feast, by De la Barthe, about 1790

View from the balcony of the Palace of the Kremlin, looking toward the Moscowa Bridge, by De la Barthe, 1790

View from the balcony of Ostankino's Palace near Moscow, by De la Barthe, about 1790

XXXI

The Banks of the Neva River, by T. Alexeiev

XXXII

finitely more masculine than feminine," but at the same time a person endowed with the liveliest sensibility—good, tolerant, and understanding toward the whole world, one to whom no one could talk for a quarter of an hour without feeling he had known her for a long time. Moreover, she was physically attractive ("certainly a highly interesting face and one which pleased at first sight," "the attributes of a very agreeable woman"), and it was therefore perfectly natural that she should be courted, and consequently tempted, and could not always resist temptation. "Whatever else people may tell you on this score is mere prudery, not based on the human heart, and no one holds his heart in his hand, to open and close his grasp on it at will."

This then was her plea, and it was more "feminine" than Catherine would care to admit. It took no account of the concrete facts on which she was to be judged, but simply pleaded that it was cruel and unjust to blame a person gifted with such high qualities. She forgot to add that for all her philosophy, she had resorted to the English ambassador to pay her expenses, and had certainly been plotting with the chancellor to keep her husband from power, and if she did admit in passing to having some such intention, then it was entirely because her husband was a man who could do nothing but harm to Russia.

It was not as a philosopher or as a "frank and loyal knight" that she went to talk to the Empress; it was as a woman who has made up her mind to play a part, and play it perfectly, in order to regain the imperial favor and, at the same time, to take a step forward to gaining power for herself. It is hard to blame her. She was not a philosopher but a creature of action and passion, and she was fighting for the thing that made her life worth while.

Catherine was granted her audience but she was still not to see the Empress alone, face to face. Her accusers, the Grand Duke and Alexander Shuvalov, were also present, and from that moment on the Grand Duke was her declared enemy: "I learned afterward that on that very day he had promised Elizabeth Vorontsova that he would marry her if I should die, and that they were both delighted at my condition." (She is referring to her feigned illness.)

The interview took place in a long, candlelit room, "with three windows with tables between them on which stood the Empress's gold toilet set." Facing the windows were some large screens in front of which a sofa had been placed. Catherine learned later that the Empress's favorite, Ivan Shuvalov, was hidden behind these screens; but at that moment she was ignorant of the identity of the person or persons concealed there, although she guessed there was someone.

Alone, then, in the presence of her judge and her accusers, the Grand Duchess began by using a woman's most natural weapon: she fell on her knees and burst out sobbing. She was now a woman of thirty, worn out by sickness and misery, humiliated and abandoned by all, and she no longer desired anything but peace. Let them send her back to her family (this was not so simple: her mother was in Paris and her brother was having serious trouble of his own with the King of Prussia). The Empress tried to make her rise but Catherine remained on her knees and continued her entreaties. Elizabeth, who was easily moved, had tears in her eyes. "How do you expect me to send you away? Do you remember you have children?" Catherine could not but realize the bitter irony of the remark: "My children are in your hands, and could not be in better."

"But what could I tell the people was the reason for your dismissal?"

"Your Majesty will say what she thinks proper, the reasons that have brought upon me your displeasure and the Grand Duke's hatred."

She knew that Elizabeth would never think it "proper" to give these reasons. The Empress tried to reason with her: "What will you live on? Your mother is a fugitive who has been obliged to leave her own house and go to Paris."

"I know: people thought she was too closely attached to Russian interests."

Already disarmed, Elizabeth was now almost beginning to try

to justify herself: was the Grand Duchess accusing her of lack of affection toward her? "God is my witness how I wept when after your arrival in Russia you lay sick almost to death; and if I had not loved you I would not have kept you here." Then she began thinking of reasons, none of them very good ones, to explain her coldness. Wasn't Catherine ridiculously proud? Hadn't she once, four years ago, neglected to salute the Empress so pointedly that she had been compelled to ask her whether it was a stiff neck that made her hold herself so erect? Catherine protested, and we may believe her, that she would never knowingly show the Empress a lack of respect! Elizabeth retaliated (with more justice): "You imagine that no one is cleverer than yourself." Catherine parried this attack as best she could, but in any case these were not criminal accusations; in fact, Elizabeth seems to have behaved like an aunt scolding her niece for some small peccadillo.

At this point the Grand Duke, urged on by Shuvalov, intervened, but speaking very much from the wings. "She is," he said, "dreadfully unkind and extremely headstrong." "I am unkind," Catherine retorted, "to those who advise you to behave unjustly, headstrong because I have seen that my complaisance merely succeeded in making you my enemy." This reference to injustice was aimed at the Holsteiner Brockdorffs, and Elizabeth, perhaps thinking she was illustrating Catherine's sense of justice, committed the most monumental *gaffe*. "Oh," she said, "you don't know how much she has said to me against your advisers and against Brockdorff on the subject of the man you have had arrested."

Catherine was thunderstruck at this. She was terrified at the idea that Elizabeth's stupidity would make the Grand Duke hate her more than ever. Why, just at that moment, did there have to be this traitorous blow which compromised still further—if that were possible—her chances of ever making peace with her husband? She had once been weak enough to talk to the Empress too freely about the affairs of Holstein and now the Grand Duke was bound to lose all confidence in her and range her once and for all among those who spied on him. Whatever happened, the die was all but cast.

Oddly enough, although the Grand Duchess was disgraced mainly on suspicion of having reached a secret understanding with Prussia, it was the Grand Duke, a dyed-in-the-wool Prussian, who appeared to be accusing her. He had good reasons. To begin with he did not wish suspicion to fall on himself, and the other reason, the true one, was that Catherine had been working for her own interests, with the secret design of preventing him from seizing power. The Empress broached the subject all the same: "You meddle in many things that do not concern you. I would not have dared do as much in the time of the Empress Anna. How, for example, have you dared to send orders to Marshal Apraxin?"

Orders? Never! Catherine had caught a passing glimpse of some letters lying in one of the gold basins: the evidence for the prosecution. "Your letters," Elizabeth told her, "are in that bowl. You were forbidden to write." The Grand Duchess insisted on the purity of her intentions, the perfect innocence of the letters, which were merely friendly notes. The Empress answered: "Bestuzhev says there are many others."

It may have been true. Catherine denied it: "If Bestuzhev says that, he lies."

"Well, if he is lying about you, I will have him put to the torture."

Calmly Catherine maintained that she had written only these three letters. They were in fact perfectly harmless, and who could swear that there had been others more compromising, if Apraxin had destroyed them as soon as he had read them? There was no proof. Elizabeth strode up and down the room, distractedly speaking now to Catherine and now to her nephew and to Shuvalov. "I perceived in her Majesty," Catherine said, "more anxiety than anger."

It was the Grand Duke who attacked and he did so clumsily, as usual, with a fierce brutality which could not help but antagonize the Empress, who already had small patience with him.

Catherine does not say what he said but she claims that "it was as clear as daylight that he was aiming to sweep me away, in order to fill my place, if he could, with his mistress of the moment." Probably Peter accused Catherine of trying to get rid of him. Elizabeth now found herself faced with two rivals, two candidates for power, both equally unacceptable. Did she believe she could reconcile the husband and wife?

What is certain is that the Empress's sympathies were all on the Grand Duchess's side. She came over to Catherine and told her in a low voice: "I have a great many more things I must say to you, but I cannot talk because I do not wish to make the quarrel between you worse." The young woman could not resist this unexpected mark of confidence. ("I became all heart," she says.) "I too am unable to speak," she said, "however urgently I desire to open my heart and soul to you."

If Catherine was moved, Elizabeth was much more so, for in the face of the obvious sincerity of these last words the tears sprang to her eyes and she dismissed her visitors in order to hide her emotion. Catherine had carried off a decisive victory, although this was not entirely due to her own cleverness. Elizabeth's weary heart still retained enough of the milk of human kindness to be capable of a surge of ordinary sympathy.

Once back in her own apartment, Catherine received a visit from Alexander Shuvalov, who told her that the Empress "had charged him to convey her compliments [to her] and to beg [her] not to be anxious, because she would have a second conversation with [her] alone."[2]

Catherine waited for this promised conversation for three weeks before she finally obtained it. Meanwhile she had continued to express her wish to be sent home to Zerbst, rather than continue to suffer constant slights and injuries. Her enemy, who was now the Grand Duke's ally, Michael Vorontsov, came to entreat with her on behalf of the Empress, and she stood firm. When she heard that the Empress had condescended to drink her health on her birthday (April 21), a signal favor, she sent a message to her Majesty, "to thank her for being so good as to remember my unhappy birth, which I would curse were it not that on that same day I received baptism."

When the Grand Duke learned of the honor bestowed on his wife, he in turn hastened to let her know that he was drinking her health. Altogether, from being in disgrace, she had so successfully turned the tables that everyone was anxiously trying to reassure her, and even the Empress herself all but asked her forgiveness. Either through laziness or through fear of committing herself too far, because she knew herself easily softened, Elizabeth kept postponing the promised interview, until she finally realized that Catherine was not a woman to be put off with airy promises. At last she permitted the Grand Duchess to see her children. Not that Catherine was greatly interested in them at that moment. Neither Paul, who was now three years old, nor four-month-old Anne, whom she had not seen more than once since she was born, could awaken any maternal feeling in her, for when she was already resigned to being deprived of them, one meeting lasting a few hours at the very most could make little difference. What did matter was that this concession was followed by the other great and long-awaited favor. Elizabeth would talk to her, or rather she would allow Catherine to do the talking.

They were alone together in a room where there were no screens. "I insist that you answer truthfully all the questions I am about to ask you." Catherine swore to tell only the exact truth, and we shall never know what she said. Perhaps she really was sincere, and in this case her confessions would duplicate her memoirs, which she saw fit to interrupt at this point.

What does seem certain is that this conversation, the first real contact between the two women, tightened the unspoken bond which, despite all appearances, had bound them for a long time.

Catherine had serious causes for complaint against the Empress, and in her memoirs and in her correspondence she does not always spare her. Sometimes she seems to be unjust toward her predecessor in order to emphasize her own merits, but she does appear to have loved her sincerely. This love seems at times almost uneasy, she was so attracted by Elizabeth's beauty. It is a somewhat abject feeling, too, like the love of a slave for the master from whom the merest smile seems an undeserved reward. There was also something of frustrated and unsatisfied filial tenderness in her love, and of the fidelity of a subject toward her sovereign. All in all, despite Elizabeth's obvious weaknesses, Catherine seems to have felt, intuitively, the kind of authentic grandeur and primitive strength which formed the basis of the Empress's character, as though Elizabeth had been a diamond of the first water whose natural brilliance Catherine, as a stone cut and polished endlessly, knew she could never hope to equal.

Elizabeth was lazy and disorganized. Since she was a young girl she had slept with servants, and danced in peasant costume with the village girls. To force her to accept the crown she had to be shown pictures which had been specially made for the purpose: one depicting her in an ermine mantle and a crown, the other shut up in a convent wearing a nun's habit with her head shaved. When she lost her temper she would swear like a vulgar fishwife, and she reminded her entourage at every opportunity that "in the time of the Empress Anna" she had lived humbly but respectably without asking anything of anyone. She was as superstitious as any peasant woman and capable of seeing an affair of high treason in the discovery of a tuft of hair wrapped around "a vegetable root" under her mattress. She was timid and continually believed she saw conspirators under her bed or behind her screens, though she did not take offense when she found a handsome young man behind those same screens. But she did possess the inimitable art of being always natural and completely unselfconscious even in her follies and mistakes. Even in her worst extravagances Peter the Great's daughter was an Olympian.

Catherine, with her sound education, intelligence and culture, her knowledge of men and her political sense, her exquisite and studied good manners, and her love of order and hard work, would never achieve the simple and unconscious majesty of a woman who never in all her life made the slightest effort to please or make an impression.

Catherine sensed this and it filled her with more admiration than jealousy. Elizabeth was subtle enough to see that this was more than simply a courtier's admiration, and that the young woman was sincere. Not that Catherine's feelings were in any way reciprocated: Elizabeth's heart was large, much too large; it was a heart open to every wind, incapable of passion, spontaneously good when an immediate opportunity of showing goodness presented itself. It was this that had made her watch, weep and hope for weeks on end at the bedside of a child with the smallpox, an impossible child whom she did not even like. It was an idle heart, dulled by pleasure, sated with flattery, and with few serious attachments. Apart from her two great favorites, Razumovsky and Ivan Shuvalov, no one kept the Empress's favors for very long. For Catherine, she was for many long years the most domineering and tyrannical of stepmothers, but the moment they found themselves face to face the younger woman's gentleness and sincere respect seem to have succeeded in disarming Elizabeth.

The Empress had brought Sophia of Anhalt-Zerbst to Russia in order to provide her nephew with a sensible, worthy companion who would not prove too demanding, in fact as the good little wife strong-minded mothers dream of for their sons. Fifteen years had passed. The marriage had turned out to be a disaster, but Catherine was after all the Grand Duchess and the mother of the heir to the Empire. The conjugal happiness of princes counts for little in politics and Elizabeth did not love her nephew. She ranged herself alongside the Grand Duchess out of feminine solidarity. But things had reached a state in which the Empress was beginning to realize more and more clearly that the husband and wife would never reign together: that each, in a more or less open manner, was trying to rid himself of the other.

The Bestuzhev affair was hushed up, especially as the chancellor whose fall had caused such a stir was generally regarded by the public as innocent and the only real evidence against him involved the Grand Duchess. The old man, for whom there had originally been talk of the death penalty, was merely deprived of his property and exiled to his estates at Gorelovo. His "accomplices," all intimate friends of Catherine's, were also exiled:

Elagin and the jeweler Bernardi to Kazan, and Adodurov to Orenburg, while Bestuzhev's confidential servant, Stampke, and Poniatowski were expelled from Russia.

Catherine was restored to favor, at least officially. It was understood that there would be no more talk of her leaving Russia, and that she would be allowed to see her children, not every day, but once a week, and even that was a great deal. She lived at the Grand Duke's palace at Oranienbaum, while the children were brought up in the imperial palace at Peterhof, fourteen miles from Oranienbaum. Catherine would perhaps have become a good mother, for she liked children and found it easy to make them like her. She had grown very fond of Maria Choglokova's little boy during the period of her enforced sterility. "I loved one of the children who used to be with her and used to kiss him a great deal: I made clothes for him, and God knows how many toys and garments I gave him."[3]

Little Paul, if his early portraits are anything to go by, was a charming little boy, as children usually are at that age, with fine features and a lively expression. Catherine might well have become very fond of him if Elizabeth's jealousy had not made her do all she could to keep mother and son apart. At these official weekly meetings, Catherine saw only a strange little boy to whom she must be careful not to speak a word out of turn. Constantly surrounded by spies and naturally cautious, at the most she was able to play for an hour or two at being a happy mother.

The young Princess Anne, Stanislas's daughter, died when she was a year old, not long after the handsome Pole's departure. Catherine wept, but it was not long before she met the man who was to make her forget the absence of her lover and the death of her little girl.

The Apraxin-Bestuzhev affair had seriously affected Catherine's position at court and had revealed to Peter and to Elizabeth, and perhaps to herself, the role which she was henceforth to play. She was well and truly set on the new path she had laid down for herself and was, as she called it "taking a road independent of all events."

Thirty-one

Love and Conspiracy

The Seven Years' War was entering its third year and the Prussian King was valiantly defending his kingdom against the attacks of the three allied powers, each of which, as tends to happen in such a situation, believed it alone was bearing the entire weight of the war. Maria Theresa of Austria and Elizabeth were indulging in mutual recriminations, each claiming the other was lukewarm and inactive. However, the Russian armies, under the command of General Fermor, were pressing the Prussians hard. In January 1758 Fermor had occupied Königsberg and on August 25 of the same year the Russians fought a battle at Zorndorf which was among the bloodiest of the century. More than ten thousand men were killed on each side. This figure may seem small enough today, but at a time when there was no such thing as compulsory military service, losses on this scale had a noticeable effect on the fighting strength of an army. Besides their ten thousand dead the Russians had more than twelve thousand wounded. The outcome of the battle was uncertain: both sides claimed control of the field and in both camps *Te Deums* were sung in thanksgiving.

The losses sustained by his army meant that Fermor could not continue to advance, and he narrowly escaped the same fate as Apraxin. Elizabeth gave her allies, and Maria Theresa in particular, to understand that she did not mean to allow Russia to pull their chestnuts out of the fire for them, but she was determined to carry on the war. In the battle of Zorndorf alone the Russians had lost twelve hundred officers, which was a considerable proportion of their total ten thousand dead, and in Russia, more than anywhere else, the military represented a political force to be reckoned with by the government. The great majority of them Russian by birth and patriots by definition, these army officers all came from a single social class, the nobility, which had the power and the means to make itself heard, and they formed, in contrast to the fluctuating, somewhat cosmopolitan circles of the court, which were swayed by every new political influence, a solid body, proud of its traditions, jealous of its rights, and ready to make its wishes felt.

During the years of war with Prussia, the army, and in particular the officers, had reached a state of extreme agitation and discontent. While the Russian troops were giving their blood and strength unsparingly, the Grand Duke, their future Emperor, was not even taking the trouble to hide his enemy sympathies, and in military circles close to the court it was whispered what no one yet dared say aloud, that the Grand Duke was shamelessly making use of the advantages of his position to betray Russia to Prussia.

It was perfectly true. Blinded by his fanatical admiration for Frederick II, Peter was deploying all the forces of his rather mediocre intelligence to keep "the King, his master" informed of what passed at the Empress's secret councils of war: with this object he had joined forces with the new English ambassador, Keith, to whom he faithfully passed on whatever he managed to learn of the plans of the Russian high command. Keith was then able to inform Frederick of these plans even before they reached the Russian army commanders themselves. By the same means the Grand Duke was receiving information about the progress of operations, and since he was totally incapable of keeping a secret, he would frequently irritate courtiers who were discussing some good news received from the front by denying the truth of whatever success had been officially announced, and saying "my information is more accurate."[1]

This scandalous behavior on the part of the heir to the throne shocked the courtiers, but many of them, regarding Peter as their future sovereign, had probably already resigned themselves in advance to one day sharing his admiration for Frederick. But the army was far from resigned and among the officers stationed or on leave at Petersburg a spirit of revolt and passionate hatred was growing up against the foreigner, the German whose dream it was to hand Russia over to Prussia.

As it happened, among the Prussian officers taken prisoner at Zorndorf was the King of Prussia's adjutant, Count Schwerin. The Grand Duke was so moved and distressed to see this man among the prisoners that he frequently sought his company, treated him with the greatest honor, almost abjectly, indeed, and allocated him a house in Petersburg, not far from the imperial palace. He assured the prisoner of his friendship and told him: "If I were Emperor you should not be a prisoner of war."

This noble prisoner had been placed under the surveillance of a young officer in the Russian army, an ordinary lieutenant who had distinguished himself in the course of the battle of Zorndorf. Three times wounded, the young man had continued to fight like a lion at the head of his troops. His superiors had sent him to Petersburg for a rest, with the honorary duty of escort to Count Schwerin. Since his new occupation gave him few worries, the young officer spent most of his time in taverns and gaming houses, but he also found time to appropriate his superior officer Peter Shuvalov's beautiful mistress, Helen Kurakina.

His height, strength, already legendary courage and remarkable good looks had already won Gregory Orlov immense popularity with his men. He was now beginning to acquire a somewhat dubious but highly flattering reputation in army circles and even to some extent in Petersburg society. Women admired him and men treated him with respect, although he was still regarded as nothing more than a charming and dissipated young scoundrel. Orlov did not come of noble family: his grandfather had been an ordinary archer in the guard of the Muscovite tsars. When, with a brutality which the Russian people were never to forget, Peter the Great had crushed the revolt of the too powerful Archers' Guard in a welter of blood, the grandfather Orlov had escaped from the massacre thanks to the courage he displayed in mounting the scaffold. Pardoned by the Tsar, he served him faithfully and obtained army rank. His son, Gregory, rose to the rank of lieutenant colonel and had five sons: Ivan, Gregory, Alexei, Feodor and Vladimir. All of them were soldiers and they made short work of getting through the modest fortune left them by their father.

Though the Orlov brothers had nothing in the world but their swords and a great reputation for strength and courage, they formed a tightly knit clan, consulting one another on all occasions, showing proper respect for the authority of the eldest, and remaining faithful to one another in good and bad fortune alike. Fanatically devoted to their regiment and to their honor as soldiers, great lovers of fighting, drinking and women, they were in fact the kind of small-time professional officers that were to be found in Russia by the thousands. Accident, or an unexpected piece of luck, was to make two of them, at least, the most powerful men in the Empire.

Nothing is recorded about the beginnings of the affair between Catherine and Gregory Orlov: neither the two people concerned, nor the few who were in their confidence, have written a word on the subject. All that we have is second-hand accounts, gossip and stories handed down by word of mouth. One fairly well authenticated version has it that the Grand Duchess's passion for Gregory began in the following manner: after a particularly stormy scene with the Empress she had rushed to the window of her room in floods of tears to get a breath of fresh air. It so happened that on that particular day Count Schwerin was at the palace as a guest of the Grand Duke and her eye lit on the young officer who, as part of the count's escort, was standing guard outside the palace. The young man's imposing height, his martial good looks and—we may imagine—his expression of respectful admiration at the sight of the Grand Duchess, are said to have conquered Catherine's heart on the spot, and she thought of nothing but how she might make the handsome officer's acquaintance.[2]

This time there was no amorous badinage: Orlov, even had he wanted to, was not in a position to court her according to the rules, like Saltykov or Poniatowski. He was too far below Catherine in rank as well as by birth to be admitted even to the title of *chevalier servant*, and, with the connivance of her friend Countess Prascovia Bruce, the Grand Duchess was reduced to meeting her new worshipper secretly in a little house situated on Vassilievsky Island. Neither the Empress, the Grand Duke nor even Catherine's own most intimate friends were to know anything of this liaison. Such a love affair would have degraded the Grand Duchess in the eyes of the public. Besides, this time Peter showed not the slightest intention of playing the complaisant husband.

The beginnings of this affair date from the spring or summer of 1759. How the clever, prudent Grand Duchess, so anxious— since her recent disgrace—to appear irreproachable, ever allowed herself to be seduced by a man of humble origin who was already only too well known for the kind of brutally debauched life which was the pride of young soldiers on leave seems a mystery, but her choice may in fact have been dictated by a kind of cynical caution. Since she could not do without love Catherine might well have preferred to choose a lover whose inferior position provided a guarantee of discretion. (Gregory was in fact anything but discreet, but he was not seen at court.) At the same time, the young officer's handsome figure, his prestige with his men, and his outstandingly good fortune, all of which were commented on with approval and secret approbation, even at court, all served to assure her that she was not making a mistake by granting this man her favors.

It seems unlikely that from the very beginning Catherine looked on Orlov as a possible instrument in her future rise to power. Popular as he was with the artillery and the imperial guard, Orlov was neither a field marshal nor a general; he was crippled with debt, and he had recently escaped from imprisonment or exile to Siberia in consequence of his affair with Princess Kurakina, as though by a miracle, when the celebrated beauty's accepted lover, the artillery general Peter Shuvalov, had died suddenly. To seduce this young daredevil with political ends in view would have been a somewhat unconventional idea on the part of the second lady of Russia. Catherine's passion for Orlov was undoubtedly sincere and, at the outset, almost entirely physical, for the lovers had practically nothing in common, either in tastes, education or character, and at the very time she was giving herself up to the young officer's embraces, the admirer of Plutarch, Voltaire and Montesquieu was still writing extremely affectionate letters to her dear Stanislas, in exile far away from her, who was capable of understanding her thoughts and sharing her feelings.

Gregory Orlov was twenty-five and Catherine already thirty. In an age when girls were married at fifteen and considered old maids by twenty-five, thirty was already mature, if not actually elderly, but Catherine's life as a woman had begun relatively late, indeed abnormally late, given her sensual and emotional precocity. In some ways it seems as though she never caught up after this belated start and that all her life, even in her worst excesses, she retained a schoolgirl naïveté and sentimentality. She had a fierce need for affection, and she needed to believe (sometimes against all probability) that each new lover was the last and only one.

There is no doubt that she had loved Sergei Saltykov deeply and truly and had not lightly brought herself to put another man in his place. When he had disappointed her she had consoled herself with a young man who was too ingenuous and who, as a lover, cannot altogether have satisfied her. This was her third experiment. In her still precarious position, with her growing ambition and the court intrigues in which she was playing an increasingly active part, how long could she allow herself to remain the mistress of a man like Gregory Orlov?

One thing is certain: Catherine did possess a remarkable faculty for making her amours coincide with the interests of her ambition. No one had forgotten the way in which Elizabeth had seized power, and in the barracks of St. Petersburg it was remembered more vividly than elsewhere. Gregory had no secrets from his brothers, so the whole Orlov tribe knew of the honor which had fallen on one of their number. The Orlovs were not the men to despise the Grand Duchess for such a choice and they were well aware that Elizabeth had distinguished, and was even said to have secretly married, a man of much more humble origin than theirs.

There was even a story that Elizabeth and her ladies in waiting used to go in person to the barracks and make the soldiers drunk in order to make them favorable to the princess's cause. Catherine had no idea of permitting herself a similar freedom, but in what was perhaps a somewhat unforeseen way, she had acquired in military circles (not in the high command, which was too dependent on the fluctuations of politics, but among the lower ranks who for this reason were closer to their troops) partisans who were fiercely devoted to her person and ready to risk everything for her sake.

Gregory Orlov was not a common adventurer, nor a drawing-room Don Juan like Sergei Saltykov; his was an ardent and simple soul. Even his ambition was only the manifestation of a kind of simple pride. He was very handsome: portraits painted when he was already somewhat past his prime show him with features running a little to fat but smooth and regular, large dreamy eyes, strong brows, and a delicate, well-shaped mouth. Also he was five years younger than Catherine, but of the two he seems to have been the more genuinely in love. This woman who possessed neither the freshness of her first youth nor real beauty did have much more than that: she had all the prestige belonging to a princess of the imperial house, allied to the charms of a lively intelligence, a quick wit and a sophistication which it had hitherto been beyond the ex-archer's grandson to even imagine. In addition to all this, this admirable woman loved him with a genuine passion; she was unfortunate, perhaps in danger, openly neglected and persecuted by an unworthy husband, and this husband was also the very Prussian Grand Duke who had for years been the army's *bête noire*.

Even to a man of Gregory Orlov's limited brain power, the problem of the succession and the Grand Duchess's future must obviously have appeared a difficult one to solve. The Empress was sick and not expected to live much longer. Should the army remain faithful to an emperor who was a traitor to his country? In the event of the Grand Duke's being compelled to abdicate, what would become of his wife? Unfortunately she was a German —she could not open her mouth without betraying her origins— but she was also an Orthodox believer, she loved Russia sincerely, and she was as patriotic as the best. Inevitably, in the circles where he had some influence, Gregory did his best to defend the Grand Duchess, and praised her piety and virtue: he could do no less.

The third of the five Orlov brothers, Alexei, who was a little younger than Gregory, was at least as well known for his courage and physical strength. He was not as handsome as his elder brother; a sword cut received in a brawl had split his left cheek and this accident had earned him the nickname of "Scarface." He was a man of a quite different stamp from his brother: intelligent, ambitious, hard and unscrupulous. Alexei was a man of action. The idea of a possible *coup d'état* and the forms it could take must have germinated in Alexei's brain long before the death of the Empress. Furthermore, the example of Elizabeth herself had inspired more than one hothead among the officers of the imperial guard, only until now no one had thought that the claimant to be put forward might be the Grand Duchess.

At court the intrigues were coming along nicely. Count Panin, a former attaché to the Swedish embassy, who in 1760 had been appointed tutor to the Tsarevich Paul, was a politician of the new school, a cultivated man of liberal outlook, with a dream of reform. He was a friend of Bestuzhev, had remained in favor in spite of the chancellor's disgrace, and naturally became an ally of the Grand Duchess. His secret aim was to have the Grand Duke set aside, after the Empress's death, to place his pupil, young

Paul, on the throne and to ensure the continuation of the government by a council of regency presided over by the young Emperor's mother. Catherine did not approve of this plan: she considered, and there were strong arguments to support her, that an autocratic regime in the full meaning of the word was the only one which would work in Russia: in other words, she wanted all power for herself, and herself alone. Meanwhile, it was best not to make plans or to come to any definite agreement either verbally or in writing. The precedent of the Bestuzhev affair showed only too clearly the danger of such steps.

Everyone waited. The war was still going on: in 1760 the Russian armies, commanded by Count Saltykov, occupied Berlin, but the victory was still not won, for Frederick was a terrible fighter. The French and Austrian courts were beginning to watch their giant northern ally with some anxiety, as she succeeded in holding their common enemy in check: the fate of the war, and possibly even the future of Europe, hung on the resistance of a woman who had for months been fighting a losing battle against a death that everyone knew to be imminent.

Elizabeth was fifty and was now a complete invalid, dragging herself painfully on her swollen legs from a sofa to her bed and from her bed to an armchair. She had not given up her disorganized life, her gargantuan meals and late nights, and she used up the little strength she had left in praying on her knees in the private chapel of her palace. She was the kind of woman who refuses to take care of herself just because she is so afraid of dying. Very little remained of her famous beauty; her face was the color of lead and puffy with fat. She was not thinking now of balls and masquerades; it was all she could do to dress herself.

"I intend to continue the war," she told the Austrian ambassador on January 1, 1760, "and to remain faithful to my allies, even if I have to sell half my diamonds and my dresses."[3] Poor Elizabeth had little use for diamonds and she clung to a war which—at the cost of a terrible effort—maintained the prestige of the Russian armies in the eyes of Europe. It was as though it were her last reason for living. The fear of approaching death was becoming confused in her mind with the fear which was gradually invading those around her, her court, the army and the two capitals. At court people were beginning to talk quite openly of the deficiencies of the Grand Duke, of placing the Tsarevich Paul on the throne and exiling either both his parents or his father alone to Holstein. Paul was not yet six. Elizabeth feared the confusion which was bound to result from putting a minor on the throne. Peter's unpopularity was such that in any case trouble of some kind appeared inevitable. Russia was at war, the state treasuries were empty, and secret negotiations and bargaining were proceeding at an ever more frenzied pace in the antechambers of chancelleries and embassies, while the Empress, informed by her spies, no longer seemed to take any interest. She knew that for her the die was cast: the atmosphere of fear and uneasiness that hung around her had no other cause beyond the certainty of her own approaching death.

One man at least was passionately longing for the Empress to die: this was her old enemy, Frederick of Prussia. But there was another who waited for her death with scarcely less impatience. The Grand Duke Peter now knew that his aunt would have neither the time nor the strength to disinherit him. Catherine may be exaggerating when she says that ever since 1749 he had been "dying to reign," but in the last years of Elizabeth's reign he too had certainly been infected by a feverish desire for power. Moreover, he was no longer a timid small boy amusing himself by hanging rats and beating his dogs. His ambitions were growing in proportion as he saw himself nearing the end of the long, weary captivity in a gilded cage which had been his lot ever since childhood.

He was now over thirty, his mind addled by drink and his character still oddly childlike, but at least, with the obsessional determination of a dreamer, he knew for certain what he wanted to do: first he wanted to stop the war with Prussia and fly, if he could, to his idol's assistance; secondly he wanted to reconquer the lands which Denmark had taken away from his Duchy of Holstein, and thirdly, to marry Elizabeth Vorontsova. Being anything but a man of action, Peter seemed deliberately to choose goals that were to all practical purposes unobtainable, at least to someone in the position in which he found himself. He may not even have known that he already had a dangerous rival in the person of his wife, all ready to snatch from him the power he coveted.

He had installed Elizabeth Vorontsova in his own apartments and was treating her less as a mistress than as a future wife. He was talking openly of repudiating the Grand Duchess. Perhaps, after all, his passion for Elizabeth Vorontsova was the principal reason for his outspoken hatred of his wife. Certainly, in spite of his debauchery, which was more gossiped about than real, what he needed more than anything was a "sister of mercy"; and the ugly, gawky, lumpish Elizabeth, who at least shared his tastes and did not make him conscious of his physical and moral inferiority, may have succeeded in awakening in his frozen heart some feeling akin to love. If this were so, then Elizabeth's influence is quite enough to explain Peter's attitude to his wife. The Vorontsovs must surely have kept Peter amply informed of the role Catherine was preparing for herself.

Nevertheless, Michael Vorontsov found himself in a somewhat embarrassing position: he had small chance of seeing his niece crowned Empress and meanwhile his family had to put up with the scandal of a public concubinage. In addition to this, seeing that their enemies the Vorontsovs enjoyed the Grand Duke's favors, the Shuvalovs were ranging themselves more or less openly on the side of the Grand Duchess and indicating that they were quite prepared to support Catherine in the event of a palace revolution finally taking place. Elizabeth's favorite, the handsome Ivan Shuvalov, was courting the Grand Duchess in such an unequivocal fashion that he was suspected of trying to occupy the same place in relation to the future Empress as he had done with Elizabeth.[4] Catherine discouraged no one: she needed friends and supporters desperately. It was not hard for her to make friends at this juncture; Peter's blunders would have made popular a much less able woman and one less determined to please.

She had already succeeded in winning Count Panin over to her side and he, as chamberlain and chief tutor to the Tsarevich, was bound to play an important role in any future government. Besides the Shuvalovs and the Razumovskys, with whom she had always maintained friendly relations, she enjoyed the support of the French and English ambassadors, who were vying with one another in their generosity toward her in the hope of making her serve the ends of their respective countries. She was also being wooed, with the utmost discretion, by Frederick II, who still hoped to win, if not her friendship, at least her neutrality. (This in itself shows how little anyone believed in the possibility that Peter III would reign.) Through the efforts of the Orlov brothers, to whom she distributed as much money as she could afford, she was in the process of winning the active sympathy of the regiments of the guard.

Meanwhile she led a retired life, showed herself very little in public—she had excellent reasons for this—and posed as the oppressed wife resigned in advance to whatever blows fate might deal her.

This was a wise move, but the Grand Duchess had not chosen it altogether voluntarily: in fact, during these last months of Elizabeth's reign, at a time when she should have been free to act and attempt to forestall her husband's accession to the throne, she found herself hamstrung by the most ordinary and untimely of accidents: she was pregnant. It was common knowledge that she and her husband had been living virtually apart for two years and now, at the very moment when the Grand Duke was talking of repudiating her, she was determined not to give him a ready-made excuse.

She therefore concealed her pregnancy with the utmost care, spending her days in an armchair in her own room and receiving hardly anyone. All this time the Empress was dying, already deserted by the crowd of courtiers who were anxious above all for their own futures. Besides, the end was already in sight, and there was no longer any practical reason which could prevent the Grand Duke's accession to the throne of his fathers.

Elizabeth was dying, but her condition was still being hidden from the Grand Duke and Duchess. The news traveled in whispers from one room in the palace to the next, and rumors, some true, some false, were circulating constantly. No one dared to act for fear of making a mistake and compromising himself. Then one night Catherine was awakened by her maidservant, who announced that the young Princess Dashkova had come to see her. It was typical of a seventeen-year-old girl to burst into the Grand Duchess's room in this way, in order to tell her—what? To tell her that she had friends on whom she could rely. From then on Catherine was to live in an atmosphere of conspiracy, feverish intrigue, and active and conscious preparation for a *coup d'état*.

Catherine Dashkova, *née* Vorontsova, was one of the younger sisters of the very Elizabeth Vorontsova who was dreaming of taking the Grand Duchess's place. She had recently married Prince Dashkov and was a fervent admirer of Catherine's. She was a remarkably intelligent girl, an infant prodigy, who was later to dazzle Voltaire and Diderot by her immense knowledge and high moral principles; she was dynamic, idealistic, generous and enthusiastic, and her friendship for the Grand Duchess bordered on idolatry. In spite of her extreme youth, Catherine Dashkova was already a personality at court: she talked a great deal, and well, and she was one of the Egerias of the "liberal" party of which Count Nikita Panin was at that time the head. She was also, it so happened, the Grand Duke's goddaughter. He had a soft spot for her, and tried to warn her against the Grand Duchess: "My dear," he told her, "remember it is safer to have to do with a fool like me than with those sublime intellects who squeeze all the juice out of a lemon and then throw it away,"[5] words which prove that Peter was far from a fool; did he think of himself as a squeezed lemon, thrown away by Catherine?

However that may be, the girl was outraged by her godfather's behavior to his wife and by the part played by her own sister in the Grand Duke's life, and she flung herself wholeheartedly into the Grand Duchess's party. Now she rushed to her friend and idol in the middle of the night, feverish and shivering with cold, in order to promise her assistance and support and to swear eternal devotion. "The Empress has only a few more days to live, a few hours maybe! What are you going to do? What are your plans? Give me the word to act and I will do whatever you tell me to do!"

But how could Catherine "act" when she was six months pregnant? Evidently the innocent Princess Dashkova did not perceive this fact, and saw nothing beyond the ample folds of Catherine's nightdress and dressing gown, but the Grand Duchess firmly took refuge in sad and noble passivity: "I have no plans . . . God is my only hope and I place all my trust in him." The girl was on fire with impatience and the desire for sacrifice: "Your friends must act, they will act!" Was the Grand Duchess afraid of being compromised? She, Catherine Dashkova, would never harm her by her devotion; but her friends would act alone, if they must, and they would be able to protect her, for did she not see that she was in danger?[6]

Catherine allowed her young friend to go without having said anything either to encourage or discourage her. Yes, she did have supporters. Yes, perhaps she really was in danger, in more danger even than her friends suspected, since if her pregnancy were discovered she would have to expect the most ignominious repudiation. Elizabeth might die within a few days or a few hours but the child Catherine carried inside her would not be delivered for another two or three months. It was due, no doubt, to this child that the Grand Duke was allowed to ascend the throne and believe that he would reign.

On December 23 Elizabeth had a stroke and this time it was the last. In the presence of the Grand Duke, the Grand Duchess and the Razumovsky brothers, the Empress received the rite of extreme unction and repeated after her confessor the words of the *Otkhodnaia*, the prayer for the dying, which she asked to have said twice. She was still lucid enough to make her farewells to all those present, asking them, according to custom, to forgive her her trespasses. At last, at four o'clock in the afternoon of Christmas Day 1761, Prince Nikita Trubetskoi emerged from the sickroom, now transformed into a mortuary chamber, and announced to the assembled courtiers and dignitaries that the Empress was dead and the reign of a new Emperor, Peter III, had begun.

Thirty-two

❦❦❦❦❦❦❦❦❦❦❦❦❦❦

Mock Emperor

For six weeks, according to custom, the dead Empress, watched over by ladies of her court and officers of her guard, received the homage of her people. Ten days before the funeral the body was taken to the Kazan Cathedral, where Elizabeth lay in state on a great catafalque surrounded by candles, dressed in a gown embroidered with silver and adorned with lace, painted and bejeweled, with a golden crown on her head, while the citizens of Petersburg, pilgrims and representatives from distant provinces came and bowed before the coffin and prayed for the dead woman's soul. She was sincerely mourned. The people had not known her well but they had loved her.

She had reigned for twenty years; a remote tsarina, immured in the splendors of her palace, with her dresses encrusted with precious stones and her golden carriages. As lovely and majestic as a queen in a fairy tale, pious and spendthrift, the daughter of Peter the Great had succeeded, almost unconsciously, in reestablishing the people's respect for the imperial power. They forgot or did not know her faults; they merely looked among all the gold and the lace at the massive yet pitiful remains of the Mother of Her People.

Peter III ascended the throne, and according to custom the nobility, the clergy, the army, and representatives of the citizens and the craftsmen's guilds came and swore fealty to him, and never were oaths of fealty more unwillingly sworn. The army, always the first to raise its voice, was murmuring aloud.

They had good reason. With an insulting disregard for public mourning, the new sovereign did not even deign to watch beside his aunt's coffin; and on the rare occasions when he did appear it was still worse, because he talked at the top of his voice, joked with the ladies and made fun of the priests. The rest of the time he stayed in his own apartments, holding riotous supper parties and even plays, and compelling his guests to wear holiday attire instead of the mourning which was obligatory at court, getting drunk, shouting and laughing immoderately, and altogether behaving as though the Empress's death had sent him delirious with joy. This was probably the truth, but however anxious the nephew may have been to inherit his aunt's kingdom, such an open display of cynicism was bound to cause a scandal.

Throughout the ten days that the Empress's corpse remained on view in the cathedral, the Grand Duchess, or as she now was, the new Empress, stayed kneeling at the foot of the coffin, shrouded in long black veils, weeping and praying. However sincere Catherine's grief, this public demonstration of piety was principally a method of drawing public attention to herself. Her pallor, her tears and the obvious fervor of her prayers touched the hearts of the crowds who filed past the catafalque; and for once this crowd really was made up of the people, the ordinary people, great and small, provincials, minor clergy—all Russia, in fact. They were able to stare with their own eyes at the Empress Catherine, wife of the Emperor and mother of the heir to the Empire, the hitherto unknown German princess; and she wore neither crown nor diamonds and was weeping real tears, crossing herself and prostrating herself like a real Russian, and grieving like a girl who has lost her mother. The French ambassador, Breteuil, reported that by her conduct the young Empress was "winning the Russians' hearts more and more."[1]

In the decisive battle she was about to fight she needed them: she was known to be in disgrace and under threats; now she presented herself in the church like a suppliant seeking asylum at the altar.

On the actual day of the funeral, however, Peter surpassed himself by disrupting the entire procession more than once, by first slowing down his pace and then starting to run so fast to catch up with the coffin that the old courtiers who carried the train of his huge mourning cloak could not keep up and were obliged to let go of the cloak and leave it flapping in the wind. Peter was almost thirty-four years old but seemed to think, like a little boy, that being Emperor was simply a matter of being able to do exactly as he pleased. In one sense he was not mistaken: he had with his own eyes seen his aunt indulging in behavior that must have astonished him by its extravagance and led him to this perfectly logical conclusion. But he was forgetting the fable of the donkey and the little dog, and was trying to exceed his own capacities. He was incapable of doing anything properly: his extravagances were no more than pitiful clowning; his attempts at authority, absurd whims; his gaiety heavy-footed; and his eagerness to please, a familiarity unworthy of a ruler.

Foreign diplomats could only conclude that "he has none of the air of a sovereign." The English ambassador, Keith, who was on good terms with Peter, told one of the ladies of the court: "Your Emperor must be mad to act as he does." In fact, far from adopting a more dignified attitude and more solemn manners as the proprieties would have appeared to demand, the ex-Grand Duke, now Emperor, seemed to take a perverse delight in exaggerating still further the eccentricities which had already brought him into disrepute a long time ago, both at court and in the city.

In the middle of the celebration of Mass he would suddenly put his tongue out at the officiating priest; he would burst out laughing in the middle of a ministerial conference; he swore and made obscene remarks in public and altogether behaved like a complete fool, as though the title of Emperor of Russia were in his eyes a mere bauble which he wanted to shatter at all costs. This German prince would have made a wonderful character in a Dostoievsky novel.

He was probably not responsible for his actions: outclassed and fearfully out of his element in the role he had to play, he was like a bad actor with an insuperable attack of stage fright; he seemed to revel in piling one *gaffe* upon another as though some infallible instinct were driving him to the course most likely to destroy him.

He had not, however, seated himself upon the throne of Peter the Great simply in order to play the fool. On the contrary, he was in a hurry to begin to act. As was only to be expected, his first concern as soon as he was proclaimed Emperor was to give the order for the cessation of hostilities, repudiate Russia's agreements with Austria and France, and restore to Frederick II all the territory which the Russian armies had gained in five years at war. As a disciple of Frederick the Great he could hardly do less, and he dreamed of doing much more. As a faithful vassal, the Duke of Holstein considered it his duty to take advantage of the accident of his birth to serve the King of Prussia to the best of his ability. As master of Russia, he wanted to reign in order to ensure the triumph of a man who, for him, was the incarnation of the sovereign Good on earth. "The will of Frederick," he used to say, "is the will of God," and he carried the portrait of his king always with him, set in a ring.

Since he lived surrounded by German soldiers, hated and despised the Russians, and did not even stop to consider that the people he thought so backward might possess opinions and feelings of their own, he believed that one stroke of the pen would be enough to compel an army which had fought for five years side by side with the Austrians against the Prussians to suddenly turn around and march alongside the Prussians against Austria. Since this was the Tsar's command, the war was now at an end; but not merely the soldiers themselves but their families, and the fathers and brothers of officers killed in action, were anything but prepared to sit back and see so much sacrifice rendered useless and so many deaths in vain, simply by the whim of one man. Peter had neither the time, nor perhaps the courage, to order his generals to place themselves at the disposal of the King of Prussia, but this was his cherished dream.

Not content with earning himself from the very beginning the irrevocable and outspoken hatred of the army, Peter was then foolish enough to try to impose new regulations on it. He wanted to introduce a discipline based on that of the Prussians, and as usual he began with details: he ordered the regiments of the guard, and in particular the famous Preobrazhensky regiment, which had been the pride of Peter the Great, to give up their traditional uniforms and replace them by new ones exactly like those worn by the Prussian officers and men. Naturally, he himself was never so happy as when wearing his uniform of an officer of Holstein.

Having made himself loathed by the army, the new Emperor then did his best to make himself equally obnoxious to the Orthodox Church. He was as convinced a Lutheran as any "enlightened" person (and for all his ignorance, Peter did belong among the "enlightened") in the eighteenth century could be, which is to say he regarded the Lutheran faith as the only reasonable one. Seeing nothing in Greek Orthodoxy beyond a collection of barbarous superstitions, he undertook to reform the Church, of which he was, after all, officially the head. In point of fact technically he was not, as yet, but it was in vain that Frederick II urged him to hasten the date of his solemn consecration in Moscow. Peter promulgated decrees and ukases ordering the removal of all sacred images from the churches with the exception of those of Christ and the Virgin and the closure of all private chapels (every noble and even bourgeois household made it a point of honor to have its own chapel). He decreed that in future all priests were to shave their beards and wear short gowns like Lutheran pastors. He had a Lutheran chapel built in his own palace and granted Russian Protestants freedom to practice their religions. He also ordered more tolerant measures toward Russian "heretics," the *raskolniki* or Old Believers. He promised an amnesty to dissidents who had fled abroad and offered them land in Siberia for colonization. Lastly, he crowned all these abominations by ordering the confiscation of the wealth of the Church and making all clerics civil servants paid by the state.

Some of these measures—such as the confiscation of the wealth of the Church—although sweeping, were clearly not altogether unreasonable, and some were actually generous and humane. But they were poisoned at the source; Peter's folly and incompetence made even his well-intentioned actions ridiculous.

It is easy to imagine the effect produced by these ukases, which were promulgated in the very first weeks of his reign by an emperor who was already unpopular before he started. The Russian clergy were rich, influential and jealous of their independence. The Church paid no taxes to the state and owned vast estates. At a census taken in 1738, out of an over-all total of five million peasants (only the men were regularly entered at the census) there were estimated to be more than a million serfs working on Church lands. Every tsar since Peter the Great had been tempted to channel into the public coffers at least some part of this vast wealth, which was doing nobody any good since the bishops and superiors of convents treated their peasants just as harshly as the laity, if not more so. It took the madman Peter III to dare utter the fateful words "confiscation of the wealth of the Church," and it is easy to understand why Catherine made increasingly obvious demonstrations of her own piety. The Tsar was denounced from the pulpit as a heretic, a Lutheran and a servant of Antichrist, which brought on him the additional execration of the lower orders of society, the majority of whom were Orthodox believers. As we shall see later on, however, Peter had on the other hand won himself fervent and unexpected support among the Old Believers.

Peter III knew the history of his illustrious ancestor and may have thought (insofar as he was able to admire any Russian) that he was following his example: if Peter the Great had cut the beards and long robes of the boyars, there was no reason why his successor should not do the same to the priests and bishops. If Peter the Great had made the Russians dress "in the German fashion," what was to prevent Peter III from continuing along the path of progress by making them dress "in the Prussian fashion"? Why should he not combat superstition and try to make of this muddy, servile Russia a completely civilized country? But here too Peter III was exceeding his capacities, for his ideas were limited and he lacked, to a pathological degree, a sense of reality. He could only act energetically on paper and, as Catherine was to say later, paper "suffers everything."

The Russian Church, which had already anathematized Peter the Great, was soon to be quelled by a stronger will than Peter III's, but the icons, the beards, the long robes and the hieratical solemnity of the Orthodox rite have survived until the twentieth century, and will survive, no doubt, as long as believers remain in Russia.

However, the Emperor's advisers, putting a good face on a bad business, did succeed in suggesting to the new Emperor one proposed reform which was liable to gain him solid sympathy among the only class which possessed any effective power in Russia, namely the nobility. Two months after his accession (March 1, 1762) Peter III promulgated his famous "Manifesto" on the enfranchisement of the nobles. He announced that in future, considering the state of stability and prosperity which Russia had reached as a result of the reforms of Peter the Great, the nobles would no longer be liable to compulsory state service except in time of war, and that they were free to travel abroad and remain there as long as they liked, although still obliged to return to Russia at the first command of the government. In actual fact, since the time of Peter the Great the whole Russian nobility had been permanently engaged in compulsory state service, in either a military or a civil capacity: in theory every son of a noble family was automatically enlisted in the army, and young men of the minor nobility served as common soldiers until they reached the rank of sergeant or, at most, lieutenant. Those who were unable or unwilling to be soldiers served in the administration. The nobles had already tried to obtain some remission of this law during the reigns of Anna and Elizabeth, such as the right to retire at the age of forty and permission for large families to keep one son at home on the family estates.

Peter III's manifesto therefore produced a calculated effect among the nobility. Prince Dashkov (the husband of the volcanic Catherine Dashkova) announced the good news to the new Empress with tears of joy in his eyes: "The Emperor deserves to have a golden statue erected in his honor; he has freed all the nobles."[2]

Peter III wanted to be popular, or rather his councilors, and Michael Vorontsov in particular, wanted to make him so. In fact, this measure was wrung from him rather in the way a condemned man's watch and rings are taken from him before he is shot, for Peter had been sentenced long ago. He lacked prestige and authority to such an extent that his fall was only a matter of months, but meanwhile he had placed the official signature to an act which his successor, whoever that might be, would not dare to revoke.

In spite of the passing enthusiasm generated by the concessions he granted to the nobility, Peter was making himself increasingly loathed. Not content with having broken off a war that he would have had every hope of winning, to the great fury of Russia's allies and indignation of the army, he was now trying to involve the Russian armies in a campaign against Denmark with the sole object of winning back from this country his hereditary province of Schleswig, which was of no interest to Russia. Moreover, he was prepared to do so even against the will of Frederick II. In his own mind he was certainly Frederick's loyal and faithful friend, but he was first and foremost Duke of Holstein and owed it to himself to return to his country the lands which had been unjustly taken away from it. In all this Peter seemed to forget only one thing: namely, that he was also Emperor of Russia.

Instead of thinking of his new and urgent duties, Peter found himself others, older, more remote, and more in keeping with his capacities. He dreamed of his expedition against Denmark, for he, who had never been to war in his life, intended to march at the head of his army. He may have seen this campaign as a pretext to escape from Russia, where he certainly felt increasingly lost and ill at ease.

The moment his aunt was dead, Peter had recalled from Siberia the officials exiled by Elizabeth. They had all returned, all to positions of honor: the infinitely detested Biron, his old enemy Münnich—a remarkable statesman exiled because of his German origin—and their families; Lestocq; Ostermann's sons— a whole company of returning exiles, all of them ready to serve their new sovereign with sincere devotion. Among the Germans living in Russia, Peter was of course considered the best of rulers. One has only to read the memoirs of Helbig, secretary to the embassy of Saxony, to find that according to his evidence the prince emerges as a simple, generous, urbane man whose only fault was to show too much patience. When Biron remarked, after the *coup d'état:* "If Peter III had had the courage to hang and behead and break his enemies completely, he would have kept his throne," Helbig added somewhat hypocritically: "Biron's attitude may have been fair, but in practice it would have been disastrous for the Russian people." When Lestocq's wife, Marie Aurore Mengden, came to express her gratitude to Peter, one of the things she said to him was: "Your goodness will be your downfall. . . . You really ought to execute those who are your declared enemies." "Ah, Countess," replied the Emperor with a smile, "have pity on those unfortunates. Should I begin my reign with bloodshed?"[3] In fact, whatever Peter III may have been accused of afterward, during the few months his reign lasted he does not seem to have shown cruelty. In order to prove that he was a sadist, the only arguments his accusers can produce are his treatment of his dogs and of Catherine. With Catherine, from 1758 onward and especially after the death of Elizabeth, he behaved odiously.

All the same, it is hard to estimate the extent to which husband

and wife sinned against one another or to understand the real nature of the conflict between them. They are both on trial but the true verdict on their case can never be known.

Thirty-three

❧❧❧❧❧❧❧❧❧❧❧❧❧

The Coup d'État *of June 1762*

While Peter III was beginning his reign with all the clumsiness of which he was capable—and clumsy he was—Catherine, for her part, remained in her apartments to which she was confined by her advanced state of pregnancy. She had as many as three excellent excuses for leading this retired life: first, her husband was behaving toward her with the most unspeakable beastliness, pretending to be unaware of her existence and already making the court treat Elizabeth Vorontsova as the future Empress. He was talking of having the Grand Duke Paul declared illegitimate and shutting his wife up in a convent for adultery. Secondly, Catherine was in mourning for the Empress and was determined to let everyone know how deeply and sincerely she was grieving. Lastly, she had sprained her ankle badly (or so she claimed) and was unable to walk. The sprain got better not long after April 11, the date on which her third child was born. It was a son and he was baptized Alexei. The delivery was effected as quietly as possible and passed unnoticed, thanks to a trick played by Catherine's faithful *valet de chambre*, Chkurin, who set fire to his own house in the knowledge that the Emperor, who loved fires, would be bound to rush off to see the blaze, taking his mistress with him. On her birthday ten days later Catherine was already receiving the Austrian ambassador's compliments and reassuring him as to her own feelings regarding his country. Peter might indulge whatever whims he pleased: everyone knew that his reign would not last for long.

Catherine scarcely needed to act at all: Peter was doing her work for her. The insults he heaped on her earned her more popularity and esteem every day. She suffered all with dignity and in silence. The French ambassador, Breteuil, wrote: "The Empress bears the Emperor's conduct and the arrogance of Vorontsov nobly. Knowing her character and her great courage I presume that sooner or later she will resort to strong measures." On the occasion of the Emperor's birthday, which was on February 21 and so one and a half months before her baby was born, she had been forced on her husband's orders to pin the ribbon of the Order of Saint Catherine on Elizabeth Vorontsova's breast with her own hand. Only empresses and grand duchesses were entitled to receive this order, and by such a symbolic, public affront Peter thought he was honoring his mistress, who may even have been foolish enough to demand it. In fact, it was really no humiliation for Catherine, since the enormity of the insult won the Empress the sympathy of the entire court.

During the festivities which he ordered to celebrate the signing of the peace treaty with Prussia (and one can imagine the pleasure with which the soldiers present at the state banquet drank to Frederick's health) Peter allowed himself to give public expression to his hatred for his wife. When the time came for him to propose the toast to the imperial family, he sent to ask Catherine, who was sitting at the other end of the table, why she drank it seated and did not stand up like the rest. She answered that since she herself was a member of the imperial family, she did not have to rise. Peter flung in her face the word *dura* (fool); did she not know, he said, that the *imperial* family included only his uncles, the Princes of Holstein? This, without any other form of trial, amounted to a public repudiation, and although

Peter did not even have the courage to carry his attitude to its logical conclusion, it was clear that he no longer regarded her as his wife. Catherine burst into tears, and turning to her neighbor, Count Stroganov, hastily asked him to tell her a funny story.[1]

Everyone knew at once that the die had been cast. Catherine was later to write circumspectly: "It was then that I began to listen to the proposals which people had been making to me ever since the death of the Empress." We know that in fact she had been listening to them for a long time.

Peter, for his part, had been warned by his spies of the possibility of a conspiracy and was considering having his wife arrested and shut up in the prison of Schlüsselburg, a fate with which he himself had so often been threatened by his aunt. Only the entreaties of his uncle Prince George of Holstein prevented him from putting this plan into practice. The Prince, of whom Peter was very fond (he had made him a field marshal) was afraid that such a step would provoke violent reactions in the army. Peter might have tried to scotch the conspiracy without arresting the Empress herself, but by seizing Catherine's most notorious supporters. Although he was urged to it by those around him, he did not do this, perhaps through fear of making himself fresh enemies. Indeed, he might not even have been obeyed.

By this time the conspiracy was well under way. The Orlov brothers had surrounded themselves with a solid kernel of Catherine's supporters among the officers of the guard. Alexei was treasurer of the artillery of the guard, and as such, was busy secretly distributing wine and money to the soldiers in the Empress's name. In the Preobrazhensky regiment, where resentment against Peter III was fiercest since its members had not forgiven him for the matter of their uniforms, Catherine had fervent admirers in two officers named Passek and Bredikhin. One day Passek went so far as to throw himself at the Empress's feet, swearing to avenge her and kill the Emperor. In the Ismailovsky regiment, which was commanded by Kyril Razumovsky, Catherine had faithful partisans in the officers Roslavlev and

Lassunsky, and among the army regiments stationed around the capital her supporters claimed that she could count on ten thousand men ready to fight for her.

All this time Peter was busy at Oranienbaum making preparations for his expedition against Denmark. At a moment when the capital was in a ferment, when his opponents were putting the finishing touches to their proposed *coup d'état*, when his friends were continually warning him of fresh suspects, this strange sovereign had only one thing on his mind: to go and win back Schleswig from Denmark. His uncles, his German entourage, and his intimate advisers were to go with him, and so, naturally, was Elizabeth Vorontsova. Peter was already insisting that she should be treated like a reigning empress. He did not, however, mean to set out from Russia leaving the field wide open to Catherine. He had as yet taken no official measures against her, but the court and the city were expecting some kind of coup which would decide the Empress's fate. There was therefore no time to lose.

Catherine was living at Peterhof, halfway between Oranienbaum and the capital. She was not staying in the palace itself but in a summer house known as Mon Plaisir, situated by the sea about a hundred yards from the palace. There, where she was less closely watched, she was able to obtain news more easily, and if things went wrong, it would also be an easier place from which to escape. Peter had decided to spend his feast day, June 29 (the feast of Saints Peter and Paul), at Peterhof with his wife and had told her to be ready to expect him. Then on June 27, Passek was arrested. He had not succeeded in carrying out his plan to kill Peter III but he had been making a great many inflammatory speeches. His arrest provided an excuse for action.

Had Peter really meant to repudiate his wife publicly before his departure? Had he fixed June 29 as the day for the execution of this plan, or even, maybe, of one more sinister still? There are a number of witnesses, although all of them somewhat unreliable, being French and therefore hostile to Peter III, who state that he had contemplated killing his wife or having her poisoned on

that day. It seems likely that Peter was in fact secretly longing
to do this, but he was too much of a coward to commit murder.
He was afraid of Catherine and he defied her as best he could,
but he does not seem to have been capable of going further.

However that may be, the arrest of one conspirator might
easily lead to the uncovering of the plot and Catherine would
then be lost. Against the advice of Panin, who distrusted the
Empress's ambitions and had his own ideas for a *coup d'état*
which would place the Grand Duke Paul on the throne with
Catherine as regent, the conspirators hesitated no longer: Princess Dashkova and Orlov acted. The time had come to warn the
troops of what was in the wind, and the great coup was fixed for
the night of June 29.

Feodor Orlov, Alexei's younger brother, went to inform Kyril
Razumovsky of the affair with the object of getting him to throw
in his lot with the Empress. Razumovsky had long been a sym-
pathizer: he lost no time in sending for Taubert, the director of
the printing works belonging to the Academy of Sciences, and
asked him to print a manifesto immediately proclaiming the
abdication of the Emperor and Catherine's accession to the
throne. The word was out, the game begun, and it was too late
to draw back. When Taubert hesitated, Razumovsky told him:
"You know too much already. Now your head, as well as mine,
is at stake."[2]

At Oranienbaum, a former residence of Menshikov's which
Peter had transformed at first into a country residence and later
into a military camp, the Emperor, dressed in his Holstein uniform, was still giving orders for the Danish expedition and reviewing his troops, surrounded by his German friends. He was
not Emperor of Russia, he never had been in more than a dream,
and soon he would not even be that.

In her summer house at Mon Plaisir with its narrow terrace
overlooking the sea, flat, smooth, waveless and as pale as milk
on those "white nights" of June, Catherine was living in a state
of feverish anxiety, knowing that for better or worse her fate was
being decided. At dawn on Wednesday, June 28, she was

wakened by her faithful servant Shargorodskaia, who told her
that Alexei Orlov had arrived and was asking to see her at once.
This was no time for ceremony. Catherine received him as she
was, in her nightgown. Orlov told her: "All is ready. The time
has come for you to be proclaimed Empress." In a few minutes
the two women had dressed and had leaped into the carriage
which Alexei had brought with him. He himself took the reins
and whipped up the horses. They set off at a gallop; the women,
half crazy with excitement and worry and perhaps a little with
the hysterical exhilaration that goes with the approach of danger,
were roaring with laughter because one of them was still wearing
her slippers and the other her nightcap. The horses were exhausted and dragging badly, so they borrowed some from a
peasant who luckily happened to be going by in a cart.

When the travelers were some miles from the capital Gregory
Orlov came to meet them in a carriage accompanied by Prince
Bariatinsky, and Catherine continued the journey at her lover's
side. At that moment Gregory must have felt like a gallant
knight of old conquering a throne for the sake of his beloved, and
Catherine, who loved him, almost certainly regarded him in this
light. Then the carriage reached the outskirts of the village of
Kalinkina, where the Ismailovsky regiment had its quarters, and
Gregory leaped on a horse and galloped on ahead to announce to
his friends the arrival of the persecuted Empress.

The carriage drove on slowly, while hidden inside the modest
vehicle, flushed and determined, sat the unobtrusive sovereign: a
small, fragile woman dressed in black, without a crown on her
head or an escort to follow her. At a signal given by the officers,
the drums began to beat the alarm, the coach stopped outside the
barracks, and Catherine got out, diffident and alone but certainly
beautiful, transfigured by the wild will to win. Her head was at
stake now, and she was not afraid.

The sight of her unleashed a flood of enthusiasm, which although it had been boiling up for a long time was still unexpect-
edly strong. At this decisive moment Catherine rose to the
situation and played her part with gracious authority. Now

she had only to show herself to provoke a storm of acclamation. "Hurrah! Hurrah for our Mother, Catherine!" The officers crowded around her, kneeling and kissing the hem of her cloak, and the regimental chaplain, Father Alexei, came to meet her with a crucifix in his hand.

On this cross the men of the Ismailovsky regiment swore allegiance to the Empress and Autocrat Catherine the Second. Their colonel, Kyril Razumovsky, came in person and knelt before the new Empress, and when Catherine continued her journey she was accompanied by this influential officer and by the chaplain. She went from one barracks to the next, just as Elizabeth had done. Now she had the Ismailovsky troops to escort her, and to these were soon added those of the Semenovsky regiment. Some of the officers of the Preobrazhensky regiment had been unaware of the existence of the conspiracy, but after some understandable hesitation this regiment too acclaimed the oppressed sovereign of yesterday, already triumphant, and the troops marched into the capital along the Nevsky Prospekt to the cheers of the assembled crowds of citizens who flocked into the street and filled every side turning. Only three hours after Alexei Orlov had burst into her bedroom at Mon Plaisir, Catherine mounted the steps of the Kazan Cathedral.

Slowly, escorted by the Orlov brothers and Razumovsky, Catherine walked forward under the massive vault of the huge cathedral where the priests were already awaiting her. The bishop, dressed in the glittering gold and silver robes of his priestly office with the miter on his head, and surrounded by the cathedral clergy, solemnly blessed the Autocrat Catherine and also her son, "the heir to the throne, Paul Petrovich."

It was in fact high time someone thought of this son. In their chivalrous enthusiasm for the cause of a woman who had been unjustly persecuted and who had come to place "her person and that of her son" under their protection, the officers of the imperial guard had meekly followed the conspirators' lead and had proclaimed Autocrat a woman who was, properly speaking, only Empress Mother. Catherine was taken in procession to the Winter Palace where Count Panin was waiting for her with the child. Little Paul, who cannot have been a very early riser, was got out of bed in his nightshirt and Catherine went out onto the palace balcony to show the little boy to the crowd. When they saw him, with his long golden curls, his little face still flushed with sleep and his eyes wide and terrified, the people roared and shouted with joy. From that moment, Catherine knew that her seven-year-old son was her most dangerous rival, and that the crowd's cheers were less for Catherine II than for the mother of little Paul.

Meanwhile the Grand Duke's extreme youth was used to explain the apparent irregularity of the proceedings, and it was Catherine who was proclaimed Autocrat and to her that the people swore allegiance, just as barely six months earlier they had sworn it to Peter III. But on this day the entire capital was in joyous revolt, in the certain knowledge that it was in the right. The army too, or such troops as were in and around St. Petersburg at the time, had marched like a single man. In the city the revolution was taking so much the same course as that which had brought Elizabeth to the throne that demonstrations against the Germans were already beginning to occur.

When Catherine left the Winter Palace accompanied by her son, she found herself being frantically acclaimed by the men of a regiment she did not recognize. They turned out to be the Preobrazhensky guard. The moment the *coup d'état* became an accomplished fact, officers and men rushed to get out their old uniforms, which had been stowed away ever since Peter III had suppressed them, and came to salute the new Empress dressed like soldiers of Peter the Great. The Good Mother Catherine was never to forget that she was loved and accepted because, in her heart at least, she was a Russian.

Catherine had only a few regiments, while at Narva Peter had assembled a considerable force, already equipped and ready for war. Instead of leading them against Denmark he could quite well march with them on the capital, in which case the rebellion would be crushed in a few hours. In theory at least, this was a very real danger. Moreover Petersburg was a maritime city, dominated by the island fortress of Kronstadt where the entire fleet of the Russian navy lay at anchor. It seemed obvious that Peter had only to take a boat across the few miles of sea separating Oranienbaum from Kronstadt to make himself master of the citadel and, from there, to send his warships to attack Petersburg. To forestall this, Catherine and her supporters immediately despatched Admiral Talysin to Kronstadt, empowered to take full command in the name of the Empress.

Sentries had been posted on all roads leading out of the city in order to prevent news of the coup from reaching Oranienbaum. When Peter arrived at Peterhof on the morning of the twenty-eighth of June, just as Catherine was in the process of being proclaimed Empress and acclaimed by the people of Petersburg, he was taken completely by surprise to find no preparations made to receive him and to learn that the Empress had departed that very morning.

At that time the Emperor was still surrounded by faithful friends. With him were his personal suite from Holstein, the Prussian ambassador Goltz, Marshals Münnich and Trubetskoi, the chancellor Michael Vorontsov, and his brother Roman Vorontsov, Elizabeth's father. When all these men realized what was happening, and then when they found out what had occurred in Petersburg, they were not niggardly of good advice. While Münnich, old soldier that he was, was urging the Emperor to ride with all haste to the capital to recall the disaffected troops to their duty, Goltz was advising him to send the army concentrated at Narva, which was all ready to march, against Petersburg. The Holsteiners, who were better acquainted with their Emperor's character, recommended him bluntly to flee to Holstein. Peter, bewildered and terrified, was incapable of taking any decision whatever. When he finally made up his mind to send emissaries to Kronstadt it was too late: Admiral Talysin was there already with the news of the *coup d'état* and orders from Catherine.

In the belief that the fortress was still faithful to him, Peter embarked in a schooner, together with his Holsteiners, Elizabeth Vorontsova and her ladies in waiting, and appeared before Kronstadt at about one o'clock in the morning. It was a bright night and visibility was almost as clear as daylight. Peter stood on the bridge, near the prow of the ship, a tall thin figure in a white uniform, crying out that he was the Emperor and must have entrance to the port.

He was answered that there was no longer an Emperor, there was only the Empress Catherine, and that if his boat did not remove itself instantly from the vicinity of Kronstadt it would be chased away by "bombs."

This was Peter's last and only attempt to assert his personal authority. He collapsed among the weeping, wailing women, almost unconscious and as weak as a woman himself. He even refused to listen to his friends when they urged him, very sensibly, not to return to land but to escape by sea to Revel and from there to Holstein. Why, since he was in no condition to fight, did he not at least try and save himself? Instead, he went back to Oranienbaum. With the ridiculous obduracy of the weak, he refused to take any decision. He seemed unable to understand that in the space of a few hours he, who yesterday had been Emperor, had become a thing of no account, that he had always been of no account, and the coup had only succeeded so smoothly because where Peter III, Emperor of Russia, should have been there was nothing, a mere ghost.

No one, in fact, himself perhaps included, had ever really believed in his reign, had ever believed that he could rule. His friends, dazed and bewildered by recent events, were beginning to realize this. They tried to behave as though nothing out of the ordinary had occurred, as though a reasonable solution could still be found; but the man before them, uttering screams of rage, weeping, swooning, babbling incoherent threats and flinging himself despairingly into the arms of Elizabeth Vorontsova —his last refuge—was nothing more than a broken doll.[3]

Thirty-four

Assassination of the Emperor

Catherine did come to Peterhof on the feast of Saints Peter and Paul, but not to celebrate her husband's feast day. She came in force at the head of her loyal regiments and ready to fight should Peter take it into his head to send his troops at Narva against her. Not for nothing had she been a tomboy as a child: she loved a fight and always regretted she had not been born a man. If she had to fight she would be capable of leading her men into battle herself, but she knew, as all the world knew, that Peter would not try to defend himself and that not a single arm would be raised in his cause.

Marshal Trubetskoi and the chancellor Vorontsov came to see the Empress on Peter's behalf to put a proposition to her: Peter acknowledged his past errors and promised his wife to allow her a share in the government. Catherine did not deign to answer. Alexei Orlov, at the head of a detachment of guards, easily disarmed the Holsteiners encamped at Peterhof and then rode on to Oranienbaum where he posted sentries at the gates of the town. Peter was virtually a prisoner.

At Peterhof, Catherine received a second letter from her husband. In it, Peter said that he would make no more demands; he renounced all his rights, begged his wife's forgiveness and asked simply to be allowed to retire to Holstein with Elizabeth Vorontsova. Catherine's only reply was a note, carried by General Ismailov and Gregory Orlov, in which she requested her husband's signature to the act of abdication. Peter signed, almost without looking at it. Then, accompanied by his faithful Elizabeth and the adjutant general Gurevich, he was taken under heavy guard to Peterhof.

If he hoped to obtain an interview with his wife in order at least to appeal to her pity, he was mistaken. Catherine was not insensitive, but she had no intention of giving herself the chance to weaken. She would not see him.

In his former apartments at the Peterhof, Peter was stripped of his decorations, his Russian uniform and his sword. He was beyond showing any emotion and was barely able to stand upright. It was Count Panin who had to undertake the painful duty of telling the former Emperor that he was, henceforth, a prisoner of state, and that he should hold himself ready to leave the palace and go to live at Ropsha, one of his country houses, until his final place of residence was assigned to him. What this would be Peter knew only too well: the fortress of Schlüsselburg.

Panin has not recorded what passed during this interview. It must have been a terrible one, for many years later he wrote: "I regard it as one of the greatest misfortunes of my life that I was compelled to see Peter at that moment." Peter must have been in a state bordering on nervous collapse: probably he wept and entreated, crawling abjectly before the man who was his son's tutor. All we do know is that he asked for just one thing: not to be separated from Elizabeth Vorontsova. This favor was denied him. The Vorontsovs, like nearly all Peter's other supporters, had already gone over to Catherine's side and the Empress could not be expected to accede to a request that was both immoral and a personal outrage to herself.

After heartbreaking farewells, Elizabeth was carried, unconscious, to the carriage which was to take her back to Petersburg. Peter, sobbing and all but fainting himself, was bundled into another carriage, surrounded by a strong-armed guard.

On the evening of June 29, roughly thirty hours from the

moment when he had arrived at Peterhof and found the palace empty, Peter reached Ropsha. He was locked in his bedroom with a sentry outside his door, and the house was closely guarded by soldiers.

To ease the rigors of his captivity, Catherine sent him his violin, his Negro servant Narcisse and his favorite dog, Mopsy. She even agreed to let him have his German servants and his French valet, Bressan, to wait on him. For several days she waited anxiously for news. The former Emperor was reported to be ill; he was suffering from violent headaches and he had sent for his doctor from Holstein, who was the only one he trusted.

But the invalid got better. Then the doctor again sent for more medicines. It was a false alarm: there was no hope there. There did not seem to be anything seriously the matter with Peter, beyond a violent nervous disorder. He was alternately prostrate and feverishly excited, and lost his temper with his servants continually. He was living in a state of fear and growing nervous tension. Fearing poison, he insisted on drinking only milk. This state of affairs lasted for a week. On July 6 Alexei Orlov, Prince Feodor Bariatinsky and a number of other officers went to visit him, on the pretext of inspecting his guards. The same day his valet, Bressan, was seized by soldiers as he walked in the garden, gagged, flung into a carriage and driven away from Ropsha. The next day it was learned that the ex-Emperor was dead.

The manifesto by which Catherine announced to the people the abdication of Peter III and her own accession had just been made public and solemnly read before the Senate. Without once mentioning Peter III by name (in order to avoid provoking some untimely surge of loyalty) the Empress declared that the Russian nation was in danger; that the most sacred traditions of the Orthodox Church were threatened and it was even menaced with subjection to an alien rite; that the prestige of the Russian army was suffering from a peace concluded, with complete disregard for the country's best interests, with the enemies of yesterday; that the system of government on which the unity and well-

being of the whole nation depended was being completely over-
thrown and that in consequence of all this, and in view of the
danger threatening her loyal subjects, calling God and His
Justice to come to her aid and knowing herself strengthened
by the express will of her subjects, she, Catherine, had been
compelled to mount the throne as Autocrat of all the Russias.

The official announcement of Peter's abdication coincided
with the news of his death. The same evening Catherine learned
that she was free of her husband forever (so, at least, it seemed
to her then). The next day, July 7, she had another proclama-
tion issued announcing that the former Emperor Peter III had
succumbed to an intestinal hemorrhage. She ordered a post
mortem, in order to put it on record that there was no question
of poisoning. Whatever were the actual causes of death, the
doctors could only state that the Emperor had not died as a
result of poisoning. The body lay in state in the convent of Saint
Alexander Nevsky, where the people had an opportunity to file
past and pay their last respects to the grandson of Peter the
Great.

It is hard to know whether the people of Petersburg believed
the official explanation they were given. Peter was known to be
in delicate health and it was therefore hardly surprising that,
under the stress of violent emotion, his condition should suddenly
have worsened. In the exhilaration which followed the new
Empress's accession to the throne, the people may not have been
disposed to wonder too much. But Catherine knew very well that
this sudden demise left her open to the most damaging suspicions.
She fainted when she learned of her husband's death, and when
she came to herself, she cried out: "I am lost; they will never
believe that I am innocent!"

There can be no doubt that it was assassination. There is
evidence of the deed. Catherine held the proof, although she never
admitted to it, but kept it locked up in a box which was not
opened until after her death.

On July 6, Alexei Orlov wrote her a short note which was
brought to Catherine that very evening. The letter ran:

LITTLE MOTHER, MERCIFUL EMPRESS. How can I explain, how describe, what has occurred? You will not believe your devoted servant, but before God I am telling you the truth. Little Mother, I am ready to die, but I myself do not know how this misfortune came about. We are lost if you do not forgive us. Little Mother—he is gone. But it was through none of our desire, for how should we have dared to raise our hand against our sovereign? But, Majesty, this misfortune has occurred. He started to quarrel with Prince Feodor [Bariatinsky] during dinner; we were unable to part them before already he was no more. We cannot even remember what we did, but all of us, down to the last man, are wholly guilty and deserve to die for it. Have mercy on me, if only for love of my brother! I have confessed my sin and there is nothing more to say. Forgive me, or have me put to death. My life is a burden to me; we have offended you and we are damned for all eternity.[1]

This is the only eyewitness report we possess of the tragic event. On the other hand Bressan, who was not present at the time, may have managed to question some of the servants who were in the house at the moment the crime took place. A number of rumors were soon in circulation in circles hostile to Catherine which may possibly have been inspired by Bressan's account, but they may equally be regarded as pure fiction. Helbig in particular claims that the role of executioner was assumed by Englehardt, a guards officer of German origin, who was very close to the Orlovs. According to him, those who took part in the murder were, besides Orlov and Prince Bariatinsky, Razumovsky's son-in-law Teplov, and the celebrated actor Volkov. The murderers first tried to strangle their victim by means of a scarf and then stifled him under a mattress. Alexei Orlov, unable to bear the horror of the scene, rushed out of the room and waited on the terrace until the execution was over. Helbig was unaware of the existence of Orlov's letter, but he wrote that some who saw Alexei coming back to Petersburg "said that his face, which was naturally gross, was still more frightful to behold" on that day.[2]

The actual letter (says Princess Dashkova, who saw it with her own eyes) was written in a hurried, unevenly penciled scrawl and obviously under the stress of drunkenness or some violent emotion. It seemed to betray some remorse, or at least the fear of displeasing the Empress. Alexei Orlov must have acted on his own initiative in the murder without consulting Catherine, and he was trying to make her believe that the crime was not premeditated. All the same he had gone to Ropsha remarkably quickly, before the government had had time to make arrangements for transferring the prisoner to the dungeon reserved for him in the fortress. Another incident in his life gives ample proof that Alexei was a man who would stop at nothing, however violent, criminal or underhand. There is no reason to be certain that the remorse he betrays in his letter is sincere, nor for that matter any reason to suppose that the murder was not in fact carried out on Catherine's orders. Orlov might very well have received more or less oblique instructions to eliminate the former Emperor, and have merely panicked when the victim showed more fight than had been anticipated and the marks of violence were only too clear. Certainly he was too intelligent to believe that Catherine would take him at his word and, as he put it, have him put to death. Whether or not she had wanted it to happen, he had made her an accessory to the crime.

Was this a crime dictated by ambition or for political ends? Probably both at once, for clearly, by eliminating Catherine's husband, Alexei thought he was leaving the way clear for his brother. But apart from that, as one of the principal architects of the *coup d'état* he could not leave the job unfinished. Catherine was a woman, and possibly unaware of the character of the Russian people and intoxicated by her initial success, she may still have cherished some illusions: Peter was merely a puppet, a hated "German," and his ephemeral reign had collapsed like a house of cards. But Petersburg was not the whole of Russia and it was perfectly possible that in a month, or six months, the very officers and nobles who had acclaimed Catherine on the morning after her coup might remember her husband's generosity and hold over the Empress the threat of reinstating Peter III. A dethroned emperor could not be allowed to remain alive.

If Catherine had really intended to leave her husband to rot for twenty years in the dungeons of Schlüsselburg, then she had little political sense. If she had hoped to hasten his end by keeping him in close confinement, then she might have had a long time to wait. The young Ivan VI, who had also been imprisoned in Schlüsselburg, had survived in the most wretched conditions for seventeen years and seemed in no hurry to die. If Catherine imagined she could rid herself of Peter by some more "gentle" means and have him poisoned in his prison, then it could be said that Alexei Orlov's action, though it may have been inopportune, at least left the Empress's conscience free of a crime which she had meant to commit in any case.

There was no going back now. Peter III was well and truly dead: probably strangled after a fierce struggle, for those who saw him lying in his coffin reported that his face was almost black and his neck muffled up to the chin in a thick scarf, while his hands, which it was the custom in the Orthodox Church to leave in view, were hidden by heavy gauntlets. Although he was a descendant of Peter the Great he was not buried as an emperor. Dressed in the pale blue uniform of an officer in the Holstein dragoons, without decorations, the Duke of Holstein received what was simultaneously the insult and the supreme consolation of going to his grave in the costume which he had always preferred to that of Emperor of Russia.

It seems that even to drown a dog people generally feel the need to accuse it of being mad. When the victim is an emperor this need is even greater. Peter III was the first tsar of Russia to die by assassination, though not the last. What explanation could be offered for such a breach of the divine right, beyond that of declaring the dead man to have been a monster and a madman? He was neither of these things; he was only a man who was pitifully unequal to the role he had to play. His German origins and even more his ridiculous attachment to his native land and to Prussia had been, much more than his vices and his weaknesses, the real cause of his downfall.

The *corrida* was over, and the matador, though threatened for an instant by a clumsy and stupid bull, had only to salute the crowd. "Fortune is less blind than we imagine. It is largely the result of strong, definite measures which pass unnoticed by the majority, which have gone before the event. More, and more particularly, it is the effect of qualities of character and personal conduct."[3]

Eighteen years earlier an adolescent girl had written this little note to her cousin and playmate who was ill in bed with the measles:

> MY LORD. Having consulted with my mother, knowing that she has great influence with the Grand Marshal, she has promised to speak to him and make them let you play on your instruments. She has also charged me to ask you, my lord, whether you would like some *Italians* this afternoon.
>
> I assure you that in your place I should go mad if everyone were kept away from me. I beg you in God's name not to show him this letter.
>
> CATHERINE.[4]

Life had turned the betrothed children into deadly enemies. The stronger had crushed the weaker. We do not know whether the shade of her assassinated husband haunted Catherine's dreams, but she had a long life in front of her and she dedicated it to the task of proving to the whole world her nobility of character and grandeur of soul.

Thirty-five

(◆+(◆+(◆+(◆+(◆+(◆+(◆+(◆+(◆+(◆+(◆+(◆

She Who Would Reign

In 1757 L'Hôpital wrote: "It would be unwise to maintain too close links with the princes [the Grand Duke and Duchess] but in the future one might regret having neglected to cultivate them."[1] In November 1760 Choiseul was writing to the Comte de Breteuil: "You can assure the Grand Duchess that I shall look into the matters concerning her brother. Although this princess has very little influence it is still wise to humor her, but this must be done with great circumspection in order to avoid arousing the jealousy of the Empress and her ministers."[2]

In fact, in 1760 the princess who had "very little influence" was already the first candidate for the imperial throne. For years, ever since her early youth, she had been preparing herself to rule. She had not succeeded in influencing Peter, although she had lavished on him the best advice in the world; she had failed as a woman to cope with a husband who was both self-indulgent and semi-impotent. Theirs was a case of a mutual frigidity, for which neither husband nor wife was probably to blame, but which rooted in Catherine with an incurable bitterness. We do not know what Peter's feelings were, but the dislike he showed for his wife during the last years of his life seems to have its deepest cause in a lively physical aversion. Their mutual loathing which was to end in the husband's tragic death must have grown and worsened in the privacy of their marriage bed.

At one given moment Catherine had realized that she would never reign at Peter's side.

While aimless intrigues were being woven around the dying Empress, while Gregory Orlov was proselytizing among the army on behalf of his mistress and Count Panin was drawing up his proposals for a government with Paul as Emperor under the regency of his mother, Catherine was thinking for herself, and jotting down the fruits of her reading and her reflections on random sheets of paper.

"As He is my witness, I have no other wish or desire beyond the good of the country to which God has sent me. The nation's glory is mine also. This is my principle, and I am only too happy if my ideas can contribute to it."

"To join the Caspian to the Black Sea and both to the North Sea; to establish trade routes from China and the East Indies through Tartary, would be to raise this Empire [Russia] to a degree of power above that of the other empires of Asia and Europe. And who can resist the *unlimited power of an absolute prince governing a warlike people*?"

With clearly expressed dreams of grandeur, dreams of "unlimited power"—and it was not for Peter that she desired it—were mingled meditations inspired by her reading of the *Philosophes*. She meant to reign as absolute monarch but she intended to use her power for the good of her people: "It is against justice and the Christian religion to make men (who are born free) slaves. . . . Liberty, soul of all things, without you all is dead. I want people to obey the laws but not to be slaves. . . . Power without the trust of the nation is nothing."

"Servitude is damaging to the state, it kills emulation, industry, the arts, sciences, honor and prosperity."[3] (This quotation was taken from the *Journal de l'Encyclopédie*, March 1761.) Catherine was against slavery, and against serfdom, the greatest social evil of Russian life. This, however, did not mean that she intended to abolish it; she did not have her head in the clouds to that extent. The "means" which she envisages, in a purely hypothetical light, is this: "To make such a sweeping change [as the enfranchisement of the serfs] would not be the way to make oneself loved by the landowners. . . . But there is a simple way: to make a ruling that henceforth whenever anyone sells land, the moment it changes hands all serfs shall be declared free. Now, *in a hundred years*, nearly all the land will have changed hands and you will have a free people." (The answer to Catherine's scheme might well have been that in that case no one would ever sell any land, since they would not find customers to buy such devalued goods.)

Apart from this agreeably unrealistic proposition, Catherine devoted very little thought to concrete ways of combatting serfdom. But she did think of the well-being of the people: "Go to any village: the number of children born to most peasant families is ten, twelve, often as many as twenty. Yet only one, two or maybe four of these are living. Reduce the mortality rate, consult doctors, do something about the care of young children. . . . They run about naked in their shifts in the snow and ice. Those who survive are healthy, but nineteen out of twenty die, *and what a loss to the state.*"

These are her views on the policy to be adopted toward a newly conquered people: "Peace is necessary to this vast empire. We need populating, but not devastating. We must make our huge deserts swarm like an ant heap if that is possible, and to achieve this I see no point in forcing those of our people who are not Christians to adopt our religion." This may look like a spirit of tolerance, but far from it: "plurality of wives helps to increase the population."

As far as the dominant classes were concerned, and the nobility in particular, Catherine considered making the law on compulsory state service less harsh: a father who had three or more sons was to be able to keep one or two at home. At forty or forty-five a gentleman should be free, because families and estates suffered in the absence of their heads. (If she was thinking in this way to please the nobility she was to find herself very soon outdone by her husband in the most radical fashion.)

Property is sacred: "I abhor nothing more than the confiscation of the goods of convicted men, for who can oust children from their inheritance which they hold *from God himself?*"

On the conduct of rulers, she thinks they should impress by their wealth. "Opulence must reign," but a real opulence, not one based on debt. Rulers should take care to avoid making a law and then revoking it. They should rather inspire reforms than order them. In his relations with his entourage a ruler should give merit its due. "He who does not seek for merit and find it, is unworthy to reign." "I want to establish that I am told the truth by way of flattery." "Grant only favors requested personally, so that people may be obliged to you and not to favorites."[4]

These reflections were put down during Elizabeth's lifetime —some perhaps in the first months of the reign of Peter III— but on reading them we receive the impression that they are the words of a woman who has been seated on a throne for a long time, or is at least certain of ascending one in the normal course of events. Catherine forged for herself the soul of a ruler. The *coup d'état* which took only a few hours to accomplish had been prepared down to the minutest detail by the Orlovs, Princess Dashkova, Panin, Razumovsky and Catherine herself. Catherine's rise to power, which seemed in the eyes of the people a spectacular show, had long been prepared for in the secret heart of a resolute woman who was already more preoccupied with power than with her private loves and sorrows.

Catherine was ruling at last, with opulence, with *panache* and also with a latent, obsessional fear of (as Breteuil put it) "losing what she had been bold enough to take." The revolution had been not so much *for* her as *against* Peter III. She began by giving pledges to everyone. For the Orthodox Church, her uncertain ally (for was she herself not also a German and a former Lutheran?) she rescinded Peter's ukase confiscating the wealth of the clergy (leaving herself free to reinforce it later on when she felt stronger). For the army, there was, of course, to be no war against Denmark and no treaty of alliance with Prussia. There was not to be war either, because she did not want to make an enemy of Frederick; but there was to be friendship with Austria and France.

She gave generous rewards to those who had taken part in the conspiracy: all, down to the humblest soldier, were placed on a list, held by the finance department of her chancellery, of those to be given gifts of either money or land. At its head were the Orlov brothers, Panin, and Razumovsky. The gifts given to these principal architects of her success totaled as much as 526,000 rubles, besides eighteen thousand peasants—these last came from those attached to "crown" lands (lands where the peasants were still to all intents free). This was an odd way of going about easing the burden of serfdom; but these crown lands were an easy way of making loyal servants.

With Panin, whom she could never quite forgive for his intention to have young Paul proclaimed Emperor, and with Catherine Dashkova, both influential representatives of the party who looked to her for reforms, she continued to parade her liberal outlook, and in this she may have been sincere: yes, she said, certainly she meant to put the ideas of the *Philosophes* into practice, but later, when she had consolidated her position . . . For the time being, she knew and all the world knew that she was merely a usurper, who had come to the throne as a result of the enforced abdication and suspicious death of her husband. She was no daughter of Peter the Great. She could distribute all the gifts, smiles and promises that she liked; she was still only a petty German princess, a high-flown adventuress, carried to power more as a result of her husband's ineffectiveness than by her own merits. Her reputation was not stainless; her love affairs with Saltykov and Poniatowski were known to every court in Europe, quite apart from the Russian one, and now she had a new threat hanging over her in the person of her lover of the moment, her paladin and accomplice Gregory Orlov, who, seeing her a widow, was beginning to make insistent demands for the reward he considered his right.

Catherine began by silencing possible sources of intrigue by proclaiming her wish to be solemnly crowned Empress in Moscow, where all the tsars of Russia had been anointed since the time of Ivan the Terrible. Once crowned, and anointed of the Lord, she would be Empress in earnest.

Thirty-six

᚛᚛᚛᚛᚛᚛᚛᚛᚛᚛᚛᚛

The New Empress

On the seventh of July—the day on which news of Peter III's death was made public—Catherine announced her intention of being consecrated in Moscow, and fixed the date of the ceremony for September. Clearly this left barely enough time to arrange the details and make the preparations, for she meant to inaugurate her reign with all the pomp which she herself had advocated in her notes.

She was aiming not merely at appealing to the people's imagination with a show of wealth and a display of religious and civil pomp and ceremony, but also at attracting the sympathies of the second capital. In Catherine's eyes Moscow was provincial, strongly traditionalist, inert, and retrograde, but it was still powerful, and closer to the rest of Russia than the cosmopolitan and somewhat artificial St. Petersburg.

It would be impossible to attempt a description of the pomp and ceremony of the coronation, which was to surpass in magnificence all those which within Russian memory had been celebrated in the massive and hieratic Cathedral of the Assumption, right in the middle of the Kremlin. The cathedral was of modest size compared with those of Petersburg—the Saint Isaac and the Kazan, built on the model of Saint Peter's in Rome—but it was very old. This Russian cathedral dated from the fifteenth century and Catherine thought it more than a little barbaric. The huge iconostasis was adorned with fine icons by Andrei Rublev, all covered in gold, silver and precious stones, and the massive pillars and vaulted roof were painted with frescos owing something to both Byzantine and Eastern traditions and reminiscent of what Romanesque churches must once have been like. The Russian Church, immensely rich and its riches continually increasing as a result of pious donations, devoted a great part of its wealth to embellishing God's houses with a luxury on a par with that of the imperial household.

Russian museums still possess these solid gold and silver crosses encrusted with diamonds, miters studded with precious stones, and priestly vestments sewn with seed pearls weighing in all well over forty pounds. For herself, Catherine had an ermine cloak made which took four thousand skins, and commanded her goldsmiths to make an imperial crown for which she gave a pound of gold and several pounds of silver, not to mention jewels. A hundred and twenty kegs full of silver pieces were to be distributed among the people, and all the craftsmen in both capitals worked feverishly, day and night, to prepare a celebration the like of which had never been seen.

Catherine was not idle in the two months preceding her coronation: with an energy surprising on the part of a young woman who still looked to all appearances fragile and unused to this kind of work, she made it her personal business to supervise all diplomatic correspondence, kept herself informed of all details of finance and administration, presided over all councils of ministers, all meetings of the Senate, keeping senators and high officials on their toes by her minute and extremely pertinent questions, her demands and her incessant appeals to their civic responsibilities.

No Russian sovereign since Peter the Great had ever taken the trouble to really go into this somewhat bureaucratic and technical side of his royal duties at all seriously. Catherine, however, threw herself into the rather stern and unrewarding work with the eagerness of a starving man falling on food. She had much lost time to make up. She would work ten, twelve, fifteen hours a day: she wanted to be, like Peter the Great, the first worker and the first servant of her country, a country that was hers at last. She had prodigious reserves of common sense, and a gift for organization and administration which she had hitherto had little chance to display. Like an actress who finally manages to get the leading part she has always dreamed of, she developed almost overnight a dazzling authority, wit and eloquence, and a graciousness at once smiling and distant—for she was still at the stage of playing at being Empress.

She felt herself so infinitely above all her ministers with their private interests, her idle or ignorant civil servants, that she was determined to give them all lessons in civics, economics, politics and diplomacy, for had she not the immeasurable advantage over them of having read *L'Esprit des Lois*, Bayle's *Dictionnaire* and Voltaire's *Histoire Universelle*? She had her work cut out for her: in Elizabeth's time—and in Anna's also—the greatest disorder had reigned in all branches of the administration, and it could be said that despite the efforts of Peter the Great, Russia was still governed by much the same system as it had been under Tsar Alexei Mikhailovich. The administration was in fact empirical and based on custom. Thousands of regulations existed on paper which were never applied in practice, and the various ministries and chancelleries were independent bodies and never worked together. Things were in such a state that Catherine, who possessed an innate love of order and clarity, felt like Hercules cleaning out the Augean stables. The senators and ministers who listened to her could not help giving vent to murmurs of approbation, as they wondered whether this romantic and extravagant foreigner would entertain herself for much longer with playing the statesman.

It was Catherine's honeymoon with power. She gave herself to it completely. She was not niggardly with promises nor of generous intentions: she says that she herself studied every petition, and she wanted to right every wrong. She proposed to increase the salaries of higher and lower civil servants (this with the object of combatting corruption). One day she herself intervened between the police and the crowd which had pressed too close as she passed along a street. Publicly in the Senate, she renounced her right to the "Chamber funds," money set aside for the Tsar's personal expenses, which amounted to one and a half million rubles. She hoped this would set an example and encourage officials of Elizabeth's time to resign their monopolies on major industries with a good grace, since these monopolies were paralyzing the import and export trades.

The treasury was empty, and the state on the verge of financial disaster. Catherine spent money recklessly on her coronation and to reward her friends, taking back with one hand what she gave with the other. What did it matter? It was a good investment and she had a head for business. A state does not become more powerful by cutting expenses, but by creating new sources of income and increasing its credit. To increase her popularity she stopped the balls and masquerades which Elizabeth had enjoyed so much and at which, in former days, she herself had so often been bored. Otherwise her shows were more impressive: for every ruble that Elizabeth had managed to spend, Catherine would spend a hundred, but in such a way that the whole of Europe would have to bow before the brilliance and splendor of her empire.

She began at the beginning, that is to say with her coronation. In that month of September 1762, Moscow plunged for weeks on end into an atmosphere of carnival, and forgot the short interregnum that had been the reign of Peter III, until it seemed to have been merely an unfortunate mistake. Dancing, drinking, singing, cheering the new Empress, seeing daily processions of gilded coaches with soldiers in glittering uniforms and great ladies in jewels and fine clothes, hurrying to stare at firework displays, sporting contests and *tableaux vivants*, the people of Moscow were learning that the new Empress was an Orthodox

Russian who loved her people and who was still young, pretty and smiling. Moreover, she had been crowned with a golden crown in the Cathedral of the Assumption, dressed in a purple cloak, anointed by the hands of the Archbishop of Novgorod, and proclaimed Autocrat of the Russian Empire and temporal head of the Orthodox Church.

It did not occur to anyone to condemn her for failing to wear mourning for her husband, nor for the untimely nature of the festivities which followed so hard upon the death of Peter III. It was as though this ephemeral emperor had never existed, which in its way was true enough. Yet even so the Muscovites, strongly conservative and distrustful as they were, would have preferred to honor Catherine as a mother who had just crowned her son: for them, the Grand Duke Paul was the real heir to the throne of his father.

Now the child was ill, so ill, in fact, that eight days after his mother's coronation he was actually hanging between life and death and the rumor was already spreading among the people that Catherine, having rid herself of her husband, was trying to kill her son by slow poison. In desperation, and knowing very well that her son's death at such a time was likely to lose her the crown just as she had won it, Catherine spent her days and nights at little Paul's bedside. The child got better, and in gratitude Catherine had a hospital built in Moscow to commemorate his recovery. She had had a narrow escape—but for how long? Paul's health was delicate and she had no other heir; even crowned and anointed with holy oil, she still reigned only on sufferance. She had not yet had time to manifest the "qualities of character" which would make her worthy of the throne.

She was beginning to realize that, behind her few more or less steadfast supporters—the Orlovs, the Razumovskys, the Panins —behind the court which was always prone to discontent and intrigue and the army which was more than ever sure of its own strength, there lay something she had not as yet encountered or even guessed at. Behind these were the people, and the unobtrusive but powerful minorities constituted by the minor nobility,

265 · *The New Empress*

the clergy, the merchants, and all those who in Russia represented public opinion. To these people she was a foreigner, an
unknown. It was a matter of complete indifference to them
whether or not she wore the crown of diamonds and an ermine
cloak.

When she finally sensed this indifference she responded to
it by an equal indifference herself. In reality she was never
interested in anyone who could not either serve or love her.
Few women have been so greedy for love.

Catherine was thirty-three. Favier, her French secretary,
describes her like this: "One cannot say that she is a beauty; her
figure is tall and slender but not supple; she has a noble carriage, an affected and somewhat ungraceful walk, with a narrow
chest, a long face, especially about the chin, an eternal smile
on her lips, a deep-set mouth, a slightly aquiline nose, small
eyes, an agreeable expression, and a face marked by smallpox
[she had not had it, so the marks must have been left by chicken-
pox]. She is pretty rather than ugly, but not so as to inspire
violent feelings. Her height, medium; rather thin."[1] It is a
well-made portrait and on the whole coincides with that left by
her portrait painters, although these, in the eighteenth century,
were generally gallant enough to flatter their female subjects.

Catherine's face, even as a young girl, was neither pretty
nor really attractive; the mouth, under the "eternal smile," was
tight-lipped, hard and sensual, and the eyes, though sparkling
with life, were cold. Her chin was decidedly too long and with
age was to become really prominent. While priding herself on
being not in the least mannish, Catherine had in fact a somewhat masculine cast of countenance, but even if (as is fairly
clear) she did not inspire any violent feelings in Favier's bosom,
the secretary must be said to speak only for himself, for Catherine obviously was attractive and many men were attracted
to her. She was able to inspire sincere passion, a devotion which
could withstand every test, and many lasting friendships. She
possessed the charm of a supple and inquiring mind, natural
gaiety, and a real gift of sympathy and understanding for the

person to whom she was speaking. She knew how to put everyone at their ease and she had the desire to please which Saint-Simon attributed to Fénelon, and which meant that everyone she talked with felt at ease and pleased with their own wit. Her cordiality and the simplicity of her manners contained no trace of affectation.

For a grand duchess and the wife of an emperor, this charm had been the most precious of qualities; in an autocrat, too much affability could be taken for a want of dignity, and Breteuil wrote at this period: "At the great court assemblies, it is curious to watch the care with which the Empress sets out to please everyone, the freedom and importunity with which everyone speaks to her of their affairs and opinions. . . . She must believe herself very little independent to endure that."[2] She was, indeed, "very little independent" as yet, and it takes more than three months to shed a habit of eighteen years. Catherine was conciliatory. But with the years she was to develop an awe-inspiring natural majesty.

For all her intelligence and good will she was still, in matters of government, no more than an amateur. She had left affairs in the hands of the old team which had directed them throughout the time of Elizabeth and Peter III. Count Michael Vorontsov was still chancellor, although he had formerly been Catherine's declared enemy. The most capable man of the last years of Elizabeth's reign, Peter Shuvalov, was dead. Panin, to whom Catherine entrusted the direction of foreign policy, was a staunch ally, but not always an easy one, for he had ideas of his own. Old Bestuzhev, recalled from his exile and treated with the greatest honor (Catherine would rise and go to meet him when she saw him enter the council chamber) would have been glad to regain some of the power he had once enjoyed, but Catherine knew him too well and distrusted his ambitions. Her most loyal friends, the soldiers who had put her on the throne, were uneducated men, with no experience of affairs of state.

She herself had once written that "he who does not look for merit . . . is unworthy to rule," but men of real merit have a

tendency to act on their own initiative, and Catherine was unwilling to risk losing, through lack of experience, the power
she had bought so dearly. She was realizing, also, that not only
her ministers but the humblest of her early supporters believed
that they had a right to impose their will on her. "The meanest
soldier of the guard," she wrote, "thinks, when he sees me, that
I am the result of his work."[3]

Thirty-seven

◄◆◄◆◄◆◄◆◄◆◄◆◄◆◄◆◄◆◄◆◄◆

The Faithful Servants

She had to begin by neutralizing her own friends.

From the first days of her reign the Empress set about indicating to Catherine Dashkova that there were limits to the claims
of friendship. Before the *coup d'état* this young woman had been
a most precious auxiliary: she had taken an active part in the
conspiracy, although she obviously paints an exaggerated picture
of it in her memoirs; above all, she had exercised a real moral
influence on "liberal" circles close to the court, and had persuaded Panin to give up insisting on the rights of the Grand
Duke Paul. She was an idealist, and one who could not be
made to keep quiet by being loaded with money and honors.
Neither did she aspire to power. What she wanted was to be
admired. Moreover, she loved Catherine passionately and did not
mean to be disappointed in her.

But the Catherine of Dashkova's dreams did not exist: the

day the young princess discovered that her beloved friend was having an affair with Gregory Orlov she was deeply hurt by it, for she was—a rare thing at the court—both naïve and puritanical. She drew a veil over her idol's weakness but she continued to hope and to make demands. In drawing rooms she was always discussing reforms; she talked to ambassadors and boasted indiscreetly of her influence over Count Panin and the Empress, claiming that she was their confidante, their best friend, even their inspiration. She did this to such good effect that foreign diplomats began to talk, ironically, of "Dashkova's government."

Catherine herself, in a letter to Stanislas Poniatowski, complains of her friend's presumption and tries to minimize the part played by the young princess: she has had enough of people who regard her as "a tool in their hands." The young woman's uncle, the chancellor Vorontsov, was beginning to be afraid that the girl would draw the Empress's displeasure on herself by her indiscreet behavior and become, through her independent character, the cause of the family's disgrace[1]—a curious apprehension when the princess's sister, Elizabeth Vorontsova, had been forgiven and honorably married off to the senator Poliansky. Catherine was generous to her enemies, at least to those who could no longer do her any harm. She was less so to her friends.

Catherine Dashkova was merely a nuisance on account of her youthful indiscretions. More important were the masculine ambitions with which the Empress had to deal. These were more difficult to control, for she was still not strong enough to be able to afford to make enemies.

One of the principal authors of the *coup d'état* had been Kyril Razumovsky, the brother of Elizabeth's favorite but more ambitious than his elder. He was a gallant in the best sense of the word and had long admired Catherine. He was also an educated man (his brother had sent him to Berlin to study and he had remained there for a number of years), honest, generous, universally esteemed, and immensely rich because Elizabeth had granted him the title of hetman, or governor, of the Ukraine and the rank of colonel in the Ismailovsky regiment. Kyril, who was neither an administrator nor a soldier, reaped no other advantages from this privileged position beyond a comfortable income. Now he hoped for more: he was a Ukrainian and he had in mind making his title of hetman hereditary and acquiring practical control over the government of his native province. Catherine did not disabuse him, but the part she gave him to play in affairs was almost entirely an honorary one. At the beginning of her reign she could still allow herself to show gratitude to her supporters by heaping on them marks of friendship, marks which left them everything to hope for in the future.

Two years later she felt herself strong enough to rebuff Kyril's demands. She maneuvered him into resigning his post of hetman and, at the same time, abolished the hetmanship altogether, thus taking away from the Ukraine what little independence it still retained.

The Orlov brothers, for their part, considered that the Empress owed everything to them, and in fact she did owe them a great deal. The day after her coronation she granted Gregory and Alexei and the three other Orlov brothers the title of count, and she loaded them with lands, gifts in money and in kind, swords with hilts studded with diamonds, and decorations (the orders of Saint Andrew and Saint Alexander Nevsky). Neither Gregory nor Alexei was prepared to consider himself paid off for so little. In fact, Catherine's lover aspired to nothing less than marriage; whether or not he had had anything to do with the assassination of Peter III, he was well aware that Alexei had made Catherine a widow so that he, Gregory, could marry her.

Simple men, and as ignorant of politics as they were unscrupulous, the Orlovs imagined that, since they had been strong enough to make an empress, one of them might just as well put the imperial crown on his own head, or at least obtain the title of prince consort. Gregory had his pride and he was not at all disposed to play the subordinate and humiliating role of a woman's clandestine lover, to be received at night and blushed for during the day. Catherine's relations with Gregory Orlov were no longer a secret from anyone. Princess Dashkova, in her memoirs, describes Gregory nonchalantly sprawling on a sofa in the Empress's apartment and opening official communications addressed to Catherine; then when she arrived and ordered the meal to be served, the table was pushed up to the sofa because Gregory refused to disturb himself. This incident occurred during the days immediately following the *coup d'état*, while Peter was still alive.[2]

What Catherine needed least was to be thought of as a weak or loose-living woman, dominated by a baseborn lover. Her prestige suffered greatly. As a result of their brash arrogance, the Orlovs soon made themselves unpopular not only at court but also among the army officers, with whom they had formerly enjoyed some influence but where they were now making themselves an increasing number of enemies. There is no doubt that Catherine was thinking of a secret marriage, for she loved Gregory Orlov and was concerned to safeguard his pride. She even entrusted the chancellor Vorontsov with a delicate mission to Alexei Razumovsky which hinted that if the former master of the royal hunt would provide proof of his marriage to the late Empress, he would have the right, as the widowed prince consort, to the honors due to members of the imperial family, and to a substantial pension besides. But the old Ukrainian was not interested in honors, and did not need money because he was already one of the richest men in Russia. Tradition has it that before Vorontsov's eyes he took out a certain piece of paper tied with a pink ribbon, carried it piously to his lips and then threw it in the fire. He was not going to furnish a precedent for the Empress's marriage to such a man as Gregory Orlov.

Not long afterward a plot, or the beginnings of a plot, was discovered. A young officer named Khitrovo, with a number of his friends, was proposing to kill the Orlov brothers (they were aiming at Alexei in particular, as the most dangerous of the gang) in order to prevent the Empress from marrying Gregory, because they considered that such a marriage would be a disaster for the country. Under interrogation Khitrovo defended himself bravely and declared that his plan was inspired solely by love of his country, and that he and his friends asked nothing better than to see the Empress marry again, provided only that it was with a man worthy to wear the crown.

This, Gregory Orlov, in the eyes of public opinion, was certainly not. Nor was he in Catherine's. He was neither intelligent nor cultivated, and was not even of noble birth. Furthermore, there were already rumors abroad among the people attributing Peter III's murder to the Orlovs. Catherine loved him in spite of his jealousy, unreasonableness and bad temper—not, perhaps, as much as she had in the first months of their affair, but in the way that any reasonable woman loves the man with whom she has chosen to make her life.

More than a lover, more than a favorite, Gregory was to hold for ten years a position which was not altogether that of a morganatic husband but which was remarkably like it. He owned a splendid palace in Petersburg and a house just outside it, at Gatchina, set in the middle of an enormous park. He was given huge gifts of land in Russia, Livonia and Estonia, he received countless decorations, and he alone was privileged to wear in his buttonhole the Empress's portrait set in diamonds. Without actually being a member of the government he kept himself informed on affairs of state, and Catherine consulted him on everything, or at least made a pretense of doing so; and although he may not have been competent to carry out the administrative tasks assigned to him, he was at least, for Catherine, a devoted servant.

But it had taken him time to resign himself to the subordinate position in which he was forced, partly by the Empress's will and partly by the pressures of public opinion, to remain. On the eve of her coronation, he had told Catherine publicly that he was strong enough to dethrone her "in one or two months." ("In that case," Kyril Razumovsky had retorted, "we won't wait a month. We'll have you hanged in a fortnight.") A lion with his claws drawn, Gregory was never truly happy, in spite of the riches and honors rained on his head, and he suffered cruelly from a position that would have fulfilled the dearest wishes of many other men, more self-interested or less proud than himself.

As for Alexei Orlov, he was to find in the services an employ-

ment worthy of his abilities. He became admiral of the Russian
fleet on the Black Sea and covered himself with glory in the
war against the Turks. For him, at least, when all was said and
done, the coup of June 28 was an unqualified success.

Thirty-eight

[◦[◦[◦[◦[◦[◦[◦[◦[◦[◦[◦[◦

The Neglected Lover

A few days after her dramatic accession to the throne, Catherine
wrote the following short note: "I urgently pray you not to hasten
to come here, because your presence in the existing circumstances
would be dangerous for yourself and very harmful to me. The
revolution which has just occurred in my favor is miraculous:
it is incredible with what unanimity it was carried through. I
am terribly busy and cannot relate everything at length. All my
life I shall seek only to serve and honor both you and your
family, but everything here is at a vital and critical stage at
present. I have not slept for three nights and have eaten only
twice in four days. Goodbye. Stay well. CATHERINE."[1]

The recipient of this note was all too likely, at the first hint
of the revolution and news of the death of Peter III, to dash to
Petersburg like a madman, with the object of at last holding
in his arms the woman for whom he had been pining for almost
four years. But Stanislas Poniatowski was not to see his beloved
again until thirteen years later, and then only for a few minutes.

Prudence, pity and the remains of a sincere affection had

restrained Catherine from admitting to Stanislas that she had betrayed him. Moreover, she differed from the majority of unfaithful women in that she continued to write to her former lover, and there was nothing in her letters to indicate to the young Pole that she no longer loved him. It is not necessary to accuse Catherine of deceit here, for she felt morally isolated and she had a great need for the affection and understanding which a man of his sensibilities could give her, and the remembrance of him consoled her for the coarseness of her handsome Gregory. She may also, even at this stage, have been thinking of using Stanislas for political ends.

She had barely got over the first shock of her startlingly rapid success when, a month after the coup, she wrote a long letter to Poniatowski, telling him in detail her version of the events which had taken place in June and giving him to understand that she would support his candidature for the throne of Poland after the death of Augustus of Saxony.

To Stanislas, who was not very much interested in being a king, such a suggestion could have only one meaning: Catherine wanted him crowned so that it would be easier for her to marry him. He wrote to her: "Do not make me a king! Only call me back to you! . . . That any other woman could have changed I would believe, but you, never. What is left for me? Emptiness, and a frightful weariness of heart. Sophie, Sophie, you make me suffer terribly!" Here was a man who loved her truly and without calculation, and there is no doubt that he would have been happy to see Catherine lose her throne and marry him, but he knew, too, that above all else his beloved wanted to rule.

More honest than Catherine, after remaining absolutely faithful to her for two years he had thought it his duty to write and tell her of his decision to take—for the time being—a mistress. He was the more determined to do everything possible in order to marry Catherine because his mother, horrified to learn that her son had committed adultery, had made him swear on her deathbed to regularize the situation as soon as the opportunity occurred. It was not an easy promise to keep even if he had to allow himself to be elected King of Poland to make the marriage possible.

The Polish throne did in fact become vacant in 1763 when Augustus of Saxony died, and Catherine gave the *Sejm* (Diet) to understand that she would support the candidature of Stanislas Poniatowski with all her might. Frederick II showed himself equally disposed to approve of this candidate. Both of them had excellent reasons for this. The candidate chosen by the Polish nobles was Count Adam Czartoryski, a cousin of Stanislas. He was an able man, immensely rich and well known for his patriotism, and he had plans for reforms which could save Poland, a country politically backward, without frontiers, and watched on all sides by greedy and powerful neighbors only waiting to pounce. Such a king would not have suited the book of either Prussia or Russia, both of whom had long regarded Poland as a cake which they could nibble at if not cut up completely. Frederick appealed to the German and Protestant minorities, Catherine to the Orthodox Ukrainians, both of whom were harshly oppressed by the Polish government, which was traditionally Catholic, extremist and racially prejudiced.

The two monarchs therefore found themselves in agreement in deciding that the dangerously able and popular Adam Czartoryski should be set aside in favor of his young kinsman who was easier to manage. How easy this was, Catherine knew better than anyone. Stanislas accepted the throne to become a puppet in the Empress's hands.

He was not rewarded for his devotion as he had hoped. Rumors had begun to circulate to the effect that Catherine was trying to put her future husband on the throne and so unite the Polish and Russian crowns. Stanislas was made to realize that in order to silence these rumors he would have to marry, or at least announce his impending marriage. He held out against it vainly until he finally understood that his "Sophie" herself wished to see him married to another, and then the wretched lover steeled himself, with death in his heart, to make a promise that immediately after his election to the throne he would choose a wife, any wife, provided only she was a Catholic and preferably Polish. But he never kept his word.

In order to guarantee the "freedom" of the elections Catherine sent troops into Poland, and under the threat of the Russian army, on August 26, 1764, the Polish Diet pronounced, with the unanimity required by the constitution, in favor of Stanislas Poniatowski, who became King of Poland under the name of Stanislas Augustus.

Catherine's gentle lover moved into history, and the hero of a charming, melancholy love affair was unknowingly to dig the grave of his country's liberty. Catherine saw in him the Polish king of her dreams—weak, ineffectual and ultimately of as little account as a king can be.

Thirty-nine

The Empress

Catherine reigned for thirty-four years. She was thirty-three when she came to the throne, and of the two halves of her life the second was undoubtedly the most spectacular, the most well known, and the most brilliant. Yet in this book I do not intend to dwell on it for long.

We have seen her as a child, as a young girl, as a young woman, and then as a mature woman increasingly aware of her real desires and capabilities. Gradually stripping away her prejudices, scruples and sense of shame, her beliefs and her principles, one great ambition finally brought her to the point of realizing a dream which few women in history have achieved: to rule as absolute mistress of a great nation, while owing her crown neither to hereditary right nor to the love of a reigning sovereign. As she herself proclaimed, she was a self-made woman, for the Grand Duke Peter's wife might easily have suffered the fate of so many other princesses who were the victims of an unhappy marriage and court intrigue. She proclaims it aloud in her memoirs: she struggled hard to maintain her position and to survive; she did not go mad, she did not die of grief; she spent eighteen years allowing people to trample on her heart, swallowing insults, gritting her teeth and forging herself nerves and a heart of iron.

She had made cunning her second nature and she had learned to see in people, things and events only that which could serve her goal. Power once hers, she struggled first and foremost to keep it. When her authority was assured she gave herself up to her passion for ruling with an eagerness and fervor which compels admiration: ten, twelve, fourteen hours of work a day, meetings of the Senate, councils of ministers and personal control of all the machinery of government. Catherine insisted on being her own minister of finance, war, home and foreign affairs. Her ministers were only there to carry out her orders and sometimes to advise her. She would read personally all the papers she was given to sign (she speaks with great contempt of Elizabeth who nearly always signed without reading). She would look after her own diplomacy by personal correspondence with all reigning monarchs. She would make it her business to instill some order into the more than somewhat chaotic legislation of her empire and would convene a Commission, a kind of parliamentary assembly, with the object of finding out the country's real needs and providing a fresh basis for legislation.

All her life she was seized by sudden bouts of "legislation mania" but she legislated alone. She was also, almost continually, in the grip of a passion for building and filled her capital of Petersburg with magnificent stone buildings (she had suffered

enough from uncomfortable wooden houses in her youth), and
the environs of Petersburg and Moscow with delightful palaces,
country houses and parks. She also had a mania for collecting
works of art, pictures, statues, carpets, gold and ebony work,
collections of coins, precious stones and so forth, and her busy
agents, recruited from among the best minds in Europe, literally
stripped the private collections of France, England and Italy.

She was also to become the enlightened Maecenas, patronizing
poets, writers and philosophers, from whom she asked nothing
in return beyond a little flattery. She built schools and hospitals,
and busied herself personally with making textbooks for the use
of Russian children. Better still, she turned writer herself and
was the author of satirical comedies and moral fables. She edited
a literary review—the earliest in Russia—and organized theatrical
performances. In her palace, whose splendor outshone that of
Versailles, she gave receptions that were rich beyond even the
dreams of Louis XIV. Besides this, she conducted long and
ruinously expensive wars against Turkey, victorious wars at
which she was only present in the persons of her generals but
the day-to-day operations of which she controlled in her voluminous correspondence with the heads of her armies. Her victories,
too, were the excuse for lavishly stage-managed celebrations, on
a scale such as even the most ambitious film directors of our own
day could scarcely dare to imagine.

She took a personal interest in everything, which did not
prevent her from keeping up a lively correspondence with such
illustrious friends as Voltaire, Diderot, Madame Geoffrin, and
Baron Melchior von Grimm. To Grimm more than anyone else
she poured out her thoughts and feelings, but she wrote them
all letters that were ten or twenty pages long, for letter writing
was another of her most devouring passions. Even Dumas *père*
never came anywhere near covering so much paper as this woman
absorbed in her countless occupations.

Her love life was at first monotonous and trying, during the
ten years in which Orlov remained her "husband" in all but name.
Later, she experienced a deep love for a man who was both in-

tellectually and morally her superior: Potemkin. After this came a series of relatively short amorous interludes which have left in the history books an indelible and grossly exaggerated picture of Catherine as a Messalina. None of this prevented her from being the kindest and most devoted of grandmothers and taking a personal interest in the education of her grandsons. (She did in fact subject Paul's wife to exactly the same treatment that Elizabeth had inflicted on her by depriving her of her son.)

In short, she was to be the Catherine the Great, Great Catherine, the woman who, through her fortunate wars (and the *fortunate* partition of Poland), through the almost fairy-tale brilliance of her court, her refined tastes and broad culture, was to place Russia among the great powers of Europe and make possible the flowering of an authentic Russian culture, give her name to a whole era of Russian history and be, in the generally accepted meaning of the term, a *great* monarch.

I shall confine myself here to a brief survey of the principal events and most characteristic aspects of a life which was henceforth to be so rich in events and yet for all this monotonous. Catherine ruled and she had a passion for ruling, a happy passion since she was able to satisfy it completely. Before we return to Catherine the Great, we must forget for a moment the official portraits, the diamonds and the lace, the praises and the twenty-page letters to Voltaire, the love affairs, and the very real nobility of character of this magnificently ambitious woman, and look at the price she paid to win the indisputable grandeur of her reign.

Catherine was not a showman; she would not be satisfied with "pulling the wool" over the eyes of visiting foreigners. The opulence which she regarded as essential had to be real, and she managed to acquire it at the cost of incessant effort, and decrees which show remarkable good sense, coming as they do from a woman who was not a trained political economist. She succeeded in reorganizing trade; she managed to rebuild and repopulate cities which had been practically dead, to centralize administration and to colonize desert provinces, though in all this, it is true, she was assisted by an exceptionally able man whom she was fortunate enough to choose as her lover. Under her rule Russia acquired new territories totaling a quarter of the area of European Russia: she created outlets to the Black Sea and the Baltic, and doubled the strength of the army and the Russian fleet. During her reign Russia exported twice as much as in the time of Elizabeth and imported three times as much.

By her imperialist and expansionist policies, based on long-term planning, she succeeded in making Russia a much more rich and powerful state than it had been under her predecessors.

And yet, one needs very little imagination to perceive the other side of the picture. The richness of "Catherine's" palaces (and in Russia this word is used to mean "of Catherine's time"); the splendor of which today only the still-dazzling traces remain; the pictures and descriptions by admiring contemporaries portraying entertainments worthy of the Thousand and One Nights: all this alone (for it is almost impossible for us to conceive what the day-to-day pomp of this life can have been like for the hundreds of favored people who lived and moved in this setting of almost unbearable luxury) is enough to make us ask: Where did all this money come from? Whose hands built and decorated and maintained all this? Catherine was not a fairy; her will was only metaphorically like a magic wand. The truth is that never had greater luxury, wealth and refinement been based on a more shameless exploitation of the misery of the people.

Russia was a vast country but it was, as we have seen, under-populated and economically backward. Industry was as yet only in its infancy and it made little progress during Catherine's reign —in fact it showed a tendency to decline. (For reasons which, all things considered, conform very well to approved Marxist theory, no one was interested in creating a working class.) Russia's greatest and principal source of wealth came from the exploitation of the land and the products of the land. This exploitation was not organized: the peasant toiled with a wooden plow just as he had done in the Middle Ages and made his own harrows, scythes (also of wood), sleighs, carts and harness, while his wife spun and wove the wool and linen herself.

Communications were nonexistent, and the life of the people was organized around their skills along strictly local lines. Production, considering the richness of the soil, was extremely low, usually for lack of able-bodied men. It was on this wealth that the state had to draw to pay for its expenses. How many bushels of wheat were needed to pay for a single diamond, or for one golden snuffbox which Catherine gave to Voltaire or Grimm? The peasant had rudimentary tools which served, although they were continually having to be replaced. But for the most part he had no furniture and went barefoot. The women wove, and on feast days they wore their sober, dignified and attractive folk costumes, but for the rest of the year they dressed in rags and their children went almost naked, for the wool they spun and the cloth they wove belonged to others. The bread harvested by the sweat of his brow did not belong to the farmer; he was entitled to only a small fraction of the fruit and vegetables he grew, just enough to prevent him from dying of hunger. The condition of peasants was hard in every country. In the West, as in Russia, the people were liable to forced labor, loaded with taxes and frequently compelled to sell a horse or a house to pay their annual dues. In Russia, however, the poverty was worse because the conditions of work were harsher and also because, in the eyes of the law, peasants had obligations but strictly no rights: the majority of peasants were serfs.

Serfdom was already an ancient institution in Russia, but it only became really widespread in the time of Peter the Great. We know that in 1738 three million peasants out of five million were serfs belonging to landowners and more than one million were serfs belonging to the Church. In spite of a heavy infant mortality rate, the population was growing fairly fast, but cultivation of the land, badly directed by landowners who were nearly always absentee, produced insufficient food to feed all these new mouths, while the landowners, over and above the compulsory taxes they levied to pour into the state coffers, were free to demand of their serfs as much work as they pleased or as was physically possible. (In Radishchev's famous *Journey from St. Petersburg to Moscow*

he describes finding a peasant working on Sunday because that
was the only day on which he was allowed to work to feed his
family, all the other days being devoted to the toil exacted by his
lord.)

The landed proprietor counted his wealth not only in land but
in the "souls" attached to it, who were his absolute property. Although the law did not allow him this in so many words, he had
in practice absolute rights over his serfs and could dispose of
them in exactly the same way as his cattle or his dogs. The serf
was not merely a peasant from whom forced labor was exacted;
he was whatever his master wished him to be: valet, footman,
coachman, hunter, builder, carpenter or even, if he was lucky and
possessed the talent, an actor, dancer, musician, accountant, fool
or even poet, and he could at any moment be flogged and sent
back to the plow or to whatever task his master's whim imposed
on him.

As the Russian nobility "polished" themselves in European
fashion, they were quick to realize the advantages which absolute
power over their fellow men could bring them. A wealthy landowner might own tens of thousands of "souls," a poor or relatively
poor one only a few hundred. Russian gentlemen employed six
times as many servants for their personal service as people of
the same rank in Europe: the domestic staff of a great lord would
number several hundred servants (*dvorovye*), and that of a less
wealthy man a minimum of at least twenty.

So many servants toward whom a man had no obligation whatever and who cost him literally nothing—except for their food
and the cost of their training—were a boon indeed. Moreover
these people were generally model pupils, clever and gifted, for
woe to the one who proved unworthy of the care lavished on
teaching him. These children of peasants or domestic servants,
selected for their intelligence or good looks, were trained in every
conceivable craft, for the estate of a great landowner was like a
Roman villa, a kind of autonomous community able to supply all
its master's requirements.

The great lord had his own tailors, shoemakers, goldsmiths

and ebony workers, to say nothing, of course, of the servants employed in everyday tasks, such as cooks, bakers and grooms, and these tasks were as varied as they were numerous, with usually several servants assigned to each job. Besides all this, the Russian lords were great lovers of spectacles and often had their own theaters, orchestras and ballets, and even their own regiments, composed of serfs dressed as soldiers and trained to carry out parades and mock battles. Altogether, in the eighteenth century and in Catherine's reign in particular, the Russian nobility was in the process of unconsciously recreating a vast system of slavery similar to that which existed in imperial Rome.

Naturally the vast majority of the serfs were ordinary peasants, although the peasants too had numerous obligations and, depending on the season of the year and the whim of their master, might be employed in the building, repair and upkeep of roads, in woodcutting or even (as in the case of the Count Razumovsky who wanted to hear the nightingale when the river was in flood) in building dikes and changing the course of rivers. The nobleman who wished to erect a pavilion or a triumphal arch in a single night had only to call up the peasants of one or two villages, and with these all assembled and all put to work, the job could be finished in a few hours and not a penny to pay for the cost of labor. (The peasants must have been extremely versatile and directed by capable foremen, for we know that whims of this kind were far from unusual in the eighteenth century.)

The peasant women were never idle: when they were not weaving linen or wool for their lord and his family (the needs of noble families were immense and included trousseaux containing dozens and dozens of sheets and table linen, to say nothing of personal linen, which not everyone possessed the means to order in the city or from abroad), they sewed; when they were not sewing or helping their husbands in the fields, they spent their days gathering mushrooms and berries—work usually reserved for children and young girls—although they were not, of course, permitted to keep any for themselves. In *Eugene Onegin*, Pushkin describes a moving scene in which peasant girls busy gathering raspberries are made to sing in chorus "so that their naughty mouths do not, from time to time, eat some of the seignorial berries." And here the poet is portraying a family of good land-owners.

There were probably many "seigneurs" like this among the lesser nobility in remote districts where life was backward and still close to the soil. Toward the end of the century, there were also a number of great lords of "liberal" or at least enlightened views who believed in being gentle and humane, realizing that slaves worked better when well treated. But by its very nature, the system of serfdom as it existed in Russia was such that it led increasingly to masters abusing their power: those who did not oppress their serfs or bleed them totally white could already be looked on as benefactors.

In the end this passion for grandeur on the part of the Russian nobility, which was for the most part a nobility of recent date, created what was almost a new social class: a class of serfs who were not simply domestic servants but craftsmen and artists. But however numerous these must have been, when one considers that each great family possessed hundreds of serfs who were qualified in various ways, they were still infinitely more dependent on their master than were the peasants. Their lives were often easier, for a good tool is to be cared for. It was even possible for their master to grow fond of them and discover that they were human beings: Prince Sheremetev, for instance, fell in love with a serf who was the prima donna in his theater and married her. This woman's portrait, which shows a nobler and more sensitive face than Elizabeth's own and one almost imperceptibly marked by suffering, now hangs today in the room in the Hermitage Museum which is devoted to the Russian theater, next to the excellent model sets designed (just as the actual sets themselves were built) by serf craftsmen.

Few actresses and singers were lucky enough to become prin-cesses. For the most part they were simply human cattle, subject to the whims of their masters, favorites for a day or for a year, but always liable to be sent back to their villages. Those who loved their work—and among the serfs there were many extremely talented performers, both men and women—the thousands of singers, dancers, actors and musicians would have dreamed, as though of paradise, of the proud, poverty-stricken lives which have been the lot of actors in all countries and in all periods of history, and would not have asked for so much as "a little bit of earth obtained by a prayer."[1] They did not have to travel the road, dreaming of success and a good box-office take, but they risked a flogging when their master did not like the play. (An illustration of this is the account of one noble lord suddenly seizing a singer who was playing the part of Dido and slapping her face, promising her that when the play was over she would be properly thrashed in the stable. Dido, her face scarlet from the blow, had simply to go on singing.)[2]

Orchestras of more than a hundred pieces, ballets requiring hundreds of dancers—including on occasion naked girls; teams of decorators, painters, sculptors, a whole world of artists who were often taught at great expense by French and Italian masters: all this wealth of human talent was debased less by actual ill-treatment than by the humiliating condition which made men and women, who were frequently the intellectual superiors of their masters, into mere chattels. Serfs became theologians, engineers, mathematicians, astronomers and architects. They received no salary and could not move a step without risking imprisonment. Some of them, musicians and painters in particular, were sent abroad to perfect their technique and their lords might justly be proud of their generosity to them. But more often than not, when the serfs returned to Russia they would take to drink because they were unable to reaccustom themselves to the state of slavery after the liberty they had glimpsed in Rome or Venice.

Slavery. Not all were beaten, and not every day, but there were nobles like Count Skavronsky, who was besotted about opera and commanded his servants always to speak in recitative. Great lords, and those not so great as well, would be waited on by fifty servants at a time, keeping one simply to open one door and another for the next, one to be always ready to bring his master his pipe, another his glass of water, a third a book, a fourth a handkerchief, and there was no allowance made for confusion or division of labor. Imagine the life of a man compelled to be continually on the alert for the moment when his master might want a handkerchief.

Besides this monstrous waste of manpower, there was also the inhuman exploitation of the laborer, who was looked on as nothing more than a tool. There are many objects in museums which bear witness to this: mosaics which have to be looked at through a magnifying glass before one can see that they are not paintings; inlay work of a delicacy and intricacy which it makes one dizzy to contemplate; lace so fine that no worker could have continued at such a task for more than five years without going blind. The term "serf's work" became synonymous with work of such perfection that no one today could possess it at all: the cost would be too high.

Whether he was a forced laborer, an artist or craftsman, or the most idle of lackeys, the serf was a human being suffering perpetual humiliation because he had no rights. He was married off or forbidden to marry, separated from his family, forced to move house or change his job without being able to utter a word of protest. He could be sold. During Catherine's reign the trade in serfs who were specialized in some useful craft reached hitherto unimaginable proportions, and it was at this period in particular that serfs began to be looked on as marketable goods by definition. Advertisements appeared in the newspapers: "For sale, a barber and also four bedposts, an eiderdown and other pieces of furniture." "For sale, two banqueting cloths and likewise two young girls trained in service and one peasant woman." "For sale, a girl of sixteen, of good behavior, and a ceremonial carriage, hardly used." "For sale, a girl of sixteen trained in lacemaking, able to sew linen, iron, starch and dress her mistress, in addition having a pretty face and well formed."

The price of a serf, even a highly trained one, was often less than that of a pedigreed dog. A specially skilled worker might fetch as much as a thousand rubles; in general the average price was between two and five hundred rubles for a man and from fifty to two hundred rubles for a woman. Compare this with the value of the rings and necklaces which Elizabeth gave to the young Grand Duchess, which were worth sums like five, ten and fifteen thousand rubles. Later Catherine presented Orlov with a service of Sèvres porcelain worth 250,000 rubles; young Korsakov received from her, as payment for his services, diamonds to the value of 150,000 rubles. The presents Catherine sent to her illustrious French friends—small mementos such as snuffboxes, writing desks, expensive furs and so forth—added up to thousands of rubles in all. These few figures provide some kind of scale.

Naturally these sales took place without regard to the family circumstances of the interested parties. Lords who did take this into account were regarded as good and generous. In this way the serfs, who in theory were attached to the land, had lost even that poor shadow of independence which consisted in having their own house and family.[3]

At the time of Catherine's accession there were not very many free peasants in Russia, but nearly half a million of them (this, with their wives and children means something like a million and a half people) worked on the so-called "crown" lands, where the peasants were dependent not on a lord but on officials appointed by the government. Their position was roughly the same as that of peasants in Western countries: apart from taxes and some obligations to work, they were to all intents and purposes independent.

The Ukraine, which had only been annexed to Russia for a century or so, enjoyed a special regime of its own. There the peasants were free and not subject to taxation. Very early in her reign (in 1764) Catherine took advantage of Kyril Razumovsky's move to gain independence when as hetman of the Ukraine he claimed to be protecting the rights of landowners in that district. She refused point-blank to give way to her former ally's demands and drove him to resignation. With Razumovsky out of the way, Catherine then decreed the introduction of serfdom in the

Ukraine, and several million peasants who had been rich and free and owned their own land became serfs overnight as a result of a stroke of the pen by a so-called enlightened empress.

Moreover, in the thirty-four years of her reign, Catherine distributed crown lands generously among her servants and favorites, together with the "souls" attached to them, until there were no longer any free peasants left in Russia. The *people* to whom Catherine meant to do good were actually limited to the ruling classes, or rather to the strongest of all classes, the nobility. In practice, they alone had the right to consideration, if not always to free speech (for woe betide the nobles who attempted to criticize her regime). The *kuptzi* or merchant class, wealthy, greedy for gain, as ready to oppress the lower classes as the nobility itself, had already been relegated by the nobles, and by Catherine herself, to the rank of second-rate humanity, tolerated by reason of their usefulness but kept in an inferior position by the fact that they did not have the right to own land (although men not of noble birth could rent farmland). As for the clergy, they would have reason to repent the assistance they had given the Empress when she seized power. In 1764 Catherine went back on her decision to abolish Peter III's decree. She confiscated all the wealth of the Church and placed all Church land under the jurisdiction of the College of Economics. The state thereby gained vast estates and nearly a million serfs, and archbishops, bishops and convents were reduced to living on subsidies allocated by the government. (On this account Catherine ordered the complete closure of 252 religious institutions, and a further 161 were in future only permitted to exist on charity.) The Metropolitan Archbishop of Rostov, Arsenius Matsievich, who violently opposed Catherine's policy, was deposed by the Holy Synod and exiled. The Church, which already had very little influence over affairs of state, was now reduced to the rank of a mere government institution, wholly and officially dependent on the secular authorities.

Thus Catherine governed through the support of the nobility, the only social class she really knew. Nothing could have been more natural. But then, why did she proclaim across the length and breadth of Europe, with such insistence, so much false modesty and real self-satisfaction, her love of progress and freedom and her hatred of oppression, and a great deal more besides? Why should the most slave-driving ruler that Russia had ever known want at all costs to gain a reputation as a friend of enlightenment? It almost reads as though there has been some misunderstanding, as though in her mind the words *light, progress* and *freedom* were never to be applied to any but the nobility and that it was to them that she meant to give these benefits. But no, she does not forget that the rest of the people also exist, and she claims to bring happiness to everyone. All the same, the fact remains that both directly, by reducing the Ukraine to slavery and by giving away state lands, and indirectly, by indulging in unheard-of expenditure and encouraging the nobility to an excess of luxury and prodigality, she was responsible for carrying the system of serfdom to the extreme limits of injustice and absurdity.

She found good excuses for herself. It was the ill will of the nobles and the incompetence of the representatives whom she summoned to her Commission in 1767 which were responsible for making her plans for reform miscarry. The plans were there— there was, of course, no question of effective measures for the enfranchisement of the serfs, but her *Nakaz* (Instructions), written with a view to the work to be done by the Commission, were so liberal in inspiration that in France there was even some doubt as to whether they ought to be published.

The *Nakaz* consisted mainly of somewhat arbitrary maxims inspired by Montesquieu's *L'Esprit des Lois*, by Beccaria's *Of Crimes and Punishments*, by Bielfeld's *Treatise of Jurisprudence* and by Turgot's *Treatise on the Growth and Distribution of Wealth*, all works which offered no help in solving the concrete problems of Russian economy and administration. Catherine advised all the representatives to read her *Instructions* daily, or even several times a day, in order to draw from them ideas for future reforms. But these declarations of principle—aphorisms on freedom and its limitations, on the need for tolerance, on the benefits of education and so forth—could not teach anything to men who had come from every corner of Russia to formulate precise demands or suggest improvements in local administration. Moreover, Catherine's Commission had never been taken seriously except by the members of the middle class—merchants and citizens not of noble family—a class which was still far from numerous but active and eager to obtain new advantages.

The nobles (totally uninterested in the whole business) sent only 61 representatives; the free peasants (whose representatives were actually appointed by the nobles of their regions), 73; the various branches of the administration, 28; the Cossacks, 88; and the cities (i.e. the middle classes), 208. The Commission was solemnly inaugurated on June 30, 1767, and remained in session in Moscow for five months. Then Catherine decided to move it to St. Petersburg and suspended it for two months. At the end of 1768 the debates and discussions were still going on, without reaching any concrete results, and Catherine grew tired of her subjects' apathy and sent the representatives home again. She had more urgent matters to worry about.

This attempt at a parliament was a failure largely because neither Catherine nor the representatives had any clear ideas about the reforms to be undertaken. The former was chiefly concerned with displaying her talents as a legislator and her liberalism; the latter's views were limited to their own local or professional interests. Furthermore, Catherine must have felt as though she were casting her pearls before swine: the representatives, who possessed more good sense than she credited them with, must certainly have understood the one essential fact that the Empress wanted to reign alone and at her own good pleasure, and that all the rest was nothing more than play-acting. No one thought of contesting her right to rule.

She actually began the second chapter of her *Instructions*[4] with this declaration: "The extent of her [Russia's] territories demands that the person who governs shall be accorded absolute power." She also added that the hour of the decline of an empire has struck when "the spirit of equality, having reached the supreme degree, takes such root that each man wants to be equal to the one who has been ordained by law to be his superior." This cannot be meant in a purely administrative context, for Catherine, despite her protests ("the serf is a human being" and so forth), was a convinced adherent of the caste system. For her the superiority of the noble over the non-noble citizen was a primary and indisputable truth: the free man was *essentially* superior to the serf; a merchant must never believe himself the *equal* of a noble.

Realizing that the Mother of Her Country was trying first and foremost to serve the interests of the nobility, the representatives could only say amen and fall back on details of local interest. At all events, the Empress, after spending days on end reading the minutes of the meetings, did have herself depicted by the painter Levitsky as a legislator, wearing classical robes, smiling graciously and pointing with one hand to a heap of scrolls. In his portrait, she is beautiful, still young and slim, and the expression on her rosy lips, though somewhat pinched, displays an invincible self-satisfaction. In the years to come this expression would rarely falter.

Forty

The People

"The disposition toward tyranny is cultivated there [in Moscow] more than in any place on the inhabited earth; it is inculcated at the most tender age by the cruelty with which children see their parents behaving toward their servants, for there is no house which does not contain iron collars, chains and whips, and such other instruments intended to crucify for the slightest fault those whom nature has placed in that unfortunate class, who cannot break their chains without also breaking the law. One hardly dares to say that they are men like ourselves, and though I say it myself it is at the risk of finding myself stoned; how I have suffered from the voice of a cruel and insensate public whenever some matter relating to this subject arose in the Commission on the Laws."[1]

The author of these words is none other than Catherine herself. She did not really have to suffer, since the nobles could not permit themselves, like the Metropolitan of Rostov, to brand the Empress a heretic and call down the divine wrath on her head. The archbishop had been dismissed on Catherine's orders and had been condemned to imprisonment for life in a monastery under the insulting name of Andrei *Vral* ("liar," or more accurately, "slanderer"). The nobles, moreover, would not throw stones at the Empress for the excellent reason that she never spoke to them of freeing the serfs: the very most she advocated was "some improvement in the present condition" of farm workers. But she herself acknowledged that nature had placed the serfs in the condition in which they were, nature and not human law, and that this unhappy class could not break its chains without committing a crime. Catherine did not come out against serfdom, only against the abuse which those who owned slaves made of their inalienable right.

Now she was the first to admit that this was a generalized evil ("there is no house," etc.), but she was satisfied to preach gentleness and humanity instead of promulgating a ukase forbidding the use of iron collars, chains and whips, and other instruments of torture.

To do her justice, she herself was not cruel; she was humane and capable of showing a sympathy toward those beneath her of which the society in which she lived offered few examples. Little Figchen of Anhalt-Zerbst, who had served her apprenticeship in social life playing with the daughters of the citizens of Stettin, and the young Grand Duchess who had lived as a semiprisoner in her palace with no other friends than her servants, was not the woman to turn her whole household upside down in order to move a jug or pick up a handkerchief. She had an inborn respect for other people's work, and in the morning (for she was an extremely early riser) she would often light the fire in her stove herself rather than wake her servants. One evening, when she had an urgent message to send to one of her ministers and found her four footmen engaged in a game of cards, she sent one of them to take the message and took his place at the table so as not to disturb the game.

This good-natured familiarity, without a trace of condescension, had always earned her the affection of those of the lower classes who were lucky enough to have anything to do with her. If all serf owners had resembled her, serfdom might not have been such an inhuman institution. But it must also be admitted that throughout her reign she was, through either opportunism, calculation or a prejudice in favor of the nobility, the most zealous defender of the very people whose cruel and arbitrary behavior she denounced.

"One scarcely dare say that they are men . . ." Catherine herself says it, and thinks herself a heroine for doing so, but woe betide the Russian who dared to say it louder than she did. The writer Radishchev, whom she considered "more dangerous than Pugachev," found that out when he was condemned and exiled. Woe above all to the common people who dared demand for themselves the title of men, even though they had not read the Empress's generous letters. (It is quite true that these declarations of principle were in no way intended for the people, but for "enlightened" men, such as Voltaire, who himself took care that his servants were not by when he was talking about freedom of thought.)

The people themselves were in no doubt as to their rights, for, whatever anyone may say, there have never been in any country or in any age human beings who were so downtrodden as to doubt

their own status as men. Even the most oppressed and wretched
have a general tendency to believe themselves the only real men.

The condition of the Russian peasants was dreadful, and in
many ways it resembled that of the Negro slaves in America
before the Civil War: there was the same cruelty, the same
arbitrary treatment, the same tendency to ignore the most ele-
mentary human rights. But the Russian serfs were not people of
a foreign race, violently deprived of their own language and
traditions and their own religion and artificially implanted in a
strange land. The peasant was the original master of the land he
cultivated, proud of his religion and his customs, and tending to
despise his masters for being contaminated by a "German" un-
godliness. Although usually weighed down by work and starva-
tion and obliged to bend their necks through fear, the peasants
were in a state of perpetual revolt. They retained a respect for
the person of the Tsar which was entirely a matter of principle;
he was just by definition, as God is just, and one of their favorite
sayings, showing all the philosophical cynicism of the oppressed,
was: "God is too high and the Tsar too far away." The nobles
were in general hated, unless they were absent and as inaccessible
as the Tsar, and in that case the hatred devolved on their sub-
stitutes, the overseers, who were simultaneously hated and
despised, as were all those such as agents of the law and the
army who in any way represented the power of authority.

The people lived their own lives, as withdrawn and suspicious
as though they were under foreign occupation. They took refuge
in a piety that was mingled with superstition and in customs
harking back to pagan times. They celebrated their own festivals,
sang their own songs and invented their own legends, knowing
as little of the world of their masters as their masters knew of
theirs. But they did possess a growing, fierce, exasperated aware-
ness of their own misery. To those who expressed astonishment
at the indifference they showed to the pain of a flogging, the
peasants would answer: "What does it matter? My back's not my
own, it's my master's." Their contempt for their masters was
such that it was no longer possible to humiliate them; they simply

endured like some anonymous, nonhuman force. Young unmarried men deserted by the thousands and fled either to Poland
or toward the Caucasus and Siberia. The boldest of them became
Cossacks, but the majority were recaptured and treated as severely as deserters from the army.

In the eighteenth century peasant revolts were frequent and
bloody, and always harshly suppressed. These suppressions, news
of which traveled quickly through the country provinces, nourished a perpetual atmosphere of dull resentment and defiance.
"And they often get their throats cut by their peasants,"[2] Catherine wrote underneath a poem in praise of the idyllic life of the
country landlord. "Bad" masters were in fact murdered fairly
frequently; this was the only form of justice for which the people
could hope, since the serf had no other recourse to save him from
his master's will.

In August 1767, at the very time when she was advising the
representatives to treat the serfs kindly, just when she feared
being "stoned" for her liberal views, Catherine signed a ukase
which sentenced any peasant who dared complain against his
master, or so much as have anything to do with any petition aimed
at protesting against ill-treatment, *to the whip and forced labor
for life*. Even before this decree, peasants who were bold enough
to complain rarely received satisfaction. Catherine was depriving
them of their last resort, the last right still remaining to them,
and she cannot, like Elizabeth, be accused of failing to read the
papers she signed. She read them all and took pride in it.

She had great faith in progress: she dreamed of a country in
which gentle, humane landlords would rule with paternal care
over groups of obedient serfs who worshipped their masters.
Catherine cannot even be excused on the grounds that this cruel
measure was dictated by understandable terror at the mass revolt
of the peasants, since this occurred six years before the revolt.
(Neither had she waited for Pugachev before enslaving the
Ukraine.)

There were some men in Russia who succeeded in speaking
the language of freedom aloud, outside the literary salons; Cath-

erine was wrong to claim a monopoly in this. In 1774, at Chelyabinsk in the Urals, the following manifesto was distributed and read in the city:

Our Lord Jesus Christ deigns to desire, through Holy Providence, to free Russia from the yoke of servile toil, a toil, I tell you, which is known the world over. . . . You yourselves know how Russia is being used up and by whom: the nobility own the peasants, and although it is written in the law that they are to treat them like their children, yet they look on them merely as slaves, and lower than the dogs they keep for hunting hares. . . . Factory owners have set up a mass of factories and they work their serfs so that nothing like it is seen even in the prisons. How many are the tears shed by the workers and their wives and their little children! But, like the Israelites, you shall be delivered out of bondage.[3]

The author of this pamphlet was an old soldier who had set himself up as leader of a band of peasants and Cossacks who revolted and incited the garrison and people of the town of Chelyabinsk to declare for the "lawful Emperor" Peter III, who they claimed had returned to Russia after ten years' absence to free his people from the yoke of slavery. Peasants from the Urals and all over the southwest of Russia left their homes by the hundreds of thousands and set out, armed with forks, scythes and axes, to win their freedom and a better life. Led by a phantom emperor, providentially reincarnated in the person of a daring adventurer, the people rose in a body, seeking their own rights more than those of their so-called tsar, but all moved by the same wild hope.

In June 1773, while she was still engaged in her long and costly war with Turkey, Catherine heard the news that her dead husband, Peter III, miraculously saved from the hands of his assassins, had reappeared at Yaitsk in the Urals, and was scouring the country at the head of a band of Cossacks, writing incendiary pamphlets and promising the people freedom in return for placing him once again on the throne of his fathers.

The authorities did not take the curious news very seriously to begin with: they were used to periodical revolts among the Cossacks because Catherine II's government was aiming at increasing restrictions on their freedom. Two years earlier a revolt in the Urals district had been cruelly suppressed. The government had good reason to distrust the Cossacks: they were fine fighters, but they were a foreign body in the state, a small people composed largely of adventurers of all nationalities who obeyed only their own leaders and acknowledged only their own laws, and the more unmanageable in that they were mostly Old Believers. The government repeatedly made determined attempts to assimilate them into the regular troops, but for the Cossacks the worst thing that could happen would be to find themselves transformed into ordinary "soldiers," for the soldier was by definition a slave, and moreover they would then be compelled to shave their beards and cross themselves in the Orthodox fashion. A rebellion in the name of "the cross and the beard" had become their most sanctified watchword.

For this reason, it was originally thought that this was simply one more Cossack revolt, but one which had had the bold idea of claiming Peter III himself as its leader. Already between 1765 and 1773 at least five spurious Peter III's had turned up in the southwestern provinces, the last of whom, Bogomolov, had succeeded in rousing the Cossacks of the Astrakhan region. There was nothing astonishing in the appearance of another one. The people, seeing no way out of their wretchedness, were inventing "liberators" to suit themselves. Tsar Peter III had disappeared after a six months' reign; he had been killed (for no one believed that he had died a natural death) and therefore he must have been a good man. From this conclusion it was only a short step to raising the dead. Rumors that the Tsar had miraculously escaped from his murderers circulated with such persistence among the people that unscrupulous mountebanks would sometimes pass themselves off as Peter III simply because they thought they could make something by it, and it was not difficult for them to find an audience willing to believe them.

As a result, Catherine found that her husband, who had been so unpopular at Petersburg and with the army, had already acquired a legend of his own and was in the process of becoming a national hero, a liberator tsar, while she herself was the tyrant tsarina, the servant of the nobles. Peter, it was said, had been eliminated in order to prevent him from freeing the serfs. This legend had some real basis in fact, because at the time when Peter had released the nobles from their compulsory service a rumor had circulated among the people to the effect that the liberation of the serfs was imminent, and in actual fact, since the people were originally obliged to serve the nobles in order that the nobles might better serve the state, the enfranchisement of the nobles should, in all justice, have been followed by that of the serfs. A perfectly logical though not perhaps a very realistic conclusion. Catherine's attitude made short work of this slender hope, but did not stop the people from dreaming.

Peter III, transformed through no fault of his own into a martyr for the cause of the Russian people, continued to exist in the person of his "double," Emelyan Pugachev, a Don Cossack, an experienced soldier and a man of energetic, restless and compelling character. It seems that he had once been told that he looked like the Emperor, and he had fought gallantly in the ranks of the Russian army during the Seven Years' War, finally ending up, after a great many wanderings, on the banks of the River Yaik (the modern Ural) where he began sowing the seeds of revolt among the oppressed Cossacks. Pugachev's portraits show abundantly that he bore no physical resemblance to Peter III, as do the eyewitness accounts, which describe him as a man of medium height and solidly built, whereas Peter had been tall and narrow-shouldered. Pugachev's early followers did not take him seriously. A Don Cossack he was and a Don Cossack he would remain: the Cossacks were not to be deceived in a matter like that. But they also said: "What difference does it make to us whether he is the Tsar or not: we can make a prince out of a turd. If he doesn't succeed in conquering the Empire of Moscow,

The People · 298

then we will make ourselves a kingdom on the Yaik."⁴ Thus it
was as a Cossack revolt that the affair had really begun.

But the popular movement which the history books were later
to refer to modestly as "Pugachev's uprising" was in fact a real
attempt at a social revolution, a revolution pure and simple and
the greatest mass rising of the people against the landowners
experienced in Russia prior to 1917. Pugachev served as the
pretext for this revolution, and as its head, since the people were
naturally law-abiding and were not yet ready to revolt in the real
sense of the word. They could only rise in the name of a lawful
sovereign, and it was the name of Peter III much more than
Emelyan Pugachev's personal prestige which drew the enthusiasm of the crowds. Strange as it may seem, Pugachev really did
succeed in passing himself off as the Emperor: wherever he
appeared he had to produce proofs of his identity, arrange for
special effects, bring forward soldiers who, so they said, had seen
the real Emperor, make a show of fatherly affection for the
Grand Duke Paul, and so forth.

A consummate actor and expert at handling crowds, he was
extremely convincing. The people of the southwestern provinces
had never seen a tsar in their lives, and this stout fellow with the
black beard, gold-embroidered caftan and fur cap covered in
medallions managed to pass in their eyes for an acceptable
sovereign. How were they to know that the real Peter III had
been a German who knew scarcely any Russian and a weakling
who could barely raise a sword? The Peter III who roamed the
countryside at the head of his army of Cossacks and Kirghiz
tribesmen, surrounded by his splendid, black-bearded officers—
part lords, part beggars—with sabers flashing and banners wav-
ing, this Peter III was a magnificent soldier, a war lord who
made the government armies retreat before him, took fortresses
by storm, authorized the pillaging of seignorial estates with royal
generosity, and published manifestos in which for once a tsar
spoke the language the people dreamed of hearing him speak.

Perhaps at the outset Pugachev may simply have intended to
exploit the people's credulousness in order to further the ambi-

tions of the Cossacks who, tired of being oppressed by leaders in the pay of the government, were trying to free themselves and carve out a kingdom of their own in the Urals. To this end, they had gained the sympathies of the indigenous populations along the shores of the Caspian and the Lower Volga: Kirghiz and Bashkirs, Moslem Mongols who had been recently subdued by the Russians and were the more hostile to them because there had been some attempt to convert them to Christianity by force. These men, seminomadic, tireless horsemen and as famous for their love of plunder as for their contempt for death, were precious allies for the Cossacks, at least to begin with. But they were unreliable allies, always ready to pick a quarrel with their friends of yesterday and totally indifferent to the cause of the "great sovereign" Peter III and the emancipation of the Russian serfs.

As it moved westward the revolt rapidly took on all the appearance of a popular rising, for to make himself new allies Peter III—Emelyan Pugachev, that is—promised the people to suppress serfdom, punish their wicked masters and distribute land to the peasants; in short, like anyone who has ever led a rebellion, he drew up in advance a program calculated to satisfy everyone's dreams and ambitions.

It does not seem to have been long before he began to take his role seriously. Gifted with a vivid imagination, this extraordinary man identified himself with the person of a tsar whom he himself, aided by popular legend, had invented and soon he was talking, apparently with sincere conviction, of justice, of the rights of the people, and of freedom, of freedom above all. "You, such as you are, I enfranchise you and give eternal freedom to your children and grandchildren. . . . You will no longer work for a lord and you will no longer pay taxes: if we find you toiling on behalf of another, we will massacre you all. . . . We grant all those who have hitherto been peasants and the serfs of landowners the privilege of being the most faithful slaves of our own crown; we make them a gift of the cross and of their ancient prayers, of the long hair and the beard, of liberty and independence. . . . When we have destroyed their enemies, the guilty nobles, each man will be able to enjoy a life of peace and tranquillity which shall endure for hundreds of years."

The people flocked to follow him. Everywhere Pugachev and his lieutenants appeared the peasants came out to meet them, whole villages and whole districts at a time, hailing them as liberators. Men deserted their homes and families to swell the troops of this emperor who had been saved by a miracle. As was to be expected, those of the nobles who were caught on their estates, deserted by their servants who were either terrified or delighted at the chance to revenge themselves on their hated masters, were for the most part slaughtered without mercy. Few were the families so loved by their serfs that they escaped the terrible fury of the self-styled emperor and his soldiers. The people abandoned themselves to an orgy of cruelty: nobles were burned and flayed alive, mutilated, or torn to pieces by screaming crowds, while their womenfolk were only spared long enough to be raped first, unless they were pretty enough to become the spoils of victory of the victorious leaders. But so great was the hatred the rebels felt for anything that was noble that even Pugachev himself was not able to keep his pretty widow, Elizabeth Kharlova, for long and had to give her up to be shot.

This martyrdom of the noble families who were caught up in the flood of popular fury has seemed, in the eyes of history, infinitely more cruel and revolting than the agony of the tens of thousands of serfs who were two years later to pay for their crimes a hundred times over. Pushkin in *The Captain's Daughter* later immortalized the heroism of the slaughtered officers, but he took good care not to celebrate the courage of the rebels: even to suffer and die was a privilege of noble birth.

Pugachev made the imperial power totter and shook the system of serfdom to its very foundations. The revolt spread like wildfire to provinces that had never seen a Cossack or a Kirghiz, provinces populated by "good mouzhiks" who were supposed to be piously resigned, submissive to God and to the Tsar. Submissive to the Tsar they still were, but he was a tsar who commanded them to rid themselves of their masters, "forbade" them to toil and personally dealt out justice to the overseers and officials who oppressed them. It was too good to be true, and this providential tsar himself was only a man of the people and an imposter in the bargain.

While this was going on, Catherine was receiving Diderot in St. Petersburg and negotiating a peace with the Turks which had become the more vital because she needed the troops to fight Pugachev. She remained calm and pretended not to regard the "Marquis de Pugachev," as she contemptuously refers to him in her letters, as anything more than a "highway robber." Nevertheless, the revolt was gaining ground and in the winter of 1763–64 Pugachev came within 120 miles of Moscow, which was practically undefended. The rebel army—already it was an army fifteen thousand strong—marched on the old capital. The population was panic-stricken. The police hunted down Pugachev's emissaries in the streets when they came to bring manifestos promising liberty to the people, severe punishments for the nobles, and for Catherine a convent.

Noble families who had escaped the massacre fled to the two capitals and increased the atmosphere of panic by describing the scenes of horror they had witnessed. Catherine considered going to Moscow herself to organize the defense of the city and was only with difficulty dissuaded. Moscow was really believed to be in danger. The situation appeared so grave that at court there was already talk of reform and even of a change of government. Count Panin, Princess Dashkova and Prince Nikolai Repnin had succeeded in recruiting the Grand Duke Paul to their party and were thinking of satisfying the rebels by dethroning Catherine in favor of her son, then aged nineteen. Catherine was informed of the plot, thanks to the vigilance of Gregory Orlov, and after eliciting a confession from her son she generously forgave the culprits.

The Turks, on whom the Russian army and fleet had inflicted severe defeats (at Chesme in 1770, under the command of Alexei Orlov, and in the Crimea in 1771, under Prince Dolgoruky), dragged out the peace talks interminably, finding in Pugachev a valuable and unexpected ally. Meanwhile the Grand Vizier's envoys were inciting the Moslem tribes of the Urals and the Caspian to come to Pugachev's assistance while the Turkish armies attempted to regain the ground they had lost.

The Russian armies, inferior in numbers but well disciplined and commanded by such great generals as Suvorov and Rumiantsev, held out gallantly, counterattacked, and finally defeated and took prisoner the entire Turkish army at Shumla on the Danube. In July 1744 a peace was signed at Kuchuk-Kainardji by which Russia gained the Northern Caucasus and access to the Black Sea, while the Khanate of the Crimea became a Russian protectorate. Russia's most precious gain was the release of her army, which was now able to march north to attack Pugachev's forces.

When Pugachev learned that peace had been signed, he fell back toward the Volga, burning and devastating the land as he passed. The revolt had already reached the proportions of a national catastrophe and brought unspeakable misery on the people who had risen. Peasants who had deserted the land were roaming in ragged armed bands with their wives and children, burning and pillaging, with no object beyond that of finding somewhere, God only knew where, justice. There would be no toil and no harvest that year on most of the land overrun by the rebels; nothing was left of the goods they had plundered and the threat of famine, ever present in those arid regions where cultivation was poor, hung over the people. Pugachev saw his army melting away before his eyes and his soldiers turning into marauding vagabonds. The fortresses had reorganized their defenses, Suvorov's armies were inflicting defeat after defeat on the Cossack bands, and in the end the false Peter III was handed over to General Peter Panin (the minister's brother) by his own lieutenants, who had been secretly negotiating with Catherine for their own pardon in return for this act of treachery.

On October 30, 1744, Panin wrote to the Empress to tell her that he had seen the "infernal monster." Pugachev made no attempt to sustain his imposture in the presence of men who he knew only too well could never believe it. He fell on his knees

before Panin and declared publicly that he was Emelyan Pugachev, a Don Cossack fugitive. He said that in parading himself
under the name of the late Emperor, Peter III, he had sinned
greatly before God and man.[5] He was taken to Moscow in an iron
cage, barely large enough to allow him to stand upright. This
cage was merely an instrument of torture, not intended to humiliate him, because they did not dare show him to the people.

Pugachev was not tortured—Catherine having forbidden the
use of torture—but his interrogators did not spare their cuffs and
blows. At all events it was a man physically and morally broken
who was taken to Moscow for trial: he was so exhausted that
more than once he collapsed unconscious and his judges were
afraid that he might die of weakness before the trial got under
way. "The Marquis de Pugachev," Catherine wrote to Voltaire,
"of whom you continue to speak to me, has lived as a ruffian and
will die like a coward." As a coward, no, for it is hard to call a
man a coward when he has been reduced by ill-treatment to the
condition of a mere rag of humanity. The man who had been
able to quell the crowds by putting on a false name now had
difficulty in holding up his head once he had confessed to his
imposture. He was no longer anything but a Cossack named
Emelyan Pugachev.

He did not die like the seventeenth-century Cossack hero
whose name the people still revered—and still revere today—as
a hero of freedom, Stenka Razin. Razin had laughed and sung
while he was being tortured and had defied the executioner with
his last breath. Pugachev had only the strength to cross himself
and lay his head on the block. He was executed with his principal
lieutenants (the ones who had handed him over to Catherine
were honorably granted their lives). He was not, like the famous
Stenka, tortured to death in the public square. Customs had
changed and Catherine was concerned not to exacerbate public
resentment any further by too harsh a punishment.

"He could neither read nor write," she wrote to Voltaire in
October 1774, "but he was an extremely bold and determined
man. So far there is not the least indication that he was the tool

of some foreign power. . . . It is to be supposed that M. Pugachev is simply a robber baron, and not the servant of any living soul. No one since Tamerlane has done more harm than he has. He hopes for clemency because of his courage. If he had offended only myself his reasoning would be just and I should pardon him, but this cause is the Empire's and that has its own laws." We can feel through Catherine's words her involuntary sympathy for a beaten foe; she respected "courage" in whatever form it showed itself. Moreover, from her own point of view she was right in seeing Pugachev as nothing more than a brigand, for certainly he was, beyond all possible doubt, a shameless liar.

It would be interesting to know whether she was angry or amused when she read reports telling her that this Cossack who called himself her husband had surrounded himself with other Cossacks whom he christened Orlov, Panin, Chernyshev and so forth, had created an improvised court, had given his Cossack wife so-called ladies in waiting and had even talked with a good imitation of tenderness about his son Paul. Extravagant, shameless liar he may have been, but the man was brave. "One cannot sufficiently wonder," wrote Professor Rychkov, "at the speed and sureness with which this rebellious coxcomb put into action his nefarious intentions."

But General Bibikov, who was ordered to put down the rebellion in 1773, wrote: "What matters is not Pugachev, but the general state of discontent." Catherine was not easily disposed to admit this. Her views on the real wretchedness of the peasants were no more than purely theoretical, and she preferred to believe that they were not really as miserable as all that, or that if they were, then they were resigned to their suffering. Pugachev was a criminal and those who had followed him had been accessories to a crime. They could in the last resort plead ignorance but their rebellion was beyond all possible doubt a crime. They had attacked the laws of the Empire, and that first law of all, which states that all property is sacred. On that account, Catherine was not to be softened. She saw to it that order was re-established by the army and by the landowners themselves with the severity traditionally shown by the strong toward the weak who dare to rebel. True, she recommended clemency, fearing that excessive severity might soon lead to fresh revolts; but these recommendations did not weigh heavily in the face of the atmosphere of hatred and vengeance which reigned among the nobles after the massacres of 1773. The persecution continued until the end of 1775, and every village had its scaffold set up in the main square. The death penalty may have been suppressed in the towns and for the nobles, but serfs were still condemned to death without trial and exterminated like wild beasts.

In the regions through which Pugachev's bands had passed, not one village had stood out against the uprising and not a priest was left anywhere among them: every one of them had been turned out for having, willingly or unwillingly, welcomed the imposter and prayed for him. When Catherine realized the extent of the damage, she did not try to remedy it but merely increased the penalties for attempted rebellion and gave the landowners, police and administration even greater powers over the mass of the peasants, on the assumption that these people were clearly not ripe for progress and, like wild beasts, should be firmly chained.

The River Yaik was expunged from the map and rechristened the Ural, and it was forbidden to utter Pugachev's name. The name of Peter III did however survive among one sect of the Old Believers who adopted him as their Messiah. The gulf of mutual distrust, incomprehension and silent hatred grew deeper still between the ruling classes and the people. Catherine still talked of improving the condition of the peasants but she no longer spoke of emancipation, if indeed she had ever contemplated it.

In 1774 she wrote to Diderot, who was naïvely concerned about the wretchedness of the Russian peasants: "The bread which nourishes the people and the religion which comforts them, these are their only thoughts. They will always be as simple as the earth itself. The prosperity of the state, time and the generations to come are words which cannot touch them: they belong to society only by their sufferings, and of all that immense space we call the future they perceive only tomorrow. Their wretchedness deprives them of any further interest." And this wretchedness of which Catherine nevertheless does have some vague idea and this ignorance which she exaggerates, she took care not to try and overcome. Above all else, the people must not begin thinking about anything beyond religion and tomorrow's bread, since they were too dull to realize that their wretchedness was necessary to the "prosperity of the state."

Forty-one

Private Life of an Empress

Catherine II, Autocrat of all the Russias, was thirty-three when she ascended the throne. She was no longer, according to the view of her time, a young woman, but she was a woman who was still youthful, reasonably pretty and attractive, and no one regarded her as a model of chastity.

Her affair with Gregory Orlov did a great deal of harm to her reputation, largely on account of her lover's arrogant and indiscreet behavior. But Catherine was a strong woman and she could take slander and calumny. She conducted her domestic life in such a way that Gregory was admitted and tolerated everywhere with the prerogatives if not the title of a prince consort. Officially he was only one of the Empress's advisers, but in her letters she is continually being betrayed into praising him in a way that shows perhaps more pride than love. According to her, Gregory's only fault was that he was too lazy to make the most of his immense talents.

Gregory was not, properly speaking, lazy; he was only a man without great intelligence or education who suffered cruelly from the intellectual superiority of the woman whom he lived with but was unable to marry. Nevertheless he did his best to be something more than simply the Empress's lover. He spent part of his fortune playing the Maecenas, protecting the great scholar Lomonosov, building an observatory on the roof of the Summer Palace (for he developed a passion for astronomy), and even engaging in a correspondence with Jean-Jacques Rousseau which did not altogether please Catherine. In 1765 he founded something he called a "patriotic society" through which he tried to spread liberal ideas, and produced a report dealing with opportunities for helping young peasants to own their own land.

At last, during the plague of Moscow in 1771, he had a chance to display some initiative in personally organizing the fight against the terrible sickness which ravaged the capital and killed half its inhabitants. By his dynamic energy, his courage and the efficacy of the measures he ordered, he earned great respect and did in fact succeed in controlling the epidemic. In passionate gratitude Catherine had a triumphal arch erected in his honor and a medal struck showing Gregory as the Roman Curtius flinging himself into the midst of the flames. The wording on the medal read: "Russia too has a son like this." Gregory, finding the praise somewhat overdone, begged the Empress not to denigrate Russia's other sons and Catherine agreed to change the wording to "sons."

Catherine was certainly prepared to spend the rest of her life with Gregory Orlov, although she felt quite free to deceive him from time to time when he was away: she had one short affair with a young man named Vyssotsky. She is credited with three sons by Orlov: the eldest, Alexei Bobrinsky, born while Peter III was still alive, was brought up in the imperial palace and was almost officially acknowledged as the Empress's son. Although

Catherine was by no means a devoted mother to him, she did take an interest in young Alexei and supervised his education; but she was unable to prevent him from falling under the evil influence of courtiers who flattered and coaxed him because, at least as he grew older, he was believed to have a great influence over his mother. The boy was given the title of count when he was five years old, and was later sent to study in Paris where he led an extremely dissipated life. He lived to a great age and his descendants are still alive today.

Catherine dared not openly acknowledge her two other pregnancies, and Orlov's other two children were brought up with the other little "protégés" whom Catherine educated in her palace. They were never the objects of any special distinction, and their contemporaries were never able to agree altogether as to their identity. A son was born in 1763, and another in 1771. But Catherine could not permit herself to lead a normal family life with her lover and the children she had by him. In the eyes of the public she had only one child: Paul.

Although Catherine's relations with her favorite were an open secret, the Empress was determined to keep up appearances and Count Orlov (later she bestowed on him the title of prince) was officially only one of the principal servants of the state. His services to it (apart from his fight against the plague in 1771) were in themselves unremarkable. Moreover, when Gregory availed himself of his rights as a councilor to meddle in politics, he did so in such a blundering fashion that he made Catherine very angry. At the time of the peace talks with Turkey, he was the only person not to want peace, and he stuck to his position so firmly that negotiations were finally broken off. Catherine promptly fell ill, "in consequence," wrote the Prussian ambassador, Soms, "of troubles which might be termed domestic." However, this last remark could equally well apply to a state of advanced pregnancy as to a quarrel with Gregory.

After twelve years of semimarried life, Catherine was beginning to tire of her favorite. He was quite unconditionally devoted to her service, but he was limited, quick-tempered, susceptible and, as a lover, unfaithful. Catherine pretended to ignore several of her friend's passing affairs but she was deeply hurt when she found out that Gregory was deceiving her with Princess Golitsin. She was now past forty and was becoming jealous and touchy. Acting on the advice of Orlov's old enemy, Nikita Panin, she made up her mind to sever a connection which was becoming, for her, more and more of a tie. After all, she was not married; she was free to break off the affair.

It would appear, though, that Empress and Autocrat though she was, she did not easily bring herself to face a rupture, not so much because she was still in love as out of a kind of feminine diffidence, a natural dislike of change. Although she was still youthful and agreeable to look at and, having put on some weight, did not look her age; although she still believed what flatterers still told her every day, that she was a beauty, she was well aware that people were capable of making love to her more out of self-interest than desire. Although it was a great effort to do so, and must have been like setting out on the most perilous kind of adventure, she resolved to embark openly on a new love affair, in such a way as to put any reconciliation with Orlov quite out of the question.

Gregory had been sent to Focshani to negotiate the peace with Turkey, and he was dragging out the discussions to inordinate lengths, offending the Turkish ambassadors and plenipotentiaries by his arrogance. Word reached him that a young man named Alexander Vassilchikov, a nice-looking boy of good but not outstandingly brilliant family, was occupying his apartments in Petersburg. Beside himself with rage, Orlov rushed back to Petersburg with the intention of punishing his faithless mistress and her new lover. On Catherine's orders he was kept prisoner in the Gatchina palace on the outskirts of the capital, supposedly on account of quarantine regulations, and although he was kept under strict supervision Catherine was so afraid of him that she had new locks put on all the doors in her palace and surrounded her apartments with armed guards. The slightest noise made her imagine that Orlov was coming; she was always ready to rush out of the room, or hide behind her courtiers, and altogether showed every sign of being in a state of abject terror, like an adulterous wife caught in the act. Her behavior was oddly out of character for a woman with her great natural courage and complete self-control who was generally so careful of her reputation. She told everyone repeatedly: "You don't know him [Orlov]! He is capable of killing me, and of killing the Grand Duke."

Gregory did not come and threaten his mistress and his rival with his sword, although perhaps, at the bottom of her heart, this may have been what Catherine wanted. She refused to see her former lover but sent him messages containing quantities of promises and entreaties to the effect that he must be reasonable and go away and travel for the good of his health. Gregory retorted that he had never felt better in his life. He refused to return the portrait Catherine asked for and merely sent back the diamonds from the frame. In the end, having rejected the Empress's offer of a million rubles and held out against threats of destitution and exile—to Ropsha of all places—after storming and raging for weeks on end, he suddenly gave in and reappeared quite calmly in Petersburg and in the imperial palace, filling Catherine with mortal terror. However, he showed himself a graceful loser, merely smiling bitterly at his mistress's fears and even displaying a sudden liking for young Vassilchikov. Then he allowed himself to be loaded with gifts, for Catherine knew only one way to beg for forgiveness. Six thousand serfs, a salary of 150,000 rubles, a service of Sèvres porcelain worth 250,000 rubles, and finally a palace made entirely of marble. True, in order to avoid any imputation of mercenary motives, he gave the Empress in return a superb solitaire diamond, a unique stone which cost him 460,000 rubles. It is still in the imperial treasure today and is known as the Orlov Diamond.

Then, unable to bear the fact that he was no longer the favorite, he did set off on a journey to Holland and soon consoled himself for his rejection by falling madly in love with his young and charming niece (she was, in reality, his second cousin), Catherine Zinovieva. The Empress, although somewhat piqued to find herself so quickly forgotten, interceded with the Synod to allow her ex-lover's marriage. In 1777 Orlov was at last able to marry, but his bride's health was always delicate and she died in Lausanne only four years later.

The deposed favorite's life had an unhappy ending. He trailed his melancholy and disappointment from one country to another, vainly lavished every possible care on the girl with whom he had hoped to remake his life, and finally returned to Petersburg, where he gave free rein to his naturally restless and uncontrollable temperament, continually making himself fresh enemies by his blunt speaking. He was now playing the upright man of integrity, the man who has known unlimited power and has no longer anything to fear or to lose. He openly criticized the government's policy and proclaimed his attachment to the Grand Duke Paul (whom he had formerly been unable to stand). The present favorite, or at least the man in power, was Potemkin, whom he loathed.

Catherine protected and humored this man right up to the end. Early in 1782 Orlov's eccentricities grew worse and he began to show all the signs of grave mental disturbance. He lapsed rapidly into madness and is said to have suffered from hallucinations: he believed that he was haunted by the bloodstained ghost of Peter III. In his will he left his immense fortune to Alexei Bobrinsky, the son Catherine had had by him, and died, oblivious of everything, on April 12, 1783, at the age of forty-six.

The day after his death Catherine wrote a long letter to Grimm in which she said that she was deeply grieved, but she did not omit to draw a long and extremely well-argued parallel between the characters of Gregory Orlov and Count Panin, who had died a few days earlier. "These two men . . . will be very much surprised to meet again in the next world." Of the love she had once felt for Gregory not even the memory remained. She also had these unconsciously cruel words to say of her dead lover: ". . . a genius; extremely brave, strong, decisive, but as gentle as a lamb: he had *the heart of a chicken*." A strange funeral oration for the brilliant artillery officer, the idol of his men and the bold conspirator of 1762, but Catherine, who knew him better than anyone, was no doubt the best judge.

Catherine had made up her mind in a fit of lover's spite or exasperation to replace this "chickenhearted" man, whom she must have despised in her heart because he had never succeeded in dominating her entirely, by another, but she had replaced him very badly indeed. Alexander Vassilchikov, whom she had elevated with great pomp to the rank of her favorite simply to annoy Orlov, turned out to be a fool. For his sake she had broken the relatively discreet code of conduct which she had hitherto imposed on herself. Although not actually mentioned in official records as the Empress's lover, Vassilchikov had been presented as such to the entire court. He found himself installed in the apartments which had formerly been Orlov's, next to those of the Empress; he was given the rank of aide-de-camp and a gift of a hundred thousand rubles: all this without possessing any title to such favors other than a handsome face and the luck that it had appealed to Catherine.

But as it can readily be imagined, her new choice made his mistress horribly unhappy not because he possessed a bad character, was unfaithful, cold or jealous, but simply because he was unintelligent. Catherine was bored to death with him. Before long his company became such a trial to her that Catherine was able to say (and she had known much worse sorrows than this) that she had never been so unhappy in her life. She spent her nights weeping and wailing over her stupidity, like a girl who has allowed herself to be persuaded into a marriage of convenience and then finds herself condemned to spend the rest of her life enduring a man she does not love. Although she was later to gain the reputation of a perfect example of the woman who changes her lovers as she changes her clothes, Catherine remained, in her heart of hearts, a German princess with a yearning for respectability and even, it can be maintained, a loyal person. At this time she sincerely believed that her union with Alexander Vassilchikov had very nearly the sanctity of a lawful marriage.

And yet—whether she knew it herself we shall never know, since for all her artfulness she could on occasion be terribly naïve—she was already, and had been for nearly ten years, secretly in love with another man. This was not yet a great love but simply what we should today call a weakness, a very strong attraction stifled by a sense of duty and the need to keep up appearances.

Gregory Alexandrovich Potemkin had first attracted Catherine's attention in 1762, not long after the *coup d'état*, when she was reviewing her regiments, dressed in the uniform of an officer of the guard. She noticed that the knot of her sword was missing. A young officer rode out from the ranks and presented her with his own, and tradition has it that at that moment Gregory Potemkin fell in love with Catherine. He had certainly been among the officers concerned in the *coup d'état*, and was a close friend of the Orlov brothers. His name figures high on the list of those whom Catherine rewarded for their faithful service in July 1762. At the coronation he was promoted in rank and received the sum of ten thousand rubles, together with four hundred peasants and the title of lieutenant of the guard.

It is clear that from their first brief interview Catherine had liked Potemkin: she praises his behavior during the *coup d'état*, exaggerating both the gallant officer's youth and his merits. (She says he was seventeen when he was in fact twenty-three.) With her own hand she crossed out the word "ensign" (the rank to which the young man was to be promoted) and replaced it with "lieutenant." In 1762 Gregory Potemkin was a dark, slim young man, tall—too tall—and with a face that was extremely attractive rather than strictly handsome. He was "a veritable Alcibiades," fiery and excitable, and possessed a shining intelligence and the kind of face that is not easily forgotten.

He was originally a country boy, born in the region of Smolensk. He studied brilliantly but erratically in Moscow, then enlisted in the cavalry at Petersburg, where he distinguished himself chiefly by the dissipated life he led. He was poor and piled up a heap of debts, as young officers of the period tended to pride themselves on doing. His comrades liked him because of his quick wit, his fine voice and his talent for mimicry. It was these talents which brought him to the notice of the Empress as one of her private circle of friends.

One day the Orlov brothers thought they would amuse Catherine by bringing her their young friend, whose extraordinary gift for mimicry they had already praised to her. When Catherine insisted on a demonstration of his talents the young officer took it into his head to give an imitation of the Empress herself, reproducing her atrocious German accent to the life. Catherine burst out laughing in spite of the horrified expressions on the faces of those around her, and from that day on Gregory Potemkin's became a familiar face at the little Hermitage where the Empress was in the habit of entertaining her personal friends several times a week.

Not the least of Catherine's many enthusiasms was her fondness for the pleasures of conversation, and drawing-room conversation, as it was understood in the eighteenth century, was one of the necessary qualifications of a gentleman. She herself had a great deal of wit and a lively personality. When she became Empress she found that her courtiers gave her credit for being a great deal wittier than she was, and this had the effect of heightening her natural liveliness and gaiety. Her little soirées at the Hermitage were one of the great pleasures of her life. Since she had little opportunity for a private life, she tried to make up for it with her friendships and liked to have a crowd of friends constantly around her, real friends who could forget that she was the sovereign, and with whom she could let her hair down as she had done in the days when she used to play blindman's buff with her companions.

She was no longer a young woman; her courtiers never forgot who she was and the brothers Orlov, who were among the few people who did not consider themselves obliged to humor her, were not exactly what might be termed "drawing-room beaux," but Catherine, who had a vocation for being the life and soul of the party, managed to amuse herself all the same. Young Potemkin amused her from the very first day, amused and intrigued her because he was not like anyone else. She could feel in him a powerful personality, perhaps a nature that was genuinely great, even in its faults, and beside which her own—official—greatness was no more than a shadow. She was fascinated by him from the outset. She tolerated his subtle and harmless impertinences, defended him to the Orlovs and altogether paid him a more than flattering degree of attention without perhaps even thinking of him as a possible lover. At that time she was much too afraid of Orlov.

But these gracious attentions did finally awaken the suspicions and anger of the Orlov family. One day Gregory and Alexei invited Potemkin to their house, tried to pick a quarrel with him over some trifling matter and beat him up so thoroughly that he had to be carried out half dead. According to some stories it was on this occasion that he lost his right eye, but another and better authenticated version attributes this infirmity to a neglected abscess. However it may be, now that he was blind in one eye, the young Alcibiades lost all hope of pleasing the lady of his heart and decided to become a monk.

Potemkin really was a sincerely devout man, deeply interested in theology, and in his early youth he had considered taking orders. However in the end, after a retreat from the world lasting a year and a half, he realized that he was not cut out for a monastery. Assisted in his decision by the fact that Catherine was good enough to inquire after him frequently, he turned up at court again and held several official posts as a result of the Empress's constant good will and protection. He was in turn assistant to the procurer of the Holy Synod, a member of the Commission on Civil and Religious Affairs, protector of the Tartars and other Asiatic peoples, and court chamberlain. Then he left the capital and joined the army in the hope of distinguishing himself in the war against the Turks, and did in fact succeed in doing so, as much by his personal bravery as by his talents as a leader of men. Once the war was over it was Catherine who summoned him back to Petersburg in a letter which gave him a great deal to hope for.

Catherine had in fact been corresponding regularly with her

protégé and found the means, in the midst of all her other occupations, to keep herself regularly informed of the impoverished young officer's activities, for although he had no influential connections she felt herself drawn to him by an overpowering attraction. In the letter which recalled Potemkin to Petersburg, after lavishing a great deal of praise on him she wrote: ". . . as I desire to keep men about me who are zealous, brave, intelligent and discriminating, I beg you do not waste time wondering to what end this has been written. I can answer you that it is to give you some confirmation of my regard for you, since I am, as always, your well-wisher, CATHERINE."

This practically amounted to a declaration of love. Deeply disillusioned with Vassilchikov, Catherine was at last summoning back to her side a man of whom she must have been dreaming secretly for a long time. But Potemkin, who knew nothing of what had been going on and thought that Orlov was still in favor, hurried to Petersburg and found a new favorite installed in his old enemy's place. He was bitterly disappointed. Orlov's disgrace seemed to make little difference to him when there was now a handsome young man as his rival instead. There was no denying that in ten years Potemkin had altered terribly. Far from resembling an Alcibiades, he was now, to judge from the accounts of numerous people who saw him, more of an object of revulsion: he had only one eye, his face, ravaged by his excesses, had become bloated, and his once slim body was now massive and shapeless. For all his thirty-four years he was no longer any more or less than a "Cyclops." (This is how the English ambassador, Sir Robert Gunning, describes him: "He is of gigantic height and ungainly proportions, and his appearance in general far from pleasing.")

Jealous of Vassilchikov and hoping to pique Catherine's imagination, Potemkin, who made no secret of his passion for the Empress, once again announced his intention of taking orders, as a result of unrequited love. He was actually in a monastery when Catherine's friend and confidante, Countess Bruce, came to find him and promised him on her mistress's behalf all the favors he could hope for. He would be made an aide-de-camp; Vassilchikov would be ordered to travel for the sake of his health, and be paid off with a hundred thousand rubles, plus seven thousand peasants, sixty thousand rubles in diamonds and a pension for life of twenty thousand rubles a year. This young man who had remained in favor for less than two years commented afterward: "I was nothing more than a kept woman."

Only too pleased to be rid of her tiresome suitor, Catherine gave herself up, for the first time in her life, to a love that was free, complete, passionate and totally disinterested. The letters she wrote to Potemkin, and she wrote to him daily even when they were only twenty yards apart in adjoining rooms, show a woman dazed and bewildered by the experience of being really in love for the first time. With Potemkin she was all tenderness, humility and submission, patient even in her reproaches, full of loving fears and constant care for the welfare and the moods of the man she loved. Few of Potemkin's letters have survived, for Catherine burned them, while Gregory kept those of his mistress, carrying them in his waistcoat pocket, next to his heart.

Was he driven more by ambition than by love? Ambitious he certainly was, in the extreme, but the two passions went together. But no doubt such overwhelming submissiveness from a woman who, if not actually aging, was already past her prime, could sometimes have been irritating to a man of the world, used to having all women on their knees to him. For it is a fact that even if he was ugly, women never seemed to think so: Catherine in particular was always praising his looks, and his feminine conquests were innumerable. Perhaps, after all, Gregory Potemkin may have been disappointed to find in the Empress only a mistress like any other. In her letters she reveals herself so much a woman, and like all women loving, monotonously loving, with an ordinariness that is disarming, even somewhat touching. But Potemkin's was an eccentric character and he loved the unexpected. His periodical fits of mysticism and neurasthenia were not accidental. He was not a man to be satisfied with the love of one woman.

Catherine wrote as she talked, as she breathed: having at last found a lover whom she could, in all honesty, look on as her equal, she gave vent to her passion in long missives filled with careless lovers' chat, and certainly in writing to Potemkin she was not thinking of the judgment of posterity. Sometimes she seems to be frightened by the strength of her love, and she shows signs of at least trying to resist it. "I have issued strict orders to my whole body, even down to the smallest of my hairs, no longer to show you the smallest sign of love. I have locked up my love in my heart ten times over; it is stifling there, it is uneasy and I fear it will explode." "A whole river of ridiculous words is flowing through my head. I don't know how you can bear a woman with such muddled ideas!" and she adds, in French, without modesty: "Oh, M. Potemkin, what a damnable miracle you have worked in so deranging a head which was always used to be considered by the world as one of the best in Europe!" She adds, speaking to herself: "You will disgust him with your foolishness."

Did she really disgust him? Her own passion was excessive, overflowing and indiscreet. We have only to look at the names she called her lover, names which many men would certainly have found trying: dearest pigeon, golden pheasant, *coq d'or*, peacock, cat, tiger, lion of the jungle, wolfbird, my marble beauty, my darling like no king on earth, my little heart, my darling, my dearest doll, my dear toy, and a great many other appelations all equally bizarre when applied to a giant with a "far from pleasing appearance." Nonetheless this stormy happiness, disturbed from time to time by Potemkin's fits of anger and retrospective jealousy, seemed made to last a number of years and there appeared to be no external obstacle that would put an end to it. The pair were fully aware of the profound sensual, emotional and intellectual understanding which reigned between them, and they had no prejudices to hold them back.

More important still, Potemkin was not, as Orlov had been, a respected but subordinate companion, reduced to carrying out the orders of his imperial mistress. In a very short time he became the real master of Russia. Catherine decided nothing without him, bowed to his opinion and let him act for her, realizing that for once she had come across a man of exceptional range. If Catherine's reign was great, then a large part of the credit for it must go to Potemkin.

Did Catherine go so far as to marry in secret the man she loved? No document exists to prove it, but certain phrases in Catherine's letters ("Have I not, for two years, been bound to you by the most sacred ties?" "I belong to you in every possible way.") suggest that this may be so. According to a story handed down by the Comte de Ségur, the marriage must have been solemnized toward the end of 1774, at the church of Saint Samson in Petersburg. There is no proof of this: it is not unlikely, but Potemkin never publicly attempted to assume the title of morganatic husband. Whether or not Catherine ever became Madame Potemkin matters relatively little: the two lovers possessed so few moral prejudices that in their eyes the marriage sacrament can have had little more value than the passionate vows they exchanged every day.

In letter after letter Catherine complains—tenderly, shyly, sometimes with a little asperity—of her "Grisha's" coolness toward her: "I come to you to tell you how much I love you and I find your door shut." One day, when he had refused to see her because he was busy talking to his friend Fonvizin, she wrote to him: "I perfectly understand that this man may amuse you more than I do, my dearest, but I pray you remember that I love you while he loves only himself." It is highly probable that Potemkin's pride suffered, as Orlov's had done, from his position as "favorite." We know too that he was jealous: one day he even went so far as to accuse Catherine of having had fifteen lovers before himself. In such a notoriously cynical libertine, jealousy is in itself a proof of love.

Catherine retorted to this accusation that the number of her lovers was only a third of what he supposed: "I took the first because I was compelled to and the fourth because I was in despair . . . as for the other three, God knows it was not from debauchery, for which I have never had any inclination. If in my youth I had had a husband whom I could have loved, I should have remained faithful to him all my life. It is my misfortune that my heart cannot rest content, even for an hour, without love."

Potemkin demanded other proofs of her love besides words and caresses. He could not forgive Catherine for the care she took of Panin and the Orlovs, his declared enemies. But the Empress was sorry for her former lover and she needed Alexei Orlov and Panin. She stood firm and Potemkin was sensible enough not to make an open issue of it. Age and illness were soon to relieve him of Panin, whom he replaced as minister of foreign affairs in 1775. Gregory Orlov, reduced to traveling "for his health" and later for the health of his young wife, had adopted an attitude of proud but powerless opposition to the regime. Alexei, more capable and less ambitious, commanded the operations of the Russian fleet with considerable success. Potemkin reigned.

But even power could not satisfy him, and he suffered from frequent fits of depression. Catherine, in one of her letters, explains him by telling him that he is a man torn between his desire to annihilate himself in God and his own overweening pride. As well as being dreadfully ambitious, jealous, possessive and domineering, with a consuming need for activity, this inconvenient lover had the additional disadvantage of being a failed mystic; his violent, restless faith plunged him from time to time into deep pits of desolation and self-disgust, and were one more obstacle between himself and Catherine. This, like music, was a world into which, because of a natural insensitivity, she was incapable of following him. She was satisfied to try and understand, and to love him.

After two years of reciprocal and sincere if not altogether happy love, Potemkin yielded his place in the Empress's bed to a young and charming Ukrainian by the name of Peter Zavadovsky.

This affair caused a great stir at the court. The all-powerful minister was thought to be in disgrace and everyone was expecting terrible explosions of anger, but nothing of the kind occurred. Potemkin continued to be received by the Empress with the same regard, the same demonstrations of friendship; he lived in the imperial palace as before, and seemed to be on the best of terms with his young rival. Potemkin's enemies, foreign diplomats and the rest of the court were reduced to making wild guesses at what lay behind it, and historians, to this day, must do the same. The truth, which everybody would know before long, seems to defy all probability: the man whom Catherine had loved passionately, and undoubtedly still loved, had renounced his office of lover and himself undertaken to find for his mistress the fortunate young men destined to take his place.

Had Potemkin seen that Catherine's sexual passion was cooling and was he trying to ensure the continuation of his own power by becoming simply a friend and adviser? Was he himself so tired of his mistress that he wanted to resign in favor of others an office which had become a burden to him? Did he, with a perversity worthy of his restless, temperamental character, think to acquire a more lasting ascendancy over her by means of a succession of handsome young men chosen by himself? Or had age made of Catherine an ogress, seeking younger flesh to devour and incapable of remaining faithful to a man who was no longer very young? (He was thirty-six; she, forty-six.) There is probably some truth in all these explanations, but none of them is complete. However, it does look as though it was Potemkin who drove Catherine into the paths of vice—there can be no other word for it—and that once he had perverted her he adopted toward her an attitude that had a good deal in common with that of a pimp prostituting his girl. True, it was always Catherine who paid, but the young men of her choice also paid—with Catherine's consent—some tangible tribute to Potemkin when they took over their duties.

All Catherine's behavior toward Potemkin shows that she continued to love him, that she could not do without him near her, and that he was the only man she feared, esteemed and looked up to. Whatever else she may have been, she was too much a woman to humor a man to this extent simply because she wanted a capable and energetic minister. There can be no doubt that she would have remained faithful to him had he wished it, for where he was concerned she was humble and eager to show herself devoted, submissive and tender. It is therefore probable that the first move in this semirupture came from Potemkin. He may have known that in the end his difficult temperament would make him tire of even the most patient of women, and Catherine was not always patient.

The fact remains that he ordered Catherine's private life so efficiently that she was compelled to make her choice from among the candidates sent her by Potemkin with his official sanction. Zavadovsky was the first of the series. There were fifteen of them in all and only one exception to the rule. This was the last, Zubov, and Potemkin never forgave the Empress for her mistake. These favorites normally lasted for a period of two years, at the end of which time they temporarily disappeared from court, loaded with expensive presents. They were "kept women," just as Vassilchikov had been, but now when Catherine tired of her lovers, she no longer spent her nights weeping and her days moaning. It was all much simpler now. Yet she had once written to Potemkin: "I have burned my fingers with that fool Vassilchikov. The thing I fear most of all is that habit may make me wretched all my life or even shorten my days. If that fool had stayed with me another year and you had not come—or if I had not found in you the man I wanted—it is quite likely that I should have grown used to him and habit would have won."

But with the men who succeeded Potemkin she had no such qualms. The new favorite was generally petted, adored, praised to the skies and presented to the Empress's numerous correspondents as the model of all human perfections. He was paraded at Catherine's side to all official receptions, not openly acknowledged as her lover, not able to permit himself the slightest misplaced familiarity in public, but permanently on duty, expected to be absolutely faithful, a male odalisque, a luxurious doll, flattered, adulated, sometimes—just a little—feared, and dismissed without ceremony when she no longer liked him. Then Potemkin would make it his business to find the Empress a new aide-de-camp.

The two, now platonic, lovers carried on this game with the utmost frankness between them. When young Ermolov had been disgraced, Potemkin presented Alexander Dmitriev-Mamonov to the Empress. He told the young man to take her Majesty a particular water color, which Catherine afterward returned to him with these words scribbled on the back: "The outlines are good but the choice of colors is less felicitous." This meant neither more nor less than that the boy was well formed but that his complexion left something to be desired. (She took him all the same and he remained in favor for two years, but then unfortunately he fell in love with a girl of his own age. Catherine raged, wept—and married the guilty pair on the spot.)

One of her favorites, Mamonov's predecessor Ermolov, was foolish enough to oppose Potemkin and try to fly with his own wings. He was swiftly put in his place: in the throne room, before the whole court, Potemkin summoned the Empress to choose between himself and the young man, adding: ". . . and I hope that in future I shall be more fortunate in my choice of a man to please you." Catherine gave in at once and told Potemkin to get rid of her too presumptuous lover straight away. Submissiveness of this kind shows that, on an emotional level at least, Catherine had abandoned all pride: Potemkin dominated her because he was stronger than she was, and with him the Empress was simply a frightened woman, anxious to justify herself.

What did she see in these young lovers, all handsome, all charming, respectful, tender and ardent? Catherine was getting old, but her favorites remained the same age, all between twenty-two and twenty-five years old. Certainly she was looking for physical vigor, which she was afraid she would not find in a man of her own age; but besides this, youth awoke in her some thwarted and frustrated maternal instinct and in her own way she found in this a solution to her own Oedipus, or rather Jocasta, complex. Since she did not love her own son—or sons—she leaned with a somewhat equivocal but real affection toward these young men who were all so handsome and so dependent on her. She tried to educate them, instruct them and turn them into good servants of the state. She encouraged, without understanding, the musical talent of the young Ivan Rimsky-Korsakov (who was ungrateful enough to deceive her with Countess Bruce). She enjoyed forming the character of young Alexander Lanskoi, who had actually been brought up in the imperial palace since adolescence, and whom she treated so much like a son that some have believed her feelings for him really were purely maternal. Her last favorite, Plato Zubov, was also a former "pupil" of the Empress's.

Lanskoi, stricken by scarlet fever and angina, died in the space of a few days, leaving her in despair. She wept for six months for the "child" in whom she had hoped to find "a support for her old age," and her despair could have been that of a lover or an adoptive mother. In her letters to Grimm, Catherine cheerfully keeps us informed of the character, tastes and preferences of each successive favorite, quite shamelessly, since they were supposed to be merely agreeable young men whom she had taken upon herself the task of educating. Of some, Dmitriev-Mamonov for example, she speaks in a tone of kindly banter: "We are as clever as the very devil . . . we adore music . . . we hide our fondness for poetry as though it were a crime." She uses this "we" in the same way when talking of her grandsons, aged one or two, and describes the temper and tastes of her favorite dogs, the "Anderson Family" and "M. Thomas," with the same seriousness. She is overflowing with a lively, genuine and somewhat superficial affection, although her grief shows that her feeling for Lanskoi was deep enough. "I drag myself about, like a shadow . . . I cannot set eyes on a human face without the tears choking my words." This was not love, but neither was it altogether licentiousness: it was a practical way of solving the problem of her demanding sensuality.

One thing is certain: that the quasi-official manner in which her favorites were appointed appealed to people's imaginations and earned Catherine a reputation she never thought she deserved. All her life she was so concerned about appearances that she almost succeeded in convincing herself that no one could see what she was up to. One well-established tradition which was going the rounds of every court, and circulating in every scurrilous pamphlet even in the Empress's own lifetime, has it that Catherine's choice of a lover was made each time according to an unalterable formula which went as follows: the young man was first informed privately of the Empress's interest in him; he was then examined by a doctor, next "interviewed" by Countess Bruce, who satisfied herself as to his intelligence and qualities of character, then *tested* by the same countess in regard to more intimate matters, and only then approved by the Empress herself. Things may possibly have happened in this or some very similar way two or three times, or even more often, but for obvious reasons there can be no official documents in existence to prove it. The fact remains that Catherine and her "testers" (first Countess Bruce and afterward Madame Protassov) were the laughingstock of all Europe, and it would be hard to say whether the story was pure fabrication or whether it was based on actual fact. In any case, biographers who state that after her rupture with Potemkin Catherine led a vestal life, satisfying herself with "educating" worthy young men to whom she gave presents of thousands of serfs and hundreds of thousands of rubles out of the pure goodness of her heart, seem to be painting an altogether too idyllic portrait of the Empress.

At the age of sixty, in consequence of an unhappy love affair which happened while Potemkin was away, Catherine took a lover whom he had not recommended. This was Plato Zubov, and it is an indication that Potemkin in general knew what he was doing that on the one occasion when he had not approved the choice of a favorite, this choice turned out to be a somewhat unfortunate one. The handsome Plato was hard, ambitious and scheming, and in the end he acquired over the aging Empress, who was dominated by her sensual desires, an influence totally out of proportion to his abilities.

Potemkin remained in favor to the end. When he died in 1791 during a campaign against the Turks, Catherine was inconsolable. She was ill with grief for several days; she ordered the court to go into mourning, and for weeks refused to see anyone, even her grandchildren. "My pupil, my friend, my idol I may say, Prince Potemkin of Taurida, has died in Moldavia after a month's illness," she wrote to Grimm. She was so broken that she could only repeat over and over again: "Whom can I rely on now?"

Her life as a woman had been over for a long time; all that was left to her now was the fierce call of a sensuality the more tyrannical in that out of an ineradicable habit of prudishness she persisted in disguising it as mere affection. There were times when Zubov, by his unreasonableness, callousness, and nicely calculated favors, almost succeeded in reducing her to dotage.

So much for Catherine's private life, or at least that part of it which concerned her love affairs. She was also a mother. She was also, before all else, a sovereign. She was, lastly, the woman who in her own lifetime succeeded in creating and maintaining her own legend, and this was not the least, or the least successful, of her undertakings.

Forty-two

❧❧❧❧❧❧❧❧❧❧❧❧❧❧❧

Mother and Grandmother

We shall never know whether or not Paul was the son of Peter III and so lawful heir to the throne of Russia. Very probably he was not. In her memoirs Catherine made a point of hinting that she herself believed her son to be the fruit of her affair with Sergei Saltykov. The case of a sovereign leaving such an admission for posterity is almost unique, but Catherine had good reasons for doing so, since she herself, in the eyes of a large section of the community, had been a usurper, if not ever since her accession to power, then at least since Paul's coming of age. She was occupying a place which rightfully belonged to her son.

It could have been to her advantage to allow it to be thought that Paul had in fact no rights, that his only rights came from her, and that she was therefore stealing nothing from him.

But bastard or no, Paul was her legitimate son because he had been publicly acknowledged as such. The people did not forget it, and Pugachev knew it very well, for he had taken every opportunity to proclaim his affection for the young man. On one occasion, when the Grand Duke was visiting Germany, the actors in the Vienna theater refused to play the tragedy of *Hamlet* in his presence in case Paul should see in it allusions to his own situation. Catherine, in spite of the respect and admiration which people felt for her statesmanlike qualities, remained, in the eyes of the majority, an unscrupulous woman who had had her husband assassinated and was keeping her son from the throne.

Young "Hamlet" grew up with a mother who, although she may well have loved him, certainly loved her lovers more, and even more than her lovers, loved power. She took an interest in him; her fantastic energy gave her the time, even in the midst of her numerous other occupations and amusements, to spend a part of her day in the children's apartments, and sometimes play with the little boy and supervise his lessons. Since 1760 Paul's tutor had been Count Panin, a conscientious tutor, although one too much occupied with affairs of state, and the boy was brilliantly, perhaps too brilliantly, taught. From the age of ten or eleven he began studying the works of Leibnitz and D'Alembert, and though intelligent, Paul was by no means an infant prodigy.

He was a difficult child, sickly, chronically nervous, and the charming irregularity of his features changed with age and became frankly ugly. Brought up until he was eight by an irrational great-aunt who swamped him with care and affection, surrounded him with nurses and would not allow him to move a muscle or do a thing for himself for fear of tiring him, he had got off to a bad start. Catherine could not mend the harm done by Elizabeth. As an affectionate or at least a well-meaning mother she tried to make friends with the little boy who had hitherto been a stranger to her. He loved her and was promptly jealous of Orlov, who on his side was jealous of the boy, and from this classic case of jealousy the child suffered a great deal more than the tough soldier who had other things to worry about.

As an adolescent Paul quickly realized that his mother was usurping his rights, that his father had died in suspicious circumstances; there was even one pamphlet by Rulhière which directly accused Catherine of her husband's murder. Paul learned the torments of Hamlet at an early age, and since he was still little more than a child, they marked him for life. Already corrupted by the knowledge that he was a prince, abnormally proud, haughty and domineering, he retreated increasingly into an attitude of barely concealed rebellion against his mother. His behavior toward her was cold and mistrustful, and effectively discouraged the affection which Catherine still felt for him. He began to idolize his father—a father he had to all intents never known—and to imitate him as far as he could. He could not be unaware that Peter III had been passionately fond of military exercises and of everything connected with the army, and he too became devoted to playing soldiers. Before long this game became a veritable mania. Since his character was naturally much more violent than Peter III's had been, as he grew older his mania began to assume the proportions of insanity.

Catherine no longer loved her son. As he grew up his defects of character, his ugliness and his obvious hostility toward her repelled her the more in that she saw him not only as a son but as a rival. People were already saying out loud that on the day of the *coup d'état* she had promised Gregory Orlov that she would abdicate in favor of her son on the day he attained his majority. She felt not the slightest inclination to do so, especially as she considered herself, not without reason, a good sovereign and Paul did not seem to possess the requisite qualities for a ruler. Catherine's enemies claimed that she had purposely instructed one of her councilors, Teplov, to discourage the young man from showing any interest in affairs of state. Teplov was supposed to have compelled the Grand Duke Paul to study heaps of documents and state papers, each more boring than the last, and so filled him with a horror of any work of the kind, but there was no need of any calculated guile to put this capricious and undisciplined young man off serious study.

Paul was definitely not to reign when he came of age and was not to be brought into the government in any way whatsoever. His ambitions were deeply repressed because of his fear that his mother might try and rid herself of him as she had of his father, and he did not even manifest any desire to claim such power as was his right. He remained, on the surface, a respectful and submissive son. Wishing to ensure at the same time her son's happiness and the future of the dynasty, Catherine married him off very young (he was nineteen at the time) to Princess Wilhelmina of Hesse-Darmstadt, who became Grand Duchess under the name of Natalia Alexeievna. It turned out to be an unfortunate choice, for though Paul seemed to be passionately in love with her, the young bride was ambitious, extravagant, frivolous and self-centered. Three years after their marriage she died in childbirth after bringing into the world a stillborn infant. The young husband's distress was terrible, and there were fears that he would put an end to his life or allow himself to die of grief, and at the very least, that he would refuse to marry again. Catherine resorted to a cruel remedy: she showed her son some letters which had been found in a box belonging to the late Grand Duchess. They were love letters addressed to another man and Paul's despair grew, if possible, even more violent. The man with whom she had been deceiving him was his best friend, Count Razumovsky.

In the end youth had its way and Paul agreed to be married a second time. This time the marriage was a success. Young Sophia Dorothea of Württemberg, or Maria Feodorovna as she became, was a good, simple, sweet-natured girl, always prepared to worship her husband and close her eyes to his ugliness and unpleasant character. She loved him faithfully and over the years he came to love her. They had many children.

But still they were not allowed to be happy. Their two eldest children, both boys, were taken away from their parents almost at birth: their grandmother was determined to bring them up herself. As for the girls, Catherine was well content to leave their education to the Grand Duchess. But the Empress's interest in the boys was more than just a sorrow to their parents because they were unfairly deprived of their sons. Paul must have realized from the beginning that his mother intended that she personally should be the one to educate the future Emperor, and that she aimed at disinheriting him in favor of his eldest son, Alexander.

Catherine was a passionately devoted grandmother, as her

letters to Grimm bear witness. From the first days, the first weeks, she adored little Alexander, her "Monsieur Alexandre" as she called him, and her faithful correspondent was kept constantly informed of everything concerning his character, the details of his education, his first childish words, and the plans for his future which the doting grandmother was already making on his behalf. If we are to believe Catherine, the child was exceptionally gifted. At three, he already had the intelligence of a six-year-old, he understood everything, he was gay, sensitive, affectionate and as pretty as a cupid. All grandmothers talk like this. Catherine was forty-nine when Alexander was born and she had not been allowed to bring up her own children. Now she was making up for lost time, and in her view, it was just too bad for his mother, who was a silly, empty-headed young woman and would certainly have ruined the child's naturally charming character by educating him stupidly.

Over and over again she says: "I am crazy about him. . . . I am crazy about this child." It was perfectly natural. Alexander adored his grandmother, and Catherine was finding out, for the first time in her life, the charm, innocence and affection of a very young child turning trustfully to those it loves. Alexander would spend hours playing in her apartment, watching her work. She invented games for him, went into raptures over every word he uttered and everything he did, studied his awakening personality, and was continually astonished to find in him a liveliness and depth which all children in fact possess but which she believed to be the sole prerogative of Alexander. The pretty, bouncing child flattered her pride the more in that she considered him her own work; his father and mother would never have succeeded in developing the little boy's intelligence and sensitivity as she had done, and besides, it was all very simple: he loved only her and was happy only when he was with her, would only do as she told him. "He loves me instinctively."

Catherine was proud of her talent for education and was naïvely astonished when anyone complimented her on it. Was she forgetting that her entourage was obliged, on pain of disgrace, to find everything she did excellent? She made up a little alphabet for her grandson's use; she invented a particular type of garment for children—extremely practical, she said—and sent the pattern to the King of Sweden and the Prince of Prussia. Both expressed themselves delighted with her brilliant idea, and who should wonder? Besides, the results were there to be seen. Alexander was the most wonderful child that ever was, his grandmother bore witness to it, and no courtier was likely to say differently.

Alexander and his brother Constantine (so named because Catherine hoped one day to see him reign over the Empire of Constantinople) were both brought up by their grandmother, spoiled, coddled, and kept as far as possible away from their parents' influence. Alexander was always the favorite. As he grew up the child, who was extremely intelligent, realized the equivocal situation in which his parents' semidisgrace placed him, and he learned to regard his grandmother as considerably less perfect than he had in his childish ignorance believed. It was not long before his sense of propriety was shocked and hurt by the spectacle of a woman who seemed to him even older than she was just because she was his grandmother, surrounded by her youthful favorites. Tugged incessantly between his parents whom he respected and his grandmother whom he no longer respected but loved all the same and had to treat carefully, the young man became canny, indecisive and somewhat hypocritical. When Catherine told him one day that she meant to have him proclaimed Emperor instead of his father, on account of the latter's unreliable character, Alexander categorically refused. Catherine had not succeeded, either by her excellent education or by her passionate love, in winning her grandson's heart. Faced with the choice between her and his oppressed father, he chose his father, although once that father had become Emperor, the son felt at liberty to take part in the conspiracy which was to end in Paul's death.

Forty-three

ເເເເ

The Sovereign

It is hard to know how to take leave of Catherine the Great.
It would take so long to draw up a balance sheet of her thirty-
four-year reign that one might be tempted to copy the formula
which Catherine herself used in one of her letters to Grimm
in 1779:

Governments created on the new plan	*29*
Cities built	*144*
Agreements and treaties concluded	*30*
Victories won	*78*
Memorable edicts, laws and statutes	*88*
Edicts to improve the lot of the people	*123*
	492

Between 1779 and 1796 the list of cities built, treaties concluded and so forth lengthened further still. Catherine was a
magnificent architect of Russian greatness.

Catherine remained faithful to the system named after Peter
the Great, and she pursued Russia's expansion to the south and
west. Her successful wars against Turkey enabled Russia to
establish herself firmly on the Black Sea and to incorporate the
Crimea and the Caucasus into a protectorate which under the
following reigns was to develop effectively into a conquest. She

did not realize the dream of the Empire of Constantinople which, for more than a hundred years, was to be an obsession with imperial Russia, but this great dream haunted her and shaped her foreign policy, since, while she despised the Greeks and the "Western Slavs" who were then under the domination of the Ottoman Empire, she hoped one day to unite them all under the rule of a Russian Empire which should stretch from the Arctic Ocean to the Adriatic.

Like Napoleon's generals after them, Russian generals took the names of their victories: Alexei Orlov became Orlov-Chesmensky, from the naval victory of Chesme in 1770. General Rumiantsev was given the name Zadunaisky (Transdanubian) in memory of his crossing of the Danube, and Potemkin was Tavrichesky, Prince of Taurida (the Crimea). Certainly in Russian eyes Catherine's chief claim to greatness lay in this brilliant revenge on the Moslem and Ottoman East, and over "Tartary" in particular.

Toward the end of her reign, Russia had acquired possession of Latvia, Lithuania, White Russia and Volynia, territories which had formerly been part of the Kingdom of Poland (it was not until after 1815 that Russia annexed the greater part of Poland properly speaking, including the capital city of Warsaw). The operation was carried out in three stages, in 1772, 1793, and 1795. By the end of this period what little was still left of Poland had been divided between Prussia, Austria and Russia. In the space of twenty years a kingdom which was, territorially speaking, one of the greatest in Europe, had been wiped completely off the map. Anarchy, political weakness, the disparate elements of which her population was made up, the absence of natural frontiers and the increasing aggressiveness of Prussia and Russia between whom Poland found herself caught as in a vise, had made possible a scandal hitherto unheard of in a Europe which even then possessed some kind of tacit but real "international law": a whole nation, an independent, civilized country proud of her traditions and her past, was divided up like a cake among her neighbors.

Polish resistance was bloody, and Russia (much more than Prussia) became in the eyes of Europe a symbol of despotic power carried to extremes, a symbol of oppression and injustice. Public opinion in Russia itself felt no remorse at this unjustifiable annexation: the people had a hatred of Poland which was both ancient and tenacious, and under Catherine's rule national pride swelled to hitherto unimaginable proportions.

Russia's expansion to the west brought her rich provinces whose populations could in future be exploited for the benefit of the Empire: in the south she acquired the steppes, vast but sparsely populated regions which had to be made to yield. With Potemkin's help Catherine busied herself there successfully, and the famous "Potemkin villages," villages artificially created within a few weeks by the enterprising and eccentric favorite on the route the Empress was to take during her tour of the Crimea, have become a byword.

But this development was more than simply a matter of Potemkin villages; it was the beginning of real colonization. Catherine does not boast idly (even as early as 1779) of having built 144 cities. There have been few builders like her in history: in her reign old ruined cities which had become little more than sprawling, dirty villages were adorned with public buildings and palaces of stone; new cities were founded and in a short space of time became important centers, and a number of them bore her name: Ekaterinoslav(Catherine's Glory), Ekaterinburg (City of Catherine), Ekaterinodar (Gift of Catherine) and so on. Catherine succeeded in spreading her fame throughout her empire by means of concrete and lasting monuments. She was no dreamer; she was a worthy successor to continue the work of Peter the Great.

She set up a bronze equestrian statue to the great master whose lessons she never forgot. This statue, which was the work of Falconet, stood poised on the crest of a rising wave carved out of a single huge block of granite. Peter, dressed in Roman fashion and crowned with laurels, was stretching out his right hand before him while with the other he held his rearing horse, and the horse's hoofs were crushing a serpent. On the rock were engraved these words: PETRO PRIMO CATHERINA SECUNDA. The Empress did not wish, she said, that people should think it was his wife, Catherine I, who had erected the monument. By this signature she proclaimed herself the second, the disciple, the woman who wanted to sow the land which the great cultivator had plowed.

In history and in the memory of his people, Peter, the Bronze Horseman, still outshines Catherine the Great, but on many counts Peter the Great might well have been proud of the clever little German princess who, less disinterestedly but almost as energetically as himself, struggled for thirty years to make Russia great.

Catherine loved Russia. She was a German but she was a Russian patriot first and foremost, because Russia was the country she ruled, her kingdom, her reason for living. Because she herself had to forget, and make Russia forget, that she was only a stranger in the land and as such always suspect, that she did not even speak its language perfectly and did not understand its religion or its ways: because of all this she was determined, with the fanaticism of the converted, to be more Russian than the Russians.

"There is no single nation," she wrote in 1791 to Princess Dashkova, "which equals the Russian in courage, strength and wisdom and which possesses such a healthy administration." (In 1791 this administration was already the work of Catherine herself, or at least she could flatter herself that this was so.) "Never has the universe brought forth an individual who is more masculine, more complete, more open, more humane, more kindly, more generous or more able than the Scythian [i.e. Russian]. No man is his equal in regularity of features, in beauty of countenance, clarity of complexion, height, stature and dignity. . . . No history can furnish better or greater men than ours. . . . This nation possesses men of an outstanding merit who have all the qualities which make heroes." The Russians themselves did not have such high standards. They did not know they were so admirable. Catherine was to teach them, since she herself dictated the form of Russian history books, and in this, as in many other things, she was a pioneer.

Catherine was genuinely in love with Russia to the point of infatuation, and more than anything else, the fact that with the exception of Poniatowski all the men she loved were Russians, although there was no lack of foreigners at the Russian court, shows that her partiality must have been spontaneous and uncalculating. But there was also on her side a strong desire to make Russia, *her* Russia, great in the eyes of other nations and to show Europe that she, Catherine II, did not rule over a barbarous and backward people but over a nation which was the equal and even the superior of other nations. All her life she cared more about public opinion in the West than in Russia itself.

She had some trouble in getting others to acknowledge this superiority and she did not, in fact, achieve it. Russia had a very bad reputation. Such prestige as she had was due mainly to her wealth (which was grossly exaggerated) and to her military strength, and even this strength was generally attributed to the savagery of the Russian soldiers, the ferocity of the Cossacks, and the cruelty of Russian military leaders who would not shrink from sacrificing human lives. Europe saw the Russians simply as upstarts, the *nouveaux riches* of Western culture, without recognizing the real worth of a people, cut off from their past and several hundred years behind the West in their development, who were, all things considered, doing extremely well. Thirty years after Catherine's death, Russia already possessed a literature of the highest order, and it was a literature of Western inspiration.

Russia should not be judged either on the dirt of her villages or on her insolent display of wealth. The "Scythian" may not have been "more masculine, more open, kindly, humane" and so on than other men, but he was certainly no less so, and the Russian people (this meant in practice the Russian nobility, since the people hardly entered into it) lacked neither intelligence nor energy. To Catherine must go the great credit of having created a favorable climate for the blossoming of a real Russian culture.

The odd thing is that this Russian patriot, who wrote manuals of grammar and Russian history books and herself composed a great many plays and novels (not very good ones) in Russian, actually reigned over a largely French-speaking society in which Russian was a language reserved for the use of servants and often spoken very badly, and where almost everything written down was in French. In fact, in the eighteenth century French culture was *the* culture, and Mademoiselle Cardel's pupil was no exception to this rule. In order to westernize the Russians it was necessary, after having dressed them "in the German fashion," to educate them "in the French fashion." This process of Frenchifying the court and the upper classes in general had already begun to happen under Elizabeth, but Catherine gave to it a brilliance and *cachet* which enabled her court to rival Versailles.

When she set out to win her country—and herself—the esteem of Europe, it was toward France that Catherine resolutely turned her face.

Forty-four

❦❦❦❦❦❦❦❦❦❦❦

The Semiramis of the North

She courted Voltaire in the most unequivocal fashion: by means of a constant, playful flattery, so clever and at the same time respectful that the patriarch of Ferney could not help but return his illustrious correspondent's tribute in kind. Catherine's correspondence with Voltaire does not contain the best work of either. On both sides there was probably little enough sincerity, on both sides a pleasurable sensation of being praised by an eminent personality, and on both sides a clear calculation which amounted simply to *quid pro quo*.

Voltaire spread the legend of the Semiramis of the North throughout Europe (although he did not refer to her as this in his letters since, by an unfortunate coincidence, in his own tragedy *Semiramis* the heroine was a woman who has seized power after killing her husband: so does history repeat itself endlessly). Catherine loaded her old friend with gifts and busied herself spreading his works in Russia.

Voltaire was one of the great architects of Catherine's legend in the West. He did not stint his praises, but on the principle that however lavish the boast there will always be something left over, a tenth of his eulogies would have been enough to fix in the public mind the image of a just, liberal, generous woman, the most admirable sovereign the world has ever known, and this was an image which no amount of libel or slander could destroy. In the eyes of posterity Catherine would have her heaven and her hell: she was to pay dearly enough for the inhuman perfections attributed to her by flatterers because, not unjustly, her enemies made up for it by blackening her out of all probability. But the image propagated by Voltaire—and by Catherine herself through Voltaire and others who flattered her —is the strongest in spite of everything because, in good and bad alike, it is still linked indissolubly with the idea of greatness.

"Do you know where is the earthly paradise? I know: it is everywhere that there is Catherine II. Prostrate yourself, like me, at her feet!" (September 17, 1771) "I throw myself at your feet with worship and idolatry." (February 2, 1772) "You have become my overriding passion . . . I throw myself at your feet and kiss them with much more respect than the Pope's." Could Voltaire really have felt this adoration? Could he believe that Catherine took him seriously? She did not lack either irony or a sense of humor, and her own blandishments were more subtle.

Since she was a woman and could hardly kiss the philosopher's feet, she would "willingly kiss the hand that has written so many fine things."

Voltaire was her "master in thought"; she claimed to be his disciple, saying that since she was a child she had read only his works: an obvious lie, but was there any other way of pleasing —or of not displeasing—a famous writer? The day she received Diderot at St. Petersburg, Voltaire was so jealous that he sent the Empress a letter "breaking off" their relationship. ("I can see clearly that there is no passion which does not come to an end. It is a thought which would make me die of spleen but for the fact that I am already on the point of dying of old age. Let your Majesty deign to receive this letter as my last will and testament. Your admirer, your neglected, your old Russian of Ferney.") Catherine scolds him gently, affectionately, and soon Voltaire willingly goes back on his "last will."

Certainly he had no need to be jealous of Diderot. No one could rival him in the art of worshipping the *Incomparable*, and Diderot swiftly offended the Empress by his indiscreet questions, his even more indiscreet advice, and the persistence with which he harped on the rights of man and the wretchedness of the people. Anyone who could, in the heat of conversation, tap Catherine familiarly on the knee and call her her "my good woman," and who never so much as contemplated kissing her feet, could not expect to be understood or appreciated by a woman who had already lost the ability to see the difference between the Good and her own interests. She would be a hundred miles from imagining that this untidy, exuberant, argumentative, enthusiastic man, with his incorrigibly middle-class jollity, could be a superior creature to herself, "one of the best brains in Europe."

Let no one presume to teach her a sovereign's job. "You work only on paper, which suffers all, while I, a poor empress, I work in human skins which are a great deal more irritable and ticklish." Diderot knew that better than she, and it was in the name of these very "human skins" that he was demanding a little more justice for the common people, but Catherine's "irritable and ticklish" human skins belonged to the nobles; the serfs were, or ought to be, beyond any such feelings. Decidedly Diderot was no statesman, but then why did Catherine claim the title of philosopher for herself?

Voltaire on his part was better able to appreciate his Cateau's feelings. At the time of the first partition of Poland he actually wrote: "Quite disinterestedly, the Empress wishes to establish freedom of conscience in Poland." True, the Poles were fanatical Catholics and Voltaire loathed fanaticism, but this loathing could surely not make him rate aggression against a Catholic country as invariably right. A more prosaic suggestion is that, at the bottom of his heart, he really did not care in the least what went on among distant and barbaric nations.

In 1778 he considered making a journey to St. Petersburg in order to pay his tribute to the great sovereign in person. Catherine opposed the idea, and quite rightly, for he was old and ill and she was not exactly burning with desire to see him. "For the love of heaven," she wrote to Grimm, "advise the octogenarian to stay in Paris! . . . Tell him that Catherine is only worth seeing from a distance." She was perspicacious enough to realize that her old admirer only covered her with praise because she was at a distance, because Russia mattered very little to him and he was free to indulge in illusions about it which entailed no practical obligations. In Russia injustice, despotism and intolerance bore another name, and Catherine's subjects were merely Russians, who could not be regarded as possessing the human dignity of men like Calas or the Chevalier de la Barre, on whose behalf he pleaded so eloquently.

When Voltaire died Catherine was sincerely sorry. She was, at the best of times, a sentimental woman and was always upset to hear of anyone's death, even when he was not a personal friend. But her "master" would have been very much surprised if he could have seen the picture this friend of philosophers would draw of him: "Since he is dead, it seems to me that there is no more honor in good humor, for he was the mirth and spirit of it. . . . When I talk of the god of pleasure, it is Voltaire I mean."

What, was he nothing more than an entertainer? Had this master of thought taught Catherine nothing but mirth, a mirth which she had never lacked? No, she thought better of this, and in the same letter to Grimm she wrote: "Besides, he was my master. It was he, or rather his works, which formed my mind and my brain." This was clearly not true, for Catherine's brain had not waited for Voltaire: Tacitus and Montesquieu, Brantôme and good King Henry had been considerably more influential teachers, and her real masters were still Frederick II, Elizabeth, Bestuzhev and the life of the court. But she had to pay this posthumous tribute to the great old man who nevertheless prided himself on being something other than the god of good humor.

Catherine did not like France and she did not understand it. For her, when all was said and done, it was simply a land of gaiety, frivolity and "wit," and gaiety was not the most important thing in her life.

Infatuated, even though purely in theory, with liberal ideas, she owed a great deal of this liberalism to the influence of the Englishman Hanbury-Williams, but to all philosophers she was tempted to retort: "You work on paper, which suffers all," or in other words, as Napoleon put it: "You are dreamers." Decidedly, she thought, France's great contribution to humanity's intellectual patrimony was still "good humor."

Catherine was too much a German to comprehend that Racine was something more than a master of verbal felicities, that Molière was not merely funny, that the works of Rousseau, Bayle, Montesquieu, Diderot and even Voltaire were heavy with explosive thought, heavy with moral demands strong enough to burst apart her own sensible, narrow, realistic world, the universe in which, like a great businesswoman, she moved.

The day the French Revolution broke out, Catherine was horrified and indignant. She did not understand. To her, the crime of high treason committed by an entire people was a personal injury; it was a scandal in an age to which she, Catherine the Great, had set an example of what the wisdom, magnanimity and grandeur of an absolute ruler could be! She had long ago allowed the constant exercise of power to go to her head, had long been used to confound truth with flattery and to think of herself as a model of virtue even in her worst weaknesses, a model of equity even in her injustice, a model of humility even in her boasting. This old despot, boasting of her "republican spirit," could see nothing in the fall of the Bastille and the Declaration of Human Rights beyond a wicked conspiracy carried out by dangerous visionaries, unscrupulous adventurers, or brigands of the kind that Pugachev had been. Even with Pugachev, she had never understood why the people followed him.

She wrote to Grimm: "I am awaiting the time when it will please you to exonerate in my mind those philosophers and others who have taken part in the revolution." If Voltaire, her "god of pleasure," had ever taken part in this abomination she, Catherine, would have been compelled to accuse herself of nourishing a snake in her bosom. She herself, to some extent, might even be responsible for the excesses of these madmen who were seeking to destroy order, to violate the law of nature and the law of God.

Catherine hated the Revolution with all her strength, and on that subject there was to be no more compromise, no more attempts to flirt with republican ideas. For once she would be sincere. "I am an aristocrat, that is my job." She was hard on the Russian "Jacobins," and declaring the radical Radishchev more dangerous than Pugachev ("He praises Franklin!"), she had him tried, condemned and banished to Siberia. She also persecuted unmercifully the Freemasons and other associations suspected of "heretical" or liberal tendencies.

She despised Louis XVI's weakness (the same fate would not happen to her!) but she was terrified at the news of his death. She, who had done nothing to prevent the murder of a lawful sovereign and had covered the murderers with honors, now condemned the execution of the King as the greatest crime against humanity. All things, after all, are relative. There are some crimes which sovereigns may commit but which the people may not.

Forty-five

(<-(<-(<-(<-(<-(<-(<-(<-(<-(<-(<-(<-|

The Empress Dies

Catherine died at the age of sixty-seven, of a stroke which seized her in the lavatory. She was a healthy old woman, full of energy, and there had been nothing to foreshadow such a sudden death. Two months earlier she had received a cruel blow in the failure of her plan to marry her granddaughter Alexandra to King Gustavus IV of Sweden. At the last moment the young king had refused because of some argument over his bride-to-be's change of religion. It had been a public affront and Catherine was very much mortified and upset by it. It was then that she had had her first stroke, although only a slight one.

The second, which followed such a short while afterward, proved fatal. She did not regain consciousness. After lingering painfully for thirty hours—although she was probably not aware that she was suffering—the old Empress passed away, leaving behind her dismay, disorder and a feverish agitation as the court turned to look, not without apprehension, at its new master. A great reign was over.

She who had held the reins for so long had suddenly dropped them and as her old body, still living, lay gasping and panting like a helpless animal on the great bed with its heavy canopy, it was still less an object of pity than of anxious calculations: would she recover consciousness, speak, decide once again, with her last living breath, the fate of the Empire? She was known to have been on the point of disinheriting the Grand Duke Paul in favor of his son Alexander. The dying woman could still proclaim her last will. But no: Catherine's lips did not move to speak again, and she carried her last will with her to the tomb: it was the revenge of the son she had sacrificed.

Paul was proclaimed Emperor. He was forty-two; he had always been excluded from affairs of state, and had been given no chance to prepare himself for the duties of a ruler. He did not weep for his mother, but Catherine was mourned, sincerely, by all those who had worked with her, by the army, and by the people of the capital: she had been the Mother of Her Country for a very long time. She was admired, and she was loved. She had succeeded in imposing her powerful personality so that she was already a legend in her lifetime, and had become the idol of the herd, who instinctively love the strong. She had also, when all was said, done much good.

Paul had his father's body exhumed from the grave in which it had been buried at the convent of Saint Alexander Nevsky, and Catherine II's coffin lay in state in the cathedral of Saints Peter and Paul next to that of Peter III. The Empress's funeral was a double funeral, and in it the place of honor went to the husband who had died thirty-four years earlier. Side by side, the Emperor and Empress were censed by the priests, united again for all eternity. In this macabre encounter the still-fresh corpse of an old woman and the shriveled remains of a young man were lighted by the same candles and saluted by the same mourning chants.

Under the names of their Imperial Majesties Peter Feodorovich and Catherine Alexeievna, the Russian Church sent to their last rest a Lutheran prince and princess, Karl Peter Ulrich of Holstein and Sophia Augusta Fredericka of Anhalt-Zerbst, second cousins who had come to that country as children to find unhappiness for the one and glory for the other. Now they were equal, reunited by the will of a son who was publicly passing judgment on his mother.

Paul did not succeed in rehabilitating his father's memory,

nor in destroying the work of the mother whom he had loathed. He was violent, tyrannical, ill-prepared to reign and even slightly deranged. Four years later he, like his father, was assassinated by conspirators who wanted to put his son on the throne. Catherine was avenged in her turn.

Forty-Six

❧❦❧❦❧❦❧❦❧❦❧❦❧❦❧❦❧❦

Conclusion

From then on she belonged to legend: she had done everything necessary to create the "personality cult" which many absolute sovereigns have used as a weapon: long before Catherine, Louis XIV of France and Elizabeth I of England had excelled in the art of making the person of the monarch into an idol.

In Russia, right up to the Revolution, Catherine remained officially what she had wanted to be: a woman of genius endowed with every personal virtue, an ardent Russian patriot, a magnanimous and victorious sovereign, a simple, charitable woman with a tender concern for all outcasts, a gay, brilliantly witty woman, a patron of the arts and a friend of philosophers. It was undoubtedly a pretty picture that, for a hundred years, Russian history books, portraits and historical paintings taught people to know and respect. Historians who deviated, however slightly, from the official line had to publish their works abroad.

The West which Catherine had cultivated so assiduously, whose approval she had so desired, was much less kind to her. The partition of Poland and Russia's reactionary policy encouraged the spread of pamphlets, lampoons and vicious rumors which tarnished forever the memory of the enlightened despot. In Europe Catherine left behind her the reputation certainly of a masterful and energetic sovereign, but also of a debauched and unscrupulous woman.

She was neither the one nor the other, but because there is more human truth in the unfinished creature who was as yet no more than an ordinary human being, in this portrait I have tried above all to depict her as the Grand Duchess and the young Empress. The other Catherine, the Great one, could not open her mouth or take up a pen without being conscious of herself as admirable and admired.

She was a woman who knew how to value the praises of courtiers at their true worth, but ultimately she was caught in the trap. It seemed natural for the world to adore her; she did not see how she could moderate the chorus of praise which rose toward her on all sides, she was sure it was sincere . . . she was such an ordinary woman! Two men among those who surrounded her were exceptions to this rule: Orlov and Potemkin, and even Potemkin was intelligent enough to make use of every weapon. "Flatter her," he would say, "and you will get anything you want." She had her differences with her less malleable colleagues such as Princess Dashkova, whose pride and presumption she scoffs at in her letters. She bore with Diderot on account of his bourgeois peculiarity. In the end she could no longer bear not to be an idol.

Diderot was not deceived. Catherine, he said, believed in God because "she loves to convince herself that she has a patron in heaven who watches her behavior and who, seeing her walk with such goodness, such nobility, such grandeur and humanity, smiles on her and rejoices in a sight which is not often seen on earth." *Noblesse oblige* and convictions of this kind can compel a monarch to make real efforts to show wisdom and humanity. She loved to convince herself—and her too supple mind convinced her of so many things that ultimately she was never sincere: temperamentally an atheist, she had not the courage to carry her beliefs to their conclusion, even in her personal correspondence, and though a natural cynic, she never had the courage to admit to it openly. God? She was the nominal head of the Russian Orthodox Church, but she never understood that the ritual of this church was anything more than a masquerade, made necessary by reason of "the brutishness of the people": her God was the philosophers' God, He existed for her own convenience: she needed Him for her moral comfort, and she regarded anything which might upset that comfort as sacrilege.

She held all the trumps but here the cards were subtly stacked. She was intelligent, but not a genius. She was sentimental, but she was not really good. She was capable of passion, but not of self-forgetfulness. She was neither cruel or mean, a virtue rare enough in a despot, but it was a result of calculation, not of nobility of heart.

She claimed to govern alone, but in fact she was guided entirely by the interests of the ruling class. She claimed to be liberal and was in fact reactionary. She was wildly generous, but in giving she never deprived herself of anything. She patronized art and letters so that artists and writers would glorify her, but she did not really like them, for her taste, like her intelligence, was superficial. She was a great worker, but for this she is no more deserving of praise than a Ford or a Rockefeller. She had great abilities, but she came to resemble a pilot who regards himself simultaneously as the creator of the airplane and the absolute master of the lives of the passengers.

Catherine meant the story of her life to appear a brilliant success, brought about by her own strong character and shining intelligence. She was a woman so drunk with pride and intoxicated with flattery that she could even allow herself the luxury of being honest: she knew herself. Whatever the weaknesses which can be laid to her charge, however much she may have compounded with truth and with heaven, she herself must have known all about them in her heart of hearts.

Furthermore, she was not oblivious to the slanderous pamphlets which circulated clandestinely in Russia and quite openly abroad, dragging her character in the mud. Nor, after Pugachev's rebellion, was she unaware of what the people, some of them at least, thought of her. She knew that the staffs of foreign embassies in St. Petersburg were using their diplomatic immunity to propagate the most damaging information about her. She knew that even her great admirer, Voltaire, believed her capable of the murder of Peter III and thought it necessary to make excuses for her. However conscious she may have been of her own merit, she knew she had too many detractors not to be continually tempted to plead her own cause.

If we look more closely, we shall find, beneath the mask of unbearable self-satisfaction which was almost second nature to her, the face of a woman who is never relaxed; who is too anxious to please, not to give offense, to justify herself. Before whom? She was past conceding that anyone had the right to judge her, and she continually exposed herself, quite complacently, to the judgment of all: Madame de Geoffrin, Voltaire, Grimm, Poniatowski, nearly all her correspondents—and she had a good many—were treated to confidences in which she describes, discusses and analyzes herself at length, answering the flattery, sincere or otherwise, of her friends with a fresh set of meditations on herself.

Like all chatterboxes, she says a great deal without, in the end, ever getting to the point. She is full of news, unable to help telling all about her passing love affairs, inexhaustible on the subject of her delightful grandchildren, her friends, her dogs and her gardens, but she never tells us the secret of her relationship with Potemkin or her real feelings about her son. Nor shall we ever know whether she felt at all remorseful or even uncomfortable about the way in which she rose to power. She was never allowed to forget that she was, after all, a usurper. Her own son regarded her as one, and hardly troubled to hide it.

It is a sad fate for a mother to see her son grow up in the belief that his father was assassinated, and by her own hand. We know that Paul was effectively smothered with kindness and care, kept up to the age of forty-two in a state of enforced idleness which was made harder by the atmosphere of fear and suspicion in which he was condemned to live. He was the heir to a throne and yet, although passionately fond of soldiering, never commanded a regiment, was never allowed to meddle in politics, and could not move a step without the government's good pleasure. Even when he was sent abroad to travel under an assumed name it was without knowing whether he would return home only to be imprisoned and deprived of his rights. He was a Hamlet who went mad in earnest, a martyr to political necessity, but his jailer was his own mother, a mother who claimed to love him, who, at least in her letters to her friends, manifested a constant fondness for him, took a close interest in his consecutive marriages and his family life, and shared his joys and sorrows.

The sight of a dominating mother treating a grown-up son as though he were still a child is no doubt common enough, but less common is the bitter, enforced resignation of a son living for thirty years obsessed by the memory of his murdered father. When Paul discovered Orlov's letter he might have exclaimed, "Thank God, my mother was innocent!" when all Catherine's behavior (and the very fact that, knowing the truth, she had rewarded Alexei Orlov) proved at least a tacit complicity. Her son imagined much more, much worse. Did Catherine know this? Had she tried to explain to her son? It seems unlikely: she did not possess that kind of courage.

The tragic doubt which made the heir to the throne the Empress's enemy, instead of her ally, still lies heavily on Catherine's memory.

Historical justice is not like the justice of men. In accordance with what might almost be termed a natural law, the strong had eliminated the weak and there can be little doubt that Peter's removal was a blessing for Russia: he was a prince with all the qualities to make a terrible ruler. Catherine's rise to power was brought about by Peter's enemies and by public opinion: as far as the actual *coup d'état* went, she was very little to blame. In the circumstances, to have rejected the "proposals" which were made to her would have been heroic—or downright cowardly.

But if we go back a little further and look at the question from a moral standpoint, can Catherine be said to have been entirely innocent in the matter of her husband's downfall? The life of an insignificant creature such as Peter certainly counts for little in itself, and Catherine ruined many other lives besides: there can be little comparison between this life and those of the countless thousands of peasants who suffered under her rule. Yet even so, there was a time when Sophia Augusta Fredericka was a little girl, betrothed to a little boy who was her cousin.

On the whole, historians have dealt harshly with Peter. He was first and foremost a child, and he remained a child for far too long. But at the time Catherine knew him, at the time of the failure of their marriage, they were both children (Peter much more so than Catherine) and most of our information concerning the reasons for the marital disaster which ended in Peter's death and Catherine's accession comes from one child's verdict on another. When Catherine tells us that she was, for a long time, the Grand Duke's sincere, loyal and devoted friend, we should take her at her word. We may even believe that she meant well. Love, or even affection, cannot be had for the asking.

Of Peter himself, we know nothing. Like all maladjusted persons, he was at once garrulous and secretive, but even if he was mortally wounded by his future bride's shudder of disgust when she saw him disfigured by the smallpox, he wrote no memoirs to tell us so. When he accuses his wife of being "horribly ill-natured," Catherine is the only one able to tell us that she was not, in fact, ill-natured. What little we know of Peter's thoughts and feelings, we know from Catherine, who is a shrewd though partial judge. From her description, we can imagine a proud, complex, hypersensitive boy, driven, either through timidity or fear of ridicule, to act the clown: in short, a human being maimed, but still not incurably so. However, a child of fifteen was scarcely the person to rehabilitate or even understand him. In Catherine's relations with her husband we should at least see that the blame is not all on one side.

Madame de Maroger has pointed out quite rightly[1] that Catherine does not condemn her husband out of hand. She pities him and, comparing him with herself, observes that two people, one of whom is weak and the other strong, may react to the same situation in diametrically opposite ways. One might add that in such a situation one reaction usually tends to strengthen the other, so that the more Russian Catherine became, the more Peter determined to be Prussian, and vice versa. A young boy who has been moved by force into surroundings he detests (and with some reason, since he was a prisoner there), can hardly be blamed for remaining in a state of total rebellion against this environment to the bitter end. It might even be said that such an attitude is no more than the natural one for a boy with any pride. Catherine was more malleable because she was a girl and had been brought up to be docile and obedient from infancy. In comparing herself with Peter, Catherine forgets that he was in the more delicate position: he and not she was the heir to the throne, and of the two he was the more severely oppressed and threatened.

Catherine was much too prudish to complain of her husband's impotence in her memoirs. To begin with, as a complete innocent to whom her mother had imparted the facts of life only on the eve of her marriage, Catherine must have waited, fearfully at first and then with growing curiosity and impatience, for a consummation which never came. It may be that Peter, concealing his mortification under a pretense of platonic passions for various ladies of the court, was more sensitive to his wife's charms than Catherine realized. Another famous royal couple, the young Louis XVI and Marie-Antoinette, experienced similar difficulties in the first years of their marriage, but Louis XVI was a more stable character than Peter and more capable of affection. He was able to love his wife and—once in a position to lead a full married life—to become an acceptable husband. At least he was not sterile, while Peter almost certainly was. Today we should find a great deal to excuse in a young man placed as he was.

Peter has been condemned for failing to attract the sympathies of others, for not having had any friends, but in fact, as we have seen, it was not easy for him to make friends when everyone for whom he seemed to show any affection was promptly removed. He endured the torments of Tantalus while he was still young and by the time he was twenty-five or so and his keepers began to relax their strict supervision a little, he was already a creature driven mad by loneliness, a slave to drink, and incapable of establishing any human contact with his fellows, however hard he tried.

The job of understanding and loving this boy, for which Catherine had been brought to Russia, was not going to be an easy one, Catherine was an egoist and quite unsuitable for the part. But then, how many girls of fifteen are prepared to sacrifice their lives of their own accord? All we need say is that the young couple were both victims, first of their environment and then of each other. Catherine makes it clear in her memoirs that in practice it was she who first deceived her husband, and that by the time the marriage was finally consummated she already had a lover. This being so, Peter's resentment against her is, after all, sufficiently understandable, especially when we know that Catherine was naturally prolific and that Peter had every reason to believe himself not the father of her children. For a long time he even appears to have accepted the situation quite equably, and he certainly put up a generous show of delight when Poniatowski's daughter was born. Catherine can hardly be blamed for taking lovers, but she had no right to complain of her husband's infidelity.

Catherine's friends—and even Frederick II, who was not exactly a friend—excused her revolt against Peter III after the event on the grounds of self-defense, asserting that Peter was fostering such sinister designs against the Empress that she was compelled to safeguard her liberty and even her life. There can be no doubt that, at the time of the *coup d'état*, Peter was preparing to rid himself of his wife in one way or another. But for both sides it was only a matter of time. Peter knew very well that he was engaged in a duel to the death, that Catherine's aim was power, and that if she won, he was lost. If it seems astonishing that he should have taken such pains to humiliate beyond bearing an antagonist from whom he had so much to fear, at least his hatred seems to be borne out by the facts, since Catherine was the person responsible for his own death. Peter had lived with fear from his childhood, and always said that he was doomed to die in Russia. He was not the man to cherish any illusions as to the fate which awaited him if he ever fell from power. Moreover, when Peter came to the throne, he had already been aware of his wife's intentions for a long time. He knew her very well and had a very high opinion of her abilities. During the last four months of his reign, Peter shows us the strange spectacle of a man threatened by a dangerous enemy, delighting in taunting and humiliating her in public while still leaving her complete freedom of action. True, Peter considered having Catherine arrested and was dissuaded by his uncle, but this was because Catherine was already so strong that her arrest would have provoked a rising by the army. There remained the possibility of having her murdered, and it has been suggested that Peter was planning this, but we cannot tell whether he would have carried it through. Peter was fascinated by his wife, like a bird by a snake, and he certainly feared her even more than he hated her, but it seemed as though not even fear could drive his erratic nature to decisive action. (We know that Catherine herself did not actually give the order for her husband's murder, and her character was a great deal more energetic than his.)

From the moment it became clear that the only way either partner could reign was *without* the other, it is fair to say that both were squarely on the defensive. For Peter, to lose his throne could only mean a sentence of death. Catherine might perhaps have envisaged the possibility of going to live abroad, of trailing from one court to the next as a princess without honor, little better than an adventuress, but she would undoubtedly have preferred death to such a fate. As we have seen, it can only have been her highly inopportune pregnancy which compelled Catherine to let Peter mount the throne, to the consternation of the army and the court. To Peter himself his accession came as a surprise, such a surprise indeed that he appears to have gone mad with joy and not without reason, since once out of power he had, at best, only the fortress to look forward to. For six months he dared not lift a finger against Catherine, while everyone, and the Empress's friends in particular, expected to see him strike and believed Catherine lost. In fact, his behavior seems to suggest that he was in the grip of a masochistic desire to make his adversary's task easier. With a perverse efficiency which amazed all observers, he did his utmost to provide his enemies, especially Catherine, with the best possible reasons for getting rid of him. The instinct for self-destruction works in mysterious ways.

"Child as I was," Catherine once wrote, "the title of queen sounded sweet to my ears." Understandably enough. But for little Peter Ulrich of Holstein, forced to endure tiresome lessons in Swedish and Russian because, he was told, he was to become either King of Sweden or Emperor of Russia, the titles sounded on ears full of childish rebellion as nothing more than symbols of dreary labor. The title which, in her innocence, young Figchen coveted like a pretty toy was no sinecure. Catherine soon realized this and, in spite of all obstacles, she did her best to make herself worthy of it. Peter, weak, lazy, and terrified by the shadow of responsibility, seems to have done all he could to make himself unworthy to reign. Probably he did not do so consciously, but people in those days did not talk about the subconscious. In the eyes of history, the young royal couple, placed by chance on the steps of a throne, still have a curse on them: behind the tough, glorious figure of the woman reigning *alone* stands the shadow of the man who did not reign—the other side of the coin.

Peter was more than a victim: he was Catherine's tragic double. Of the two children, superficially so alike and suffering the same trials, one had within her the will to live at all costs and to play the game of life to the bitter end, while the other had only the negative qualities of refusal, rebellion and escape. "A strong character," Catherine once remarked, "is not made to advise a weak one." Especially, she might have added, in matters concerning such an exceptional burden as a crown. Peter's weak spirit, hopelessly ill-prepared for the fate which hung over him from childhood, was crushed by it more surely than by his poor health and misfortunes. But Catherine was the strong character, and she emerged from the trial which shattered the heart and spirit of her partner hardened, battle-scarred, debased and depersonalized. She survived, thanks to her powerful, almost animal, vitality. The story of her reign would no longer be the story of one woman, but of that "great, noble and delicious"—and also terrible—profession of kingship.

APPENDICES

CHRONOLOGICAL TABLE

	Russia	*Principal Events in Other Countries*
1682	Accession of Peter the Great	
1708	St. Petersburg founded	*Circa 1740:* Prussia: accession of Frederick II
1709	Russians defeat Charles XII of Sweden at Poltava	Austria: accession of Maria Theresa
1725	Death of Peter the Great. Accession of Catherine I	Alliances between England and Austria, and between France and Prussia
1727	Death of Catherine I. Accession of Peter II	France: Louis XV on the throne. Fleury as chief minister
1730	Death of Peter II. Accession of Anna Ivanovna	
1740	Death of Anna Ivanovna. Accession of the infant Ivan VI and regency of Anna Leopoldovna	
1741	November 25: *Accession of Elizabeth*	
1742	Peter Ulrich of Schleswig-Holstein taken to Russia, proclaimed heir to the throne and received into the Orthodox Church under the name of Peter Feodorovich	Treaty of Berlin

1744	January: Sophia Augusta Fredericka of Anhalt-Zerbst and her mother invited to Russia by the Empress Elizabeth with a view to marriage with the Grand Duke Peter	France at war with England
	June 29: Sophia of Anhalt-Zerbst received into the Orthodox Church under the name of *Catherine* Alexeievna, and officially betrothed to the Grand Duke	
	August 28: Wedding of Catherine and the Grand Duke Peter. Departure of the Princess of Anhalt-Zerbst	Frederick II defeats the Austrians at Kesseldorf. Armistice
1746	Death of Catherine's father, the Prince of Anhalt-Zerbst. The young Grand Duke and Duchess kept under close observation by the suspicious Bestuzhev	Battle of Fontenoy. Peace of Aix-la-Chapelle
1752	Catherine's affair with Sergei Saltykov	
1754	September 20: Birth of the Tsarevich Paul	
1756	Hanbury-Williams appointed English ambassador to Russia. Catherine's affair with Stanislas Poniatowski. Peter's affair with Elizabeth Vorontsova	
1756	Beginning of the Seven Years' War	
1757	August: Russian army defeats the Prussians at Gross-Jägersdorf. Marshal Apraxin retreats. Elizabeth ill	Pitt Prime Minister Choiseul Minister
	Catherine intrigues with Bestuzhev to keep the Grand Duke from the throne. Birth of Catherine's daughter, Anne	French defeated at Krefeld Loss of the Indies
1758	February-April: Catherine in semiofficial disgrace. Arrest of Bestuzhev and a number of the Grand Duchess's friends. Catherine achieves a reconciliation with Elizabeth	
	August 25: Battle of Zorndorf (issue undecided). Death of Princess Anne. Catherine meets Gregory Orlov	

1760	Russian army, under the command of Count Saltykov, occupies Berlin. Count Nikita Panin, formerly attached to the Russian embassy in Sweden, appointed tutor to Tsarevich Paul. Elizabeth ill. Plans for the accession of Paul. Unrest in the army	Accession of George III of England
1761	*December 25: Death of Elizabeth. Accession of Peter III*	
1762	March: Peter III's *Manifesto* on the enfranchisement of the nobility. Peter III confiscates the wealth of the Church for the state	The Calsas affair
	April 11: Birth of a son to Catherine and Orlov: the future Count Alexei Bobrinsky	Treaty of Paris: end of the Seven Years' War
	June 9: Catherine publicly insulted by Peter at a banquet to celebrate the peace treaty with Prussia. Preparations for war against Denmark	Death of Augustus III of Poland
	June 28: Coup d'état. Catherine proclaimed Empress	
	June 29: Abdication of Peter III. The ex-Emperor confined at Ropsha	
	July 6: Peter assassinated. July 7: Catherine's manifesto to the people	
	September 22: Catherine crowned in Moscow	
1763	Confiscation of the wealth of the Church, and trial of Arzenius Matsievich, Metropolitan of Rostov	
	Panin plans reforms	
1764	Resignation of Kyril Razumovsky and subjection of peasants in the Ukraine. Treaty of Alliance with Prussia.	Publication of Voltaire's *Dictionnaire Philosophique*
1765	Stanislas Poniatowski elected King of Poland	Joseph II's rise to power
1767	Meeting of the Great Commission	Lorraine returned to France (1766)

1768	Russo-Polish treaty: Poland becomes a Russian protectorate. War with Turkey. The Great Commission dissolved	France buys Corsica
1769	Russo-Danish alliance. Alliance between Russia and Prussia renewed. Russian troops occupy Moldavia. Russian fleet appears in the Black Sea September: Sea battle at Chesme: Russian fleet under the command of Greig and Spiridov destroys the Turkish fleet. Anxiety in France and Austria on account of Russian successes	
1770	Frederick II sends his brother Henry to Petersburg to intercede for Turkey. Negotiations between Frederick II, Joseph II and Catherine over the partition of Poland	Marriage of the French Dauphin to Marie-Antoinette. Fall of Choiseul
1771	Plague of Moscow	
1772	Failure of Russo-Turkish negotiations at Focshani. Fall of Gregory Orlov. Vassilchikov in favor	
1773	Cossack revolt on the Yaik, led by Pugachev, under the name of Peter III. Diderot in Russia. The heir to the throne, Paul, married to Princess Wilhelmina of Hesse-Darmstadt	
1774	Orenburg besieged by Pugachev. Vassilchikov replaced by Potemkin End of the war with Turkey: Treaty of Kuchuk-Kainardji: July 21. Russia gains northwest Caucasus, ports on the Sea of Azov, and protectorate over the Crimea and Orthodox Balkan peoples Pugachev makes ready to march on Moscow. Government forces under Suvorov rout the rebel armies. Pugachev given up to P. Panin	Death of Louis XV. Accession of Louis XVI. Turgot chief minister
1775	January: Trial and death of Pugachev. Bloody reprisals in revolting provinces.	

1776	Zavadovsky in favor. Grand Duke Paul married again to Sophia Dorothea of Württemberg (Maria Feodorovna)	U.S. Declaration of Independence
1777	Birth of Paul's son Alexander. Zorich imperial favorite	
1778	Rimsky-Korsakov imperial favorite	Lafayette to America
1779	Peace concluded between Prussia and Austria at Teschen, through Catherine's mediation. Birth of Paul's second son, Constantine	Deaths of Rousseau and Voltaire
1780	Joseph II seeks alliance with Russia against Turkey and Prussia. Lanskoi imperial favorite. Commission on schools for the people	Death of Maria Theresa
1783	Annexation of the Crimea. Establishment of a Georgian protectorate. Death of Lanskoi. Ermolov imperial favorite	Resignation of Necker (1781) England recognizes U.S. independence (1782)
1784	Treaty of Constantinople: Turkey accepts Russia's annexations and grants free passage through the Dardenelles and access to the Black Sea. Potemkin occupied with development of conquered territories, builds port of Sebastopol and founds Ekaterinoslav	Treaty of Versailles Calonne chief minister Death of Diderot
1785	Fall of Ermolov. Mamonov imperial favorite	The affair of the Queen's necklace. La Pérouse expedition
1786	Statute of Education. Preparations for Catherine's state visit to the southern provinces	Death of Frederick II

1787   Catherine's journey: great demonstrations of power and prestige, directed by Potemkin. "Dream of the Thousand and One Nights." Imperial train travels via Kiev, down the Dnieper, and halts at Bakchisarai (formerly the seat of the khans of the Crimea) and at Sebastopol. Last brief meeting between Catherine and Poniatowski. State visit by Joseph II who takes part in the festivities
August: Alliance with Austria and declaration of war on Turkey. Russian armies under the command of Rumiantsev and Suvorov

1788   Siege and capture of Ochakov, after fierce fighting
June: Gustavus III of Sweden declares war on Russia (Sweden was laying claim to Finland)

Convocation of the States General in France
Meeting of the States General. Oath of the Jeu de Paume. Storming of the Bastille

1789   August: Russo-Austrian victory over the Turks at Focshani (Rumiantsev and Coburg). October 11: Suvorov victorious at Rymnik. Potemkin takes Bender, Akerman and Kilia
Manonov unfaithful. Zubov imperial favorite

1790   Swedish fleet threatens Kronstadt and St. Petersburg. Suvorov's Balkan campaigns. Peace between Austria and Turkey
August: Gustavus III signs peace treaty with Russia at Verela.
Publication of Radishchev's *Voyage from St. Petersburg to Moscow*. The author disgraced and exiled

Belgian independence. Death of Joseph II

1791   October 5: Death of Potemkin at Jassy
December 29: Peace of Jassy with the Sultan: Turkey yields all the region between the Bug and the Dniester to Russia and confirms her rights over the Crimea

1792 Russia intervenes once more in the affairs of Poland. Polish government reforms the constitution toward liberal reforms, but threatened by Russia, King Stanislas Augustus (Poniatowski) revokes the new constitution

France at war with Austria. French victory at Valmy

1793 January: Catherine II, with the agreement of Frederick William of Prussia, annexes east Lithuania and the provinces of the Ukraine west of the Dnieper, while Prussia occupies Danzig and the whole of East Prussia: the first partition of Poland. Stanislas Augustus signs treaty at Grodno recognizing Russian rights over occupied territory
Diplomatic relations between France and Russia broken off

Execution of Louis XVI
Execution of the Girondins
France at war with England

1794 Polish rebellion led by Thaddeus Kosciuszko. October 10: defeat of Kosciuszko and capture of Warsaw by Suvorov (November 4). Massacre of the population. Second partition of Poland: Russia annexes Kurland, and the rest of Lithuania; Prussia, the Polish territories on the Niemen and the Vistula, including Warsaw; Austria, Galicia, including Cracow

The Terror
The 9 Thermidor
The Directorate

1795 Treaty of alliance with England. War against Persia

1796 Proposed marriage between Catherine's granddaughter Alexandra and King Gustavus IV of Sweden falls through
*November 6: Sudden death of Catherine
Accession of Paul I*

Last Tsars of the Muscovite dynasty (the "Rurikoviches")

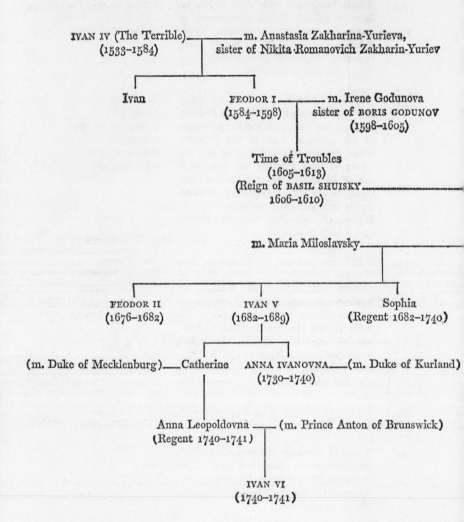

IVAN IV (The Terrible)_____ m. Anastasia Zakharina-Yurieva,
(1533–1584)   sister of Nikita Romanovich Zakharin-Yuriev

Ivan

FEODOR I_____ m. Irene Godunova
(1584–1598)   sister of BORIS GODUNOV
                  (1598–1605)

Time of Troubles
(1605–1613)
(Reign of BASIL SHUISKY_____
1606–1610)

m. Maria Miloslavsky_____

FEODOR II   IVAN V   Sophia
(1676–1682)   (1682–1689)   (Regent 1682–1740)

(m. Duke of Mecklenburg)__Catherine   ANNA IVANOVNA__(m. Duke of Kurland)
                                      (1730–1740)

Anna Leopoldovna ____ (m. Prince Anton of Brunswick)
(Regent 1740–1741)

IVAN VI
(1740–1741)

GENEALOGICAL TABLE OF THE ROMANOV DYNASTY

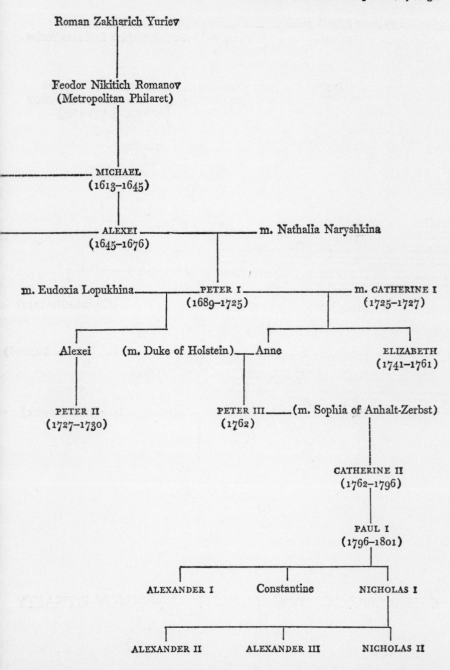

The Romanovs

The dates indicate the periods of reign

Roman Zakharich Yuriev

Feodor Nikitich Romanov
(Metropolitan Philaret)

MICHAEL
(1613–1645)

ALEXEI ——————— m. Nathalia Naryshkina
(1645–1676)

m. Eudoxia Lopukhina —— PETER I —— m. CATHERINE I
(1689–1725)   (1725–1727)

Alexei   (m. Duke of Holstein) — Anne   ELIZABETH
(1741–1761)

PETER II   PETER III —— (m. Sophia of Anhalt-Zerbst)
(1727–1730)   (1762)

CATHERINE II
(1762–1796)

PAUL I
(1796–1801)

ALEXANDER I   Constantine   NICHOLAS I

ALEXANDER II   ALEXANDER III   NICHOLAS II

Note on The Princess of Anhalt-Zerbst

A long time after she had left Russia, Johanna Elizabeth was still try-ing to work her way back into the Empress's favor, or at all events to turn her position as the mother of the Russian Grand Duchess to some practical advantage. After the death of her husband in 1746, her in-trigues aroused the suspicions of the King of Prussia. At the beginning of the Seven Years' War, the Princess and her son were stripped of their possessions on suspicion of being secretly in league with the Russian court: the Princess was obliged to flee to Paris while her son, Prince Frederick, took service with the Austrian army. The King of Prussia's troops moved into the principality of Anhalt-Zerbst.

In Paris the Princess lived far beyond her means, maintaining her own small court and making no secret of her relations with a young French-man named Monsieur de Pouilly. She applied to Elizabeth repeatedly for payment of the pension which had been allotted to her on her departure from Russia, and received a mortifying refusal from Vorontsov which was the more unjust in that she had lost everything she possessed on account of her connection with Russia.

She made several attempts to communicate with her daughter. Prus-sian diplomats appear to have tried to use her influence over the "stub-born and romantic" Grand Duchess whose fondness for England was far too pronounced. Johanna Elizabeth was very well aware of the climate of opinion in the Russian court and was unwilling to compromise her daughter: their clandestine correspondence was limited to half a dozen letters at the most, and of these only one letter of Catherine's and one of her mother's have survived. At the time of Bestuzhev's disgrace the Princess, fearing the worst for her daughter, sent her, through L'Hôpital, a moving letter begging Catherine to appear submissive, to give way to the Empress in everything, and so on. This letter shows more affection and maternal feeling than the Princess is generally credited with possess-ing. The letter reached Catherine, but she did not dare to take it for fear of compromising herself further still.

The Princess died of dropsy in 1760, at the age of forty. She had long been hounded by her creditors and she left enormous debts amounting to four hundred thousand pounds. Although Catherine dared not write to her mother she had at least managed to send her some small presents, but these were merely tokens: in 1760, for example, she sent her some tea and some rhubarb. She was unaware of her mother's illness and was deeply grieved by her death. She made a point of paying her mother's debts in order, as she wrote (in Russian), to "avoid shame," for Johanna Elizabeth's jewels were to be sold by public auction in Paris. Catherine begged the Empress for an advance on her yearly allowance which she promised to pay back within ten years. After the *coup d'état* she was in a position to discharge this debt more quickly.

Catherine appears to have been particularly upset by the fact that her mother's papers had been seized by the French authorities, since, more than anything, she feared that the papers would be handed over to the Russian government. She approached French diplomats personally in order to get the papers into her own hands, and she was successful. She had undoubtedly been a good deal too outspoken in her letters to her mother, and it is also possible that the younger woman had plunged far deeper into the paths of political intrigue than she ever admitted. However that may be, she need not have worried: her mother had had the sense to burn all her letters before she died.

Her mother's death completed Catherine's break with her own family and country. In 1761 we still find her approaching Choiseul with the object of obtaining an indemnity for her brother Fritz—the boy whom, in moments of depression, she wanted to have to live with her. When he died young, she took almost no further interest in her family and did her best to make people forget that she was a German.

BIBLIOGRAPHY

PRIMARY SOURCES

Archives de Paris, "Russie," especially volume 53.

Catherine II, *Memoirs.*

Dashkova, Princess Catherine, *Memoirs.*

Poniatowski, Stanislas, *Secret Unpublished Memoirs.* Ed. Leipzig, 1862.

Recueil des Publications de la Société Impériale de l'Histoire de Russie (This source is indicated in the notes by the abbreviation "Sbornik").

Vorontsov, Prince M. L., *Archives.*

SECONDARY SOURCES

(These consist of memoirs, reports of ambassadors not found in "Sbornik," political documents and pamphlets, etc.; only the principal sources are cited here.)

Castéra, J. H. *Vie de Catherine II.* Paris, 1797.

Catherine II, Literary Works, Correspondence with Voltaire.

Frederick II, *Memoirs.*

Helbig, G. A. W. von, *Russische Gunstlinge.* Tübingen, 1809.

Lettres d'amour de Catherine II à Potemkine. Paris, G. Oudard, 1934.

Ligne, Le Prince de, *Mémoires.* Paris, 1860.

Radishchev, A. N., *Journey from Moscow to St. Petersburg.* 1790.

Rulhière, C., *Anecdotes sur la Révolution de Russie en 1762.* Paris, 1819.

Ségur, Le Comte de, *Mémoires.* Paris, 1859.

WORKS ON CATHERINE II

(*Only the most known and most recent are cited here.*)

Russian Historians

Bilbassov, V. A., *History of Catherine II.* Berlin, 1900.

Kluchevsky, V. O., *The Course of Russian History*. Re-edited Moscow, 1923.

Platonov, S. F., *History of Russia*. St. Petersburg, n.d.; French edition Paris, Payot, 1929.

Soloviev, S. M., *History of Russia*, St. Petersburg, n.d.

Others

Bryanchaninov, N. V., *Catherine II, Impératrice de Russie (1729–1796)*. Paris, Payot, 1932.

Gaïssinovich, A., *La Révolte de Pougatchev*. Paris, Payot, 1938.

Grey, Ian, *Catherine the Great; Autocrat and Empress of all Russia*. London, Hodder & Stoughton, 1961.

Lavater-Sloman, M., *Catherine II et Son Temps*. Paris, Payot, 1952.

Michel, R., *Potemkine*. Paris, Payot, 1936.

Polovtsof, A., *Les Favoris de Catherine la Grande*. Paris, Plon, 1939.

Soloveïchik, G., *Potemkine*. Paris, Gallimard, 1940.

Vallotton, H., *Catherine II*. Paris, Fayard, 1955.

Wormser, Olga, *Catherine II*. Paris, Club Français du Livre, 1957.

NOTES AND REFERENCES

CHAPTER 1: CHILDHOOD
1. Catherine II, *Memoirs*

CHAPTER 2: WHAT DO LITTLE PRINCESSES DREAM OF?
1. Catherine II, *Memoirs*
2. *Ibid.*
3. *Ibid.*

CHAPTER 3: THE KING OF PRUSSIA
1. Catherine II, *Memoirs*
2. *Ibid.*
3. Quoted by Bilbassov, ch. 1
4. Bilbassov, ch. 2
5. Catherine II, *Memoirs*

CHAPTER 6: PETER'S SUCCESSORS
1. Quoted by Bilbassov, ch. 3

CHAPTER 7: ELIZABETH
1. *Cf.* Helbig
2. Sbornik, vols. 1 and 7

CHAPTER 8: THE CHILD OF KIEL
1. Bilbassov, ch. 7
2. Stehlin, quoted by Bilbassov, ch. 7
3. Stehlin, quoted by Bilbassov, ch. 7

CHAPTER 9: ELIZABETH AND HER NEPHEW
1. Letters from Stehlin, quoted by Bilbassov, ch. 7
2. *Ibid.*, ch. 7; Sbornik, vol. 7
3. Sbornik, vol. 6

CHAPTER 10: CINDERELLA AT COURT
1. Sbornik, vol. 7
2. F. Siebigk, *Katharinas II. Brautreise nach Russland 1744-1745*
   (Dessau, 1873), quoted by Bilbassov, ch. 6.

3. Sbornik, vol. 7
4. Quoted by Bilbassov, ch. 6
5. Sbornik, vol. 7

CHAPTER 11: SOPHIA

1. Sbornik, vol. 7
2. Bilbassov, ch. 4
3. Catherine II, *Memoirs*
4. Sbornik, vol. 7
5. Siebigk, quoted by Bilbassov, ch. 11
6. Quoted by Bilbassov, ch. 9
7. Catherine II, *Memoirs*
8. Sbornik, vol. 7

CHAPTER 12: YOUNG LOVE AND COURT INTRIGUE

1. Siebigk, quoted by Bilbassov, ch. 10
2. Catherine II, *Memoirs*
3. Bilbassov, ch. 10; Sbornik, vol. 7

CHAPTER 13: THE GRAND DUCHESS CATHERINE

1. Sbornik, vol. 7
2. Catherine II, *Memoirs*
3. Sbornik, vol. 7
4. Siebigk, quoted by Bilbassov, ch. 11
5. Sbornik, vol. 7
6. *Ibid.*
7. Catherine II, *Memoirs*
8. Siebigk, quoted by Bilbassov, ch. 11
9. Catherine II, *Memoirs*

CHAPTER 14: A JOURNEY TO KIEV, FAMILY AND OTHER TROUBLES

1. Catherine II, *Memoirs*
2. *Ibid.*
3. Bilbassov, ch. 12
4. Catherine II, *Memoirs*
5. *Ibid.*
6. *Ibid.*

CHAPTER 15: A CATASTROPHE

1. Catherine II, *Memoirs*
2. *Ibid.*
3. Stehlin, quoted by Bilbassov, ch. 13

CHAPTER 16: THEIR IMPERIAL HIGHNESSES
1. Catherine II, *Memoirs*

CHAPTER 17: THE WEDDING
1. Bilbassov, ch. 15
2. Sbornik, vol. 7
3. *Ibid.*
4. *Ibid.*
5. *Ibid.*
6. Catherine II, *Memoirs*
7. Sbornik, vol. 7
8. Catherine II, *Memoirs*

CHAPTER 18: THE NEWLYWEDS
1. Catherine II, *Memoirs*
2. *Ibid.*
3. *Ibid.*
4. *Ibid.*

CHAPTER 19: POLITICS AND PLAY
1. Catherine II, *Memoirs*
2. *Ibid.*
3. Bilbassov, ch. 19
4. Catherine II, *Memoirs*

CHAPTER 20: RUSSIA
1. Quoted by Bilbassov, ch. 10
2. Catherine II, *Memoirs*
3. Sbornik, vol. 7

CHAPTER 21: THE COURT
1. Catherine II, *Memoirs*
2. *Ibid.*
3. Helbig
4. Catherine II, *Memoirs*
5. *Ibid.*

CHAPTER 22: TROUBLES FOR THE GRAND DUKE AND DUCHESS
1. Catherine II, *Memoirs*
2. *Ibid.*
3. *Ibid.*

CHAPTER 23: THE APPRENTICE YEARS

1. Catherine II, *Memoirs*
2. *Ibid.*
3. Bilbassov, ch. 24
4. Correspondence of Frederick II (IX, 33)
5. L'Hôpital, *Archives de Paris*, "*Russie*," vol. 54, p. 83
6. Sbornik, vol. 7
7. Catherine II, *Memoirs*
8. *Ibid.*
9. Bilbassov, ch. 20
10. Catherine II, *Memoirs*
11. *Ibid.*
12. *Ibid.*

CHAPTER 24: LOVE AND REASONS OF STATE

1. Catherine II, *Memoirs*
2. *Ibid.*
3. *Ibid.*
4. *Ibid.*
5. Castéra; Catherine II, *Memoirs*
6. Catherine II, *Memoirs*
7. *Ibid.*
8. Bilbassov, ch. 23
9. Catherine II, *Memoirs*
10. *Ibid.*

CHAPTER 25: THE SUCCESSION ENSURED

1. Catherine II, *Memoirs*
2. *Ibid.*
3. *Ibid.*
4. *Ibid.*
5. *Ibid.*

CHAPTER 26: PAUL PETROVICH

1. Catherine II, *Memoirs*
2. *Ibid.*
3. *Ibid.*
4. L'Hôpital, *Archives de Paris*, "*Russie*," vol. 53, p. 171

CHAPTER 27: LOVE AND POLITICS

1. Catherine II, *Memoirs*

2. *Ibid.*
3. *Ibid.*
4. *Ibid.*
5. Bilbassov, ch. 27
6. Catherine II, *Memoirs*
7. Poniatowski, *Memoirs*
8. *Ibid.*
9. Quoted by Bilbassov, ch. 26
10. *Archives de Paris, "Russie,"* vol. 53, p. 157

CHAPTER 28: AN ODD COUPLE

1. Bilbassov, ch. 27
2. *Archives de Paris, "Russie,"* vol. 53
3. Poniatowski, *Memoirs*
4. *Ibid.*
5. *Archives de Paris, "Russie,"* vol. 53
6. Catherine II, *Memoirs*

CHAPTER 29: NEW THREATS

1. Bilbassov, ch. 28; Catherine II, *Memoirs*
2. Catherine II, *Memoirs*
3. *Ibid.*
4. *Ibid.*
5. *Ibid.*
6. *Ibid.*
7. Catherine II, *Memoirs;* Bilbassov, chs. 28–29

CHAPTER 30: THE TURNING POINT

1. Catherine II, *Memoirs*
2. *Ibid.*
3. *Ibid.*

CHAPTER 31: LOVE AND CONSPIRACY

1. Stehlin, quoted by Bilbassov, ch. 2.
2. Helbig (G. Orlov)
3. Soloviev, vol. 24, p. 1132
4. L'Hôpital, *Archives de Paris, "Russie,"* vol. 53
5. Dashkova, *Memoirs*
6. *Ibid.*

CHAPTER 32: MOCK EMPEROR

1. Bilbassov, vol. I, p. 459
2. Dashkova, *Memoirs*
3. Helbig

CHAPTER 33: THE *Coup d'État* OF JUNE 1762

1. Vorontsov, *Archives*, vol. 25, pp. 414–15
2. Bilbassov, vol. 2, p. 21
3. Accounts of the *coup d'état:* Letter from Catherine II to Poniatowski, August 2, 1762; memoirs of Princess Dashkova; Panin's verbal account to the Danish minister

CHAPTER 34: ASSASSINATION OF THE EMPEROR

1. Vorontsov, *Archives*, vol. 21, p. 430
2. Helbig
3. Catherine II, *Memoirs*
4. Sbornik, vol. 7, quoted by Bilbassov, ch. 13

CHAPTER 35: SHE WHO WOULD REIGN

1. L'Hôpital, *Archives de Paris*, "Russie," vol. 53
2. *Ibid.*
3. Sbornik, vol. 7
4. Sbornik, vol. 7, pp. 83–101

CHAPTER 36: THE NEW EMPRESS

1. Quoted by Bilbassov, vol. 1, p. 453
2. Quoted by Platonov
3. Vorontsov, *Archives*, vol. 25, pp. 424–25

CHAPTER 37: THE FAITHFUL SERVANTS

1. Vorontsov, *Archives*, vol. 5, pp. 105–8
2. Dashkova, *Memoirs*

CHAPTER 38: THE NEGLECTED LOVER

1. Sbornik, Catherine II Correspondence

CHAPTER 39: THE EMPRESS

1. Lines by Boileau on the burial of Molière: as an excommunicate actor, the dramatist had no right to Christian burial, and this was granted him by Louis XIV in response to his widow's entreaties.
2. Cf. Soloveïchik, *Potemkine*

3. Cf. accounts by Masson and Coxe
4. Published by Yvesdon, 1769

CHAPTER 40: THE PEOPLE

1. Catherine II, *Memoirs*
2. Quoted by Soloveïchik
3. Quoted by Gaïssinovich
4. *Ibid.*
5. Sbornik